Church Dynamics

BEE WORLD

Church Dynamics

BEE World

First Edition

First Printing—June 2007
Current Printing—August 2011

© 2007, 2011 BEE World.

Every attempt has been made to provide correct information. However, the publisher does not guarantee the accuracy of the book and does not assume responsibility for information included in or omitted from it.

All scripture quotations, unless otherwise indicated, are taken from the NET Bible®, ©1996-2006 by Biblical Studies Press, L.L.C. *www.bible.org* All rights reserved. This material is available in its entirety as a free download or online web use at *http://www.netbible.org*

Scripture quotations marked as NASB are taken from the *New American Standard Bible*, Copyright © 1960, 1962, 1963, 1968, 1971, 1972, 1973, 1975, 1977, 1995 by The Lockman Foundation. Used by permission.

Scripture quotations marked KJV are taken from the *King James Version*.

Printed in the United States of America.

All rights reserved. This publication is protected by copyright, and except for brief excerpts for review purposes, permission must be obtained from the publisher prior to any prohibited reproduction, storage in a retrieval system, or transmission in any form or by any means, electronic, mechanical, photocopying, recording, or likewise.

For information regarding permissions or special orders, please contact:

BEE World
International Headquarters
P.O. Box 62805
Colorado Springs, CO 80962

ISBN: 978-1-934324-01-8

Contents

Course Introduction...1
Student Instructions...4
Unit One: Laying the Foundation—Defining the Church..5
Lesson 1: Biblical Definition of the Church..6
   Topic 1: Determining a Definition of the Church...7
   Topic 2: Examining the Etymology and Usage of *Ekklesia*.....................................10
   Topic 3: Christ's Relationship to the Church..13
   Topic 4: The Church's Role and Responsibility...19
Lesson 1 Self Check..25
   Lesson 1 Answers..27
   Lesson 1 Self Check Answers..30
Lesson 1 Articles...31
Lesson 2: Presenting the Three Lenses..41
   Topic 1: Function and Form..42
   Topic 2: The Three Lenses..44
   Topic 3: Biblical Absolutes Versus Cultural Variables...47
   Topic 4: Developing Character—Temperate, Controlled, Respectable....................49
Lesson 2 Self Check..55
   Lesson 2 Answers..57
   Lesson 2 Self Check Answers..60
Lesson 2 Articles...61
Lesson 3: Focusing on History and Culture..73
   Topic 1: History of Institutionalism..74
   Topic 2: Institutionalism in Evangelical Churches...76
   Topic 3: Lessons From Culture...78
   Topic 4: Developing Character—Hospitable, Able to Teach, Not a Drunkard........81
Lesson 3 Self Check..84
Unit 1 Exam..85
   Lesson 3 Answers..89
   Lesson 3 Self Check Answers..90
   Unit 1 Exam Answers..91
Lesson 3 Articles...92
Unit Two: Applying the Three Lenses, Part I...111
Lesson 4: Worship Dynamics...112
   Topic 1: Introducing Worship...113
   Topic 2 Defining Worship..116
   Topic 3: Participating in Worship...118
   Topic 4: Gathering to Worship (Exercise in Three Lenses).....................................120
   Topic 5: Ordering the Service...122
   Topic 6: Developing Character—Not Arrogant, Not Prone to Anger, Not Violent...124
Lesson 4 Self Check..127
   Lesson 4 Answers..129

Lesson 4 Self Check Answers..
Lesson 4 Articles... 131
Lesson 5: Edification Dynamics, Part I.. **132**
   Topic 1: Biblical Principles of Edification......................................**137**
   Topic 2: Eight Principles of Edification... 138
   Topic 3: Evaluation of Principles of Edification............................. 140
   Topic 4: Training Leaders and Teachers.. 142
   Topic 5: Church Discipline... 144
   Topic 6: Developing Character—Not Contentious, Gentle, No Lover of Money............. 146
Lesson 5 Self Check.. 150
   Lesson 5 Answers..**153**
   Lesson 5 Self Check Answers.. 155
Lesson 5 Articles.. 158
Lesson 6: Edification Dynamics, Part II... **159**
   Topic 1: Who Are the Ministers in the Church?............................ **169**
   Topic 2: Unity, Diversity, and Interdependence............................170
   Topic 3: Spiritual Gifts... 172
   Topic 4: Body Life and Small Meetings... 173
   Topic 5: Developing Character—Household Management, Good Reputation, Devoted to Goodness............179
Lesson 6 Self Check.. 182
Unit 2 Exam... **185**
   Lesson 6 Answers.. 187
   Lesson 6 Self Check Answers.. 190
   Unit 2 Exam Answers.. 193
Lesson 6 Articles.. 194
Unit 3: Applying the Lenses, Part II... **195**
Lesson 7: Multiplication Dynamics..**221**
   Topic 1: The Great Commission.. **222**
   Topic 2: Personal and Corporate Evangelism................................223
   Topic 3: New Testament Principles of Evangelism........................223
   Topic 4: Developing Character—Upright, Devout, Not a Recent Convert............225
Lesson 7 Self Check..226
   Lesson 7 Answers..**231**
   Lesson 7 Self Check Answers.. 232
Lesson 7 Articles.. 234
Lesson 8: Leadership Dynamics, Part I.. **235**
   Topic 1: The Beginning of Church Leadership, Leadership Defined.................. **253**
   Topic 2: The Beginnings of Church Leadership, Leaders' Job Descriptions..................254
   Topic 3: Developing Character—Building up, Devoted To, Honoring Each Other........... 256
Lesson 8 Self Check.. 258
   Lesson 8 Answers.. 262
   Lesson 8 Self Check Answers.. 265
Lesson 8 Articles.. 267
Lesson 9: Leadership Dynamics, Part II... **268**
   Topic 1: Leadership Qualities—Self Assessment..........................**289**
                                                           290

    Topic 2: Developing Church Leaders..291
    Topic 3: Issues in Developing Church Leaders..294
    Topic 4: Developing Character—Unity, Diversity, Instruction......................296
Lesson 9 Self Check...**299**
    Lesson 9 Self Check..300
Unit 3 Exam..304
    Lesson 9 Answers..305
    Lesson 9 Self Check Answers..306
    Unit 3 Exam Answers..307
Lesson 9 Articles...311
Unit Four: Growing Toward Maturity in Christ..312
Lesson 10: Administration and Organization Dynamics....................................313
    Topic 1: Biblical Examples of Administration and Organization.................316
    Topic 2: Principles of Administration...318
    Topic 3: Principles of Organization..320
    Topic 4: Developing Character—Greet, Serve, Carry One Another's Burdens...............**323**
Lesson 10 Self Check...324
    Lesson 10 Answers...326
    Lesson 10 Self Check Answers..**327**
Lesson 10 Articles..**349**
Lesson 11: Testing the Dynamics..350
    Topic 1: The Measure of Success—Spiritual Growth..................................352
    Topic 2: The Origin of Legalism...355
    Topic 3: Recognizing the Threat of Legalism..357
    Topic 4: Grace Against Legalism...359
    Topic 5: Developing Character—Bearing with, Submitting to, Encouraging One Another...361
Lesson 11 Self Check...362
    Lesson 11 Answers..365
    Lesson 11 Self Check Answers...366
Lesson 11 Articles..**387**
Lesson 12: Your Biblical Philosophy of Ministry..388
    Topic 1: A Review of Biblical Principles...389
    Topic 2: Developing a Relevant Strategy..390
    Topic 3: Changing Familiar Church Practices...392
    Topic 4: Discovering and Using Resources..393
    Topic 5: Formulating Your Strategy..393
    Topic 6: Conclusion..**396**
Lesson 12 Self Check...**398**
Unit 4 Exam..403
    Lesson 12 Answers...404
    Lesson 12 Self Check Answers...405
    Unit 4 Exam Answers..**406**
Lesson 12 Articles..

Course Introduction

Pastor Eugene

Young Pastor Eugene had been assigned to become the pastor of a church in a small town about forty kilometers from the capital. He found himself being tossed about, not by winds of doctrine, but by the "winds of the times." Everything was changing. A new generation of Christians had arisen and many of them were not comfortable with the old ways of "doing church" he had learned as a youth and which had been reinforced in Bible school.

While he began his new ministry with considerable energy and optimism, he gradually began to confront the realities of leading a small church and encouraging spiritual transformation in the small flock which the leaders had entrusted to his care.

It was not long before he found himself at odds with his advisors on many things. They were concerned with methods to ensure numerical growth and how to increase tithing in the congregations. He was sent to various seminars on church growth and attended many conferences throughout the country. He began to realize that there was a widening gap between what he was preaching in the pulpit and what he was discussing in the planning committee. His focus was on growth, methods, and programs; he began to realize that he was beginning to view his congregation as individuals whom he could use to achieve his vision, rather than souls which the Lord had given him who needed a transforming with the Bread of Life.

One day Pastor Eugene attended a conference where a famous church leader spoke on the definition of a church and what it really means to pastor the flock of God. While he was impressed with what the man said, he was even more impressed by who he was. As this man spoke, Pastor Eugene realized that the authenticity he craved was being lived out before him. There was total congruence between what this man believed and how he was implementing what he believed in leading his own congregation. As the Holy Spirit began to convict his heart, Pastor Eugene decided to start anew. He determined that he would, with the Spirit's aid, first understand the biblical mandates for "doing church," and then implement them in his congregation.

He wondered, "Where should I begin?" He decided to start at the beginning. With Bible in hand, he began to explore some basic questions about God's plan, not the surrounding cultures, for growing a church that would bring honor to Christ. Throughout this course, we are going to follow Pastor Eugene's quest.

Unit of Study

The lessons in this course are grouped into four units, with three lessons in each unit.

Unit 1: Laying the Foundations
Lesson 1: Biblical Definition of the Church
Lesson 2: Presenting the Three Lenses
Lesson 3: Focusing on History and Culture

Unit 2: Applying the Three Lenses, Part I
Lesson 4: Worship Dynamics
Lesson 5: Edification Dynamics, Part I
Lesson 6: Edification Dynamics, Part II

Unit 3: Applying the Three Lenses, Part II
Lesson 7: Multiplication Dynamics
Lesson 8: Leadership Dynamics, Part I
Lesson 9: Leadership Dynamics, Part II

Unit 4: Growing Toward Maturity in Christ
Lesson 10: Administration and Organization Dynamics
Lesson 11: Testing the Dynamics
Lesson 12: Your Biblical Philosophy of Ministry

As you plan your study schedule, determine the dates when you want to finish each unit. You can then divide this time into study periods for each lesson.

We suggest that you try to do a lesson a week or three lessons per month. You can do this if you study about one hour each day.

Lesson Organization

Please give careful attention to every part of the lesson:
- Title
- Lesson Introduction
- Lesson Objectives
- Assignments
- Lesson Development
- Illustrations/Readings

The title, introduction, outline, and objectives provide a preview of the lesson. Your mind will be more alert and receptive, and you will learn better because of this preview. The lesson assignments describe how and in what order to complete the lesson. The lesson development follows the lesson outline. Its comments, suggestions, and questions all help you to reach the lesson objectives. Be sure to check your answers with the ones given for the study questions. These will fix your attention once more on the main points of the lesson. This procedure is designed to make your learning more effective and long lasting. Make special note of the maps, charts, and other illustrations because they will help you to identify with the ones who followed Jesus, sharing their problems and letting the tremendous truths of this gospel grip your heart. Also, you will find these illustrations useful in your preaching and teaching.

Recommended for Further Reading

Gene A. Getz, *The Measure of a Man* (Ventura, CA: Regal, 1974)

Gene A. Getz, *Building Up One Another* (Wheaton, IL: Victor, 1979)

Textbook for the Course

Gene A. Getz, *Sharpening the Focus of the Church* (Wheaton, IL: Victor, 1984)

Student Instructions

As you read through the course Table of Contents and Introduction, you saw that this course teaches a three-step inductive approach to Bible study. In order to benefit most from your study of this material, you should plan to work through the lessons in the order they are presented. In other words, we would encourage you to work through the course systematically, rather than choosing a topic in the middle of the course as a place to begin.

You should allow yourself a minimum of six hours of study time to complete each lesson. This would include doing the required reading, answering the questions, doing the exercises, and completing the study projects.

If you plan to teach this course to someone else later on, you may want to keep track of how many hours you needed to complete each lesson. In addition, you might wish to note any problems encountered or questions raised as you work through the course.

Course Design

In the Course Introduction you also found a list of course objectives which summarize the most important things you will learn as you work through the following lessons. Study these objectives attentively and refer to them periodically to gauge your mastery of the course material. They will also serve as guidelines for the final examination found at the back of this study guide.

Since most individuals taking this course are extremely busy people, we have designed each lesson with clearly defined steps for easy reference. Also, if you study the course and lesson objectives, you will know from the start which topics to spend the most time on.

The material covered in Lesson 1 is a review of what was discussed during the first seminar. Sometime between Seminar 1 and Seminar 2, review the contents of Lesson 1, do the exercises, and answer the questions if you have not already done so. The answers will be discussed during Seminar 2.

Your group leader will tell you whether the final examination is to be done by each student at home or together as a class.

Lesson Design

Several standard components are built into each lesson to facilitate your study and develop your skills. They are explained below so that you may recognize and use them to full advantage:

1. **Lesson Outlines** provide an overview of the sections of each lesson. In this way you can anticipate the flow and sequence of the various topics to be covered before you begin your study.
2. **Lesson Objectives** are provided to help you identify the most crucial parts of each lesson. They give you guidance in the effective use of your study time and will be used by your group leader for class discussion, so be prepared!
3. **Repetition and review** are woven into the course to help you learn new concepts.
4. **Examples** are given so that you can see how the steps taught apply to the study of specific passages of Scripture. By studying these examples closely, you will not only review the steps taught, you will also have a better idea of how to proceed when asked to study a passage on your own.

5. **Summary Charts** are useful tools for pulling together materials taught throughout the course. When you want to review a given lesson, you can turn to the summary sheets and charts, which serve as a reminder of all of the steps you studied.
6. **Questions** are posed from time to time in most lessons to help you interact with the material being covered. Whenever you see the heading "Question," stop and write an answer in your personal notebook. Check your answers with those provided at the end of each lesson.
7. **Exercises** give you opportunities to practice new concepts and procedures just covered in the lesson material. Whenever you see the heading "Exercise," do not proceed further in the lesson until you have completed the required work by writing an answer in your personal notebook or doing the required reading.
8. **Study Projects** give you the opportunity to personally discover what God's Word says using the Bible study method taught in that lesson. Each project is based on Philippians 2:1-11 and should be completed before the next seminar. The projects will be discussed and evaluated during the seminar.
9. **Appendices (Articles and Textbooks at the end of the Table of Contents)** include both resources needed for lesson completion and useful reference materials that may be of benefit to you outside of the study requirements of this course.
10. **Examination** is an important component of this course. There is a final examination that is comprehensive in nature, requiring you to use the Bible study skills learned throughout the course. The exam results will contribute to your final course grade.

Materials Needed

To work through this course, you will need a Bible, preferably with cross-references, a copy of this workbook, and a personal notebook entitled Life Notebook for all written work. All the Scripture references and Scripture quotations in this workbook are from the Net Bible, unless otherwise indicated. Every time you see the heading "Question," "Exercise," or "Study Project," you should respond by writing an answer in your Life Notebook.

We suggest that you divide your Life Notebook into two major sections: the first one-third should be reserved for your answers to all questions and written assignments given throughout the course. The remaining two-thirds of the notebook should be reserved for your study projects. (NOTE: If you would like to keep a separate notebook for this second half, please do so, as it may serve as a study commentary later on.) If at all possible, keep together all the work you do on a particular book or passage for future reference.

Reference books, such as a concordance and Bible dictionary, will also be helpful in the completion of some assigned work. Instructions will indicate when the use of supplementary reference books is advisable.

Your Questions about Bible Study

What questions would you like to have answered about the study of the Bible? How do you expect to benefit by working through this course? Take a few minutes to write down your questions and expectations in your notebook. Refer to this list periodically during the course to check your progress.

Unit One: Laying the Foundations

Our human vision always has limits. In the diagram below, these limits are illustrated by the wall. This is what we *do not want to happen* as we try capturing God's vision for the church. What we do want is God's vision—*a vision without limits!*

Raising Your Vision for the Church

We want to show you how to raise your vision over the wall of human limitations.

Our concept of the church is very important. It not only provides us with hope when we are discouraged, but it also guides us in our personal ministries, especially in any leadership role we have within the church. Therefore, we begin in Lesson 1 discussing the definition of the church in the New Testament. In Lessons 2 and 3, the church is then viewed through the three lenses of Scripture, history, and culture. The lens concept is a tool to help you evaluate your church and its leadership.

Unit 1 Outline: Laying the Foundations

Lesson 1: Biblical Definition of the Church
Lesson 2: Presenting the Three Lenses
Lesson 3: Focusing on History and Culture

Lesson 1: Biblical Definition of the Church

Lesson Introduction

The first requirement for accomplishing any task is to accurately understand its nature. You, as a church leader, must understand what God intends the church to be and how it should function. This lesson will help you develop a scriptural understanding of the church's nature and purpose. This is critical to becoming God's leader, and these biblical principles will become your measuring stick as you evaluate your ministry.

Lesson Outline

Topic 1: Determining a Definition of the Church
- The Multi-Faceted Nature of the Church
- Discerning Between God's Intention and Man's Implementation

Topic 2: Examining the Etymology and Usage of *Ekklesia*
- The Local Church
- The Universal Church

Topic 3: Christ's Relationship to the Church
- The Church as a Bride
- The Foundation of the Church
- The Church as a Flock
- The Church as Branches of a Vine

Topic 4: The Church's Role and Responsibility
- The Church as a Priesthood
- The Church as a Body
- The Church Members as Disciples
- The Church Members as Brothers

Lesson Objectives

Pastor Eugene, in the midst of all the meetings and competing priorities, felt like he was somehow missing God's intended role for him as a church leader. A conference with a church leader who he admired prompted him to search the Scriptures for God's vision for this concept that we call "church." In this lesson, we will explore what Pastor Eugene found in the Scriptures, including:

- Biblical references that define the nature and purpose of the church
- How the term *Ekklesia*, the original Greek word that we define as "church," is used in Scripture
- Metaphors that provide concepts to describe God's intention for the church

Throughout this lesson, you will have the opportunity to apply what you've learned to define and refine your own definition of the word "church."

Topic 1: Determining a Definition of the Church

The Multi-Faceted Church

Diagram showing a diamond with facets labeled: Scripture, History, Culture, Ekklesia, Dynamics, Purpose, Metaphors, Leadership

If Pastor Eugene looks at any one of these facets without taking the other facets into account, he will have a one-dimensional and skewed view of the church. In order to properly define the church, we need to be sure to take God's multi-dimensional point of view, looking at the concept of church holistically, as well as from every angle.

In this topic, there are several questions we will wrestle with to establish a definition of the church:

- What are the Biblical passages that define the church's nature and purpose?
- What are the difficulties associated with defining the church?
- How can we be succinct, and yet comprehensive enough, to capture its many facets?
- How can we capture its living, dynamic nature?

The Multi-faceted Nature of the Church

We're going to start this lesson with your current definition of the word *church*. As you go through each section of this lesson, you will have the opportunity to refine your definition. The definition you have at the end of this lesson will provide a foundation for the rest of this course.

QUESTION 1

Open your Life Notebook and quickly write the words that come to mind when you think of the word *church*. These words will become your starting point as you refine how you describe the *church* to others.

QUESTION 2

Read the verses in the left-hand column and match each passage with a key concept for defining the word *church*.

Passage	Concept
John 4:20-24	Worship
Acts 2:42-47	Community
1 Corinthians 12:12-27	Edification
2 Corinthians 5:14-21	Ambassadors

- Worship means to ascribe "worth" to God; for example, to praise Him for His beautiful creation or His redemption through Christ (Ps 95:6).
- Community is the togetherness the church members experience because they are family in Christ (Rom 12:1).
- Edification means to build each other up through the gifts and love the Father has given us (Rom 14:19).
- Ambassador means that we are God's representatives to earth-dwellers (2 Cor 5:14-21).

Reading Assignment

Please read the article titled "Determining a Definition" in the Articles section at the end of this lesson.

Discerning Between God's Intention and Man's Implementation

Below are listed several possible definitions for the word *church*. Answer true if you believe it is an acceptable biblical definition of the word and false if it is not.

QUESTION 3

A church is a building where Christians meet. *True or False?*

QUESTION 4

Any group led by an ordained pastor is a church. *True or False?*

QUESTION 5

Anytime a group of Christians meet together they are a church. *True or False?*

What is a church, biblically? The three purposes of the church shed light on this important question.

- Worship is from God's people upward to Him.
- Edification is based on gifts and love proceeding from God, but shared horizontally by His people.
- Evangelism is the message from God proceeding from His people to unbelievers.

The arrows in the diagram below show the direction for each threefold purpose:

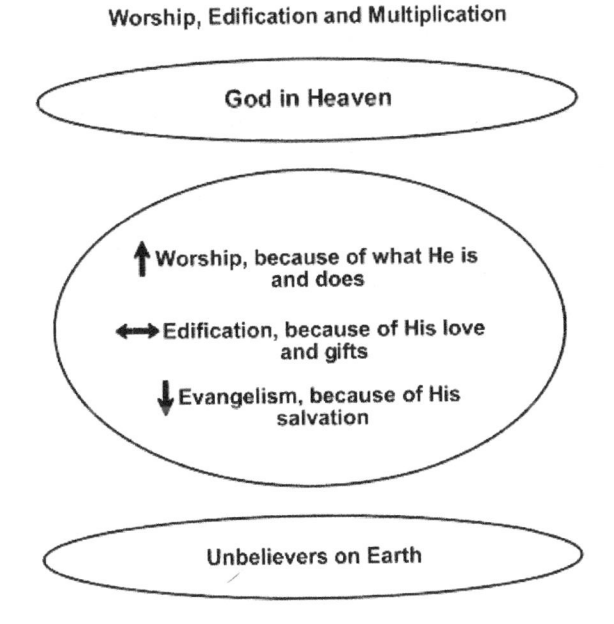

Worship, Edification and Multiplication

```
          God in Heaven

      ↑ Worship, because of what He is
          and does
      ↔ Edification, because of His love
          and gifts
      ↓ Evangelism, because of His
          salvation

        Unbelievers on Earth
```

QUESTION 6

If a Christian spends time in personal worship, reading the Bible, singing to God, and preparing evangelistic materials for others to use, then this is church. *True or False?*

QUESTION 7

The church is the living community of believers in Christ Jesus, who meet regularly to fulfill a threefold purpose: worship, edification, and multiplication. *True or False?*

Any definition of the word "church" must include all these aspects to be considered valid:

- Living Community: For the local church, this means Christians who are living on this earth at this time, but the universal church includes all believers in Christ from Pentecost on, alive or with the Lord (because these believers are eternally alive and still part of His bride, the Church).
- Community/Group/Corporately: There must be two or more believers to make a church.
- Threefold purpose: A church's purpose is worship, edification, and multiplication.
- Meet regularly: A church must consistently meet to fulfill these three purposes.

From the questions above, you may have noticed that it is difficult to write a definition that encompasses all of the dimensions of the church. We tend to define the church from our experience or from a limited number of Bible passages. This may cause us to view the church from a limited understanding, perhaps incorrectly.

Topic 1 Key Points:

- Defining the word *church* requires a complete, multi-faceted approach. Trying to define the church in a simplistic way does not accurately represent the nature and the purpose of the church.
- The key concepts that are important to include in the definition of the church are:
    Community of believers

> Worship
> Edification
> Multiplication

- To form, grow, and refine your congregation, it is important to be able to describe what God intended the church to be, as well as identify unbiblical misconceptions.

QUESTION 8

Review the words that you wrote in Question 1 and compare them to what you have learned in this lesson. Open your Life Notebook and record your thoughts about how your experiences compare with the biblical definition of the word "church."

QUESTION 9

Open your Life Notebook and reflect upon what you've learned and write your own definition of the word *church*, using Scripture references to support your statements.

Topic 2: Examining the Etymology and Usage of Ekklesia

The next thing Pastor Eugene did as he searched through the Scriptures was look at the original biblical language that was used to describe the church, and research what that language meant to the people in New Testament times. Pastor Eugene believed that understanding the original meaning of the word "church" would help him better understand the church's roots and God's original intention for congregations of believers.

In this topic, we will study the word translated "church" in the New Testament; the Greek word *Ekklesia*. We will study:

- How the Greeks used this word in secular society
- How biblical writers used this word in the Scriptures
- How biblical writers differentiated their use of the word from the way it was used in secular society

The Local Church

As Christians, it is important for us to:

- Understand our identity as part of the universal church *and*
- Be a part of a local family or congregation of believers.

The Greek word translated "church" in the New Testament is the Greek word *ekklesia*. This word literally means to "call out" and was used of any assembly of the citizens. Paul distinguishes between the literal, secular meaning of the term and the Christian meaning of the term by always using an article with the term *ekklesia*. So the church is not just a local or community assembly, it is limited to believers in Christ.

QUESTION 10

Match the following Bible passages, which all contain the Greek word *ekklesia* listed in the left-hand column with the locations of the churches they describe listed in the right-hand column.

Verses	Locations
Acts 11:22	Jerusalem
Acts 13:1	Berea
Acts 17:10-12	Antioch
Revelation 2:8-10	Philadelphia
Revelation 3:7-8	Smyrna

As you can see from the question above, the term *ekklesia* often refers to a local community of believers.

The Universal Church

Though *ekklesia* is often used to describe the local church, it is also used to describe the universal church. The local church is a microcosm of the universal church. When we look at a leaf through a microscope, the cells are a microcosm of the entire leaf. In a similar way, looking at the local church is like looking at a smaller version of the universal church. Universal means "including all" or "the whole." It also means "to be present everywhere." This means that the universal church includes all Christians everywhere. The universal church is the whole worldwide church. Local churches are a part of the universal church, just as all believers are a part of the universal church.

Macro and Micro-Views

Reading Assignment

Please read the following background information examining the etymology and usage of the Greek word *ekklesia*.

The word translated "church" in the New Testament is the Greek word *ekklesia*. It combines the preposition *ek*, meaning "out," with the verb *kaleo*, meaning "to call." It was used in New Testament times for calling the citizens of a town to assemble for business. The word is used in Acts 19:32, 41 for a large gathering in the theater in Ephesus. The assembly was called to judge whether the complaints brought against Christians by Demetrius were true or not. The use of this word in the early epistles means "an assembly of people coming together for a united purpose."

Paul distinguished the Christian assembly from other groups in two ways:

- First, in the Greek text of the New Testament there is a definite article. The definite article connected with *ekklesia* is not found in other Greek writings.
- Second, he uses a modifying phrase. In 1 Thessalonians, Paul uses the phrase "the church of the Thessalonians in God the Father and the Lord Jesus Christ" to distinguish the assembly of God's people from any other assembly (we find similar phrases in 2 Thess 2:1, 1 Cor 1:2, and 2 Cor 1:1).

Therefore, when we think of the church, one picture that should come to mind is the body of believers in God the Father and the Lord Jesus Christ meeting together for a common purpose.

Where are We in the Big Picture?

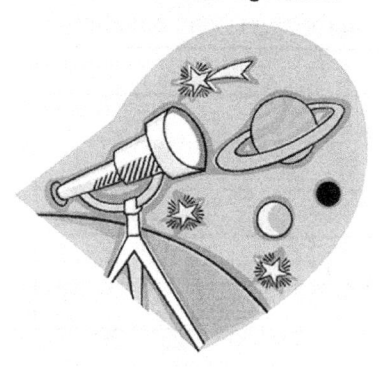

Of the 114 uses of *ekklesia* in the New Testament, most refer to a local manifestation of the church universal (the church universal being those who are in God the Father and the Lord Jesus Christ). Clear examples are seen in such expressions as "the church at Jerusalem" (Acts 11:22), "the church that was at Antioch" (Acts 13:1), and "the church of God which is at Corinth" (1 Cor 1:2).

While many passages refer to the *ekklesia* as a local Christian association, other passages (especially Eph 1:22; 3:10, 21; 5:23-25, 27, 29, 32) talk about all believers, without reference to a particular location.

We should conclude that *ekklesia* has a local sense, as well as a broader, more inclusive, spiritual sense. A complete definition should point to people—those associated spiritually with all Christians—and also to a particular group in a specific geographical location.

Because of this dual emphasis, Christians tend to capture the dual aspect of the church under the terms "universal" (our unified identity in the body of Christ) and "local" (the manifestations of the body of Christ in separate, varied geographical locations). In both aspects the people are central. With "universal," the individual is emphasized in his spiritual association in the greater body of Christ. In the "local" sense, the greater spiritual association finds geographical or corporate visible expression in the many assemblies.

QUESTION 11

Notice the different metaphors Christ uses to refer to His church. Match the verse in the left-hand column with the figure in the right-hand column.

Verse	Figure
Acts 8:1-3	People or members
Ephesians 1:5	All Christians
Acts 9:31	General fellowship

Often people's response to this dual manifestation of the "church" creates certain problems. Frustrated by the hypocrisy and sin in local churches, some people have primarily focused on membership in the spiritual body of Christ (the universal church) and neglected their association on the local level. This same reasoning leads certain people to be unconcerned about purifying their own local church. Still others stress the need for the organizational unity of Christ's church, believing the many differences among local churches are unbiblical.

Although there are two aspects of the church, in the minds of the human authors of Scripture there was not a dichotomy; the local *ekklesia* represents the universal *ekklesia*. This relationship—the micro to the macro—is seen repeatedly throughout the New Testament; the local church is responsible to represent the universal.

Topic 2 Key Points:

- The word *ekklesia* literally means to "call out" and was used to describe an assembly of the citizens of a town.

- Paul distinguishes between the literal, secular meaning of the term and the Christian meaning of the term by always using an article with the term *ekklesia*. So the church is not just a local or community assembly, but is limited to believers.
- *Ekklesia* refers to both the local and the universal nature of the church. It refers to the people as well as groups.

QUESTION 12

In this lesson, you discovered that you are part of the local and universal church. Reflect upon what you learned and refine your previous definition to include both the local and universal nature of the word *church*.

Topic 3: Christ's Relationship to the Church

Let's go back to Pastor Eugene and his search for the true definition of the word "church." Pastor Eugene knows that the Bible contains many references or metaphors that describe Christ's relationship with the church. To define the church without defining its relationship with Christ would form a rather incomplete and purposeless definition. So Pastor Eugene picked up his Bible and found all the passages that describe Christ's relationship with the Church. There are many passages, but he focused on four beautiful metaphors:

- The bride
- The foundation and cornerstone
- The shepherd and his flock
- The vine and the branches

The Church as a Bride

The first metaphor that we will discuss is that of a bride.

Reading Assignment

Please read the article titled "The Church as a Bride" in the Articles section at the end of this lesson.

Although there are few Bible references that include this metaphor, the powerful picture this metaphor paints guides our imaginations to a clear understanding of the church's purpose. The most obvious references are 2 Corinthians 11:2 and Ephesians 5:22-32.

QUESTION 13

Match the verse listed in the left-hand column with the teaching and image of the church in the right-hand column.

Verse	Teaching
Acts 20:28	Jesus describes His return for His church.
John 14:3	Christ takes His new bride to the banquet at the marriage celebration.
Ephesians 5:27	God obtained His church with the blood of His own Son.
Revelation 19:7-9	Christ's preparation of His bride

So, Christ has purchased and cleansed His bride with His own precious blood, has espoused her to Himself for that intimate relationship, and will return for her immediately before the wedding celebration. While she waits, the church prepares (clothes) herself in clean white linen by doing righteous deeds.

The Foundation of the Church

The second metaphor that we will discuss is that of a foundation.

Without a proper foundation, a house cannot stand. As a child, three tornados came through our city on one night and our house was destroyed. But we were able to build on the foundation from the previous house. Having a good foundation is vital to our survival.

In Luke 6:47-49, Jesus was speaking about people who come to Him and listen to His words and put them into practice. He said:

> I will show you what he is like: He is like a man building a house, who dug down deep, and laid the foundation on bedrock. When a flood came, the river burst against that house but could not shake it, because it had been well built. But the person who hears and does not put my words into practice is like a man who built a house on the ground without a foundation. When the river burst against that house, it collapsed immediately, and was utterly destroyed!

Building a Foundation

QUESTION 14

Match the verse in the left-hand column with its teaching on the foundation of the church in the right-hand column.

Verse	Teaching
Matthew 16:15-18	Christ is called the foundation,
1 Corinthians 3:10-15	Jesus says He will build His church,
Ephesians 2:20	The apostles and prophets are the foundation of the church,
1 Peter 2:4-8	Jesus is the only cornerstone,

Reading Assignment

Please read the article titled "The Foundation of the Church" in the Articles section at the end of this lesson.

QUESTION 15

What types of consequences may occur if we fail to keep Christ as the foundation and cornerstone of our local church?

Reading Assignment

There is a popular western hymn that was written by Samuel J. Stone in 1866 that beautifully describes the foundational relationship between Christ and the Church. Please read the words to this hymn before you answer the Life Notebook question.

The Church's One Foundation

The Church's one foundation
Is Jesus Christ her Lord,
She is His new creation
By water and the Word.
From heaven He came and sought her
To be His holy bride;
With His own blood He bought her
And for her life He died.

Elect from every nation,
Yet one o'er all the earth;
Her charter of salvation,
One Lord, one faith, one birth;
One holy Name she blesses,
Partakes one holy food,
And to one hope she presses,
With every grace endued.

The Church shall never perish!
Her dear Lord to defend,
To guide, sustain, and cherish,
Is with her to the end:
Though there be those who hate her,
And false sons in her pale,
Against both foe or traitor
She ever shall prevail.

Though with a scornful wonder
Men see her sore oppressed,
By schisms rent asunder,
By heresies distressed,
Yet saints their watch are keeping,
Their cry goes up, "How long?"
And soon the night of weeping
Shall be the morn of song!

'Mid toil and tribulation,
And tumult of her war,
She waits the consummation
Of peace forevermore;
Till, with the vision glorious,
Her longing eyes are blest,
And the great Church victorious
Shall be the Church at rest.

Yet she on earth hath union
With God the Three in One,
And mystic sweet communion
With those whose rest is won,
With all her sons and daughters
Who, by the Master's hand
Led through the deathly waters,
Repose in Eden land.

O happy ones and holy!
Lord, give us grace that we
Like them, the meek and lowly,
On high may dwell with Thee:
There, past the border mountains,
Where in sweet vales the Bride
With Thee by living fountains
Forever shall abide!

QUESTION 16

What steps can you take as a Christian leader to keep Christ as the foundation and cornerstone of your ministry? Open your Life Notebook and record your thoughts.

The Church as a Flock

The third metaphor that we will discuss is that of the Good Shepherd and His flock.

Natural sheep left alone without a shepherd will only harm themselves, yet they readily submit whenever the shepherd guides. So they are both needy and willing to follow their shepherd (Isa 53:7). Figurative sheep, like us, however, must be reminded that submission to their leader is beneficial.

Reading Assignment

Please read the article titled "The Church as a Flock" in the Articles section at the end of this lesson.

QUESTION 17

From the following verses, identify the natural needs and characteristics of sheep as they correspond to spiritual needs and characteristics of human beings.

Verse	Characteristics of Sheep
Psalm 23:1-4	Lost sheep
Isaiah 53:6	Fearful sheep
Ezekiel 34:4, 6	Dependent sheep
Matthew 9:36	Straying sheep
Luke 12:32	Wandering and straying sheep
Luke 15:1-7	Wandering and scattered sheep
1 Peter 2:25	Bewildered and helpless sheep

A sheep left on its own certainly meets destruction sooner or later. Like sheep, as Christian leaders we must follow Christ's leadership and point the members of our flock to Him. He guides, leads, and protects us.

An Enemy of the Sheep

QUESTION 18

How are the enemies depicted by the following verses? Match the verse in the left-hand column with the corresponding depiction and danger to the flock in the right-hand column.

Verse	Depiction and Danger
John 10:1, 8	Thief and robber the sheep run from
John 10:5	Fierce wolves will not spare the flock but pervert the truth
John 10:10	Thief comes to kill, steal, and destroy
John 10:12	Stranger the sheep run from
Acts 20:29-30	Hired hand abandons the sheep when wolves come

The verses above are obviously built on Old Testament warnings (such as Ezekiel 34) and developed in the specific discussions in the pastoral epistles (1 Tim 1:3-7; 4:1-4; 2 Tim 2:16-18; Tit 3:9-11), as well as in 2 Peter 2. Thieves, strangers, wild animals, and hired hands are figures used to depict false prophets, sinful priests, false teachers, and other wrongly motivated leaders. They endanger the flock by false teaching, inadequate care, desertion in times of difficulty, and concern with self rather than the flock.

QUESTION 19

As a Christian leader, describe Christ's role and your own with regard to guiding and protecting the church. Open your Life Notebook and record your thoughts.

The Church as Branches of a Vine

The fourth metaphor that we will discuss is that of the vine and the branches.

Reading Assignment

Please read the article titled "The Church as Branches of a Vine" in the Articles section at the end of this lesson.

QUESTION 20

Match the verses in the left-hand column with the teaching about abiding in the right-hand column.

Verse	Teaching
John 13:1-38	Apart from our union with Christ, we cannot produce fruit.
John 14:15-31	Jesus will send the Holy Spirit to abide with us when He leaves.
John 15:1-17	We must each accept Jesus' sacrifice on our behalf.
John 16:1-33	The Holy Spirit plays a vital role in uniting us with Christ.

Topic 3 Key Points:

- *Bride*—Christ loves the Church as His bride and prepares and sustains her to bring her home to Himself.
- *Foundation/Cornerstone*—Christ is the foundation of the church, and also the cornerstone that provides stability and strength.
- *Shepherd/Flock*—As believers, we are the sheep that comprise God's flock. Christ bought us with His blood and now owns us, guides us, and protects us.
- *Vine/Branches*—Our connection with Christ is vital to our ability to produce results.

QUESTION 21

In this lesson, you learned about metaphors that depict Christ's relationship to the Church. Open your Life Notebook and refine your definition of the church to encompass what you learned from the metaphors of bride, foundation, shepherd, and vine.

Topic 4: The Church's Role and Responsibility

Let's go back to Pastor Eugene and his search for the true definition of the word "church." Pastor Eugene has a sense that the church and the members of the church have certain responsibilities that are specified in the Bible. The Bible describes how we are related, connected, and responsible to each other by using the following metaphors:

- Priesthood
- Christ's body
- Disciple
- Brotherhood

The Church as a Priesthood

The first metaphor we will discuss is that of priesthood.

A governmental ambassador does not represent his own interest but the interest of the country that sent him. A good ambassador improves and facilitates communication between his government and the government he is sent to. Hopefully, this prevents misunderstandings and the sending country looks good in the eyes of the receiving government. If he does his job poorly or misbehaves, it will reflect poorly on the sending government.

In the same way, we represent Christ on earth: "Therefore we are ambassadors for Christ, as though God were making His plea through us. We plead with you on Christ's behalf, 'Be reconciled to God!'" (2 Cor 5:20).

We Are a Letter Revealing Christ

Reading Assignment

Please read the article titled "The Church as a Priesthood" in the Articles section at the end of this lesson.

QUESTION 22

Read Revelation 1:4-6, Revelation 5:9-10, and Revelation 20:6. Match the truth about priests under the Old Covenant in the left-hand column with the corresponding truth about priests in the New Testament in the right-hand column.

OT Priest	*NT Truths*
Some believers were priests.	All enter God's presence.
High priests entered God's presence.	All are priests.
Once a year the high priest enters God's presence.	We are always in God's presence.
Priests were ordained.	Sacrifices are no longer necessary.
Priests brought sacrifices for sins.	None need to be ordained.

QUESTION 23

Continuing with some practical implications from the types of sacrifices that are part of the church's daily function as priesthood, match the teaching of the verse in the left-hand column with the similar teaching of the verse in the right-hand column.

Verse	*Similar Verse*
Romans 12:1-8	Pictures a sacrifice greatly pleasing to God (Philippians 4:17-18)
Hebrews 13:15	Let all conversations bring thanksgiving to God (Romans 10:9-10).
Hebrews 13:16	New believers are a spiritual sacrifice to God (Romans 15:16)
1 Peter 2:9	All life turned into a worship experience by prayer (Revelation 8:3-4).
Revelation 5:8	Daily life becomes a worship service (2 Corinthians 8:5).

QUESTION 24

Describe how your daily life can become an act of worship and sacrifice. Open your Life Notebook and record your thoughts.

The Church as a Body

The second metaphor that we will discuss is that of the body.

Many passages in the New Testament use this picture for the church. (If you wish to look them up, they are Rom 12:5; 1 Cor 10:16-17; 12:12-27; Eph 1:22-23; 2:16; 4:4-12, 16; 5:23, 30; Col 1:18, 24; 2:19; 3:15.) It is tempting for some to read meanings into the texts that are not actually there. So let's explore how the Bible uses this term.

When Paul compares the church to the human body ("the church is his body," Eph 1:22-23), he clearly describes both the unity and interdependence of all church members. When he says "one body," Paul emphasizes the spiritual unity of all believers, wherever and however they associate with each other. Furthermore, in comparing the church not just to "a body" but to "Christ's body" (1 Cor 12:27), Christ becomes the center of attention.

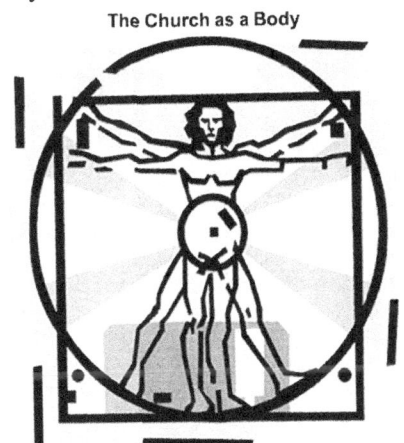

QUESTION 25

From the graphic above, which part of the body do you want in charge of the body?

　　A. Head

　　B. Feet

　　C. Arm

　　D. Tongue

The context of those exact places where the metaphor is used should determine the emphasis of the image! Churches that emphasize external organizational unity (and in that way strive for universal unity among Christians) understand the body metaphor to mean organization. On the other hand, evangelical churches that want to increase fellowship within particular local churches like to emphasize each person's individual and unique contribution and sometimes forget to emphasize submission to Christ and dependence on Him. We should, however, stick to the primary biblical emphasis of all being linked as members to their "head" and then to "each other."

Clearly, the body and bride metaphors are closely joined together. The body metaphor emphasizes the sustaining life of Christ, and the bride metaphor emphasizes the love Christ has for the church. Both emphasize growing to maturity. Both stress two aspects of the purpose of the church: one in its relationship to our Lord and the other in its relationship to the members of the church. It is hard to ponder these and not find your heart worshipping the Bridegroom and your love for fellow Christians increasing. This is exactly what these metaphors should do.

Body and Bride Metaphors Combined

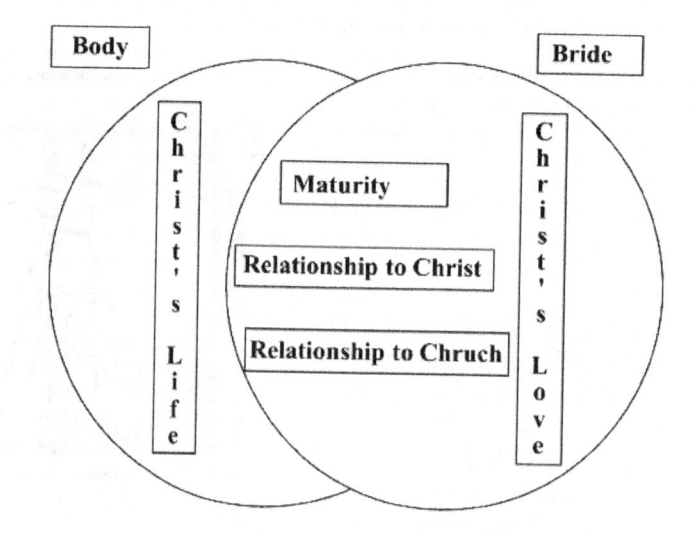

The focus of this image is "upward to Christ," then "inward to one another." The emphasis of the image is first and foremost on its head. This, in turn, results in unity and growth of the members together. Thus, we find a twofold purpose: worship (upward to Christ) and edification (inward to one another).

QUESTION 26

Describe the natural organization of the church that is highlighted by the body metaphor. Open your Life Notebook and record your thoughts.

The Church Members as Disciples

The third metaphor that we will discuss is that of disciples.

In New Testament times, the best-known rabbis had followers who left their families and livelihood to be with their rabbi full time. Their goal was not only to learn from him but to become like him. This was what the twelve disciples of Jesus did. Therefore, their purpose wasn't just edification; discipleship was about much more than just gaining knowledge.

QUESTION 27

Jesus made comments about a disciple's relationships that reiterated the threefold purpose of the church. Match the verse in the left-hand column with the corresponding purpose of the church in the right-hand column.

Verse	Purpose
John 13:34-35	Worship
Matthew 28:18-20	Multiplication
Luke 6:40	Edification

Lesson 1: Biblical Definition of the Church

Reading Assignment

Please read the article titled "Disciples" in the Articles section at the end of this lesson.

QUESTION 28

If disciples are imitators of Christ and not all Christians are disciples, then that means that churches will have members who are disciples and members who are *not* committed to discipleship. What differences do you think you might see in a church comprised of mostly disciples, compared to a church where only a few are disciples of Christ? How do you think individual discipleship affects a whole congregation?

The Church Members as Brothers

Brotherhood is also an important concept as Jesus unified the Jews and Gentiles by breaking down the wall between them (Acts 10:9-16; Eph 2:11-22). Though difficult for us to understand, this barrier seemed insurmountable during Jesus' time. To the Jews, Gentiles were unclean and must be avoided. But—and this is symbolic of all natural enemies—through Christ's work all members are brought together as a spiritual family who can truly love one another (Mk 3:31-35).

How is this novel idea built into the metaphors we have studied? Refer to the scriptural context of the metaphors to get an idea (e.g., Eph 2; Jn 10). Then relate other passages regarding unity or oneness in Christ.

QUESTION 29

Match the reference in the left-hand column with the corresponding teaching in the right-hand column.

Reference	Teaching
Ephesians 2:17-19	Members of the same household
Mark 3:35	Members of the same family
John 17:22-23	Unified members

Reading Assignment

Please read the article titled "Brotherhood in the Church" in the Articles section at the end of this lesson.

Topic 4 Key Points:

- *Priesthood*—We are Christ's representatives on earth. Every aspect of our daily life is a religious activity and a witness to others of Christ's presence in our life.

- *Body*—All church members are united in purpose and interdependent upon each other. We are the hands and feet of Christ on earth.
- *Disciples*—We are called as believers to imitate our Lord Jesus Christ, not just as individuals, but also collectively.
- *Brotherhood*—The church is a spiritual family in which we are all heirs to God's kingdom. We have a responsibility for mutual love, honor, and respect for each other in that community.

QUESTION 30

Describe what brotherhood means to a congregation. Open your Life Notebook and record your thoughts.

QUESTION 31

In this lesson, you learned about metaphors that depict the roles and responsibilities of the church. Refine your definition of the church to encompass what you learned from the metaphors of priesthood, body, disciples, and brotherhood. Open your Life Notebook and record your new definition.

Lesson 1 Self Check

QUESTION 1

Which of the following passages teaches that individuals in the church are ambassadors for Christ?

    A. Acts 2:42-47

    B. 1 Corinthians 12:12-27

    C. 2 Corinthians 5:14-21

    D. John 4:20-24

QUESTION 2

The Greek word translated "church" is _____.

QUESTION 3

Sometimes the New Testament equates members of the church with the church itself. *True or False?*

QUESTION 4

Which passage teaches about Christ taking His new bride to the banquet at the marriage celebration of the Lamb?

    A. John 14:3

    B. Acts 20:28

    C. Ephesians 5:27

    D. Revelation 19:7-9

QUESTION 5

In Scripture, Christ, the apostles, and the prophets are called the foundation of the church. *True or False?*

QUESTION 6

The metaphor that pictures how Christ now owns, guides, and protects us is the _____.

QUESTION 7

Under the Old Covenant, the priests pictured prayer by their sacrifice of _____.

QUESTION 8

Each of the truths below is emphasized by one of the metaphor/concepts studied in this lesson; which truth does the body metaphor emphasize?

    A. The church must be built upon Christ.

    B. The interdependence of church members

    C. The love Christ has for the church

    D. The protective care of Christ

QUESTION 9

The main problem with discipleship as a concept is its LACK of emphasis on_____.

    A. The corporate life of the church

    B. Imitating Christ's life

    C. Spiritual growth

    D. Spiritual maturity

QUESTION 10

At the time the New Testament was written, a Jew within the church calling a Gentile "brother" meant he fully understood the concept of _____.

Lesson 1 Answers to Questions

QUESTION 1: *Your answer*

QUESTION 2:

Passage	Concept
John 4:20-24	Worship
Acts 2:42-47	Community
1 Corinthians 12:12-27	Edification
2 Corinthians 5:14-21	Ambassadors

QUESTION 3: False
QUESTION 4: False
QUESTION 5: False
QUESTION 6: False
QUESTION 7: True
QUESTION 8: *Your answer*
QUESTION 9: *Your answer*

QUESTION 10:

Verses	Locations
Acts 11:22	Jerusalem
Acts 13:1	Antioch
Acts 17:10-12	Berea
Revelation 2:8-10	Smyrna
Revelation 3:7-8	Philadelphia

QUESTION 11:

Verse	Figure
Acts 8:1-3	People or members
Ephesians 1:5	All Christians
Acts 9:31	General fellowship

QUESTION 12: *Your answer*

QUESTION 13:

Verse	Teaching
Acts 20:28	God obtained His church with the blood of His own Son.
John 14:3	Jesus describes His return for His church.
Ephesians 5:27	Christ's preparation of His bride
Revelation 19:7-9	Christ takes His new bride to the banquet at the marriage celebration.

QUESTION 14:

Verse	Teaching
Matthew 16:15-18	Jesus says He will build His church.
1 Corinthians 3:10-15	Christ is called the foundation.
Ephesians 2:20	The apostles and prophets are the foundation of the church.
1 Peter 2:4-8	Jesus is the only cornerstone.

QUESTION 15: If we build on something else, the church will not achieve its purpose here on earth, spiritual sacrifices will not be properly made (Eph 2:20-22; 2 Pet 2:4-8), and in eternity we will lose reward (1 Cor 3:10-15).

QUESTION 16: *Your answer*

QUESTION 17:

Verse	Characteristics of Sheep
Psalm 23:1-4	Dependent sheep
Isaiah 53:6	Wandering and straying sheep
Ezekiel 34:4, 6	Wandering and scattered sheep
Matthew 9:36	Bewildered and helpless sheep
Luke 12:32	Fearful sheep
Luke 15:1-7	Lost sheep
1 Peter 2:25	Straying sheep

QUESTION 18:

Verse	Depiction and Danger
John 10:1, 8	Thief and robber the sheep run from
John 10:5	Stranger the sheep run from
John 10:10	Thief comes to kill, steal, and destroy
John 10:12	Hired hand abandons the sheep when wolves come
Acts 20:29-30	Fierce wolves will not spare the flock but pervert the truth

QUESTION 19: *Your answer*

QUESTION 20:

Verse	Teaching
John 13:1-38	We must each accept Jesus' sacrifice on our behalf.
John 14:15-31	Jesus will send the Holy Spirit to abide with us when He leaves.
John 15:1-17	Apart from our union with Christ, we cannot produce fruit.
John 16:1-33	The Holy Spirit plays a vital role in uniting us with Christ.

QUESTION 21: *Your answer*

QUESTION 22:

OT Priest	NT Truths
Some believers were priests.	All are priests.
High priests entered God's presence.	All enter God's presence.
Once a year the high priest enters God's presence.	We are always in God's presence.
Priests were ordained.	None need to be ordained.
Priests brought sacrifices for sins.	Sacrifices are no longer necessary.

QUESTION 23:

Verse	Similar Verse
Romans 12:1-8	Daily life becomes a worship service (2 Corinthians 8:5).
Hebrews 13:15	Let all conversations bring thanksgiving to God (Romans 10:9-10).
Hebrews 13:16	Pictures a sacrifice greatly pleasing to God (Philippians 4:17-18)
1 Peter 2:9	New believers are a spiritual sacrifice to God (Romans 15:16).
Revelation 5:8	All life turned into a worship experience by prayer (Revelation 8:3-4).

QUESTION 24: *Your answer*

QUESTION 25: A. Head

Most significantly, inherent in this metaphor is the relationship of the "head" to the body: "He [Christ] is the head of the body, the church" (Col 1:18).

QUESTION 26: *Your answer*

QUESTION 27:

Verse	Purpose
John 13:34-35	Edification
Matthew 28:18-20	Multiplication
Luke 6:40	Worship

QUESTION 28: *Your answer*

QUESTION 29:

Reference	Teaching
Ephesians 2:17-19	Members of the same household
Mark 3:35	Members of the same family
John 17:22-23	Unified members

QUESTION 30: *Your answer*
QUESTION 31: *Your answer*

Lesson 1 Self Check Answers

QUESTION 1:
C. 2 Corinthians 5:14-21
QUESTION 2: *Ekklesia*
QUESTION 3: True
QUESTION 4:
D. Revelation 19:7-9
QUESTION 5: True
QUESTION 6: Shepherd
QUESTION 7: Incense
QUESTION 8:
B. The interdependence of church members
QUESTION 9:
A. The corporate life of the church
QUESTION 10: Grace

Lesson 1 Articles

Brotherhood in the Church

"Brotherhood" was a term popular in many past religious orders, and it is also used in many of the newer churches of today. Although it is a technical word, brotherhood helps describe the church.

The word "brother" was already used in many earlier periods to describe relationships outside of the family. Father is used of a spiritual predecessor, or superior, and son is used of an antecessor, or inferior, without denoting a blood relationship.

The Lord Jesus gives a very pointed meaning to the term when He says, "For whoever does the will of my Father in heaven is my brother and sister and mother" (Mt 12:50). Both the equality and the spiritual bond are expressed in the rest of the New Testament when the term "brother" is used as a straightforward substitute for fellow Christians. The responsibility for mutual love, compassion, and respect within the Christian community are stipulated in 1 John consistently in terms of "brother" to "brother."

Ephesians 2:17-19 shows the significance of the church being a spiritual family:

"And he came and preached peace to you who were far off [Gentiles] and peace to those who were near [Jews]; so that through him we both have access in one Spirit to the Father. So then you are no longer foreigners and non-citizens, but you are fellow citizens with the saints and members of God's household."

A Jew within the church who called a Gentile a brother fully understood the concept of grace: Gentiles are equal to Jews within the church without having to keep the Law of Moses!

This unity of the church worldwide—across all ethnic, social, and political borders—is central in the whole New Testament. Gentiles are fellow heirs and fellow members of the body, and fellow partakers of the promise in Christ Jesus through the Gospel (Eph 3:3-6).

The fact that the church brings together, within a spiritual family, opposite groups which sometimes have strong natural dislikes for each other cannot be overemphasized. It forms the background to the many statements in the Epistles about God who in His grace forgives sinners and calls them to accept each other based on grace. Practically speaking, it becomes a tremendous testimony to the world whenever and wherever the brotherhood of Christians finds real expression.

Notice that the spiritual armament Paul describes in Ephesians, with which the church can stand strong against the attack of spiritual beings, is a list of aspects of church life described in the metaphors already.

We can draw an important inference from this truth for our definition: *We can feel free to leave the relationship of the church to Satan unspecified.* It is as if this relationship is purely negative and needs no real attention. As the church works on fulfilling its purpose, it defeats Satan and his allies.

The church becomes a training ground for believers to mature in grace and, in so doing, to become salt in this unsavory world. All of Scripture indicates how this process does currently and will lead to the greater glory of God. Again, we see the threefold purpose of the church—worship, edification, and multiplication—reflected in the concept of brotherhood.

Both technical terms, disciples and brotherhood, enrich biblical emphases on the nature and purpose of the church, truths which have already been expressed in the metaphors.

Determining a Definition

When one defines a term, the process is never purely inductive. Any comprehensive definition has deductive elements. These elements are part of the logical process. In defining the church, our definition is most comprehensive when we use relationship as a deductive concept.

Relationships are an integral part of the church. They become integral through the lives of the people who make up the church. People involved spiritually are consequently involved in interpersonal relationships as well. These relationships exist between the person and Christ, between the person and other Christians, and between the person and the outside world. God never intended for Christians to stand alone, but to interact with others and with Him. The relationships that Christians cultivate are shared with the church, thereby unifying it. In this manner, the church is bound by relational ties. (We will later learn why we can be silent about the relationship of the church to Satan.)

To determine our definition of the church, we will study metaphors of the church—body, bride, building and temple, priesthood, and flock. These will show us different aspects of the nature of the church. These aspects point out the different purposes of the church. These various purposes are associated with the three relationships of the believer—namely, between himself and God, other believers, and unbelievers. The association between the purposes of the church and relationships of the believer is summarized by three terms: worship, edification, and multiplication.

Disciples

In Protestant circles today, a new emphasis is given to the concept of discipleship. In many ways, this is a reaction to the superficial nature of much of church life. Teaching from the Bible on the metaphors of body, temple, and priesthood should suffice to give the right biblical encouragement for all believers to make their unique and corporate contribution to the growth of the church itself and in the world around them. All metaphors emphasize the relationship of the believers with their Lord Jesus Christ: their head, their bridegroom, their cornerstone, their chief priest, and their great shepherd.

Nevertheless, the worldwide emphasis in churches on gathering, and the silence or misunderstandings concerning the biblical words "church," "house of the Lord," "body," and "priest," still contribute to a lack of commitment on the part of many individual believers. Right teaching will be very important in strengthening this weakness.

The corporate emphasis of all metaphors sometimes fails to break unhealthy dependency if the flock metaphor leads to a leader-centered church structure. Many Christian leaders feel that an emphasis on discipleship is crucial to spiritual growth, outreach, and involvement of individuals in the church.

Discipleship is a call to individual believers to personally imitate their Lord Jesus Christ, that is, to grow into His image. Very little needs to be said to underline the biblical basis of the discipleship concept; every believer is called to become like Jesus Christ. God uses every circumstance in a Christian's life to mold him/her into the image of His Son (Rom 8:28-29).

Christlikeness is the very purpose of the ministry of the Holy Spirit today, who writes the law of God in each believer's heart (2 Cor 3:1-18).

The term "disciple" in itself does not designate a Christian. Every rabbi in Jesus' day called his students disciples. In the Gospel narratives, many sayings of Jesus have been written down that paint a picture of Jesus' requirements for anyone who wants to be a real student under Him.

Nevertheless, the term "disciples" was (and is) a technical term that receives its content primarily by its modifier: Disciples are students of Jesus Christ.

Many groups in Protestant churches today value this term because it calls for personal imitation of Jesus Christ by all individual believers. Anyone who denies or ignores a need for this imitation in our churches denies or ignores the emphasis in Jesus' ministry. Practically speaking, such a person creates exactly the need for an emphasis on discipleship.

If this term becomes too central in describing all of one's spiritual life, however, crucial aspects of corporate church life can be ignored. Most everything stated in the New Testament letters is said to churches—not to individuals, but to groups of Christians— associating purposefully. Also note that Jesus was a rabbi within a culture with tremendous emphasis on corporate life, and all of His calling to discipleship builds on that.

The Church as a Bride

Directly related to this implication is the exalted position of the bride in Oriental (Biblical/Jewish) culture. Edersheim gives us the following description:

> At the betrothal, the bridegroom, personally or by deputy, handed to the bride a piece of money or a letter, it being expressly stated in each case that the man thereby espoused the woman. From the moment of the betrothal both parties were regarded, and treated in law (as to inheritance, adultery, need of formal divorce), as if they had been actually married, except as regarded their living together.[1]

When we relate this to the church, we see that Christ, the bridegroom, has purchased the church with His own blood (Acts 20:28), and the church has been espoused to Him as His bride. We only wait for the presentation of the bride to the bridegroom. Neufeld describes the bridegroom fetching his bride:

> Among the wealthy the bridegroom was dressed in especially sumptuous clothes (Isa 61:10) and wore a matrimonial crown (Song 3:11). He came with a company of his family and friends (Jud 14:11; Matt 9:15) to meet his bride who was accompanied by her family and friends (Jer 2:32). The bride met her bridegroom with her face covered by a veil (Gen 29:25; cf also Gen 39:14; Jer 2:31). He brought her to his house, where all the proceedings took place by the light of lanterns to the accompaniment of music and songs (Jer 24:8; 7:34; 16:9; 25:10).

---

[1] Alfred Edersheim, *The Life and Times of Jesus the Messiah*, 3rd ed., 2 vols. (1886; reprint ed. [2 vols. in 1], Grand Rapids, MI: Eerdmans, 1971), 1:354.

When both companies met, they sang to the young couple (Jer 7:34; 16:9; 25:10; Psalms 45:16).[2]

The church should wait in anticipation for that day when her bridegroom, the Lord Jesus, comes for her (Jn 14:3). This should remind us of the words of the apostle Paul:

> For the Lord himself will come down from heaven with a shout of command, with the voice of the archangel, and with the trumpet of God, and the dead in Christ will rise first. Then we who are alive, who are left, will be snatched up together with them in the clouds to meet the Lord in the air. And so we will always be with the Lord. (1 Thess 4:16-17)

Christ not only receives His bride, but He also prepares the bride herself. He purposes to present His "church to himself as glorious—not having a stain or wrinkle, or any such blemish, but holy and blameless" (Eph 5:27). Christ is conforming the church to His image.

Yet this is not all that this metaphor tells us. Just as the final step, after the Oriental bridegroom received his bride, was the marriage feast, so it is to be with Christ and the church:

> "Let us rejoice and exult and give him glory, because the wedding celebration of the Lamb has come, and his bride has made herself ready. She was permitted to be dressed in bright, clean, fine linen" (for the fine linen is the righteous deeds of the saints). Then the angel said to me, "Write the following: Blessed are those who are invited to the banquet at the wedding celebration of the Lamb!" He also said to me, "These are the true words of God." (Rev 19:7-9)

What love the bridegroom has for His Bride! He is now preparing her and her future home. This truth should not only encourage us, but it should cause us to worship Him!

The Church as a Flock

The figure of the flock is one of the most broadly applied figures of the church. In the Old Testament, Israel is called "the flock of the LORD" (Jer 13:17, NASB; Zech 10:3). Jesus referred to His small circle of disciples as the "little flock" (Lk 12:32). Again, the term is used of the church on several occasions (see Acts 20:28; 1 Pet 5:3). There are also repeated references to the sheep that compose the flock (Jn 10:16; 21:15-17) and to the Shepherd of the flock (Jn 10:2-16; Heb 13:20; 1Pet 2:25; 5:4). Although this figure is rich with potential for application, a few things deserve special note, for this figure speaks of relationships within the church.

Significantly, for this metaphor, the Shepherd of the flock has committed shepherding to under-shepherds. Jesus gives Peter this charge three times in John 21:15-17. Writing later to the elders of the flock scattered throughout the five provinces of Pontus, Galatia, Cappadocia, Asia, and Bithynia, Peter gives the very same charge: "Give a shepherd's care to God's flock among you" (1 Pet 5:2).

In a way, the need of human beings for guidance, human leadership, and organization is far from a revolutionary concept. Leadership is needed not only among unconverted sinners but also

---

[2] E. Neufeld, *Ancient Hebrew Marriage Laws* (New York, NY: Longmans, Green, 1944), p. 149, cited by Radmacher, p. 258. We note that Genesis 39:14 probably should read Genesis 38:14. Where the original uses a comma to separate chapter number from verse number, we have substituted a colon.

among converted sinners. Although the Spirit guides growth to maturity in every saved person, no one, not even the most mature leaders, can deny their tendency to drift away and their need to be fed and guided by others. Sin must be overcome, and the strengthening influence of others blesses anyone's spiritual life. As the shepherd nourishes and protects his sheep, so God, the Chief Shepherd, provides nourishment and protection through mature fellow Christians.

This figure of the Church as a Flock corrects wrong tendencies in leaders, as well as in those being fed and led. A couple of things can be highlighted: Let us first look at how this picture of under-shepherds provides corrective encouragement for those in leadership.

The ownership of the flock: The possessive pronoun "my" in John 21:16 and the phrase "to God" in 1 Peter 5:2 emphasize a truth which recurs throughout the Bible: God owns everything; therefore, obedience goes to Him! Jesus' life (and death!) clearly set a model in this arrangement. Obviously, under-shepherds should lead as an extension of how the Chief Shepherd leads. This understanding will help eliminate being possessive, controlling, or manipulative, and eliminate timid and negligent leadership styles. The Great Shepherd gave Himself—died for—the sheep (Acts 20:28). It is God's flock, and Christ proved by His death how valuable they are to Him. God wants all leaders constantly aware of this truth! The heart of Christian leadership is service and sacrifice.

Corrective encouragement: Natural sheep left alone without a shepherd will only harm themselves; yet they readily submit whenever the shepherd guides. So they are both needy and willing to follow their shepherd (Isa 53:7). Figurative sheep, however, must be reminded that submission to their leader is beneficial. This is the flavor when the writer of Hebrews urges us to "obey your leaders and submit to them, for they keep watch over your souls and will give an account for their work. Let them do this with joy and not with complaints, **for this would be no advantage for you**" (Heb 13:17, emphasis added).

Like the teaching in Ephesians on marriage (in which the man is reminded by the Holy Spirit speaking through Paul to lead through service and sacrifice, and the woman is reminded to submit), the Bible gives no encouragement to followers to evaluate the leader or for the leader to criticize the attitudes of followers. This is crucial because the tendency is often the opposite. At the same time, the metaphor is rich enough to recognize the limits of this emphasis.

The metaphor of the church as a flock also expresses beautifully the need of servant leaders within the local church and warns us of the detrimental effects when the teaching of the metaphor is not a reality.

The Church as a Priesthood

To read about this important metaphor, we can consult several books in the New Testament, especially Hebrews. But the most specific treatment is found in 1 Peter 2:5-9 in which Peter correlates this figure with the figure of the spiritual house or temple because of logical relation between the two. The obvious resemblance to the Old Testament function of Israel is seen in verse 9 in the NASB: "a chosen race, a royal priesthood, a holy nation, a people for God's own possession" (see also Ex 19:5-6; Deut 7:6-7). Like Israel, God now calls the church to witness in this world.

A deep attitude of reverence and awe is expressed by the human builder of the physical temple: "Of course, who can really build a temple for him, since the sky and the highest heavens cannot contain him? Who am I that I should build him a temple! It will really be just a place to offer sacrifices before him (2 Chr 2:6)."

Such should be the attitude of all of us as we are involved with others in worshiping God, in edifying each other, and in reaching out to those who do not yet worship Him.

The greatest significance of the temple was the purpose of its activities: the priests offering sacrifices unto Him. Under the same words, but now as a metaphor, the New Testament pictures the activities of Christians. In the New Testament, the church is also described as a priesthood.

Under the Old Covenant, only priests could serve in the presence of God and lead people in worship. One of them, the high priest, could even enter into the Holy of Holies once a year. All others were less intimate in their contact with God. In the church, however, there are no "ordinary" people who must go through ordained priests to come to God or who cannot lead others in worship.

From Hebrews we know that Jesus is our high priest. He has gone before us and once and for all opened the direct way to the throne of grace for anyone at any time (cf. Heb 4:14-16). His sacrifice opened the way to God, even into the "holy of holies." The church no longer brings any sacrifice for sin and has direct access to God.

But the new priesthood does perform other sacrifices: the church is "a spiritual house for a holy priesthood, to offer up spiritual sacrifices acceptable to God through Jesus Christ" (1 Pet 2:5 NASB).

- The voluntary and total surrender of our whole lives to God is called our "spiritual service of worship" (or "rational service"). From 2 Corinthians 8:5, it is obvious that this is not something that pertains only to the times the church is gathered. Daily life becomes a worship service.

- This idea is also expressed in the words that flow out of our mouths. The "thank offering" from the Old Testament is directly intimated here. As His church we are God's temple, seven days a week—continuously—to let both our spontaneous conversations, as well as our special moments of attention, bring thanksgiving to God.

- Spiritual sacrifices must find practical outward expressions, such as the actual sharing of one's goods with others. This is a sacrifice greatly pleasing to God.

- These verses bring us back to where we started the discussion. The actual conversion of new believers was for Paul a spiritual sacrifice he could bring to God.

The sacrifice of incense under the old covenant was already closely connected with prayer (Ps 141:2; Lk 1:9-10). Practically speaking, each thing brought before God in prayer honors God Mal 1:11). Believer's lives can be turned into a worship experience, corporately and individually, as they walk with God in prayer.

From these many details, we should draw some general conclusions:

1. In some churches, the concept of a priesthood continues the Old Testament distinction between clergy and laity, and provides legitimate ground to present the church's ceremonies as an extension of the sacrifices. The New Testament shows us something quite opposite to that interpretation, however.

2. All believers are priests, as was emphasized anew in the Reformation era by Luther. This biblical emphasis should continue as the priesthood of believers turns every aspect of the believer's daily life into a religious activity. In terms of relationships, even the daily contacts Christians have with non-Christians are affected because they are part of Christ's priesthood. Their material life, prayer life, speech, and whole being can all be voluntarily turned into a pleasing sacrifice to God.

3. Any statement defining the church according to its purpose should connect everything mentioned so far. Although the emphasis in this metaphor is not on Christians relating to each other, their relationship with God and with non-Christians is closely connected to the metaphor. Evangelism becomes worship, and worship leads to evangelism.

4. The church as a priesthood seems diametrically opposed to human intermediaries between Christians and God. All members directly relating to the head and each having gifts to serve each other takes the focus away from having human leaders (however, a role for human leaders within the church is clearly recognized).

The Church as Branches of a Vine

In contrast to the figure from the Old Testament and synoptic gospels of Israel as the fruitless vine (see for example Mk 12:1-12), God expects the church—and individual believers within it—to produce much fruit. To accomplish this, we must be connected with Jesus. To illustrate this truth, Jesus compares Himself to a vine and believers as the branches. But what specifically does this mean?

Contextually in John 13-16, Jesus teaches His disciples that He will soon leave them, after dying for their sins in obedience to the Father's command. What teachings are in the immediate context of—and help explain—this illustration?

- In John 13:1-38 Jesus says that each disciple must accept His cleansing sacrifice on his behalf. He warns of Judas' betrayal and predicts Peter's denial, probably as negative examples of the danger of not abiding in Him.

- In John 14:1-14 He again says they need to believe in Him to glorify the Father and experience answered prayer—necessary elements of producing fruit.

- In John 14:15-31 Jesus says that He will send the Holy Spirit to be with them in His absence and that loving Him by keeping His commandments is the key to God residing with the believer. Both the Spirit and obedience are necessary elements for producing fruit.

- Then, after teaching on the vine and abiding in Him, in John 15:18-27 He teaches on how this changed life through abiding in Him will cause the world to hate the believer as it hated Jesus.

- Then, in John 16, He again teaches the vital role the Holy Spirit will have in keeping the believer and His church united to Him.

These are all key points of Jesus' teaching; these are all keys to abiding with Him.

Apart from this union with Christ we, as individuals and corporately as the church, cannot produce fruit. Programs, though not wrong in themselves, cannot produce fruit; only by remaining united with Christ and allowing Him to "prune" (lift us up) can we succeed (John 15:2).

One main hindrance to this abiding is the conflict we have with one another that cuts the church off from the vine. An example of this is given by Paul in 1 Corinthians 3:3: "you are still influenced by the flesh. For since there is still jealousy and dissension among you, are you not influenced by the flesh and behaving like ordinary people?"

Notice also that abiding in Christ is always away from the direction and approval of "the world" and that of the power of our flesh. First comes cleansing by faith through Jesus' work; then warning against separating from Him, dependence on the Spirit's power, and practical love by keeping His commandments. As the branches must remain connected to the life-giving vine to remain alive and vital, so we must remain connected to our source of life in Christ.

The Foundation of the Church

Four prominent passages dealing with the foundation of the church are Matthew 16:15-18; 1 Corinthians 3:10-11; Ephesians 2:20; and 1 Peter 2:4-6. The following harmonizes them in terms of the concept of the foundation of the church:

- **First**, in Matthew 16 Christ only says He will build His church. It is greatly debated whether He, Peter, or some other person or thing is "this rock" upon which He will build the church.

- **Second**, 1 Corinthians 3 refers to Christ as the foundation; whereas 1 Peter 2 refers to Him as only the cornerstone. On the other hand, Ephesians 2:20 seems to say that the apostles and prophets are the foundation of the church.

How do we harmonize these apparent problems? Who or what is the foundation of the church?

- **First**, calling Christ both the foundation and the cornerstone is no problem. Since the cornerstone was the most important part of the foundation, it can merely be a matter of viewing the foundation from a different perspective. Whether as foundation or cornerstone, Jesus Christ is the most important element.

- **Second**, calling the apostles the foundation can be handled in at least two ways. Most likely, the reference in Ephesians 2:20 is to the apostles and prophets as the foundation, in that they were the first leaders and proclaimers of the Gospel. The other possible way to handle this is to point out that the word "of" in the phrase "foundation of the apostles" (Eph 2:20) can mean "laid by," not "consisting of." For example, in the phrase "love of Christ" (2 Cor 5:14) Christ can be the "source" of the love (Christ's love) or the "object" of the love (love for Christ). So it is in a phrase like "the love of parents." The parents can either be the source or the recipients of the love. Thus, in Ephesians 2:20 the phrase can mean "the foundation of the apostles and prophets." Matthew 16 may be understood in the same way as the first explanation of Ephesians 2:20. It is unlikely that Jesus says that He will build the church on Himself. The text says that He will build His church on Peter, referring to Peter's foundational role in building the church through evangelism and preaching. In effect Jesus says, "I am going to build My church upon Peter's role as chief apostle." And since Peter would represent all the apostles and prophets, this understanding agrees with Ephesians 2:20.

- **Third**, in 1 Corinthians 3:10-11 Christ contextually is only the foundation of the Corinthian church. Nothing is said about the church universal. If so, the reference is to the Gospel of Christ as the only foundation of a local church and there is no explicit reference to Christ as the foundation of the universal church. If 1 Corinthians 3 refers to Him as the foundation of the universal church, the focus is either on the Gospel or on viewing the foundation from God's perspective rather than the human perspective (His church, of which He is the head).

However one views it, there is no contradiction in these various representations of the foundation and building of the church.

Lesson 2: Presenting the Three Lenses

Lesson Introduction

In Lesson 2, we will look through the lenses of Scripture, history, and culture and their relationships to church "function" and "form." **Scripture** will tell us how the church should function. **History** will indicate how the past has affected us today. Finally, we shall peer through the lens of **culture** to determine how to make the church relevant to today's needs. Looking through the three lenses and distinguishing between function and form will be helpful methods as we reflect upon our current ministries and determine how to make them more effective.

Lesson Outline

Lesson 2: Presenting the Three Lenses
- Topic 1: Function and Form
- Topic 2: The Three Lenses
- Topic 3: Biblical Absolutes Versus Cultural Variables
- Topic 4: Developing Character—Temperate, Self-Controlled, and Respectable

Lesson Objectives

As you recall from Lesson 1, Pastor Eugene leads a small congregation about forty kilometers from the capital. He was inspired by a conference to research the biblical principles around the concept of "church," and he learned a great deal from his study.

In this lesson, Pastor Eugene is in a situation in which the members of his church are disagreeing about how to best reach out to non-believers in the community. Some members believe it is important to go out and minister to the community by handing out Christian information (tracts) and inviting them to come to church. Others believe that the church must transform into a more seeker-friendly environment and by doing so non-believers would feel more comfortable and invite their friends.

The controversy stems from a lack of church growth, leading to a lack of funding for church activities. The congregation agrees that it needs to grow and that they need to reach non-believers, but they disagree about how to approach the issue. The disagreement is tearing the church apart, causing church members to become angry with one another.

Pastor Eugene is torn and does not know how to approach the issue with the congregation, let alone how to solve it. In this lesson, you will learn some concepts that will help you as you sort though issues like the one Eugene faces. The concepts we will discuss include:

- The difference between "function" and "form"
- Viewing the church through the lenses of Scripture, history, and culture
- Distinguishing between cultural and supra-cultural practices
- The character traits of temperance, control, and respectability

During this lesson, you will reflect upon your present ministry, comparing your ministry activities with essential Christian values. You will begin to formulate a plan for making appropriate changes in your own life and your ministry.

Topic 1: Function and Form

The title of this course is *Church Dynamics*. We dealt with the biblical concept of "church" in Lesson 1. Let us now define the word "dynamic." Dynamic is something in motion, full of vitality, living. In Ephesians 4:14-16 we read:

> The purpose of this is to no longer to be children, tossed back and forth by waves and carried about by every wind of teaching by the trickery of people who with craftiness carry out their deceitful schemes. But practicing the truth in love, we will in all things grow up into Christ, who is the head. From him the whole body grows, fitted and held together through every supporting ligament. As each one does its part, the body grows in love.

The picture presented in these verses is striking. The church is like the human body; it is made up of Christians vital to its proper functioning and growth. It is full of energy, and the functioning of each member makes it dynamic. Each member has a role to play, with functions and activities to perform. These functions and activities are the **individual** dynamics which make the **church**, as a whole, dynamic. It is on these dynamics that we shall focus in this course.

Form: Jumping Through Hoops

Many of us have worked for a boss that wanted a job done his or her way, but it is much more rewarding to work for someone who simply wants the job done and allows us the freedom to accomplish it our way. In the terms from our topic, this boss is more interested in form than function. Most jobs have many ways to achieve the same results, and as long as the function is accomplished, there are few reasons to worry about which form is used.

In Pastor Eugene's case, the congregation had correctly identified the biblical function of multiplication, or church growth. The controversy in the church was about how to achieve that function. This congregation was arguing over form, which is a common occurrence in churches. To learn more about form versus function, continue working through this topic.

Function Accomplished!

Reading Assignment

Please read the article titled "Dynamics" in the Articles section at the end of this lesson.

QUESTION 1

Match the word in the left-hand column with its corresponding definition in the right-hand column.

Word	Definition
Dynamic	The activities we organize to fulfill a purpose
Function	How the church is kept alive and growing
Form	A purpose for ministry

Lesson 2: Presenting the Three Lenses

QUESTION 2
Review the following list: Which of the following is a **function**?

 A. Small groups

 B. Worship services

 C. Evangelism committees

 D. Sunday school

 E. Music ministry

QUESTION 3
Read Acts 2:42-46. Which of the following activities are **forms**? *(Select all that apply.)*

 A. Learning from the apostles' teaching

 B. Devoting themselves to fellowship and prayer

 C. Selling their possessions to give to the needy

 D. Meeting daily in the temple courts

It is difficult to formulate a definition of the church from narrative literature. This type of literature is primarily descriptive, and one needs interaction with the metaphors to arrive at an accurate understanding.

For example, one could easily try to define the church from a good example in Acts as Christians meeting together regularly around the Word, in prayer, in fellowship, and for the Lord's Supper." Acts 2:42 gives us these practices of the very first church. But if, when we read on, we also want to incorporate verses 44 and 45 into the definition, a problem becomes apparent. These two verses evidently speak more about form than function. When we come to verse 46, it is clear that the emphasis is on form, because one of the two places mentioned, the temple, does not exist anymore.

The article correctly emphasizes formulating a biblical rationale behind everything we do. Yet there are other questions to address, such as how, where, when, and who. Usually we go no further than asking what, and sometimes we provide some incomplete biblical rationale or some pertinent historical or cultural *whys* for the *whats*. Getz' challenge to be biblically sound is good, though not complete. In America, everybody automatically looks for an answer to the question of *how*; whereas in Western Europe people tend to overlook this question and devote themselves primarily to finding out *why*. In your culture, other questions may be emphasized and overlooked.

Topic 1 Key Points:
- *Dynamics* are the purposes and activities that keep a church alive and growing.
- Dynamics include both *forms* and *functions*.
- A *function* is a biblical purpose for ministry.
- A *form* is the way that we organize around or express a biblical function.

QUESTION 4
Record your response to the following in your Life Notebook. Name a "form" that has caused some controversy in your church. Describe how the form is practiced, the function it serves, where and when the activity is performed, and who is involved. Discuss why that form is practiced, as well as why it is controversial.

Topic 2: The Three Lenses

Several people can look at a map and determine how to get from one place to another. Although they have the same starting point and destination, they may choose different routes to get there. Form and function are very much the same way. Function is the destination that everyone agrees upon. Form is the various routes that can be taken to get to the destination.

Form = The Various Routes

In Pastor Eugene's congregation, there is a disagreement about how the church should accomplish the biblical function of multiplication. To help Eugene think through the implications of this issue, we will use a pictorial tool, looking at the issue through the three lenses of:

- Scripture
- History
- Culture

Each gives its own unique contribution to the final process.

Has anyone asked you why you do what you do, but you have no good answer? Have you ever wondered why churches do what they do or thought there might be a better way to meet biblical goals?

- Functions are based on Scripture, yet we would not build a temple to worship God like the Jews did.
- Functions are accomplished within history, yet most Christians have not and would not follow the pattern of sharing all things in common like the early church did (Acts 4:32-37).
- Functions are achieved by cultural means yet they are realized by different forms in different cultures.

Why do you do what you do?

We will use these three lenses to know why we do what we do and to make the changes necessary to wisely accomplish our functions.

Reading Assignments

- Please read the article titled "The Three Lenses" in the Articles section at the end of this lesson.
- Please read Getz Chapter 2 on "A Look Through Three Lenses".

A **philosophy of ministry** is a strategy and plan for spiritual growth for your church or ministry. At the end of this course, you will have an opportunity to use what you learned in this course to write a philosophy of ministry for your church or ministry organization.

QUESTION 5

The development of an effective strategy for Christian ministry should start with form, not function. *True or False?*

The observations Getz makes concerning form in Acts are very important. Though the forms present in Acts are limited, it does not imply that what is there is without value. *Note: The lack of information about forms is primarily related to Luke's purpose in writing Acts; He showed how the Spirit moved the growth of the church from purely Jewish territory into the Gentile world.* He obviously did not intend to show us how to organize the church. Maybe the Holy Spirit purposefully prevented him from providing this information.

From what we have seen so far about the function/form distinction, the nature of both automatically helps us to recognize in Acts that functions are found across many different forms when the church moved into additional cultures. This example implies that this model of varying forms can be followed by us, living and working in different cultures and different situations.

QUESTION 6

Why is there a lack of information on church forms in Acts? *(Select all that apply.)*

   A. It is related to the author's purpose in writing Acts.

   B. He did not intend to show us how to organize the church.

   C. Functions take on different forms in different cultures.

   D. It is of relative unimportance.

The following are some inferences to draw from the three observations Getz makes regarding form in the New Testament:

The limited scope of forms relates to their particularity. Forms are always limited by space and time, whereas the general functions are not. Things bound by space and time are automatically self-delimiting (they create boundaries).

QUESTION 7

Forms are limited in scope because they are bound by space and time. *True or False?*

Lesson 2: Presenting the Three Lenses

One basic thing we need to remember is that change is not a goal in itself. We have stated the threefold purpose of the church as the Bible gives it. Any change we want to take place must be crucial in helping our church meet its purpose for existence. Understanding our own and others' resistance to change should stir us to greater maturity. Patience, teaching, and love are crucial. Most important, however, is the need to direct everyone's attention to the Lord Jesus. Seeing His love for us and the world for whom He died will help cultivate the right attitude in us. This attitude will involve us in fulfilling God's desire for the church's growth. The combination of truth and love in Ephesians 4:15 provides an important balance for us to keep.

Biblical Devotion: Enough?

One can be devoted to being totally biblical in one's practices yet discover tremendous inner resistance to changing old habits. Sometimes this resistance is apart from our sinfulness, especially within groups from different generations where such resistance can be readily observed. Getz provides us with some very realistic insights that help us to understand ourselves in this regard.

QUESTION 8

Match the situation in the left-hand column with the solution to it in the right-hand column.

Situation	Solution
Understanding our own and others' resistance to change	Should stir us to greater maturity
People's resistance to change	The combination of truth and love
Most important	Having patience, teaching, and love are crucial
An important balance for us to keep (Eph 4:15)	Direct everyone's attention to the Lord Jesus
Concluding something is primarily historical or cultural	This does not mean it is bad

Topic 2 Key Points:

In this topic, you learned:

- A "philosophy of ministry" is a strategy and plan for spiritual growth for your church or ministry. This will be your final work project for this course.
- To create your philosophy of ministry, you will need to view the purposes of the church (functions) through the lenses of Scripture, history, and culture to determine what forms would provide relevant expressions for your congregation.
- Forms are limited by space and time. Biblical functions are timeless.
- The book of Acts contains little information about forms because it is not intended to show us how to organize the church. The process of developing relevant forms is left in our hands with the help of the Holy Spirit.
- When dealing with people's reactions to change, biblical principles of truth, love, patience, and maturity are required.

QUESTION 9
Let's go back to the controversial form that you wrote about in Topic 1, Question 4. View that form through the lenses of Scripture, history, and culture, and record your observations in your Life Notebook. Then consider how you can apply the biblical principles of truth.

Topic 3: Biblical Absolutes Versus Cultural Variables

At this point, you should understand the importance of relating the truths of Scripture to history and culture. This process helps us to recognize and maintain a clear distinction between **biblical absolutes** and **cultural variables**.

We study the Bible to learn the biblical absolutes so we do not vary from them. But when we study we also find cultural variables. One probable example of this (and one that has puzzled subsequent churches) is 1 Corinthians 11:2-16 which deals with women's head coverings. If wearing a head covering is a biblical absolute (supra-cultural), every church anytime should obey this direction. If it is a cultural form, we should find the biblical absolute behind the form and obey that.

Americans visiting the Orient and Orientals visiting America are struck by the cultural differences. For example: Americans typically greet each other with a handshake; whereas Orientals typically greet each other by bowing. Both accomplish the same goal (absolute); they are greeting each other and showing respect. The biblical exhortation to "greet one another with a holy kiss" (1 Cor 16:20) is an example of a cultural variable that, if practiced in some cultures, may lead to misunderstandings.

There were other cultural differences in Bible times, as we saw in the topic introduction about head coverings for women. To properly apply the Bible, we must understand the difference between these two concepts. To help avoid embarrassing misunderstandings or misapplications, please continue reading this topic.

QUESTION 10
Number the lines in your Life Notebook one through fourteen (plus) depending on how many of your own examples you come up with. Reflect on the graphic below entitled "Absolutes vs. Non-absolutes," and then look at the following practices. State whether you think they are cultural or biblical absolutes and why. For each one identified as an absolute, give a Scripture to support your position. (Note: Godly Christians have disagreed on the absoluteness of some of the practices listed below. Do not regard your opinion as the last word.)

    1. Celebrating the Lord's Supper with white bread and red wine

2. Celebrating the Lord's Supper on Sunday
3. Celebrating the Lord's Supper in a church building
4. Celebrating the Lord's Supper at all
5. Having a Sunday school
6. The pastor wearing a coat to church
7. The pastor receiving a full salary from his congregation
8. Having a choir during worship services
9. Allowing guitarists to provide accompaniment during worship services
10. Distributing gospel tracts or other written portions of the Word of God among the unsaved
11. Attending to the needs of the sick and discouraged among the church membership
12. Meeting regularly in small groups for prayer and Bible study
13. Instructing believers to regularly memorize portions of Scripture

(Add some of your own that come to mind and are unclear to you.)

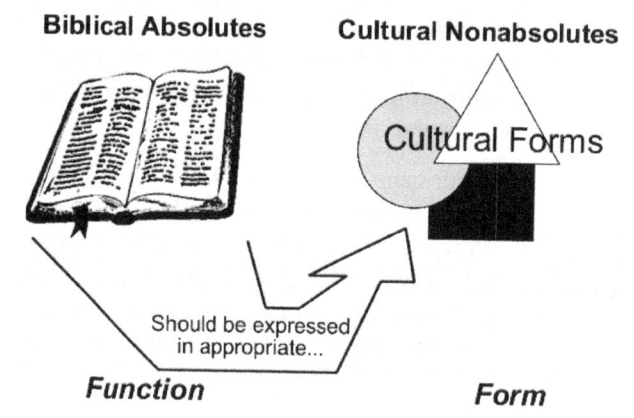

Biblical Absolutes   **Cultural Nonabsolutes**

Cultural Forms

Should be expressed in appropriate...

Function   **Form**

We must hold firmly to the absolute truths of Scripture, yet be willing to adjust our approach to ministry in order to maximize effectiveness and accomplish our biblical objectives.

A cultural norm is one which is practiced **because** of the culture in which a given church exists; a supra-cultural (biblical absolute) norm is one which is practiced **regardless** of the culture in which a given church exists. The absolute informs and influences the cultural. Function is the only absolute. If a form (cultural norm) interferes with a function (supra-cultural norm) or prevents its accomplishment, then the form must be changed.

This requirement will often lead to resistance because people generally dislike change. You may hear, "We have **always** done it this way!" or "We have **never** done it that way!" But the Bible gives us the freedom to adjust non-absolutes to be maximally effective in local situations.

QUESTION 11

If a form interferes with a function the _____ must change.

As we look through the lenses of Scripture, history, and culture, keeping in mind the concept of function and form, we not only develop biblical principles that assure we are following God's directions, but we are **set free to minister to the church and to the world**. We are committed to the functions revealed in Scripture and free to create forms to minister to our culture.

QUESTION 12
From your church, choose one form you think you could change to make it more effective to accomplish your church's purpose. Then open your Life Notebook and record your thoughts. Give scriptural references where appropriate.

Topic 3 Key Points:

- A cultural norm is one which is practiced **because** of the culture in which a given church exists; a biblical absolute is one which is practiced **regardless** of the culture in which a given church exists.
- If a form (cultural norm) interferes with a function absolute) or prevents it from being accomplished, then the form must be changed.
- The Bible gives us the freedom to adjust non-absolutes for maximum effectiveness in local situations

Topic 4: Developing Character—Temperate, Self-Controlled, and Respectable

In this topic we continue developing the character that comes with Christian maturity. Three requirements of a Christian leader are to be temperate, self-controlled, and respectable.

Pastor Eugene returned home late one night after attending a grueling four hour "elders" meeting. As he drove, a pall of discouragement swept over him while thinking about the events which had just transpired.

He remembered suggesting that they open with about thirty minutes of conversational prayer. One of the elders looked at his watch and said, "We have a lot to discuss tonight, and many of us must get home to our families. Why don't you just open us in prayer to save time?"

Then after Eugene excitedly presented his vision for the church, one elder replied, "I have been a member of this church for fifteen years; this is my church, and I will not have you changing it."

Noticing that a leading elder was missing, he asked, "Where is Bill?" They said Bill's wife was divorcing him because of years of physical and emotional abuse. Consequently, Bill wanted to withdraw from the elder board.

A question came to Eugene's mind: "How were these men selected to become leaders of the church?" A major problem in our churches is that leaders are often selected because of their position in the community, their wealth, their networks, or how many years they have been a member.

If you were selecting key individuals to invest time with, what selection criteria would you chose? 1 Timothy 3 gives us some answers.

QUESTION 13

Fill in the columns with a pen or pencil by matching the option on the left to the verses in the bottom rows.

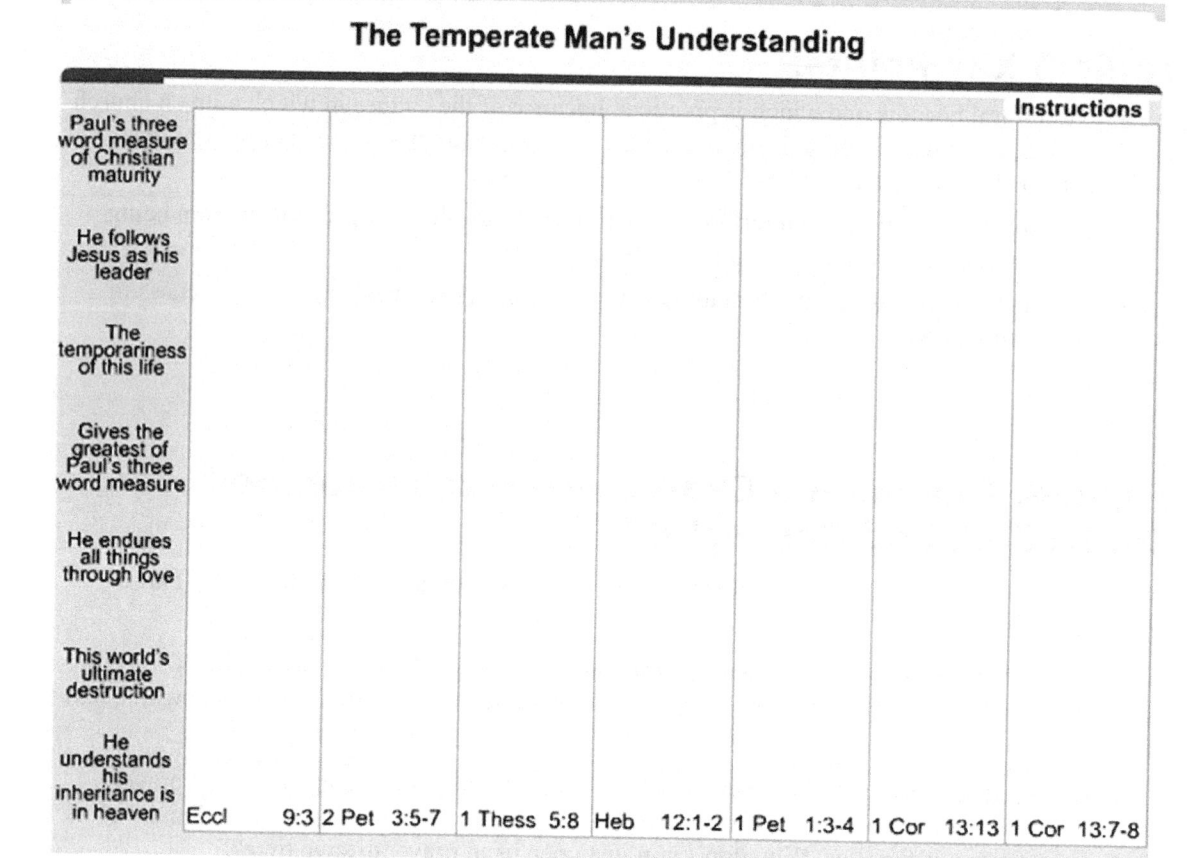

The Temperate Man's Understanding

							Instructions
Paul's three word measure of Christian maturity							
He follows Jesus as his leader							
The temporariness of this life							
Gives the greatest of Paul's three word measure							
He endures all things through love							
This world's ultimate destruction							
He understands his inheritance is in heaven	Eccl 9:3	2 Pet 3:5-7	1 Thess 5:8	Heb 12:1-2	1 Pet 1:3-4	1 Cor 13:13	1 Cor 13:7-8

Temperate

Reading Assignment

Please read the article titled "Temperate" in the Articles section at the end of this lesson.

A person who is temperate exhibits the following qualities:

- Praises God in all circumstances
- Christian faith is revealed in actions
- Hope is placed in the eternal, not in the temporary things that this world provides (Mt 6:33)
- Does not lose perspective or control in times of conflict, continues to follow God's ways and looks for God's lessons throughout the trial
- Demonstrates proper self-care (food, rest, clothing, and shelter), knowing that it is easy to lose perspective when you are emotionally or physically exhausted (1 Kgs 19:1-8)
- Courteous, sincere, humble, controlled, and selfless.

Self-Controlled

Reading Assignment

Please read the article titled "Self-Controlled" in the Articles section at the end of this lesson

Developing a proper self image helps cultivate self-control. Christians frequent two extremes: they either see themselves as nothing or they are caught up with an exalted view of themselves. An immature person vacillates between these two attitudes.

Neither approach is proper. It is vital for Christians to balance their lives. There must be a tension between two truths:

- All we are and have is because of God's grace.
- We have human and divine resources to do great things for God.

A "sound mind" enables us to maintain this balance.

There are reasons this problem of balance exists and persists. Some of these reasons are listed in the question below.

QUESTION 14

Match the verse in the left-hand column with the corresponding characteristic it describes of the self-controlled man.

Verse	Characteristic
Romans 12:3	God expects self-control from everyone in the body.
1 Corinthians 12:14-27	He counts everything he has as loss for what he has in Christ.
Romans 12:10	He knows that self-control does not lead to weakness.
Titus 2:2-6	He understands he is a sinner saved by grace.
Romans 5:8	He does not think he is God's gift to the church.
Philippians 3:4-7	He thinks about himself with sober discernment.
2 Timothy 2:7-8	He gives preference to others.

QUESTION 15

Which of the following circumstances have you experienced in your life? *(Select all that apply.)*

A. *An unfortunate series of circumstances beyond human control:* e. g. the loss of a parent or parents, bad experiences in school or in the neighborhood, bad influences from others, or hereditary factors or physical illness creating feelings of inferiority.

B. *An incorrect theology:* such as hearing for so long you are "nothing" that you actually feel and believe you are "nothing"; trying so hard to "crucify self" that you have downgraded your "self-image" and the "image of God in you"; an incorrect view of forgiveness and being right with God—that is, trying to become "nothing" before God accepts you. (*Remember:* You cannot do anything to become right with God—you cannot even become "nothing"—rather, you must come to God just as you are and accept His free gift of salvation)

C. *Parents unwise in rearing me:* either withholding praise and attention, creating an unnatural thirst and desire for recognition, or being unwise in giving me too much prominence, creating an emotional need to always be "first in line" and in the "limelight." (*Note:* Withholding praise is far more common than giving too much. Christian parents especially often withhold praise and attention from their children for fear they will create pride. Actually they achieve what they want to avoid: creating a person who is starved for attention and has a tremendous pride problem later in life because he is unable to handle success emotionally).

D. *Emotional or Psychological abuse of any type*

QUESTION 16

How do you think the experiences you selected in the previous question may have impacted your ability to maintain a sound and balanced mind in certain ministry situations? Record your thoughts in your Life Notebook.

A **self-controlled** person exhibits the following qualities:

- External appearance is considered proper, both biblically and culturally
- Items owned glorify Christ and are purchased with pure and right motives
- Her/his speech builds others up and glorifies God

Respectable

Reading Assignment

Please read the article titled "Respectable" in the Articles section at the end of this lesson.

QUESTION 17

What does a Christian dressing in a drab or sloppy fashion communicate to an unbeliever?

In everything, we must live so our lives are becoming to the teachings of God. Especially to those in authority we must be non-argumentative, and we must be honest with all people.

QUESTION 18

Match the verse that teaches about the respectable Christian's **social life** in the left-hand column with the corresponding teaching in the right-hand column.

Verse	Teaching
1 Corinthians 10:31-33	Conduct yourselves with wisdom toward outsiders, making the most of the opportunities. Let your speech always be gracious, seasoned with salt, so that you may know how you should answer everyone.
Colossians 4:5-6	Be subject to every human institution for the Lord's sake, whether to a king as supreme or to governors as those he commissions to punish wrongdoers and praise those who do good. For God wants you to silence the ignorance of foolish people by doing good.
1 Peter 2:12	And maintain good conduct among the non-Christians, so that though they now malign you as wrongdoers, they may see your good deeds and glorify God when he appears.
1 Peter 2:13-15	So whether you eat or drink, or whatever you do, do everything for the glory of God. Do not give offense to Jews or Greeks or to the church of God, just as I also try to please everyone in all things. I do not seek my own benefit, but the benefit of many, so that they may be saved.

QUESTION 19

Match the verse that teaches about the respectable Christian's **business life** and **Church Life** in the left-hand column with the corresponding teaching in the right-hand column.

Verse	Teaching
1 Thessalonians 4:10-12	And indeed you are practicing it toward all the brothers and sisters in all of Macedonia. But we urge you, brothers and sisters, to do so more and more, to aspire to lead a quiet life, to attend to your own business, and to work with your hands, as we commanded you. In this way you will live a decent life before outsiders and not be in need.
Colossians 3:23-24	But as for you, communicate the behavior that goes with sound teaching.
Philippians 1:27	Whatever you are doing, work at it with enthusiasm, as to the Lord and not for people, because you know that you will receive your inheritance from the Lord as the reward. Serve the Lord Christ.
Titus 2:1	Only conduct yourselves in a manner worthy of the gospel of Christ so that—whether I come and see you or whether I remain absent—I should hear that you are standing firm in one spirit, with one mind, by contending side by side for the faith of the gospel.

Isolate your areas of weakness and work on them. Both prayer and deliberate action are needed. If you are habitually late for work, your goal is to get an early start. Concentrate on this until it is a habit. You must put feet to your prayers and become Christ-like (respectable).

QUESTION 20

Consider the scriptural admonitions in the two matching questions above. As you work through them, ask yourself, "Are they true in my life?" Putting them into practice helps you become a respectable person, both among Christians and non-Christians. Mentally

---

Lesson 2: Presenting the Three Lenses

note (or note them in your Life Notebook) those areas in which you are particularly weak. Write your observations as you read.

A person who is **respectable** will exhibit these qualities:
- Works to support self
- Works with enthusiasm
- Is gracious
- Makes the most of opportunities
- Does good deeds
- Works on areas of weakness
- Conducts self in a manner worthy of Christ, whose name we bear

QUESTION 21
Read through the qualities of someone who is temperate, self-controlled, and respectful. From that list of qualities, select up to three qualities that you struggle with. For each difficult quality, write a plan for how you will work toward self-improvement in this area. Record your response in your Life Notebook.

In this lesson, we learned to look through the lenses of Scripture, history, and culture, keeping in mind the concept of function and form. As we do, we not only develop biblical principles that give us the assurance we are following God's directions, but we are **set free to minister to the church and to the world**. We are committed to the functions revealed in Scripture and are free to create forms that will minister to our culture. The next lesson develops the use of history and culture in greater detail.

Lesson 2 Self Check

QUESTION 1
Which of the following is a definition of function?

    A. A ministry activity

    B. The way we organize our ministry

    C. Each member's role or activity to perform

    D. A cultural norm

QUESTION 2
Which of the following is an example of a form?

    A. Sunday school

    B. Evangelism

    C. The Lord's Supper

    D. Worship

QUESTION 3
Which of the following is an example of a function?

    A. Wednesday prayer meeting

    B. Baptism

    C. Sunday morning services

    D. Church choir

QUESTION 4
The Bible gives us the freedom to adjust non-absolutes for maximum effectiveness in local situations. *True or False?*

QUESTION 5
Greeting each other with a kiss is a biblical absolute. *True or False?*

QUESTION 6
The Lord's Supper is an example of a church practice that is supra-cultural. *True or False?*

QUESTION 7
You want to institute a new form of worship into your church meetings. Before implementing your idea, you will want to look at this proposed form through the lenses of Scripture, culture, and _____.

QUESTION 8
Understanding the temporariness of this life helps someone develop the character trait of _____.

QUESTION 9
A Christian who comes to a meeting dressed in drab clothing helps communicate the humility of Christ. *True or False?*

QUESTION 10

Romans 12:3 says, "Do not think more highly of yourself," in relation to God and other Christians, "but think with sober discernment." This expresses which of the following concepts?

    A. Respect

    B. Self-control

    C. Temperate

    D. Cooperation

Lesson 2 Answers to Questions

QUESTION 1:

Word	Definition
Dynamic	How the church is kept alive and growing
Function	A purpose for ministry
Form	The activities we organize to fulfill a purpose

QUESTION 2:
B. Worship services

Only one of the items, worship services, is a biblical function of the church. The others are all forms, or ways that we organize to accomplish the functions. For example, an evangelism committee is a form used to accomplish the function of multiplication. Sunday school is a form used to accomplish the function of edification.

QUESTON 3:
C. Selling their possessions to give to the needy
D. Meeting daily in the temple courts

QUESTION 4: *Your answer*

QUESTION 5: False

Function answers the question, "What should be done?" Form answers the question, "How best can we do what we should do?" The development of an effective strategy for Christian ministry should start with functions. First, we must decide biblically what things should be done in ministry. Then we can plan effective ways of doing them in our culture and at our place in history.

QUESTION 6:
A. It is related to the author's purpose in writing Acts.
B. He did not intend to show us how to organize the church.
C. Functions take on different forms in different cultures.

QUESTION 7: True

QUESTION 8:

Situation	Solution
Understanding our own and others' resistance to change	Should stir us to greater maturity
People's resistance to change	Having patience, teaching, and love are crucial.
Most important	Direct everyone's attention to the Lord Jesus.
An important balance for us to keep (Eph 4:15)	The combination of truth and love
Concluding something is primarily historical or cultural.	This does not mean it is bad.

QUESTION 9: *Your answer*
QUESTION 10: *Your answer*
QUESTION 11: Form

There is freedom to adjust forms to accomplish biblical functions.

QUESTION 12: *Your answer*

QUESTION 13:

Scripture	Temperate Man's Understanding
Ecclesiastes 9:3	The temporariness of this life
2 Peter 3:5-7	This world's ultimate destruction
1 Thessalonians 5:8	Paul's three-word measure of Christian maturity
Hebrews 12:1-2	He follows Jesus as his leader.
1 Peter 1:3-4	He understands his inheritance is in heaven.
1 Corinthians 13:13	Gives the greatest of Paul's three-word measure
1 Corinthians 13:7-8	He endures all things.

QUESTION 14:

Verse	Characteristic
Romans 12:3	He thinks about himself with sober discernment
1 Corinthians 12:14-27	He does not think he is God's gift to the church
Romans 12:10	He gives preference to others
Titus 2:2-6	God expects self-control from everyone in the body
Romans 5:8	He understands he is a sinner saved by grace
Philippians 3:4-7	He counts everything he has as loss for what he has in Christ
2 Timothy 2:7-8	He knows that self-control does not lead to weakness

QUESTION 15:
**There is no incorrect answer to this question: Most of us in this sinful world have dealt with these issues and struggled with balancing them.

QUESTION 16: *Your answer*

QUESTION 17:
Drabness and sloppiness hurt Christ's cause by projecting His image as backward, uncultured, and "peculiar" in the bad sense of the word—it is not respectable!

QUESTION 18:

Verse	Teaching
1 Corinthians 10:31-33	So whether you eat or drink, or whatever you do, do everything for the glory of God. Do not give offense to Jews or Greeks or to the church of God, just as I also try to please everyone in all things. I do not seek my own benefit, but the benefit of many, so that they may be saved.
Colossians 4:5-6	Conduct yourselves with wisdom toward outsiders, making the most of the opportunities. Let your speech always be gracious, seasoned with salt, so that you may know how you should answer everyone.
1 Peter 2:12	And maintain good conduct among the non-Christians, so that though they now malign you as wrongdoers, they may see your good deeds and glorify God when he appears.
1 Peter 2:13-15	Be subject to every human institution for the Lord's sake, whether to a king as supreme or to governors as those he commissions to punish wrongdoers and praise those who do good. For God wants you to silence the ignorance of foolish people by doing good.

QUESTION 19:

Verse	Teaching
1 Thessalonians 4:10-12	And indeed you are practicing it toward all the brothers and sisters in all of Macedonia. But we urge you, brothers and sisters, to do so more and more, and to aspire to lead a quiet life and attend to your own business and work with your hands, as we commanded you. In this way you will live a decent life before outsiders and not be in need.
Colossians 3:23-24	Whatever you are doing, work at it with enthusiasm, as to the Lord and not for people, because you know that you will receive your inheritance from the Lord as the reward. Serve the Lord Christ.
Philippians 1:27	Only conduct yourselves in a manner worthy of the gospel of Christ so that—whether I come and see you or whether I remain absent—I should hear that you are standing in one spirit, by contending together with one mind for the faith of the Gospel.
Titus 2:1	But as for you, communicate the behavior that goes with sound teaching.

QUESTION 20: *Your answer*
QUESTION 21: *Your answer*

Lesson 2 Self Check Answers

QUESTION 1:
A. A ministry activity
QUESTION 2:
A. Sunday school
QUESTION 3:
B. Baptism
QUESTION 4: True
QUESTION 5: False
QUESTION 6: True
QUESTION 7: History
QUESTION 8: Correct answers include:
Temperate
Temperance
QUESTION 9: False
QUESTION 10:
B. Self-control

Lesson 2 Articles

Chapter 2: A Look Through Three Lenses

Wherever you have people, you have function. And wherever you have function, you have form. In other words, "form" and "structure" are inevitable. Put another way, you cannot have "organism" without "organization." Wherever you attempt to achieve a goal or apply a principle, you must develop a procedure or pattern for doing it. You cannot communicate a "message" without a "method." You cannot teach "truth" without developing some kind of "tradition."

The local church is no exception. Wherever you have people actively functioning in various roles, you have form and structure. You cannot have one without the other.

Note! It is possible to describe function without describing form. The authors of Scripture did it all the time. But in the outworking of the New Testament functions, you can be sure there was always some kind of cultural form.

All of us can identify with this reality. We live within the circle of form and structure. It is what gives us a sense of security. But the important question facing every church leader is what kind of form and structure should we have in our church?

An Adequate Philosophy of Ministry

We cannot answer this question for ourselves or for anyone else. Unless we have an adequate philosophy of the ministry, which raises one basic question—the question "why?" Why do we do what we do? Even as individuals we all have a philosophy that determines the way we function in life. We may not have spelled it out or articulated it to ourselves or others. But it is there, nevertheless, determining our actions and the way we function.

So it is in the church. All church leaders have a philosophy of ministry. Though it may not be obvious to the leaders themselves or the congregations they serve, it is there, nevertheless, determining how each church functions.

My concern in writing this book is to help Christians develop a biblical philosophy of ministry. It is only then that we can structure and organize our churches properly. It is only then that we can choose methods and patterns that will help the church become what God intended it to become in this world.

Interestingly, the "church growth" writers emphasize how important it is for church leaders to focus their philosophy of ministry in order to experience numerical growth. However, they seldom specify, at least in detail, what that philosophy should be. In fact, they often recognize various philosophies of ministry as being valid and acceptable[1].

Is it possible to develop a philosophy of ministry that is truly biblical—one that is recognized as what the Scriptures illustrate and teach? I believe it is—if we use an adequate research

---

[1] C. Peter Wagner, *Leading Your Church to Growth,* Regal Books, pp. 171–181, 214–216.

methodology that helps us arrive at a clear focus regarding what God is saying. Though we may have differences of opinion on minor matters, I believe it is possible to understand God's specific plan for local churches just as surely as it is possible to discover the truth regarding Christ's deity, the Trinity, salvation, and other important biblical doctrines.

To develop an adequate philosophy of ministry—one that God espouses—we must look through at least three lenses. The first is basic and foundational—the lens of Scripture. The lenses of history and culture are related in content to the lens of Scripture, but they also reveal extra biblical insights and are very important in avoiding "tunnel vision" and church-related shortsightedness as we develop a personal philosophy of ministry. Stating it positively and following through on our analogy, the three lenses can assist us in developing 20/20 vision regarding God's plan for the church.

How can we use the three lenses? This is the purpose of this book. What follows this chapter are the results of this process.

What follows immediately in this chapter, however, is an explanation with illustrations of how to use this process. In that sense, the three-lens approach comprises a method for biblical, historical, and cultural research.

The Lens of Scripture

This is the place to begin in formulating a biblical philosophy of ministry. Let me illustrate. Consider the following exhortations in the letter to the Hebrews:

> *Let us not give up meeting together, as some are in the habit of doing, but let us encourage one another—and all the more as you see the Day approaching* (Heb 10:25, NIV).

This Scripture passage delineates clearly two New Testament directives and functions. Christians are to "meet together regularly" in order to "encourage one another"; however, it is also clear that no "form" or "structure" is mentioned in this verse for these two functions. This does not mean that the author of this epistle expected Christians to meet together without form. Neither could they "encourage one another" without some type of structure.

Let's look more carefully at the first directive. These Christians were to meet together regularly. However, the passage does not specify when they were to meet, how often they were to meet, where they were to meet, or what the specific order of service should be when they would meet together.

If we look more carefully at the larger context in the New Testament—a very important aspect in accurate biblical interpretation—we will find illustrations of when the church met, how often they met, and where they met. To a lesser degree we will find a few references to how they ordered their services. However, when you look further you will notice something very significant.

First, functions and directives are often described in the New Testament without a description of forms, just as they are in the passage in Hebrews. For example, Luke recorded in the book of Acts that the apostles "never stopped teaching and proclaiming the good news that Jesus is the Christ" (Acts 5:42c, NIV). "Teaching" and "proclaiming" are functions. Though Luke made references to these functions, he did not describe the apostles' teaching and preaching methodology (form); however, we know that it is impossible to "teach" and "preach" without some kind of form and methodology.

Second, when form is described, it is always partial or incomplete. It is never possible to duplicate biblical form and structure exactly because certain details and elements are always missing in the biblical text. For example, Luke recorded in the same passage that the apostles "kept right on teaching and proclaiming" as they went "from house to house" (Acts 5:42b). Going from "house to house" is definitely form and structure. However, the process is not delineated in detail. Did they stop at every house or did they go only to the homes of those who had already believed in Christ? Did people invite their neighbors to come and hear the apostles? Did the apostles go "inside the house" or "stand outside" or "go to the rooftop"—as they would be able to do in this culture? We do not know the answers to these questions because the form described (going "from house to house") is incomplete and partial.

Third, form and structure that is partially described varies from one New Testament setting to another. In fact, we see variations within the text we're looking at. Not only did the apostles teach and preach from house to house, but they also went to the "temple courts" (5:42a, NIV).

This poses a problem immediately. We may not have too much trouble in some cultures going "from house to house" teaching the gospel of Christ. However, we would have to select our methodology carefully, for if we used the apostles' approach described in the book of Acts, we would probably be in violation of most city ordinances and find ourselves in trouble with local authorities.[2]

The problem of cultural restrictions on Christianity impacted me forcefully several years ago when I was sharing principles of New Testament church life with pastors behind the Iron Curtain.

In this particular country, it was illegal for groups of people to meet in private homes. Even relatives could not get together in large numbers. It was not just a regulation directed toward Christians. This government policy was established to avoid any possibility of a conspiracy against state authority. Naturally it restricted Christians greatly in being able to use their homes for any kind of religious service involving more than their immediate families.

Our biggest challenge, however, in any culture today would be to teach the gospel in "the temple courts." This was a cultural phenomenon related to the early days of Christianity, which was exclusively Jewish. However, it wasn't long until even the "temple courts" were off limits to Jewish Christians.

Let me summarize.

- The Bible often teaches function without describing form.
- Where it does describe form it is partial and incomplete.
- What form is described varies from situation to situation.

This leads to a very important conclusion. In church-renewal conferences, I'm often asked how it is possible to distinguish absolutes from non-absolutes in Scripture. The answer is found in these three observations regarding form in the New Testament. It is not possible to absolutize something that is not described, that is always incomplete, and that is always changing from one setting to another. This is why form and structures are not absolutes in the Bible. I have not found any that do not fit this threefold criterion. In fact, there is only one structure in the entire Bible

---

[2] The apostles definitely got in trouble for preaching the gospel. In fact, some ended up in prison. However, they were incarcerated for challenging their fellow Jewish and religious leaders theologically. Twenty-first-century city codes in most instances are designed to guarantee the right of privacy to local citizens. In this sense, we would be in violation of Paul's admonition to obey local magistrates and authorities (Rom 13:1-7).

that is described in detail—the tabernacle in the Old Testament. But even then, it is not possible to reconstruct this Old Testament place of worship without adding some details of our own.

On the other hand, functions and principles are absolute—if they appear consistently throughout New Testament history and are not self-delimiting.[3] Our challenge is to "look through the lens of Scripture" and isolate those functions and directives that are absolute and applicable in any culture.

The Lens of History

Note, first of all, that we can superimpose the lens of Scripture over the lens of history. Scripture is history that is, divine history, inspired history, or "God-breathed" history. It is here that we find absolute directives and functions that enable us to lay the foundations for a biblical philosophy of ministry.

Furthermore, we can learn valuable lessons from our forefathers. Paul illustrated this point in his letter to the Corinthians when he wrote: "These things happened to them [the children of Israel] as examples, and were written [the Old Testament] for our instruction, on whom the ends of the ages have come" (1 Cor 10:11). Today Christians have not only Old Testament history but also New Testament history—God's divinely inspired history of the church. It too has been recorded for "our instruction" to teach us how to order His church.

However, there is history that extends beyond the sacred pages of Scripture. Church history is filled with lessons for twenty-first-century Christians. It is this lens that enables us to turn the spotlight on the church in the latter part of the first century and throughout the centuries that followed. It is this process that gives us insights that will enable us to accentuate what Christians have done right, hopefully eliminate what we've done wrong, and correct what we have done poorly. This process, like the study of the church in Scripture, is open–ended.

There is, however, a special kind of history that can also be studied that offers unusual insights for Christians. Let me illustrate. Not surprisingly, social historians have discovered that wherever you have people, you have function, and wherever you have function, you have form. But they have discovered something else that is extremely relevant to our overall concern in this book.

Resistance to Change

Social historians have made two important observations. First, in studying people and their societal structures, they have discovered that over a period of time people tend to fixate—particularly on forms. People do not want to change. Studies show there is one constant in history. That constant is fixity.

However, social studies also point out that people do change their forms and structures in society, basically under one condition—some kind of *crisis*. Then, and then only, people are open to change. Usually this crisis comes because forms and structures are no longer relevant. They are no longer serving as an effective means to meet the needs of people in that particular society.

Recently this has been illustrated in an unusual way in our own society and others. For years we have built our national economy on such important energy sources as oil, gas, and coal. Understandably, these resources will someday be depleted.

---

[3] A "self-delimiting" function or directive is incapable of being repeated. For example, Paul asked Timothy to bring his cloak and parchments (2 Tim 4:13).

What has happened? This energy crisis has precipitated extensive research projects to overcome the problem. If the Lord tarries, we'll no doubt develop *new* energy sources, perhaps eventually replace the old ones entirely. Already we've learned how to use solar energy in new and different ways and we'll refine this process in the years to come.

The important point is that we would not be exploring new energy sources if we had not faced national and international crises. And so it is with the church. Christians differ little from people in general in their psychological makeup. Structure provides a sense of security. And when we tamper with societal structures, we are tampering with people's emotional stability.

This causes anxiety, and anxiety always results in resistance to change.

Let me illustrate this point with a personal experience. Several years ago I left the sacred halls of learning—the theological seminary. After nearly twenty years as a professor, first at Moody Bible Institute in Chicago and then at Dallas Theological Seminary, I decided to become a full-time pastor. I helped launch Fellowship Bible Church in Dallas, and since then a number of churches have come into existence as a result of the first church in 1972. Though in these early days I was enjoying this experience greatly, for a number of months I also experienced unusual anxiety. I couldn't understand why.

Then one day I got the answer to that question. It suddenly dawned on me that after twenty years in one kind of structure—a structure that I knew very well—I had made a dramatic change. In fact, I was pastoring a renewal church, one that started with functions first, allowing forms to develop naturally in our own cultural setting. I knew the forms forward and backward in a traditional church. I had been down that road before. But here I was, exchanging academic forms for local church forms that were new and innovative. I had not been down that path before. Had I stopped to think before I made the change, I could have predicted the anxiety that followed. It was natural. Once I understood the source of my anxiety, I was able to cope with it and eventually develop security in the new forms I was helping create.

I have often seen this psychological phenomenon in people who visit our services for the first time, particularly if they are unusually entrenched in traditional church structures. At first they feel uncomfortable. It is an understandable emotional reaction.

Lack of Understanding

We must therefore understand why people resist change. **But** we must also understand that Christians sometimes have "double-trouble." Because we believe there are things that should never change, we often confuse non-absolutes (those things that should change) with absolutes (things that should not change). Often this resistance is rooted in insecurity and fear and leads to rationalization. After all, what better way to rationalize than to think we are standing for the truth of Scripture?

However, many Christians resist change because they are honestly confused. They don't understand the differences between absolutes and non-absolutes. They put "beginning the service with the doxology" in the same category as the "virgin birth." Or, they think that "meeting at 11 o'clock on Sunday morning" is just as significant as what the Bible teaches about the "second coming of Christ." Though I'm exaggerating, these illustrations point to our problem.

It is important to help Christians understand the difference between absolutes and non-absolutes, between functions and forms, between principles and patterns, between truth and tradition, between organism and organization, between message and method, between that which is applicable in any culture and that which is purely cultural. This is why it is important to look carefully at the New Testament churches through the lens of Scripture.

And, the lens of history will help us discover our successes and failures in making these differentiations in the past.

ABSOLUTES	NON-ABSOLUTES
Function	Form
Principle	Pattern
Organism	Organization
Truth	Tradition
Message	Method
SUPRACULTURAL	**CULTURAL**

Furthermore, as Christian leaders, we have a God-given means to bring about crisis in the lives of Christians that can bring significant change. I'm speaking of the Word of God. Wherever and whenever God's truth is taught, it should create a Spirit-directed crisis in the life of every believer who is out of harmony with that truth. If we are to be in the will of God, we must change our attitudes and behavior and conform our lives to God's Word.

This is why it is important to use the lens of Scripture to help Christians understand God's plan for the church. As believers begin to comprehend what is absolute and what is not absolute; what is applicable in any culture and what is cultural; and as they understand that the Bible teaches "freedom in form" in order to effectively carry out the Great Commission of our Lord Jesus Christ in every place in the world and at any moment in history, most will be open to change in areas where they should change. At the same time, they'll be secure in the fact that they are not changing those things God intended to remain the same. When this happens, they'll understand what Paul really meant when he wrote: "And to the Jews I became as a Jew, that I might win Jews ... to those without law, as without law .... I have become all things to all men that I may by all means save some" (1 Cor 9:20-22, NASB).

The Lens of Culture

Once again, this lens is clearly related to both the lens of Scripture and the lens of history. You can't study the Bible without seeing the influence of culture. And you cannot study history—particularly social history—without encountering culture.

Jesus carried on His ministry within several cultures, and He understood those cultures very well. This was dramatically illustrated when He encountered the Samaritan woman at Jacob's well. Her culture was different. Her viewpoint on religion and life in general was very different from the individual who had a typical Jewish background. Jesus used His cultural insight to communicate effectively with this woman. It had a decided effect on His methodology in approaching her and teaching her divine truth. It also had a decided effect on her response.

Paul, more than any other apostle, illustrated how important it is to understand culture. We would expect this since his ministry was primarily to the Gentiles. As we'll see in our chapter on New Testament leadership functions and principles, Paul's insights into the Greek and Roman cultures, for example, affected his use of language.

Thus, we can build a strong case from the lens of Scripture itself showing the importance of understanding culture and how it affects the way people think and feel about life. But, as with history, we need to look beyond Scripture to gain insight and implications from culture.

Secular analyst Alvin Toffler has helped all of us understand the influence on culture much better. His book *Future Shock* was a stimulating study relative to where history is headed. However, his book *Third Wave* was particularly helpful to me personally, especially in contributing to my understanding of how culture affects form and structure. Interestingly, I first read much of this book on my way to Quito, Ecuador, to speak to missionaries on the subject of New Testament church principles. I found Toffler's insights helpful as I entered this setting to minister to Christian leaders who were working in cultures vastly different from my own.[4]

Toffler has pointed out that for years much of civilization existed in an agrarian culture. Society's forms and structures were relatively small because form "conforms" to the number of people involved in any given situation. Generally speaking, this describes the biblical culture, though certainly there are exceptions, particularly in the Roman Empire that boasted some very large cities. Even then, most structures were relatively small, with the exception of the amphitheaters and some religious temples.

Toffler further states that all of this was destined to change several hundred years ago. We moved from the "agricultural wave" to the "industrial wave" which gave birth to centralization of population, which in turn gave birth to large societal structures such as towns, cities, and suburbs. These population centers also gave birth to factories, universities, hospitals, and also churches. Large forms and structures came into existence to accommodate functions that involved thousands of people living in a particular geographical area. This is a significant cultural insight. For a time in my own church planting experience in the Dallas metroplex, I determined to keep church structures small to encourage body function. To achieve this goal, we've made multiple use of buildings a priority and started a number of branch churches. However, the more churches we started, the more growth we experienced, primarily because we were in a growing population area. The churches we started in other areas of the city did not resolve the growth problem in our home-base church.

A couple of things happened that were directly related to culture. First, we soon used up the culturally acceptable times for worship and teaching periods. Second, in about four years we had exhausted geographical areas that were potential areas to start new churches, particularly in relationship to our home-base congregation. Third, we soon reached the maximum number of people we could accommodate in our own building. Fourth, this began to lead to an "ingrown mentality"—a desire to stop reaching new people. Also, we began turning people away, causing negative feelings on the part of newcomers as well as those who were regulars.

It was then I saw that we were beginning to violate the very principles that we believed in—one being that form follows function. To solve the problem we had to change form—in short, we had to build a larger building. This, in turn, would affect the service form. And here the church-growth people have also made a very significant cultural observation. As the church grew in size, it was necessary to move to "celebration" when the church met corporately. The challenge we faced was to encourage and develop forms that would continue to accommodate body function. To do this, we developed home cells—which we call Fellowship Families and mini-churches.

In essence, I'm saying you cannot force church structures to remain small if you are located in a cultural situation that is permeated with people and large structures. That is, you cannot remain small if you're about our Father's business of reaching people for Christ. And if you are reaching these people, you must then design structures to accommodate these people in their own cultural environment without violating New Testament principles of church life.

---

[4] Alvin Toffler, *Third Wave*, William Morrow and Company, Inc.

Summary

This is a book designed to help the church develop forms and structures that are effective in carrying out the Great Commission in any given cultural setting. It is not a book about form and structures. Rather, it is a book that focuses first and foremost on New Testament directives and functions, which, in turn, can be translated into absolute principles that are applicable in every culture of the world since the first century. In that sense, if they are focused correctly, they become guidelines that apply to all cultures at all times.

The lens of Scripture is basic in formulating these principles.

The lens of history and the lens of culture add additional insights, particularly in helping us discern and apply these biblical principles. Together, all three lenses help any seeking person to formulate an adequate philosophy of ministry. It is this kind of philosophy that will enable every church leader to develop forms and structures and use methods and techniques that are contemporary and relevant but yet in harmony with biblical absolutes. It is this combination that creates dynamic churches that reflect God's purposes and plans in any culture of the world and at any moment in history.

Dynamics

Dynamics are those activities which keep the church alive and growing. The dynamics of a church are important for worship, edification, and multiplication. Dynamics are the key to the church fulfilling its purpose on earth. As a result, it is important as Christians that we consider carefully the dynamics of our churches. Every dynamic in a church can be divided into two parts. The first we will call "function." The second part we shall refer to as "form."

In order to understand the two sides of every dynamic, consider the following question: *When you think of ministry, what usually comes to your mind?* You might think of an activity, such as preaching, or perhaps a meeting, such as the Sunday worship service. Maybe you are involved in a program for evangelism, so that comes to your mind. Whether you thought of an activity, a meeting, or a program, each of these is done in a certain way. The ministry activity can be called function. The way in which we organize our ministry can be called form.

In other words, every function has a form. When you preach, you prepare your message and deliver it in a certain way. Preaching is the function; the way you prepare, organize, and deliver the sermon is the form. When you have a worship service, you include certain things and do them in a specific manner. Meeting together for worship is function; the manner in which you worship is form. When you put together a program for evangelism, you make decisions on how you will share Christ. Evangelism is function; how you do it is form.

This concept of function and form should cause us to ask ourselves some important questions: *Is what we are doing and the way we are doing it biblical?* By "biblical" we mean that our churches should reflect the principles and commands given to us in Scripture. *Should we change what we do (function)? Should we do what we do differently (form)? How has church history made an impact on our functions and forms? Does culture have anything to do with the way we do certain things?* These questions are only a few of the ones we will consider in this lesson.

Lesson 2 Articles

Respectable

*"The overseer then must be above reproach, the husband of one wife, temperate, self-controlled, **respectable**"* (1 Tim 3:2, emphasis added).

The Greek word *kosmios* means orderly or well-arranged—one who lives a well-ordered life. In 1 Timothy, Paul uses it of the way a woman should dress—proper, becoming, and modest—as a woman claiming godliness (1 Tim 3:9-10). (For both men and women) this does not mean drab or sloppy, but not attracting undue attention to oneself at the expense of Christ—inner beauty must be the emphasis—for this would be disorderly. Drabness and sloppiness also hurt Christ's cause by projecting his image as backward, uncultured, and "peculiar" in the bad sense of the word. It is not respectable!

Jesus uses the verb sense of this word to describe a well-ordered house (Mt 12:44), "decorated" tombstones (Mt 23:29), and "well-trimmed" lamps (Mt 25:7). He also describes the temple as "adorned with beautiful stones and offerings" (Lk 21:5).

A good Biblical illustration of the concept is Paul's exhortation to slaves to be subject to their masters in everything; to be well-pleasing and not argumentative and not to steal but to bring credit to the teaching of our God in all ways (Tit 2:9-10). In everything, we Christians must live so our lives are becoming to the teachings of God. Especially to those in authority, we must be respectful and we must be honest with all people. He must be a Christian gentleman in all areas of his life: his dress, his speech, the appearance of his home, his office, or the way he does business. All areas must conform to God's Word.

Note: This material is adapted from Gene A. Getz, *The Measure of a Man.* (Ventura, CA: Regal Books, 1984).

Self-Controlled

*"The overseer then must be above reproach, the husband of one wife, temperate, **self-controlled**"* (1 Tim 3:2, Tit 1:8, emphasis added).

Romans 12:3 expresses this concept: Do not think too highly of yourself, in relation to God and other Christians, "but think with sober discernment." Some in Corinth had an exalted view of themselves thinking they were "God's gift to the church" (1 Cor 12:14-27). Instead, they should give preference to one another in honor and not put each other down (Rom 12:10). Paul emphasizes this trait, more than any other characteristic of maturity, for everyone in the body. In Titus 2:2-6 he exhorts older men to have self-control, older women to teach younger women self-control, and younger men to have self-control.

An overseer is truly humble. He knows any and all gifts and possessions come from God. Without God he is nothing. He understands grace and knows he is a sinner saved by grace (Rom 5:8). Everything he has he counts as loss for the sake of what he has in Christ (Phil 3:4-7). He is trained in his Christian walk by God's grace (Tit 2:11-12). Also, only the self-controlled can pray appropriately (1 Pet 4:7).

Self-control does not lead to weakness or low self-confidence. This was an area Timothy may have had a problem with (2 Tim 2:7-8). This takes a divine balance: Paul commended himself when falsely accused and belittled, but his motives were clear; he did so because of what God had done in his life. Paul counted himself as the least of the apostles, yet he says he worked harder than all of them, but it was only by the grace of God in him (1 Cor 15: 9-10; see also 2 Cor 10–11).

Lesson 2 Articles

Note: This material is adapted from Gene A. Getz, *The Measure of a Man*. (Ventura, CA: Regal Books, 1984).

Temperate

*"The overseer then must be above reproach, the husband of one wife, **temperate**"* (1 Tim 3:2, emphasis added).

For the Christian, this word has far more significance than its common meaning to not be self-indulgent. Paul uses it to mean someone having a clear *perspective* on life and a correct spiritual *orientation*. This man does not lose his physical, psychological, and spiritual orientation. He knows the temporariness of this life and walks by God's wisdom, not man's (Eccl 9:3). He knows that this world is headed for ultimate destruction (2 Pet 3:5-7). This same word in Greek is translated "sober" throughout 1 Thessalonians 5:2-8.

Paul measures soberness the same way he measures Christian maturity: the measure of someone's faith, hope, and love (1 Thess 5:8).

The temperate man is a man of faith (Heb 11). He steps out and acts on the promises of God without a guarantee of what is ahead. He follows Jesus, his Leader and waits for and teaches others to look for His return and deliverance from "the wrath to come" (1 Thess 5:9; Heb 2:10; 12:1-2).

He is a man of hope. Our hope refers to our inheritance laid up for us in heaven (1 Pet 1:3-4; Col 1:5). This refers to both the object of our faith and our present attitude (and future) and state of being (Heb 11:1).

He is a man of love. This is the most important of the three (1 Cor 13:4-6, 13). It is foundational for the other two and it endures all things and never fails (1 Cor 13:7-8).

All three are foundational for having a clear perspective on life.

Note: This material is adapted from Gene A. Getz, *The Measure of a Man*. (Ventura, CA: Regal Books, 1984).

The Three Lenses

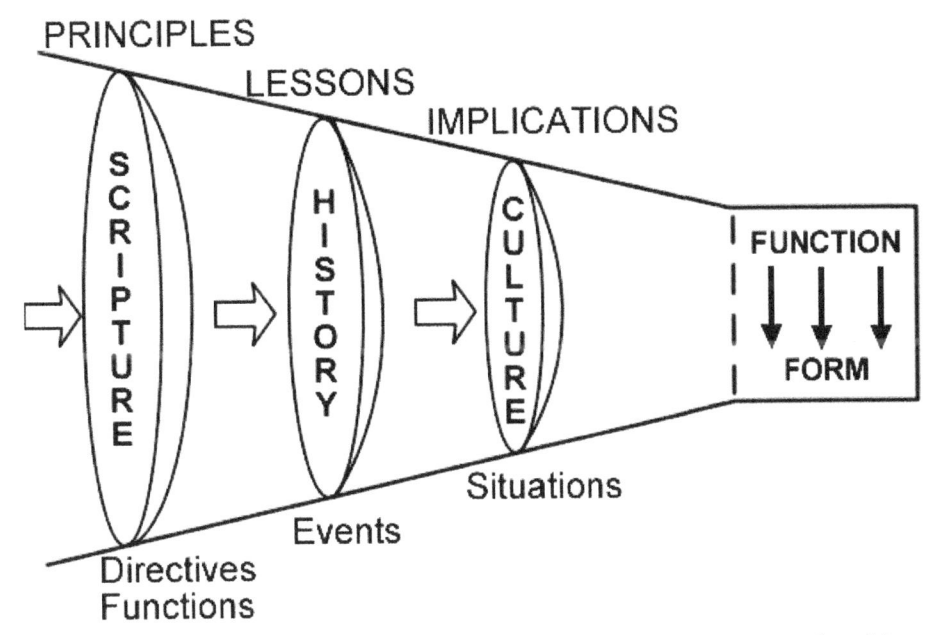

[Diagram: A funnel showing three lenses — SCRIPTURE, HISTORY, CULTURE — narrowing from left to right into a box labeled FUNCTION → FORM. Top labels: PRINCIPLES, LESSONS, IMPLICATIONS. Bottom labels: Directives/Functions, Events, Situations.]

In our study of the word *ekklesia* and the metaphors about the church, we saw that things can be more complicated than they first appear. It is one thing to discuss the biblical definition of the church, but it is another to free yourself from the influence of history and culture. As a matter of fact, it is impossible. An awareness of today and yesterday seen through a correct biblical perspective is all that is possible—and all that God wants from us.

We have learned that *ekklesia* includes two aspects of the church: the universal body of Christ and local forms in which it manifests itself to the world. The universal church, by its very nature, is invisible and perfect. On the other hand, the local church, the only aspect of the church which we experience, is visible and imperfect. In the previous lesson, we noted some differences between the universal and local aspects of the church in terms of leadership, genuineness, and continuity. The last two areas of difference show how limitations, as well as sinfulness, affect the church that is visible.

In history, churches have flourished and deteriorated spiritually. Many have continued to exist and claimed the name "church." New churches have also come into existence, and some of these have also died out. The universal church has always continued, but local churches have not. None of the churches mentioned in Revelation 2 and 3 still exist today. In other cases, forms have continued, but the spiritual functions have died out. It is absolutely necessary for us to gain a proper perspective on these developments. The distinction between function and form that Getz provides can prove to be very helpful in gaining this perspective.

"And now these three remain: faith, hope, and love. But the greatest of these is love" (1 Corinthians 13:13).

Lesson 3: Focusing on History and Culture

Lesson Introduction

The lenses of history and culture are very useful in evaluating local church ministry emphases and programs. It is difficult to separate oneself from the present and to acknowledge the influence of history and cultural norms upon one's Christian service. In this lesson, we will examine some common tendencies as churches grow older, as well as some of the common occurrences as churches try to integrate within their present cultural norms.

Lesson Outline

Lesson 3: Focusing on History and Culture
    Topic 1: History of Institutionalism
    Topic 2: Institutionalism in Evangelical Churches
    Topic 3: Lessons from Culture
Topic 4: Developing Character—Hospitable, Able to Teach, Not a Drunkard

Lesson Objectives

Pastor Eugene's church has existed for over a decade and comprises believers of every generation. Some church members have been in the church since its founding, and others have joined the church as new believers over the years as the church has grown.

The church has been holding Wednesday evening prayer meetings at the houses of the elders since its founding. The church was originally formed out of a couple of those prayer meetings, so these mid-week meetings have a strong historical tradition in the church. However, the city is hosting a series of community meetings about issues important to the health and welfare of the community; they will be held every Wednesday night for the next month.

Several church members have asked if they could hold a prayer meeting on a different night for those who will speak at or attend the city meeting. Other church members have simply asked to be excused from the prayer meetings for the month of the town meetings.

One very vocal church member accused the community-meeting attendees of being too worldly. Others say the Wednesday night prayer meetings are foundational to the church and that we should pray for the community instead of attending the meetings. Other church members think that Christians should be represented in the community and need to be salt and light at these meetings.

As you can see, Pastor Eugene has quite a dilemma on his hands. During this lesson, to help Pastor Eugene and ourselves to know the correct course, we will:

- Review historical cases of institutionalism and identify common symptoms
- Provide antidotes and hope for those who are seeing signs of institutionalism
- Review how culture affects churches
- Use a list of evaluative questions to determine the influence of your church and your culture on each other
- Integrate the Christian character traits of hospitality, lack of drunkenness, and teaching others into your life and ministry

Topic 1: History of Institutionalism

To develop a form of ministry that is both faithful to biblical principles and relevant to modern society, we must take into account the historical context. This is a complex process, one which requires insight into a variety of historical factors that influence the direction of a given ministry. Obviously, a detailed historical analysis is not possible within the scope of this course. Instead, the focus will be on one historical process which can greatly hinder effective ministry—namely, the process of institutionalism.

In Pastor Eugene's case, he needs to consider the history of both his local church and the church universal to find solutions to the Wednesday night prayer meeting dilemma.

"Those who forget history are doomed to repeat it" is a famous quote, although the author of it is disputed. This saying applies to our topic because we want to look through the lens of history to learn from its successes and avoid its mistakes. Learning lessons from history is almost like looking with wisdom into the future. To accomplish this task, please continue working through this topic.

Institutionalism is a problem in both religious and secular organizations. Getz lists eleven symptoms of institutionalism within secular groups and then traces religious institutionalism through six historical movements.

Reading Assignment

Please read the chapter titled "Institutionalism in History" from Getz' book *Sharpening the Focus of the Church* in the Articles section at the end of this lesson.

The essence and ideas of function and form are listed in the chart below. Take time to review the chart to make sure you understand the differences between absolutes (function) and non-absolutes (form). Notice how life-giving and open the absolutes are compared to how time-bound and limiting non-absolutes are.

ABSOLUTES	NON-ABSOLUTES
Function	Form
Principle	Pattern
Organism	Organization
Truth	Tradition
Message	Method
SUPRACULTURAL	**CULTURAL**

QUESTION 1

As we look at church history, when functions and forms and absolutes and non-absolutes are confused, we are in danger of _____?

QUESTION 2

Every growing movement eventually faces the threat of institutionalism. *True or False?*

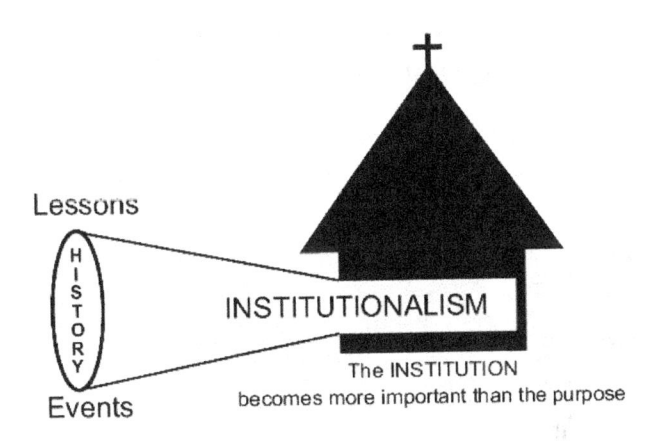

QUESTION 3

Each of the following statements was made by a parishioner about his/her church. Which of the following statements indicate symptoms of institutionalism? *(Select all that apply.)*

    A. "I learn so much about the Bible from my fellow church members."

    B. "I'm a good Christian. I go to church every week and listen to the pastor's sermon."

    C. "We were founding members of our church, and we took part in making many decisions about how we worship; we made good decisions then, and we still do everything the same way today."

    D. "We were founding members of our church, and we took part in making decisions about how we worship; but now a younger generation is involved in leading the church, and they have some great new ideas."

    E. "We must be doing something right because people are coming through our doors in droves!"

    F. "The faith of our brothers and sisters is amazing. Even through hardship, the Lord has blessed their efforts by transforming the lives of people they encounter."

According to Getz, the eleven symptoms of institutionalism are:

1. The organization becomes more important than the people who comprise it.
2. Individuals begin to function like cogs in the organizational machine.
3. Individuality and creativity are lost in the structure.
4. The atmosphere in the organization becomes threatening, rather than open.
5. The structural arrangements become rigid and inflexible.
6. People are serving the organization, rather than the objectives for which the organization exists.
7. Communication breaks down because of a repressive atmosphere.
8. Procedures are rulebooks that grow substantially.
9. People develop their own special interest groups, often creating a competitive atmosphere.
10. People lose their initiative and become discouraged.
11. As the organization grows, so does the increase in institutionalism.

QUESTION 4

Open your Life Notebook and record which of the eleven symptoms you have observed in your own church or in other churches you've participated in.

Lesson 3: Focusing on History and Culture   Page 75

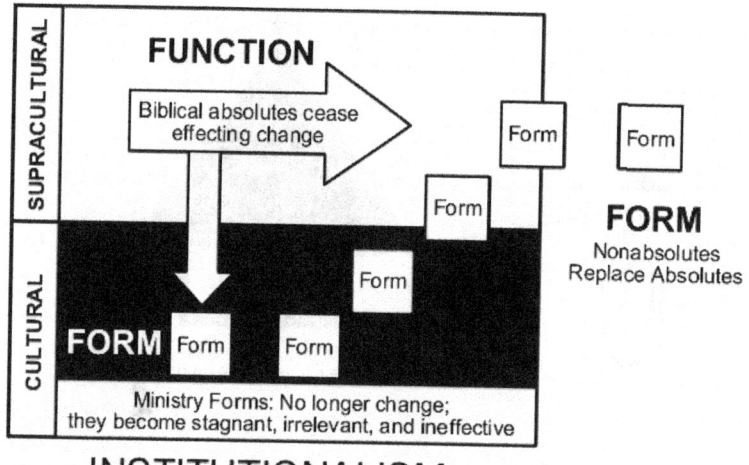

FUNCTION — Biblical absolutes cease effecting change

FORM — Nonabsolutes Replace Absolutes

SUPRACULTURAL / CULTURAL

Ministry Forms: No longer change; they become stagnant, irrelevant, and ineffective

INSTITUTIONALISM
Allows cultural forms of ministry and structure to become absolute and to replace the functions of biblical principles

Topic 1 Key Points:

- Every growing movement eventually faces the threat of creeping institutionalism.
- The key ingredients for institutionalism are people, structure, and age.
- The symptoms of institutionalism in a church are:
  - A religious system that emphasizes non-absolutes as essential. Religion becomes a matter of form and ceremony, not life experience.
  - Loss of the individual's understanding of God's truth and failure to use each one's God-given gifts to enhance the church.
  - Focus on measuring the multitudes, instead of the results achieved by the believers.
  - A hierarchy of leaders who do the "thinking" and communicating. Everyone else becomes a recipient.
- God's truth and Christian community are antidotes that counteract institutionalism.

Topic 2: Institutionalism in Evangelical Churches

Pastor Eugene had always thought that institutionalism was prevalent in Roman Catholicism and Orthodox traditions, but he didn't think that it occurred in evangelical churches like his own. Now he has begun to identify some symptoms of institutionalism in his own church. He wants to better understand these symptoms and what he can do to avoid or alleviate the problem of institutionalism in his church.

Reading Assignment

Please read the chapter from *Sharpening the Focus of the Church* titled "Reflections of Institutionalism in the Evangelical Church" in the Articles section at the end of this lesson.

Note: Since the textbook is written from an American perspective, do not take offense or put it aside as irrelevant, but look carefully as you read for those things that are universally true. Follow Getz' processes as he develops his analyses. For example, institutionalism is a common historical phenomenon in society in general, as well as in the church. You will probably find that the cultural implications outlined in the textbook relate to most cultures of the world.

In view of these historical effects of institutionalism, one could have hoped that evangelicalism would have avoided its snare, but unfortunately that has not always been the case.

QUESTION 5

One danger Getz cites for evangelical churches is that "body life" often takes precedence over a skilled individual preaching and teaching the word. *True or False?*

In your reading, Getz outlines five thought-provoking reflections on institutionalism in the evangelical church:

- Our greatest strength has helped create some of our greatest problems. (The strongest feature of the evangelical church has been its adherence to the Bible as its final authority in faith and practice.)
- Emphasizing the church as a soul-winning station has also contributed its share to the process of institutionalization.
- We are beginning to support the "institution" rather than its reasons for existing. Put another way, we are more concerned with existence than our cause for existence.
- We are emphasizing correct doctrine and frequently neglecting the quality of one's life. An important criterion for evaluating spiritual maturity is often "what one believes" and not "the way that person lives."
- We have allowed non-absolutes to become absolutes. (This way of thinking is the most subtle of all in leading the church into institutionalism. That which is meant to be a means to an end becomes an end in itself.)

QUESTION 6

Open your Life Notebook and number the lines one through five. Comment in your notebook as to how each reflection is, or could be, a problem for your church. Where applicable, speculate as to the probable cause of each condition as it applies to your church. What solutions can you think of?

QUESTION 7

Write a short paper (one or two pages) describing the historical development of your own local church. You may write this out in your Life Notebook. Describe how the various ministry forms in your church evolved. Discuss how and why they have changed, or why they continue that way today. At the end of your paper, include a paragraph discussing the symptoms of institutionalism that you see in your church.

Topic 2 Key Points:

- Failure to provide balanced New Testament experiences results in an emphasis on knowledge of correct doctrine and Scriptures, but to the detriment of other experiences that create mature Christians.
- Evangelism without edification creates shallow experiences for believers.
- Church programs should *never* become more important than the purpose of the church.
- Discipleship, which is represented by love, should take precedence over doctrine.
- Do not allow non-absolutes to become absolutes. This is an obvious symptom of institutionalism.

Topic 3: Lessons from Culture

This course—indeed our entire church ministry—must understand and employ function and form. Function is the constant, based on the unchanging and unchangeable Word of God. Form is variable, though it must always be in line with the principles of the Word. One of the most important factors, perhaps **the** most important, affecting the form through which we minister is **our culture**. Even then it is not enough to say "our culture," but rather "our culture at the present time."

By answering the previous questions, Pastor Eugene realized that within one country, one province, even one city or village, the culture changes over a period of time. The way life was lived fifty years ago is not the same as today. Therefore, it is important for Pastor Eugene (and all church leaders) to understand and accurately evaluate the present-day culture where they live to develop forms of ministry that effectively and relevantly communicate with that culture.

Galatians 4:4-5 says, "But when the appropriate time had come, God sent out his Son, born of a woman, born under the law, to redeem those who were under the law, that we may be adopted as sons with full rights."

God picked the perfect time to send His Son into the world, into the perfect universal and dominant culture of the time (Greek/Roman), for the writing and spreading of His Word. The forms He chose were also best suited to His purposes. We want to accomplish His mission for us with the same wisdom, with the best forms for accomplishing our task in our culture and time. To get help with making wise choices about forms, please continue reading in this topic.

The cultural implications which are given in this chapter are drawn from what is happening in American society. As you read, think about your own culture. Some of the observations in the readings may be equally valid for your ministry. Other observations may come to mind which are significant in your cultural context but not mentioned in the text. Be sure to make note of them for future reference. Most importantly, however, try to analyze your culture the way Getz analyzes his own culture!

For example, "The church of Jesus Christ must develop a correct perspective regarding the multiple factors at work in our society." To apply this statement to your culture, ask yourself what kind of factors are at work in your society. Are there many or are there few? Which have the greatest impact on the church?

American society is very fast moving and production oriented. Few real villages still exist. As Getz states, technology has left its effects. All people relate primarily to each other at work. Television substitutes for personal contact for many. Little time is left for meeting and knowing neighbors. Meeting your neighbor is hardly spontaneous and becomes an effort in any urban society.

This way of life affects church life. In America, planning the erection of a church building without having enough space for a parking lot reveals cultural ignorance. Sunday school teachers have to compete with television programs for the interest of the children. Many other cultural factors need noticing as affecting church life in America. These are cultural and not biblical factors, yet we must give them our conscious attention.

Reading Assignment

Please read the chapter from *Sharpening the Focus of the Church* titled "Cultural Implications for the Twentieth-Century Church" in the Articles section at the end of this lesson.

QUESTION 8

Prominent Christian personalities who walk across the pages of the New Testament could not and did not ignore cultures. In the following list of verses the person or church took into account the culture of the people they ministered to. Study the verses and incidents and then write the incident in the appropriate titles in the chart on the right.

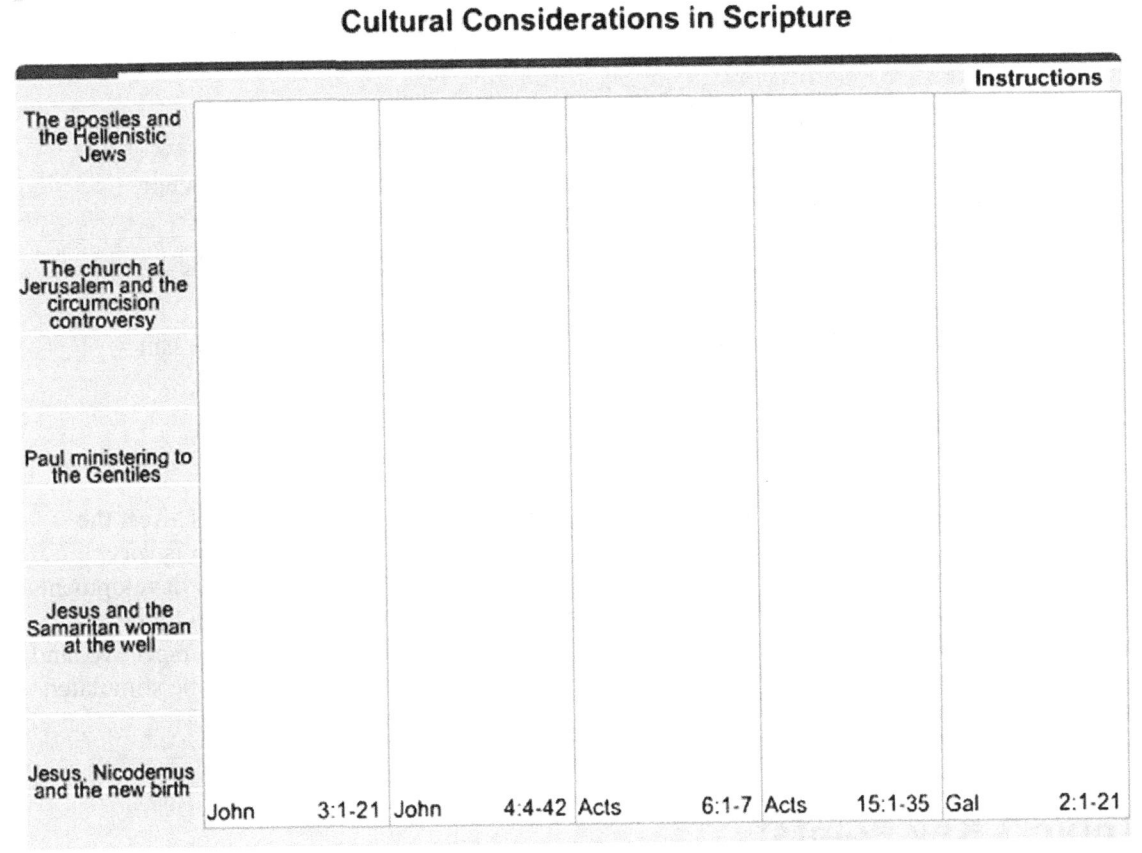

Cultural Considerations in Scripture

	John 3:1-21	John 4:4-42	Acts 6:1-7	Acts 15:1-35	Gal 2:1-21
The apostles and the Hellenistic Jews					Instructions
The church at Jerusalem and the circumcision controversy					
Paul ministering to the Gentiles					
Jesus and the Samaritan woman at the well					
Jesus, Nicodemus and the new birth					

Getz examined ten cultural implications for the twentieth-century American church. The following questions will help you consider the impact of these cultural implications for the church in your culture:

QUESTION 9

Open your Life Notebook and record your answers to the following questions: To what extent do the people in your church have a biblical view of history? Do they really believe that history will climax with the return of Christ, and do they therefore live in the light of His coming? What factors in your society make it difficult to maintain a proper view of history, and how can you resist these pressures?

When looking at the issue of culture, discussions with others will greatly stimulate your objectivity. Analyzing your culture is neither easy, nor can you accomplish it quickly. It is an ongoing process as culture is constantly changing.

QUESTION 10

Lead a group discussion around the following questions and record your observations in your Life Notebook.

1. What economical, political, and religious factors have historically determined the development of our culture to become different from those around us?
2. American culture is "production oriented." Some Western European cultures are very "discussion oriented." These characteristics are seen in church life. This orientation gives to each culture its own peculiar problems to deal with. Some cultures are very intellectually oriented. Other cultures put heavy emphasis on experience. Still other cultures value intuition and feelings. As far as they are familiar to us, how would you typify your culture according to these concepts, and what can you determine as causes?
3. To what extent are the Christians in your church adhering to values that are really based upon cultural norms rather than upon biblical principles? What effect does this have upon how the church ministers in the community?
4. "Why do people in our culture like the church, or why do they dislike the church?"
5. What are the major cultural problems which your society faces, and how can the church help solve those problems?
6. How can our church relate *optimally* to non-Christians without losing its testimony?

You can take each of the factors that describe your culture and ask, "How does this affect the culture today and the church's response?" For instance, if one's economic situation is very difficult and people lack many basic things, this situation has an impact on cultural developments, which in turn affects the church. When one has abundance, the same is true but in a totally different way. In both cases, people may become very materialistic in their daily perspective, and Christians may lose their eternal perspective. On the other hand, other people may be stimulated to hunger for eternal things when there is material poverty.

Topic 3 Key Points:

The church needs to develop a proper perspective about factors such as:
- A nation and a church's history
- Concern for government leaders
- Concern for human needs in our community
- Determining absolute versus relative truth within value systems
- Communication methods
- Lifestyle choices
- Family life

Topic 4: Developing Character—Hospitable, Able to Teach, Not a Drunkard

In this topic, we will continue developing mature Christian character. These are the same requirements Paul lists for Christian leaders. We will focus on these characteristics: hospitable, able to teach, and not a drunkard.

The widow giving her mite contrasts perfectly with the story of the Rich Young Ruler (Mk 10:17-22). In the story of the widow's mite, the widow's actions vividly illustrate Jesus' point about giving without pretension (Mk 12:41-44). It also perfectly counters the pretentious actions of the Jewish leaders that Jesus had just taught against (Mk 12:38-40). But what leads up to the widow giving her commendable offering? What source brings forth her actions? They come straight from her heart—from character developed over the years.

If developing the character that leads to these actions interests you, please read on in this topic.

Hospitable

Reading Assignment

Please read the article titled "Hospitality" in the Articles section at the end of this lesson.

QUESTION 11

Fill in the columns with a pen or pencil by matching the option on the left to the verses in the bottom rows.

Scripture	Teaching of Hospitality
Leviticus 19:4	Brotherly love shows others you are Christians.
Hebrews 13:1-2	We must love all men without partiality.
John 13:35	In response to culture, love was shown communally.
Galatians 5:14	Loving your neighbor as yourself fulfills the law.
James 2:6-9	Love the foreigner as yourself.
Acts 2:42-47	Brotherly love and hospitality must continue.

QUESTION 12

The basis for Christian hospitality is love, 1 Corinthians 13:4-7; biblical love is not a feeling but an action, so one must not wait to feel like showing hospitality. Which of the following acts of hospitality can you practice in the next month? *(Select all that apply.)*

   A. Look for opportunities to share your home with spiritual leaders like pastors, missionaries, and other Christian leaders. Invite them to dinner or to stay at your home.

   B. Look for opportunities to share your home with other members of the body of Christ from your own local church. If bashfulness or shyness prevents you, take the step of faith to invite others to your home.

   C. Begin to show hospitality to non-Christians starting with those around you: neighbors, co-workers, or others with whom you associate. You are the Christian and you should reach out with a dinner invitation or an evening of relaxation and social activity.

   D. Open your home for an informal Bible study for either Christians or non-Christians (try to do both over a period of time). Learn to love people because they are people and not just to win them to Christ.

   E. Other ways of your own choosing

Hebrews 13:2 says, "Do not neglect hospitality, because through it some have entertained angels without knowing it." Angels often appear in human likeness, so a person may not even know if he/she is entertaining men or possibly a heavenly messenger from God (for example, Gen 18 and Gen 19). Even so, it should not matter, for we should be hospitable to all alike, just as God would be (Jas 2:1-4).

Think of how you can show hospitality at church. Can you open your church and provide a free meal for the homeless or those out of work? Maybe you can also find a way to provide transportation. How about at work? Can you help someone out with a work burden without compromising the quality of your own work? The possibilities are endless; begin praying for opportunities to show hospitality and prepare to give it as the opportunities surely arise.

"Actions speak louder than words," is an expression that's used in American culture. We often think that a person who teaches is an eloquent speaker or writer. However, the basis for being a good teacher is how someone behaves, not what someone says. To learn more about being able to teach, please read the following textbook chapter.

Able to Teach

Reading Assignment

Please read the article titled "An Able Teacher" in the Articles section at the end of this lesson.

QUESTION 13

Having the spiritual gift of teaching is key to Paul's concept of being "able to teach." *True or False?*

When we think of the word "drunkard," we often picture someone who is stumbling through the street after drinking too much. This person lacks control of their physical movements. However, God's definition of the term provides a slightly different take on the subject. To learn more about how God defines this term and what is expected of you as a leader, please read the following chapter.

Not a Drunkard

Reading Assignment

Please read the article titled "Not a Drunkard" in the Articles section at the end of this lesson.

QUESTION 14

The issue with the concept of "not a drunkard" is _____ *(Select all that apply.)*

    A. Alcohol itself

    B. Abstinence

    C. Drunkenness

    D. Control

QUESTION 15

Open your Life Notebook and record your answers to the following questions:

- Are there any areas in which the quality of the life you are living harms your ability to minister and lead others?

- Do you do anything that harms your body, clouds your thinking, or brings you into bondage to yourself? If your answer is affirmative, write out a plan to address this issue.

Topic 4 Key Points:

To be an effective Christian leader, you must exhibit a quality of life that others respect and want to learn more about. The social customs that you follow may vary from culture to culture, but they will always include being in control of your body and being hospitable to others.

Lesson 3 Self Check

QUESTION 1

People plus structure plus age (more often than not) equal _____.

QUESTION 2

Decline in organizations is inevitable and the cycle cannot be reversed. *True or False?*

QUESTION 3

Which of the following is a remedy to institutionalism?

- A. Emphasizing how someone lives over what someone believes
- B. Moving non-absolutes toward becoming absolutes
- C. Emphasizing the gifted Bible teaching of one main leader
- D. Emphasizing the church's role as a soul-winning station

QUESTION 4

According to the Bible, why primarily are we to pray for our nation's leaders?

- A. To help preserve the country we live in and its values
- B. So that we may live a quiet and tranquil life
- C. To help us prosper materially
- D. So that we might right the wrongs that exist in society

QUESTION 5

When asking questions about forms in our culture, we must ask about our culture at this present time and NOT just about our culture in general. *True or False?*

QUESTION 6

According to the teachings from this lesson on Galatians 4:4-5, God picked the perfect time and culture in which to send His Son into the world. *True or False?*

QUESTION 7

Christians teach with their actions more than their words. *True or False?*

QUESTION 8

As with meat sacrificed to idols, alcohol itself is the main issue in Paul's concept of a mature Christian as "not a drunkard." *True or False?*

QUESTION 9

Overeating is just as much a sin as being a drunkard. *True or False?*

Unit 1 Exam: Church Dynamics

QUESTION 1

The word translated "church" in the New Testament is the Greek word _____.

QUESTION 2

The word translated "church" from the original Greek is used exclusively by believers in Christ. *True or False?*

QUESTION 3

The metaphor of the body best emphasizes the unity and interdependence of the members of the church. *True or False?*

QUESTION 4

Biblically, a local gathering of believers is a microcosm of the larger church. *True or False?*

QUESTION 5

The key concepts to include in a definition of the church are:

    A. The Father, Son, Holy Spirit, and Satan

    B. Unity, community, multiplication, and brotherhood

    C. Community, worship, edification, and multiplication

    D. Vertical and horizontal relationships with God and people

QUESTION 6

Under the metaphor of the church as priesthood, the sacrifice of incense under the Old Covenant was already closely connected with _____.

QUESTION 7

A "function" is a biblical purpose for ministry. *True or False?*

QUESTION 8

The most important key to the victorious Christian life is_____.

    A. Being filled with the Holy Spirit

    B. Adopting Christ-like behaviors

    C. Discovering your spiritual gift'

    D. Studying God's Word

QUESTION 9

Church "dynamics" includes both forms and functions. *True or False?*

QUESTION 10

The development of an effective strategy for Christian ministry should start with form, not function. *True or False?*

QUESTION 11

A function can be defined as a ministry activity. *True or False?*

QUESTION 12

What was the principle behind the church's decision in Acts 15:29 about meat sacrificed to idols?

    A. Gentiles should not eat meat sacrificed to idols.

    B. To respond in some situations and eat to the glory of God

    C. Eating meat sacrificed to idols is fellowshipping with demons.

    D. For Christian sensitivity to win unbelievers by not offending them

QUESTION 13

If a form interferes with a function, the form must change. *True or False?*

QUESTION 14

Which of the following is most clearly a supra-cultural absolute?

    A. Having Sunday school

    B. Ordaining a pastor

    C. The pastor receives a full salary

    D. Sunday evening services

QUESTION 15

According to the teachings from this lesson on Galatians 4:4-5, God picked the perfect time and culture in which to send His Son into the world. *True or False?*

QUESTION 16

For the Christian leader (the mature Christian), what is the most important consideration in buying a house?

    A. Motive

    B. Size

    C. Cost

    D. Location

QUESTION 17

To have proper self-control, one must keep the balance between having human and divine resources to do great things for God and remembering that all we are and have is because of God's _____.

QUESTION 18

A challenge in preventing institutionalism is to prevent forms and non-absolutes from becoming as sacred to people as their core biblical beliefs. *True or False?*

QUESTION 19

People plus culture plus age equals _____.

    A. Absolutes

    B. Institutionalism

    C. Message

    D. Organism

QUESTION 20

The problem in Acts 6 between the apostles and the Hellenistic Jews was primary caused by_____.

    A. Historical reasons

    B. Culture

    C. Traditions

    D. Different biblical interpretations

QUESTION 21

Biblically, the primary reason for praying for our nation's leaders is to help right the wrongs that exist in our country. *True or False?*

QUESTION 22

A church has a tradition of meeting on Saturday night for a fellowship meal, but participation in that form is minimal. What step(s) should that church leader take?

    A. Use the lenses of Scripture, history, and culture to analyze this form.

    B. Put continuing this form up for a congregational vote.

    C. Consider changing this meal to the traditional Wednesday night.

    D. Eliminate this ineffective form and substitute a proper function.

QUESTION 23

To Paul, the necessary ingredient for being "able to teach" is_____.

    A. Having the gift of teaching

    B. Learning effective teaching methods

    C. Motivating people to want to learn

    D. Having a quality of life that others want to mimic

QUESTION 24

Evangelism without edification creates shallow experiences for believers. *True or False?*

QUESTION 25

Alcohol itself is NOT Paul's main concern when giving guidelines for choosing Christian leaders. *True or False?*

Lesson 3 Answers to Questions

QUESTION 1: Institutionalism
The challenge is to prevent forms and non-absolutes from becoming ends in themselves and as sacred to people as their beliefs.

QUESTION 2: True

QUESTION 3:
A. "I learn so much about the Bible from my fellow church members."
D. "We were founding members of our church, and we took part in making decisions about how we worship; but now a younger generation is involved in leading the church, and they have some great new ideas."
E. "We must be doing something right because people are coming through our doors in droves!"

QUESTION 4: *Your answer*

QUESTION 5: False

QUESTION 6: *Your answer*

QUESTION 7: *Your answer*

QUESTION 8:

Scripture	Incidents
John 3:1-21	Jesus, Nicodemus, and the new birth
John 4:4-42	Jesus and the Samaritan woman at the well
Acts 6:1-7	The apostles and the Hellenistic Jews
Acts 15:1-35	The church at Jerusalem and the circumcision controversy
Galatians 2:1-21	Paul ministering to the Gentiles

QUESTION 9: *Your answer*

QUESTION 10: *Your answer*

QUESTION 11:

Scripture	Teaching of Hospitality
Leviticus 19:4	Love the foreigner as yourself.
Hebrews 13:1-2	Brotherly love and hospitality must continue.
John 13:35	Brotherly love shows others you are Christians.
Galatians 5:14	Loving your neighbor as yourself fulfills the law.
James 2:6-9	We must love all men without partiality.
Acts 2:42-47	In response to culture, love was shown communally.

QUESTION 12:
**There is no right or wrong answer to this question.*

QUESTION 13: False

QUESTION 14:
C. Drunkenness
D. Control

QUESTION 15: *Your Answer*

Lesson 3 Self Check Answers

QUESTION 1: Institutionalism
QUESTION 2: False
QUESTION 3:
C. Emphasizing the gifted Bible teaching of one main leader
QUESTION 4:
B. So that we may live a quiet and tranquil life
QUESTION 5: True
QUESTION 6: True
QUESTION 7: True
QUESTION 8: False
QUESTION 9: True

Unit 1 Exam Answers

QUESTION 1: *Ekklesia*
QUESTION 2: False
QUESTION 3: True
QUESTION 4: True
QUESTION 5:
C. Community, worship, edification, and multiplication
QUESTION 6: Prayer
QUESTION 7: True
QUESTION 8:
B. Adopting Christ-like behaviors
QUESTION 9: True
QUESTION 10: False
QUESTION 11: True
QUESTION 12:
D. For Christian sensitivity to win unbelievers by not offending them
QUESTION 13: True
QUESTION 14:
C. The pastor receives a full salary
QUESTION 15: True
QUESTION 16:
A. Motive
QUESTION 17: Grace
QUESTION 18: True
QUESTION 19:
B. Institutionalism
QUESTION 20:
B. Culture
QUESTION 21: False
QUESTION 22:
A. Use the lenses of Scripture, history, and culture to analyze this form.
QUESTION 23:
D. Having a quality of life that others want to mimic
QUESTION 24: False
QUESTION 25: True

Lesson 3 Articles

An Able Teacher

*"The overseer then must be above reproach, the husband of one wife, temperate, self-controlled, respectable, hospitable, **able to teach**"* (1 Tim 3:2; Titus 1:8, emphasis added).

The unique Greek word *didaktikos*, or "able to teach," is only used twice in the New Testament (1 Tim 3:2; 2 Tim 2:24). Normally, we think of effective communicators using skillful methods and being able to motivate learners, but these are not what Paul had in mind. Paul also is not referring to someone with the gift of teaching (1 Cor 12:28-29; Eph 4:11). Paul's concept must be developed by every mature Christian.

Paul's concept has more to do with a quality of life, as do the other concepts surrounding its use in context (2 Tim 2:23-26). A person must possess certain personal qualities that enable him to communicate with others in a nonthreatening, objective manner. He is sensitive to all— even the obstinate and bitter—and does not reciprocate when attacked. He is not in bondage to himself, but is secure as a person and in control of his personality.

He has certain convictions about the Word and is able to exhort in sound doctrine and refute those who contradict. But he is not given over to foolish and ignorant speculations (2 Tim 2:23). He must diligently study God's Word and work hard to teach it accurately (2 Tim 2:15).

To sum up, this person must be characterized by spiritual and emotional maturity and able to handle difficult situations. This person must be convinced the Word of God is true. This person must also be able to teach all people. He must learn, believe, and live the Word of God.

Note: This material is adapted from Gene A. Getz, *The Measure of a Man*. (Ventura, CA: Regal Books, 1984).

Cultural Implications for the Twenty-first Century Church

Prominent Christian personalities who walk across the pages of the New Testament *could not* and *did not* ignore cultures. Jesus Christ took into consideration cultural backgrounds, effectively demonstrated in His dealings with such people as the woman at the well, or in contrast, with Nicodemus. We see this demonstrated by the apostles, as they faced and solved the problem between the Hellenistic Jews and the native Hebrews in Jerusalem. We see it demonstrated by the church at Jerusalem, as they were confronted with the circumcision controversy. And we see it demonstrated in a most unusual way by Paul, both in his methodology and language, as he moved from the Jewish community out into the Greek culture.

We Must Not Ignore Culture

"Culture is a stern reality," acknowledged Dr. George Peters, professor of World Missions at Dallas Theological Seminary. "It is as extensive as man and as comprehensive as his ways, thoughts, sentiments, and relationships."[1] It is the all–encompassing non–biological atmosphere of his being as well as the institutions that make his life tolerable and mold him into that being.

The twenty–first–century church, then, must not ignore culture. If we do, we are neglecting a significant factor in formulating a contemporary ministry strategy that is relevant, practical and workable. What then are some cultural implications for the twenty–first century church?

Multiple Factors at Work

First, the church of Jesus Christ must develop a correct perspective regarding the multiple factors at work in our American society. We must be realistic without being pessimistic.

We must also be aware of reductionistic thinking, which causes us to say that our problems are caused by "this" or "that," or "something else." We are in trouble because of many factors.

Some Christians (along with many Americans who are Christian in name only) make the mistake of believing that a return to the "good old days" would solve our American problems. We must face the fact that those days are gone forever. They no longer exist. The population explosion, developing technology, and a big society have changed everything. We cannot return to a simple culture—apart from a nuclear holocaust which would simplify things fast, but not to our liking.

But realism must not lead to pessimistic thinking on the part of a Christian. We must realize that the church is Christ's body and bride and He will sustain it. It is through His supernatural intervention that the church survives and thrives through the ages.

There is much we can do to minister to the needs of humanity and to penetrate culture, just as the New Testament Christians penetrated their culture. And though it seems impossible, humanly speaking, to turn the overall tide in America, we can make a tremendous impact for Jesus Christ.

A little careful reflection makes it difficult for those of us who have been privileged to live in the American society to understand why God has granted us this blessing. Many Christians before us and many of our contemporaries have never experienced the religious freedom and material blessings that we enjoy.

But one thing is sure: with privilege goes responsibility—the responsibility to be totally Christian in all of our relationships and activities. We must, as Jesus commanded, love the Lord with all our hearts, and all our souls, and with all our minds, and our neighbors as ourselves (Mt 22:37–39). This, of course, means both vertical and horizontal responsibilities. At the divine level we are to maintain a dynamic relationship with God, keeping ourselves untainted from this world system (1 Pet 2:11). At the human level we must love all men, both Christians and non–Christians.

Develop a Correct View of History

Second, the church must develop a correct view of history. Life on this earth will not continue indefinitely. History is inevitably moving toward a great culmination. Eternity, for all men

---

[1] I George Peters, *Saturation Evangelism*, p. 193.

It is recognized that there is some problem in establishing the connection between verse 2 and verse 3. However the total context seems to point to the fact that the salvation of all men is directly related to both prayer and an environment that is conducive to dynamic Christian living and witness.

collectively, will eventually begin. Time as we know it will cease to exist. Most Christians, of course, "know" this "theologically," but we seem to live as if it is not true.

This correct view of history gives the Christian hope, no matter what happens in our society. It was a significant factor in sustaining the New Testament Christians, including the apostle Paul.

The church, then, must develop a correct philosophy of history, recognizing that when time runs out, our sojourn in space–time history will cease to exist. We will stand before Christ, to give account of what we have done with the time He has allotted us to carry out His purposes on earth. As modern–day Christians, we will no doubt be evaluated in the light of the opportunities we have had to live in a culture that has provided us with more blessings and resources in life than any other people before us. We need to remind ourselves of the words of the Lord Jesus Christ Himself, who said while on earth, "And from everyone who has been given much shall much be required; and to whom they entrusted much, of him they will ask all the more" (Lk 12:48).

This concept leads us naturally to the next cultural implication.

Third, the church must understand clearly why God has left us on earth, and strive with His help to fulfill that purpose. Cultural problems can blur our purpose and sidetrack us onto peripheral issues.

The Bible is clear–cut at this point. We are not here primarily to make a living, or to build material security for ourselves and our families, both legitimate objectives. We are to be everlastingly busy at this holy task of making Christ known to a lost world until He comes again.

This primary task does not mean we should not have earthly concerns: to provide for our families, both presently and in the future. It does not mean we should not be good citizens and do what we can to preserve our nation from moral and spiritual decay. *Christians: should be the best citizens.* But all of these concerns must be kept in proper perspective, and must be subordinate to our ultimate purpose for being on earth. The sooner we realize— not just in our heads, but in our hearts–that we are but "aliens and strangers" on this earth (1 Pet 2:11; Heb 11:13), the better we will fulfill the purpose God has left us on earth to fulfill.

Show Concern for Leaders

Fourth, though "this world is not our real home," the church must recognize it has a divine mandate to show a vital concern for our government leaders in the life of our nation. One of our primary responsibilities specified in Scripture is to pray for our national and international leaders. Paul made this clear to Timothy when he instructed him regarding the function of the New Testament church in relation to the political structure of his day. "I urge," he said, "that entreaties and prayers, petitions and thanksgivings, be made on behalf of all men, for kings and all who are in authority." But notice why we are to pray:" ...in order "that we may lead a tranquil and quiet life in all godliness and dignity. This is good and acceptable in the sight of God our Savior, who desires all men to be saved and to come to the knowledge of the truth" (1 Tim 2:1–4, NASB).

The church, as it proceeds to carry out the Great Commission, must not neglect to pray for our national and international leaders, with a view that they may be able to lead in such a way as to maintain a cultural environment that is conducive to living for Jesus Christ, and also conducive to sharing Him with all men.

It is also clear from Scripture that "governing authorities" and the position they hold are related to God's sovereign wishes (Rom 13:1). We must recognize this fact and fulfill our responsibility to them, even though they may be in error. This does not mean that we meekly tolerate sin and digression from the laws of God without voicing our disagreement. Assuredly, "we must obey

God rather than men" (Acts 5:29), particularly when the two are in contradiction. But it also means respecting our leaders and praying for them, and recognizing their God-ordained appointments and responsibilities.

A correct view of our culture should put all Christians on their knees for the leaders of our countries and their staff members. Their ultimate task is seemingly insurmountable and many of their problems almost insoluble. They, like the American people, seem to be shackled by the same big institutionalized machine that rumbles on and keeps them from bringing about needed changes that could, at least to a certain extent, ameliorate the American situation. And obviously they are not unaffected by the moral and ethical degeneration that is taking place in our culture.

Whatever our position and vocation in life, whether in a government role or at an ordinary job, we must remember our primary task. We are God's witnesses in this world and we are part of the functioning body of Christ, with the responsibility to contribute to the health and welfare of that body. In so doing, the church can become a dynamic force against many of the environmental factors that are leading this earth's citizens away from truth and justice.

Help Believers Relate

Fifth, the church must provide an atmosphere where Christians can relate to one another in a noninstitutionalized environment. Unfortunately many local churches have become as institutionalized as the American structures. People who are fed up with an impersonal society often find an impersonal atmosphere in the church as well. People who are tired of being "cogs" in a secular machine find they become "cogs" in a religious machine.

The "church gathered" must realize that it can become a haven for lonely and frustrated people. Through providing a place that is a dynamic and loving community, it can counteract the plastic environment in which people live. Francis Schaeffer comments relative to this point: "Our Christian organizations must be communities in which others see what God has revealed in the teaching of His Word. They should see that what has happened in Christss death and reconciliation on the cross back there in space and time and history is relevant, that it is possible to have something beautiful and unusual in this world in our communication and in communities in our own generation...."[2]

The Christian community and the practice of that community should cut across all lines. Our churches have largely been preaching points and activity generators. Community has had little place.

I want to see us treating each other like human beings: Every Christian community everywhere ought to show that we can have horizontal relationships with men and that this can result in a community that cares not only for the human race but for the individual, not only for human rights, but for the individual and all of his needs.

Unless people see in our churches not only the preaching of that truth but the practice of the truth, the practice of love and the practice of beauty; then let me say it clearly: they will not listen and they should not listen.

---

[2] 'Francis Schaeffer, *The Church at the End of the Twentieth Century*, pp. 39–40.

Provide Stability and Security

Sixth, the church must provide stability and security for people, something which culture is increasingly failing to do. In a day of unprecedented change, Christians can give people something to believe that is true and trustworthy.

Without absolutes, our cultures are like a ship at sea, caught in a storm without an anchor or a compass, with dangerous reefs nearby,

Not so with Bible–believing churches. Some may have lost their focus. Some may have become institutionalized. Others may not be fulfilling their primary purpose for existence. But we have not lost our anchor or compass. We have a foundation to which to return. We have a body of literature that can give us directives and a philosophy of life that allows us to look into the future realistically and with certainty.

Thus, the evangelical church must recognize with renewed vision that we have the only authoritative answers to our society's deepest needs. We must realize that many uncertain voices in our society today provide us with unprecedented and unparalleled opportunities for evangelism. Men everywhere are confused, but they have the potential to differentiate truth from falsehood. The Holy Spirit is still at work in the world, enlightening the hearts of men and honoring the Word of God.

Parents—many of whom hold to absolutes "in memory only" are experiencing tremendous insecurity regarding their children.

They see their own flesh and blood floundering in the mire of relativism. Though they do not understand it completely, they see the effects of movies, literature, friends, and professors. And many inwardly (and some outwardly) are crying out for stability—something to really believe in. When they attempt to give answers to their youth, their own children point their finger and cry "hypocrite," for they see clearly that the answers their parents are giving are not based on convictions believed as well as lived.

People need what the church can provide: stability and security, something to believe and to make a part of their total lifestyle and that squares with reality. Our problems can be a blessing in disguise–one that can bring many people into the kingdom of God.

A Christian Value System

Seventh, the church must help Christians to live in the world without being a part of the world. "Christians must not consciously or unconsciously adopt the aspects of the American value system that are contradictory to the Christian value system". [3]

God has not yet called the church "out of the world" (1 Cor 5:9-11). He never intended for Christians to withdraw from society and to live in a Christian community. For how else can we carry out Christ's commission to reach all nations with the good news than to be "in the world." This is one reason why we are here on earth. How unfortunate when Christians confuse "separation" with "isolation." We are not to become a part of the world—living like the world lives—but neither are we to become isolated from the world. Others need to (they must) see in us what it means to be disciples of Jesus Christ.

---

[3] John Culkin, ""A Guide to McLuhan,"" *Religious Teachers Journal,* October 1969, p. 26,

Church leaders must also help Christians who live in the midst of our culture to understand the conflicting value systems.

These conflicting value systems are separating the committed Christians from the uncommitted. In some instances, there is a great gulf between the person who is a Christian and a person who is not a Christian. This is a blessing in disguise. Most people clearly see the difference. And again this provides us with unlimited opportunities in evangelism.

The Communications Revolution

Eighth, the church must recognize and understand and adapt to the cultural effects of the communications revolution.

John Culkin, an interpreter, points out that "each culture develops its own balance of the senses in response to the demands of its environment. The most generalized formulation of the theory would maintain that the individual's modes of cognition and perception are influenced by the culture he is in, the language he speaks, and the media to which he is exposed. Each culture, as it were, provides its constituents with a custom–made set of goggles."

The important issue facing the church today is how the present communications explosion in America is modifying cognition and perception, on the part of both the Christian and the non–Christian. It is already possible to conclude that the "Sesame Street" generation is a new breed. They are used to exciting and stimulating approaches to learning. In living color, the characters of "Sesame Street" have reached out and almost touched their viewers.

Again the important issue is that the church must not—it cannot—overlook the cultural implications that grow out of our current communications revolution. Like Paul of old, who was faced with the challenge of a new mentality as he encountered the Greek culture, we, too, must adapt our communication approaches to reach people where they are. We cannot ignore their perceptive apparatus by proceeding to communicate in ways that once appealed to us, but no longer to the new generation. Whether we are ministering to children, youth, or adults, we must adapt and change in order to communicate effectively. Our message, of course, remains unchanged; our methods must be contemporary.

This, of course, raises another problem! In the church we have both the old and the new generations. On the one hand, the older generation (not necessarily in age) is threatened and feels insecure and uncomfortable with new communication forms; and on the other hand, the new generation is "turned off" by the "oldways."

This is all the more reason for all members of the body of Christ to understand culture and how it affects us all. Understanding at least helps create tolerance and acceptance and love for one another. It helps the church itself to exist in harmony and unity—an ingredient so basic to Christian growth as well as witness.

The functioning body of Christ itself is a significant answer to the communications revolution. It has always been a "form" in itself for communicating a profound message. It is a group of people who, as they function, create an atmosphere and environment that communicate the Christian message. To other Christians, the message is one of love and reality. To the unsaved, the unified body says that here are people who are followers of Jesus Christ, the God–Man.

The church, then, can become the means that can provide what the culture does not—an environment that radiates acceptance, security, and stability, and at a personal level.

Cultural Effects on Lifestyle

Ninth, the church must understand the cultural effects on lifestyle, particularly of our youth, and learn to differentiate between what is a violation of biblical principles, and what is a violation of the cultural norms we have come to accept as absolute.

One of the most tragic consequences of cultural change is that some Christians cannot emotionally tolerate a variance in lifestyle because they have come to equate certain externalities with being biblical. For example, men's hair lengths and beards have caused unusual disturbance among some Christians. Some have equated the two as being reflective of unspiritual or sinful behavior forgetting that some of our great Christian leaders in the early 1900s looked quite similar. .

It is easy to see how this false conclusion came into existence. Those who first demonstrated this "new" lifestyle were radical youth, who also went much further in demonstrating lifestyle characteristics that were definitely non-Christian. But many Christians—as we so often do—failed to differentiate between characteristics that violated Christian values and those that did not. We fell into the subtle trap of developing caricatures and forming generalizations based on false conclusions.

Even more tragic is a Christian who allows his prejudice toward Christians to also include non-Christians. When believers will not tolerate having on the Church premises non-Christian youth whose lifestyle does not measure up to certain accepted middle-class norms, we are guilty of what James specifically called it SIN (Jas 2:9). Though he was speaking in this instance in his epistle regarding prejudice toward the poor, the principle is clear. Just because a person "looks" different does not mean he is immoral, or as some would almost imply, less than human. But even if he should be all of these, he is a person for whom Christ died. He is a human being and he needs love and compassion.

God forbid that we become guilty of failing to distinguish between biblical norms and cultural norms. In the words of Francis Schaeffer when lecturing at Dallas Theological Seminary, we evangelicals have tended to lose our way. We have developed an ugliness that must be terribly repulsive to our Savior, who died for all men because He loved them. Christian ugliness is the saddest kind of ugliness, for it is demonstrated by those who should demonstrate it least.

It is unfortunate, indeed, when we who are to be the "salt of the earth" and the "light of the world" are so indoctrinated with a non-Christian value system that we no longer can feel compassion towards those who are in deepest spiritual need. May God help us all to shed our carnality and prejudice and become spiritual people–people who love all men, not just those we can tolerate intellectually and emotionally.

Strengthening the Home

Tenth, the church must do all it can to strengthen the home, and to counteract the devastating cultural attacks upon this most basic of all institutions. Family life has been hit the hardest by the American crisis. Divorce rates are increasing, while children from these broken unions are frequently the victims of an increasing adult selfishness and insensitivity, leaving children in a state of disillusionment and insecurity.

The breakdown and abandonment of the traditional approach to home life parallels a variety of marriage experiments, such as collective marriages, trial marriages, and "living together" without any legal or moral commitments.

The Christian home, too, is being affected. Divorce rates are increasing at an alarming rate among Christian families. But in Christian families that remain together, our homes are still—in many ways—being split apart.

The greatest contribution the church can make to our decaying society is to help build the home. Strong families build strong churches, and together strong homes and strong churches can do more than any one thing to stabilize and revitalize our culture.

Summary

There are many implications for the church that grow out of an understanding of culture. As a starter consider these:

- Develop a correct perspective regarding the multiple factors at work in society.
- Develop a correct view of history.
- Understand clearly why Jesus Christ has left the church on earth, and strive with His help to fulfill that purpose.
- Show a vital concern for government leaders and the state of the nation.
- Provide an atmosphere in the church where Christians can relate to one another in a non–institutionalized environment.
- Provide security and stability for people.
- Help Christians "live in the world," without being a "part of the world."
- Recognize, understand, and adapt to the cultural effects of the communications revolution.
- Understand the cultural effects on lifestyle—particularly on our youth—and learn to differentiate between what is a violation of biblical principles, and what is a violation of cultural norms we have come to accept as absolute.
- Do everything possible to strengthen the home and counteract the devastating cultural attacks on this basic institution.

Hospitality

*"The overseer then must be above reproach, the husband of one wife, temperate, self-controlled, respectable, **hospitable**"* (1 Tim 3:2; Tit 1:8, emphasis added).

Hospitality is not just a Christian responsibility. In oriental cultures, it is considered a sacred duty. In Israel, it was also commanded by God: "The foreigner who resides with you must be to you like a native citizen among you; so you must love him as yourself, because you were foreigners in the land of Egypt. I am the LORD your God" (Lev 19:34).

The hospitality instituted by God in the Old Testament is reconfirmed in the New Testament. It is a mark of Christian maturity and love and the basic motivation for reaching out to others. "Brotherly love must continue. Do not neglect hospitality, because through it some have entertained angels without knowing it" (Heb 13:1-2; also 1 Pet 4:8-9). It is the way the world will know we are Christians (Jn 13:35).

Hospitality must not stop with fellow Christians, but must extend to all humanity. Paul says that loving your neighbor as yourself fulfills the whole law (Gal 5:14). James tells us we must love all men without partiality, regardless of race, status, or creed (Jas 2:6-9).

Showing hospitality is an absolute, but how we show it changes with the culture. In Acts 2, this involved briefly living in a communal arrangement and Acts 11 shows the Christian response to widespread famine (Acts 2:42-47; Acts 11:29).

Paul says hospitality marks Christian maturity and specifically marks leaders. This characteristic is an individual responsibility but must mark everyone in the leader's home. But the context is even broader because it must mark everyone in the church. It is every believer's responsibility.

Note: This material is adapted from Gene A. Getz, *The Measure of a Man*. (Ventura, CA: Regal Books, 1984).

Institutionalism in History

The process of institutionalization is a recurring phenomenon among God's people. What makes this pitfall particularly dangerous is that it is not exclusively related to the church or other Christian organizations. It happens naturally wherever you have people who band together to achieve certain objectives. People, plus structure, plus age more often than not, equals institutionalism.

And all elements are necessary, for wherever you have people, you have function; and wherever you have function, you need some kind of form and structure. And age, of course, is inevitable, for time marches on.

But more specifically, what is "institutionalism"? Let's look at it first as a natural phenomenon.

What of the Secular World?

John W. Gardner, past president of the Carnegie Corporation, has said: "Like people and plants, organizations have a life cycle."[4]

They have a green and supple youth, a time of flourishing strength, and a gnarled old age. Rather than defining "institutionalism" per se, it may be easier to look at the symptoms of institutionalism—when has it happened? Or, when is it beginning to happen?

Institutionalism is in process when:
- The organization (the form and structure) becomes more important than the people who make up the organization.
- Individuals begin to function in the organization more like cogs in a machine.
- Individuality and creativity are lost in the structural mass.
- The atmosphere in the organization becomes threatening, rather than open and free; people are often afraid to ask uncomfortable questions.
- The structural arrangements in the organization have become rigid and inflexible.
- People are serving the organization more than the objectives for which the organization was brought into existence. In other words, means have become ends.
- Communication often breaks down, particularly because of a repressive atmosphere and lots of red tape.

---

[4] John W. Gardner, "How to Prevent Organizational Dry Rot," *Harper*, October 1965, p.20

- People become prisoners of their procedures. The "policy manual" and the "rule book" get bigger, and fresh ideas are few and far between.
- In order to survive in a cold structure, people develop their own special interests within the organization, creating competitive departments and divisions. The corporate objective gives way to a multitude of unrelated objectives, which, inevitably, results in lack of unity in the organization as a whole.
- Morale degenerates; people lose their initiative; they become discouraged and often critical of the organization and of others in the organization—particularly its leaders.
- As the organization gets bigger and as time passes, the process of institutionalization often speeds up. A hierarchy of leadership develops, increasing the problems of communication from the top to the bottom and the bottom to the top. People toward the bottom, or even in the middle of the organizational structure, feel more and more as if they really don't count in the organization.

When you have these symptoms in an organization, institutionalism is already in its advanced stages.

But there is a note of optimism that grows out of the study of the history of organizations and institutions. Again, let me quote Gardner:

> Organizations differ from people and plants in that their cycle isn't even approximately predictable. An organization may go from youth to old age in two or three decades, or it may last for centuries. More important, it may go through a period of stagnation and then revive. In short, decline is not inevitable. Organizations need not stagnate. *They often do, to be sure, but that is because organizational renewal is not widely understood.* Organizations can renew themselves continuously.[5]

The principles of organizational renewal actually work. More and more, even secularists are discovering what these rules are and are beginning to apply them in the secular community.

What of the People of God?

Church history reveals at least three major periods of institutionalism among the people of God, with many smaller segments and periods of institutionalism in between.

Judaism

The first main period of institutionalism involves the children of Israel after they returned from Babylonian Captivity. For a while, under the leadership of Ezra and Nehemiah, new life was evident among God's chosen people. But by the time Jesus Christ arrived on the scene, the nation of Israel as a whole, and its religious system particularly, had become so encrusted with institutionalism that it was impossible to recognize truth from tradition.

It was at this "religious system" that Jesus directed His sharpest barbs. For example, when His disciples were criticized by the Pharisees for plucking the heads of grain on the Sabbath, Jesus retorted: "The Sabbath was made for man and not man for the Sabbath" (Mk 2:27, NASB).

---

[5] Ibid.

In other words, He was saying that you have taken a means and made it an end in itself. You have completely lost sight of the spirit of the Law. You have lost the individual in your religious system. All you have left is an empty form.

Again and again Jesus put His finger on the devastating results of institutionalism. He reminded the religious leaders that they had successfully preserved their religious system, their "orthodoxy," and their tradition, and had even led the majority of the people into an external conformity with the outward expressions of their religion. But they had lost the individual; they had no deep understanding of God's truth; their followers had no vital and real experience with the living God.

Roman Catholicism

In the panorama of church history, the vibrant, pulsating New Testament church that grew out of Judaism eventually gave way to a stagnant, lifeless Roman church. As always, there were pockets of vitality and pure Christianity; but as a whole, the church was doomed to hundreds of years of institutionalized religion. When the Edict of Milan gave legal status to Christianity, many became "Christians" because it was the popular thing to do.

It was against this religious system that the Reformers rose up to defend biblical truth and personalized Christianity. Religion had become a matter of form and ceremony, not of life and experience. The Roman church was preserved—in all of its "bigness" and power—even to this day. Its authoritarian approach to education and its effective transmission through the centuries preserved the church's "orthodoxy," and until very recently, very few within the system questioned its demands and dogmas.

It is important to point out at this juncture that "bigness" is not necessarily a sign of true spiritual success. Numbers can be very deceiving. Followers are relatively easy to find, if one works hard enough and shouts loud enough to make his voice heard.

Let us not be deceived by numbers, for if Jesus Christ's success on earth had been measured by numbers, He must be classified as a failure. There were times, of course, when multitudes followed Him, when His disciples multiplied; but there also came a time when "many of His disciples withdrew, and were not walking with Him any more" (Jn 6:66). The price was too great for these people to follow Jesus Christ (Jn 6:60).

This is not to say that numbers are not significant. In the early days of the church, thousands were added to the company of believers (Acts 2:41), and "the number of the disciples continued to increase greatly" (Acts 6:7). But true success was measured by the results that were being achieved in the lives of people. Just so today, we must measure our success by biblical criteria—not by how many people attend on Sunday morning, or Sunday evening, or on Wednesday night, or how many we have enrolled in our Sunday school. Some even measure success by the total number of meetings that have been conducted in a given period of time.

Activity alone is not a correct measuring rod. The results of these activities (biblical results) are!

Reformation Churches

And so the reformers reacted against the institutionalism and the dead orthodoxy of the Roman church.

But with what did they replace it?

For a time, life and vitality! The authority of the Bible, justification by faith, and the priesthood of every believer became cardinal doctrines once again. Conversion became a matter of personal relationship with Jesus Christ,

However, some leaders eventually refused others the same liberty and freedom they had demanded for themselves. Education was controlled and directed by Protestant state churches, and degenerated into the same stereotyped, traditional and authoritarian system from which they came. You *cannot force* Christian community. Correct doctrine by itself was not the answer!

The Free Church Movement

Out of the institutionalized religion that soon developed in the Reformation churches came a variety of groups that wished to maintain the vitality and freshness they saw reflected in the New Testament. The discovery of America provided a natural means by which many could begin anew. But in many instances, even in these early days, the same "institutionalism" was transferred from the Continent to the New World. It was a constant struggle, as it has always been, for the true believers to keep a proper focus on biblical objectives and principles, and to keep from becoming institutionalized.

The Church at Large

The Protestant church at large is, without doubt, institutionalized. It is criticized by young and old alike. It not only has become a victim, of its form and ceremony, but it has lost its direction. It no longer has an absolute guide to determine its objectives and from which to get its principles to guide it in its function.

Many religious leaders recognize the symptoms of institutionalism in the church at large.

They are trying desperately to pump new life into a dying corpse by means of "form" changes and a renewed emphasis on the individual.

But they are no more successful than a social organization in obtaining ultimate success, for even though they can meet the physical needs of people, and in some ways their psychological needs, they have no way to change the heart, the inner being. The true message of Christianity—personal conversion and a supernatural new birth through the indwelling and living Christ—has been basically eliminated from modern theology. A comfortable universalism has replaced the hard realities of eternal lost-ness outside of Jesus Christ and "situation ethics," which has no foundations in the absolute values of Scripture, is rampant within the religious community. Without the true message of the gospel and God's eternal laws for Christlike living, all efforts toward helping people are ultimately doomed to failure.

No amount of organizational renewal can save the church at large.

Whenever sound and systematic Bible study and teaching is neglected, there will always be a lack of depth leading to superficial experience and various kinds of excesses.

The Evangelical Church

What of the Bible-believing church?

It has grown and become more popular than ever before and has penetrated society. Some of its key spokesmen are household names among the leaders of the world.

Evangelicalism has come into its own as a worldwide movement. There are many signs of encouragement. In spite of the pressures of secularism and materialism, and the obvious moral decline in our culture as a whole, evangelical Christianity is continuing to make an impact. The advent of the drug culture, sensualism, and the mystical cults actually created a vacuum into which Bible-believing Christians have been able to enter with the message of Jesus Christ. Youth, particularly, who have been subtly led into a way of life that has left them in a whirlpool of despair, are responding to the authority of the Bible and its redeeming message. Campus organizations such as Campus Crusade for Christ, Inter-Varsity Christian Fellowship, and The Navigators are experiencing unparalleled opportunities to communicate the gospel to disillusioned youth.

Furthermore, these organizations are also impacting the church in its areas of weakness.

But what about the local church in the evangelical community?

Here too there are some definite encouragements. Bible-believing churches are growing. Generally, there is a strong faith in the authority of Scripture and the need for personal salvation. Many Christians, though affected in their thinking by materialism and secularism, still have a deep desire to be in the will of God. Many pastors are teaching the Word of God as never before and there is general concern for evangelism and edification. Never have we had so many educational agencies within the church, and so many excellent materials and tools available to reach all age levels.

But somehow, with all of these strengths, the voice of the ancient apostle comes echoing across the centuries: "I know your deeds and your toil and perseverance.... I know your deeds, and your love and faith and service.... But I have this against you" (Rev 2:2, 19-20, NASB). Something is wrong with the evangelical church!

This, of course, is not strange language, for something is always wrong and will always be wrong with the church on earth. We can never be perfect while in bondage to mortality. But there seems to be something distinctly wrong in the local church, a lack of focus that need not be; something that can be corrected by means of making some proper adjustments.

Here we can learn a vital lesson from history. Every growing movement eventually faces the threat of creeping institutionalism. Evangelical Christianity is facing this threat today, particularly in an era of rapid church growth. It is in particular danger because it has moved from the crisis of fighting for its life into a period of unparalleled popularity—a trend that usually produces institutionalization.

At this juncture we need to remind ourselves of what happened to previous movements among the people of God. We need to look carefully at the results of institutionalized religion.

Reflections of Institutionalism

Judaism, Roman Catholicism, and the Reformation churches preserved their religious system, but they lost sight of the individual.

In fact, the system in each instance—its dogmas and traditions and its forms and structures—eventually became more important than the people themselves.

These movements also preserved their "orthodoxy," but their adherents failed to appropriate a deeper and personal comprehension of God's truth. People gave mental assent to doctrine, but there was little relationship to their daily living. Being a part of the movement was little different from belonging to a club, society, or group in the secular world. In many cases traditions overshadowed the Word of God.

These movements all gained external conformity on the part of their followers, but apart from inner experience. People religiously performed routines and rituals, but without true spiritual meaning. Their religion became a matter of form and ceremony, not life and experience. A personal relationship with God was replaced with an impersonal relationship with an organization.

All of these movements perpetuated themselves by means of an education that was authoritarian, stereotyped, and transmissive.

They utilized indoctrination with little room for creative thinking and freedom. The learning atmosphere became nonpermissive.

All of these movements developed a hierarchy of leaders, who in turn developed a careful and logical system of theology. It was the leaders who did the thinking and the communicating, while the ordinary people became the recipients and followers of the wisdom of the sages.

As these movements grew and enlarged, structure and form became rigid and inflexible. In fact, their means and ways of doing things eventually became ends in themselves and as sacred in the minds of people as their beliefs.[6]

Summary

It is the thesis of this chapter that history can tell us something very important. As evangelicals we often confuse functions and forms and what is absolute and what is non-absolute. When we do, our churches move rapidly in the direction of becoming institutionalized.

Not a Drunkard

*"The overseer then must be above reproach, the husband of one wife, temperate, self-controlled, respectable, hospitable, able to teach, **not a drunkard**"* (1 Tim 3:2-3; Tit 1:7, emphasis added).

The issue is not total abstinence from any form of alcohol. The Greek word *paroinos* literally means one who "sits too long at his wine." He overdrinks, is brought into bondage, and loses control. The most common meaning, from common and exegetical evidence, in the Old and New Testaments of "wine" is fermented grape juice. Drunkenness and being out of order is the issue, not abstinence per se (Prov 23:29-34; Eph 5:18; 1 Pet 4:2-3). Drunkenness is a sign of Christian immaturity.

However, Paul in Romans addresses the issue from a different perspective: Do not be a stumbling block to your brother (Rom 14:21). Cultures vary, the alcoholic content varies, and so do cultural connotations that come with drinking. The problem is not drinking or meat sacrificed to idols, but idolatrous associations or problems for the weaker brother. The higher principle must be followed wherever possible.

Another principle is not allowing oneself to be controlled by anything (Prov 23:19-21). Overeating is just as sinful as over-drinking and more common in some cultures— especially for Christians. A Christian must do nothing that would harm his body or cause him to become ineffective for Christ (1 Cor 10:31). Drink, food, tobacco, money, or even laziness can all control a Christian.

Instead, all must be done to the glory of God (1 Cor 10:31).

---

[6] For a helpful treatment of the problems of institutionalism in the church, see Findley B. Edge *A euest Sor Vitality in Religion* (Nashville: Broadman, 1963).

Note: This material is adapted from Gene A. Getz, *The Measure of a Man*. (Ventura, CA: Regal Books, 1984).

Reflections Of Institutionalism in the Evangelical Church

The phenomenon of creeping institutionalism in the evangelical church in the latter part of the twentieth century and continuing in the twenty-first century is unique. In some respects it is a different kind of institutionalism than at any other time in history. True, the institutionalism we see today has many similarities to that of the past. There are certain common elements wherever and whenever institutionalization takes place. But there are also some unique elements, the most important being our *biblical* orthodoxy. Is it possible to believe the Bible is the Word of God and to communicate it to others with expertise, and yet be a victim of institutionalism?

Problems Created

Our greatest strength has helped create some of our greatest problems.

The strongest feature of the evangelical church has been its adherence to the Bible as its final authority in faith and practice. Though there are a variety of interpretations in some areas of theology, most evangelicals are in agreement regarding the Bible as being the inspired and inerrant Word of God.

This emphasis has helped greatly to preserve historic Christianity. Wherever groups have departed from this basic starting point, history reveals there is an eventual movement away from the clear teachings of the Scriptures regarding Jesus Christ and salvation, as well as other important fundamental doctrines. But something has happened, particularly in our strong Bible-teaching churches. By emphasizing the Bible as the Word of God and rightly so—as well as its doctrinal teachings—we have put a strong emphasis on studying the Bible and transmitting it to others. This, in turn, has become a primary objective of many evangelical churches, a worthy objective, to say the least. To carry out this objective, several things have transpired.

First, we began to train qualified people to teach the Bible. Evangelical schools—first Bible institutes and colleges and later seminaries—designed curriculums to teach young men and women knowledge of the content of the Scriptures so that they might transmit it to others. Second, the people trained in these schools went into churches and taught as they were taught. Many became ardent expositors, in some instances "little professors," and the people were their "students." In Sunday morning services, on Sunday evenings, during the midweek service, and in Sunday school classes, some people have listened to three or four or even five expositions a week. However, a problem has emerged. Many laymen have become ardent "listeners." There is little opportunity for personal interaction with other members of the body of Christ, or little opportunity for expressing the Word in their own lives. In many churches the functioning body has been replaced with a trained and talented individual. Fortunately, young pastors can take what they have learned in schools and transmit it to others as they turn their churches into miniature Bible schools and seminaries. But, for the most part, those who are on the listening end in the churches absorb the Word, but have no similar outlet.

Third, church structures and patterns are often designed to carry out this Bible-teaching objective. Church sanctuaries, functionally speaking, often become "lecture halls," and educational buildings become academic centers. Preaching well-organized sermons (or put another way, delivering high-powered Bible lectures) has become the primary means of teaching the Word of God.

Thus our concentration on biblical authority and the importance of learning and transmitting its message has led some evangelicals to neglect some other extremely important emphases in the Scriptures. As we've already observed in our study, learning the Word of God is foundational to Christian growth. But what of other experiences Christians need to become mature believers?

What about the New Testament emphasis on the importance of the body of Christ functioning in all of its parts in order to build itself up? How can all members of the body participate in this process when they are consistently "forced" to sit and listen to one man teach or preach? In many instances there are *no opportunities for mutual ministry*.

And what about the New Testament atmosphere that emphasizes *koinonia*, that unique fellowship with one another where Christians bear one another's burdens and "thus fulfill the Law of Christ"? To what extent do our church structures and patterns lend themselves to bringing about this kind of New Testament experience?

And what about that unique New Testament experience of worship and fellowship with God that grows naturally out of a heart full of gratitude to God, not only for His Word, but for fellow believers? To what extent do our typical "worship services" and "prayer meetings" result in true worship?

In many churches our *failure to provide balanced New Testament experiences* for believers has resulted in an emphasis on correct doctrine and knowledge of the Scriptures, but has neglected other important needs that create mature Christian personalities.

The Soul-winning Station

Emphasizing the church as a soul-winning station has also contributed its share to the process of institutionalization.

This is really a different kind of problem than the one just described. In a sense, it is an opposite-type problem, one you don't really find in the strong Bible-teaching church. In the evangelistic-oriented church we often find a decided lack in good Bible teaching. The frequent complaint is that "all the preacher ever preaches is the simple gospel message." And often he preaches these "gospel messages" to a church full of Christians. Pastors of these churches put a strong emphasis on bringing unsaved people to the church to "hear the gospel." The church becomes the center of all activity in reaching the unsaved world. Laymen are taught by word and example that their evangelistic task is to "bring them in" to hear the gospel.

But what about the church as an evangelistic center? *First of all, one of the basic objectives of the church is to reach the unsaved world.* But the purpose of the "church gathered" as described in the New Testament is not to provide a setting for the pastor to preach evangelistic sermons to unsaved people who are brought to church by church members.

Again, don't misunderstand—this does not mean that unsaved people should not be welcomed in the church or even invited.

Otherwise, they may not see the body of Christ functioning in love and unity, a vital means of reaching non-Christians. The non-Christian, observing the body of Christ functioning properly to build up itself, would then be in a position to become convicted by the Holy Spirit and respond to the message of the gospel (1 Cor 14:24-25).

Many churches that function as evangelistic centers often have greater problems with institutionalism than the Bible-teaching churches. Without a good diet in the Word of God, activity and meetings become even more superficial and void of real scriptural meaning. Even fellowship opportunities degenerate into social contacts that are little different from social gatherings in the world.

Fellowship, or koinonia, in the biblical sense is more than "coffee and doughnuts" and human beings relating to each other on the human level. Within the context of biblical koinonia, even partaking of food will become a more meaningful experience (Acts 2:42).

An emphasis on the "church gathered" is commendable and biblical. But a church in the biblical sense is not a building or simply an organization, or even a place of meeting, but an organism, a body of believers meeting together. And "why" Christians meet is of utmost importance! From a biblical point of view, it is not to listen to a pastor preach an evangelistic sermon. Nor is it to just listen to the pastor-teacher expound the Word. Rather, the total structure of the church is to *provide an opportunity for believers to be edified through total body function.* There will need to be a time when the Word of God is taught. But there must also be times when believers can experience true family-of-God relationships. As a result of these vital experiences, they are in turn to minister to their own families, minister to other believers, and be effective witnesses for Jesus Christ in the unsaved world.

Existence Vs. Reasons For Existing

We are beginning to support the "institution" rather than its reasons for existing. Put another way, we are more concerned with existence than our cause for existence.

This problem is reflected in the way we evaluate success. As long as we have lots of activity, lots of people coming, lots of "decisions" to follow Christ, an enlarging income, a growing pastoral staff, and an ongoing building program, we feel comfortably successful and evangelical. "The Lord is blessing us," is our repeated evaluation.

"The Holy Spirit is at work," echo the church-growth people.

Frequently, we show little concern for the content of our activities, as long as they are "going on." Whether or not "decisions" for Christ result in mature discipleship is often overlooked in the midst of everything else that is "happening."

And the people who come? *Well, so long as new people are coming, it really doesn't matter who they are and where they come from and how long they stay.* When they come, we report we are reaching people. The facts seem to be that many churches grow only because Christian people are on the move—from the center of the city to the suburbs, and from city to city, and from church to church. Few seem to be new Christians, reached for Christ by the local body of believers as they share their faith with neighbors, friends, and work associates.

Yet we feel successful because we are growing—and really without reaching a New Testament objective of penetrating the pagan community in which we live.

The problem of being concerned with "existence" more than our reason for existence is also reflected in the way we evaluate "spirituality," particularly as a pastoral staff. Our people "measure up" as long as they come and listen to our sermons, bring their children to all the activities we've planned for them, support the church with their offerings, willingly serve on boards and committees, and help keep the agencies of the church functioning by filling leadership slots. *In short, as long as people support the program, we evaluate them as spiritually mature.*

But what about their life outside of the church? Is each home a dynamic force in the community, reflecting Jesus Christ? How are the church members relating to unsaved neighbors? Are church members acting ethically in the business world? Are they dynamic Christian witnesses in the way they live as well as in the way they talk?

What about other aspects of our church life? Are believers really ministering to other members of the body of Christ, or do they use all of their time and effort just to keep the machinery of the church running smoothly? Are they really growing and developing in their Christian life? Or are they frantically running on a religious treadmill, getting wearier and more numb as each week passes by, and at the same time keeping their guilt level down because of their "Christian service"?

What about the overall climate in the church? Is it warm and inviting and personal, or do people come Sunday after Sunday, sit side by side in long pews, take notes in their Bibles, say "Amen," drop their money in the offering plate, and walk out without really coming to know other members of the Christian family, and without making any contribution to other members of the body of Christ?

All of these questions can go unanswered in many evangelical churches—can even be answered negatively—and yet we can evaluate our church as successful. The truth is, it may be existing beautifully as an organization but woefully lacking as a functioning New Testament organism. It is not achieving certain fundamental, biblical objectives.

Belief Vs. Conduct

We are emphasizing correct doctrine and frequently neglecting the quality of one's life. An important criterion for evaluating spiritual maturity is often "what one believes" and not "the way that person lives."

To be sure, what a person believes is basic and fundamental, but the Bible is explicit and clear that it is both/and, not either/or. The first eleven chapters in Paul's letter to the Romans emphasize doctrine and the last five, Christian living. Likewise, the Ephesian epistle presents doctrine in the first three chapters, and the last three chapters present the Christian's walk. The Bible is clear that we are to be "doers of the Word, and not merely hearers" (Jas 1:22, NASB).

It is possible to go into some evangelical churches and discover there is little difference in the lifestyle of its members and that of non-Christians. They may know the Bible, but their lives reflect little of the fruit of the Spirit. On the other hand, many evangelical churches have developed false criteria for evaluating spirituality—an unfortunate legalism that reflects the same spiritual sickness of the Pharisees. Spiritual depth is measured primarily by externalities—certain "thou shalt nots" that have become standard in some Christian circles. If Christians *don't do* certain things, they are automatically classified as spiritual. It is possible to refrain from many activities and be extremely carnal and yet to feel comfortably spiritual. And when it comes to basic Christian attitudes toward both fellow Christians and unsaved people, particularly an attitude of love, there is a decided lack.

This is not to advocate total freedom—a concept that is very nonbiblical. But both extremes—license or legalism—are a reflection of institutionalized Christianity. Again, we must evaluate spiritual maturity by means of proper biblical criteria. And Jesus stated the most important criterion. "By this all men will know that you are My disciples, if you have love for one another" (Jn 13:35).

When Non-absolutes Become Absolutes

We have allowed non-absolutes to become absolutes.

This way of thinking is the most subtle of all in leading the church into institutionalism. *That, which is meant to be a means to an end, becomes an end in itself.* We allow ourselves to get locked into patterns and structures that are no longer relevant and adequate to help us minister to the people who live in our contemporary culture.

It is vitally important for every believer to be able to differentiate between those areas of the Word of God that are absolute and never changing, and those areas that are relative and simply illustrative of the way the people of God in years past attempted to reach biblical objectives.

It is obvious from a careful study of the Scriptures that New Testament Christians considered certain doctrines absolute: that God exists; that He is a Spirit; that Jesus Christ was God in the flesh and that He came to die for the sins of the world; that man is in need of a Savior; that salvation is by grace through faith; that there is a diabolical spiritual world which includes Satan and his evil forces; that Jesus Christ died, arose, ascended to heaven, and will come again. These and many other truths should never be changed if a church is to be "Christian" in the biblical sense.

Another area of obvious absolutes has to do with directives and objectives. The New Testament church consistently took the Great Commission seriously, both in the task of evangelism and edification. And there were certain qualifications for Christian leaders!

There was to be no "give and take" in these matters.

But there is also much scriptural evidence to show that New Testament Christians did not consider certain forms and patterns and structures to be absolute. Rather, these were but means to carry out New Testament directives and reach New Testament objectives. When patterns do appear, they vary from situation to situation in the areas of communication and organization and administration.

But it is very important to note that these biblical examples are given for a purpose: to yield absolute principles for the church. A careful study of the way the first-century church proceeded to carry out the Great Commission reveals certain obvious *harmony with the New Testament church—absolute in the essentials, and free and creative in devising contemporary approaches to evangelism, edification, leadership, communication, and organization and administration.* An important task facing Christian leaders of every generation is to make sure these principles and guidelines are accurately formulated and correctly focused.

Summary

Evangelical churches in the twenty-first century have a unique challenge to break the shackles of institutionalization that have already begun to bind and inhibit many organisms. One of the most encouraging lessons from history is that we need not be "locked in" to a continuous cycle of institutionalism. It can be broken; renewal can and must be constant. True believers, as no other group of people on earth, have the resources always to be what God wants us to be. If secular organizations can apply the principles of renewal and be successful, how much more can the family of God, particularly when it has principles that emerge from the eternal Word of God? And this is what renewal is all about.

Unit Two: Applying the Three Lenses, Part I

In this unit, we will apply the "three lenses" to our church life that makes worship and edification possible. Our goal is to help begin a practical thinking process to consistently evaluate church life from biblical and relevant points of view. In doing so, we must ensure that present forms are established on biblical principles, and that you are confident the forms are well thought-out.

Pastor Eugene's spiritual journey has presented him with many successes and challenges in the 10+ years of the church's history. As the spiritual leader of a maturing church, it is Pastor Eugene's responsibility to reflect on the church's journey to this point and to carefully plan for the future growth of the church. In this unit, we will reflect upon how he will do that with the functions of worship and edification.

Unit 2 Outline: Applying the Three Lenses, Part 1

Lesson 4: Worship Dynamics

Lesson 5: Edification Dynamics, Part I

Lesson 6: Edification Dynamics, Part II

Lesson 4: Worship Dynamics

Lesson Introduction

Worship is the main reason for a congregation to assemble, share, and learn about God.

It provides a congregation with the means to show their adoration, devotion, and respect for God through their actions and experiences. It is important to realize that worship is an essential part of a healthy and growing church.

As the spiritual leader of the church, you are responsible to ensure that *real* worship takes place each time you meet in the name of God. From our biblical study on worship, it is obvious that worship should permeate every area of our lives.

This lesson presents you with the dynamics of worship. It gives you the opportunity to reflect upon the meaning of worship and how it is manifested in an assembly.

Lesson Outline

Lesson 4: Worship Dynamics
    Topic 1: Introducing Worship
    Topic 2: Defining Worship
    Topic 3: Participating in Worship
    Topic 4: Gathering to Worship (Exercise in Three Lenses)
    Topic 5: Ordering the Service
    Topic 6: Developing Character—Not Arrogant, Not Prone to Anger, Not Violent

Lesson Objectives

Lately, Pastor Eugene's church attendance has shrunk. Some of the congregation feel that a cornerstone of their church, "Worship," has become routine and meaningless.

Pastor Eugene recognizes that a biblical study approach will allow him to clearly concentrate on the meaning of worship and how it is manifested in his congregation. His goal for the church is to worship God through all actions and experiences, allowing the life of the church to be self-sustaining.

Pastor Eugene readily accepts the responsibility to provide his church with opportunities that actively involve his congregation with *real* worship experiences. His goal is to inspire his congregation to take action and to experience God in everything they do. However, before Pastor Eugene can effectively accomplish this, he needs to pray and learn more about worship dynamics. His learning, and yours, will involve:

- Interrelating worship, edification, and multiplication
- Defining "worship"
- Evaluating your church's present worship dynamics
- Designing creative worship services from an inductive study using the three lenses
- Recognizing the advantages and disadvantages of meeting in both small and large groups
- Integrating the characteristics of being slow to anger, lacking arrogance, and non-violence into your life

Topic 1: Introducing Worship

Before looking intensively at worship dynamics, we must look at the relationship between the three aspects of the church's reason for existence. How are worship, edification, and multiplication interrelated?

Remember, the threefold purpose of the church is comprehensive and covers all spiritual relationships. We relate to God, to saved human beings, and to unsaved human beings. Scripture tells us that we should relate to fellow human beings, saved or unsaved, in the same way God relates to us (1 Jn 4:19-21; Mt 5:43-48; Lk 6:27-36; Jn 14:15, 21, 23-24).

Worship cannot be isolated as a separate purpose apart from the rest of your life (Deut 6:4-9). Notice the connections between worship, edification, and multiplication in these three definitions:

Worship is the Christian's recognition of who God is and his/her response to Him. Proper perspective and practice of worship leads to edification.

Edification is the spiritual encouragement and instruction that Christians provide one another. When Christians build each other up in Christ, they fulfill God's command to encourage fellow believers. The unity among believers, which comes from this mutual encouragement, is a witness to the world and promotes evangelism. The way Christians relate to each other affects multiplication (Jn 13:34-35; 17:20-23).

Multiplication is the process by which the number of believers is increased through the sharing of the Gospel. Multiplication results in praise and worship of God (1 Thess 2:9, 19-20).

In this manner, the three facets of the purpose of the church are interrelated: worship leads to edification, which brings about multiplication, which in turn leads to worship again. The illustration below depicts this interrelationship:

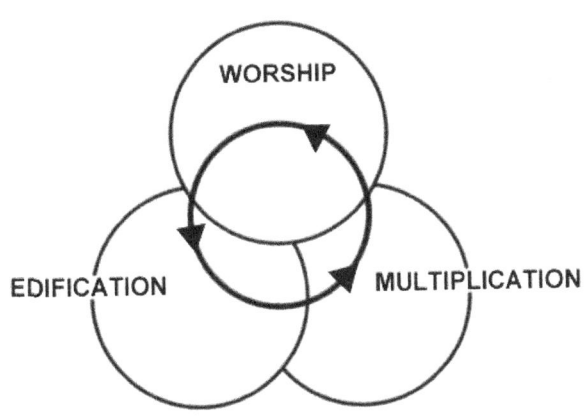

It is important to note from Scripture that there is priority in this correlation. While Galatians 6:10 shows that edification takes some priority over multiplication relationships, many verses throughout the Bible indicate how worship establishes a foundation for the other two.

    Worship
        Edification
            Multiplication

To learn how to play a sport with multiple skills, a player first works on individual skills. To play soccer, someone must learn to trap, dribble, pass, and shoot, among other skills. After practicing these skills, a person must strategically integrate these skills into play during an actual match. To achieve success, this person also must learn what skills take priority in each game situation.

Just as in soccer, the three aspects for the church's existence cannot always be exercised separately, either. When all are integrated, they all support each other. The topic of this lesson is designed to help you deepen your knowledge of the threefold purpose of the church, to practice each aspect, and to interrelate each of these aspects to succeed at "church."

It is through our relationship with God that our Christian life becomes purposeful and fulfilling. The Bible includes several verses that stress the significance of worshiping God.

Read the passages in the question below to discover ways in which worship gives meaning to edification and multiplication of the church.

QUESTION 1

Please match the verse in the left-hand column with what it says about the significance of worship in the right-hand column.

Verse	*Worship Significance*
Romans 14:7-9	Worship gives meaning to edification.
John 15:9-12	Worship gives direction for multiplication.
Philippians 1:9-11	Our relationship with God carries over into other relationships.
Romans 1:1, 5, 9	Our relationship with God is our first priority.

QUESTION 2

Worship takes precedence over the other two relationships; namely, with other Christians and nonbelievers. *True or False?*

Paul sets a clear example for us. In his ministry, he was often severely criticized. Responding to such a wave of criticism in his second letter to the Corinthians, his response betrays an unwavering attitude of integrity and confidence. This confidence originates from a worshipful sense of God's presence, which makes him rise above human criticism: "So then whether we are alive or away, we make it our ambition to please him" (2 Cor 5:9; see also 1 Cor 4:1-5).

Paul's letters to the churches demonstrate his prime directive: to glorify God. His instruction on spreading the Gospel would add to the growing multiplication of believers. Yet Paul's foundational reason for writing is so that God would receive more glory. This motivation to glorify God is also what inspires him to edify other believers (1 Cor 4:15; 2 Cor 8:19). Thus, it becomes clear that *giving glory to God through worship is the foundation for the endeavors of the church.*

QUESTION 3

When you consider the following verses, what phrase(s) show how the desire to glorify God permeates all that Paul and other New Testament apostles did? Match the verse in the left-hand column with the corresponding phrase(s) in the right-hand column.

Verse	Phrase
Acts 4:19-20	By open proclamation of the truth we commend ourselves to everyone's conscience before God.
2 Corinthians 4:2	We recall in God's presence your endurance of hope in Christ.
2 Corinthians 7:12	I wrote to you to reveal to you your eagerness on our behalf before God.
1 Thessalonians 1:3	Whether it is right before God to obey you rather than God, you decide.

Hebrews 13:20-21 has the same tenor:
> Now may the God of peace who by the blood of the eternal covenant brought back from the dead the great shepherd of the sheep, our Lord Jesus Christ, equip you with every good thing to do his will, working in you what is pleasing before him through Jesus Christ, to whom be glory forever. Amen.

The phrases "in the sight of God" (2 Cor 4:2; 2 Cor 7:12; Acts 4:19) and "in the presence of our God" (1 Thess 1:3) show how Paul and the other apostles had a keen awareness of the constant presence of the Lord. Whatever they did, they did it with their eyes turned to God. *This is worship!*

Worship must have priority in our personal lives, and it must take precedence in our ministries. Much of what we will consider is focused on worship in community. We are not neglecting the importance of private worship. On the contrary, we believe that when worship penetrates the whole life of each believer, then corporate worship is strengthened.

QUESTION 4

Consider the role that worship plays in your own life. How do you make worship a priority? If it is not a priority, then what do you think you should do differently? Record your thoughts in your Life Notebook.

Topic 1 Key Points:

- Worship leads to edification, which leads to multiplication. These church functions are tightly interrelated.
- Giving glory to God through worship is the foundation for the endeavors of the church.
- Worship must have priority in our personal lives, and it should take precedence in our ministries.

Topic 2: Defining Worship

To prepare himself to provide his congregation with a *real* worship service experience, Pastor Eugene spent time carefully reflecting on the dynamics of worship. At the center of his thoughts was the question: What is worship?

A foundational principle of his Christian belief is that Christ is the "head" of the body, our "bridegroom," the "cornerstone," our "high priest," and our "great shepherd." Using this principle as his spiritual anchor, he found that within the context of the church, "worship" refers to the *relationship* between God and the congregation of believers that make up the church.

Pastor Eugene quickly realized that the more he tried to define the concept of worship, the deeper and broader his definition became. It was apparent to Pastor Eugene that defining worship from a purely biblical perspective can easily be overwhelming because it exposes us to issues that encompass and permeate *all* of Scripture. Therefore, for the purposes of this discussion, we will limit ourselves to a selected inductive and deductive study of the concept of worship.

Spiritual Anchor: Christ is the Head

Worship in its simplest form is the believer's response to God. It is the heart's response to God revealing Himself—through His character, His works, and His bestowing of blessings on us and others. Practically speaking, we find that worship entails a specific God-directed orientation. This response broadly takes two forms: adoration and activity or submission and service. However expressed, worship is both passive and active. There is a time to stand before Him in adoration, and there is a time to be actively working for Him or serving Him.

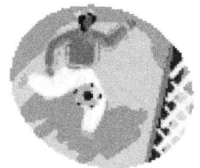

To help clarify and explain the fundamental dynamics of worship, we will use the sports metaphor of soccer. In soccer, a key position is a "forward," whose primary focus during a soccer match is to score goals. If soccer teams were unable to score, they would not win a match—it's as simple as that! Recognizing that scoring goals during a match is a *priority*, which skill do you think is most important for a forward?

Practice Key Elements

Successful forwards use a variety of skills such as dribbling, crossing, trapping, and shooting. However, the primary skill they use to score goals is shooting. To become a highly skilled shooter requires the forward to *prioritize* his or her time to practice all kinds of shots.

Christians, just as soccer forwards, must carefully define key elements of church life and prioritize the actions required to achieve a successful church.

Lesson 4: Worship Dynamics

Pastor Eugene's biblical studies have helped him to clearly define the key elements of church life as worship, edification, and multiplication. His studies also helped him to specifically *prioritize* worship as a key area of the church.

To help you gain a deeper understanding of why worship is a priority in the life of our church, please read through the following topic.

Reading Assignment

Please read the article titled "Worship as Adoration" in the Articles section at the end of this lesson, and complete the activity associated with the article.

QUESTION 5

What is the first aspect of worship as a response to God?

    A. Submission

    B. Obedience

    C. Adoration

    D. Prayer

QUESTION 6

What is/are the fundamental ideas that support worship? *(Select all that apply.)*

    A. Recognition

    B. Thankfulness

    C. Response

    D. Prayer

It is significant that the original texts of both the Old and New Testaments contain words meaning "to bow down" and "to serve." These concepts have defined worship throughout the Bible.

QUESTION 7

Many Old Testament and New Testament Scriptures suggest various elements of worship. Identify the forms indicated in the following references by matching the references in the left-hand column with the corresponding forms indicated in the right-hand column:

Reference	Worship Form
2 Chronicles 20:18; 1 Kings 8:54; Romans 14:11	Praises and singing
1 Samuel 1:3; Deuteronomy 12:26-32	Kneeling or bowing down
Nehemiah 9:3; 1 Kings 8:33-35	Offering sacrifice
Luke 2:37; Acts 13:2	Offerings and gifts
Psalm 98; Colossians 3:15-17	Reading the law and confessing
Proverbs 3:9; 2 Corinthians 9:6-12	Fasting and prayer

As we progress through these verses, the impression grows that *it is hard to distinguish outward and inward attitudes.*

QUESTION 8

Take a moment now to define worship for yourself, using the Scripture references that were provided in this topic. Open your Life Notebook, and write out your definition of *worship*.

Topic 2 Key Points:

In conclusion, let's look at three different definitions, three different ways of expressing an understanding of worship:

- Worship is pure adoration, the lifting up of the redeemed spirit toward God in contemplation of His holy perfection[1]
- Worship is an active response to God whereby we declare His worth[2]
- Worship is the dramatic celebration of God in His supreme worth in such a manner that his "worthiness" becomes the norm and inspiration of human living[3]

Topic 3: Participating in Worship

Pastor Eugene is excited about his new outlook on worship. He now realizes why some of his congregation feel that worship has become *routine* and *meaningless* in their church. His spiritual journey has enlightened and clarified his sense of what true worship is and the power it has to impact the lives of those who participate in a worship service.

Pastor Eugene's new perspective on worship has helped him to understand the complex issues that are included in a *real* worship service. By its very nature, worship can be honest and proper or false and hypocritical. It became very apparent to Pastor Eugene that worship must constantly seek to be honest and proper while not losing sight of the false and hypocritical aspects of the *worldly* worship that can be destructive to a church. Pastor Eugene keenly recognizes that we are all capable of falling into an empty formalism, which is not worship at all.

The Jewish leaders at the time of Jesus had fallen into the trap of empty formalism. Please look at the examples in the following series of questions:

QUESTION 9

In Mark 12:41-44, the widow's offering demonstrates proper worship. *True or False?*

QUESTION 10

In Mark 12:38-40, the teachers of the law exhibited proper worship. *True or False?*

---

[1] Everett F. Harrison, "Worship," in *Evangelical Dictionary of Theology* (Grand Rapids, MI: Baker, 1984), p. 1192.

[2] Ronald Allen and Gordon Borror, *Worship: Rediscovering the Missing Jewel* (Portland, OR: Multnomah, 1982), p. 16.

[3] Ralph P. Martin, *The Worship of God* (Grand Rapids, MI: Eerdmans, 1982), p. 4.

QUESTION 11

In Mark 14:3, 6-9, Mary exhibited proper worship by anointing Jesus. *True or False?*

QUESTION 12

In Mark 11:15-19 the Jewish Leaders in the temple offered the Lord proper worship. *True or False?*

Notice that all of the acts of proper worship revolve around acknowledging the character of God and being grateful for His goodness. The acts of improper worship revolve around a focus on us and rituals and ceremonies that we have created. So, in essence, proper worship is focused on God, and hypocritical worship is focused on us.

Think back to the skill that successful soccer forwards prioritize during a match. Once they have practiced their shooting skills, the time comes when they need to reevaluate their progress.

Reevaluating what they are doing can be accomplished by asking for help from a coach or a more skilled forward, or most important, checking to see if more goals are being scored. This reevaluation process allows them to refine their shooting skills and correct areas of weakness.

As church leaders, reevaluating your church's present worship dynamics is important to fulfilling God's design for the church. This reevaluation process can be done by asking yourself, your congregation, and perhaps other pastors you respect questions such as:

- Is your worship service engaging and free of false practices? Does it meet the spiritual needs of your congregation?
- Does it spiritually excite your congregation to go forth and spread God's Word?
- Is the church growing?

To help you answer these and other questions, please continue reading in this topic.

Evaluate Your Progress

Reading Assignment

Please read the article titled "Private and Family Worship" in the Articles section at the end of this lesson.

QUESTION 13

The problem Israel had in 1 Kings 18:22 was _____.

QUESTION 14

The problem Israel was having in 1 Samuel 15:22 was _____.
Idolatry and ritualism, liberalism and legalism, and wrong "functions" and empty "forms" are possible descriptive terms for the dangers of rituals. As we noticed before, there are *no* functions without forms. This concept applies in many ways to both individual and public worship. Habits can become empty, or habits can be full of devotion but for the wrong things. The function of

pure worship is expressed through forms today as well, but any form can become empty and any form can be used for the wrong purposes.

QUESTION 15

Match what God is worshiped for in the left-hand column with its description in the right-hand column.

Column A	Column B
God's works	King of the nations
God's character	Holy and true
God's position	Great and powerful

QUESTION 16

This scene in heaven shows a large group of the redeemed praising God with singing and musical instruments (Rev 15:1-8). *True or False?*

QUESTION 17

Open your Life Notebook and answer the following questions:

- What is God worshiped for?
- How is worship expressed?
- What are some of the elements of heavenly worship?

Topic 3 Key Points:

- Proper worship is focused on the character of God. Hypocritical worship is focused on our own selfish motives.
- Worship forms can become empty and/or used for the wrong purpose.
- Worship is part of our broader service to God and, therefore, is continuously expressed in both public and private settings.

Topic 4: Gathering to Worship (Exercise in Three Lenses)

An important concept Pastor Eugene has identified during his spiritual journey is that, as Christians, we are not given specific instructions on how to express our worship, especially when we gather as a church. We are given the freedom to be creative within the framework of scriptural guidelines, but not a specific model or set of instructions. As Getz puts it, there are no functions without forms. Yet we should wonder and ask ourselves, "Are there guidelines in the New Testament for forms of worship to use when the church gathers for worship?" This topic, *Gathering to Worship*, will help us answer these questions.

Let's think once again about successful soccer players that have refined their skills. Not until soccer players truly understand the fundamental skills required for the position they are playing can they begin to be creative in the execution of those skills. Often a skilled player develops a signature style or an individualized talent based on unique abilities, knowledge of the game, and vision. When this skill—this inspiration—is developed, it is usually the most personally rewarding part of the game and the most entertaining to watch as a spectator; it helps the team score goals and win matches.

Now that we have developed some skills, we will use our inspiration to design creative worship services from an inductive study using the three lenses. This topic will help you with this design.

QUESTION 18

The New Testament identifies seven aspects of worship when the church gathered together. To help you think through the Scriptures related to these experiences, match the Scriptures on the left with the aspect of New Testament worship on the right.

Scripture	Aspect of Worship
Acts 2:42	Relational experiences with each other and with God
1 John 1:3	Sharing Christ with non-believers
Philippians 4:6	Singing
Ephesians 5:19	Giving
Romans 12:13	Meals and the Lord's Supper
1 Corinthians 11:23, Acts 2:46	Biblical Instruction
1 Thessalonians 1:8	Praying together

What is edification in the New Testament sense of the word?

It is ongoing experience where biblical truth (doctrine) is learned within the context of "relational Christianity" and "dynamic Christian witness." All three experiences are needed to create a mature body of believers. To neglect any one of these facets of New Testament life is to interfere with the God-ordained plan for edification in the local church. Without these three experiences, a church will not grow to reflect the three marks of corporate maturity—faith, hope, and love.

QUESTION 19

What the forms of worship were in the Christian assemblies elsewhere remains extremely vague. It is obvious that the New Testament gives us the functions of worship but does not specify the form. Open your Life Notebook and identify each function listed in the key points below, the current form it takes in your church, and what your thoughts are in making the form as relevant as possible to your culture. What would you change? Why?

Topic 4 Key Points:

Churches develop their own forms of worship. Worship can include any or all of the following purposes:

- Vital learning experiences
- Vital relational experiences, both with one another and with God
- Corporate prayer
- Corporate singing
- Corporate giving
- Corporate eating, including the Lord's Supper and other meals

- Vital witnessing experiences

Topic 5: Ordering the Service

One element still needs considering when we discuss worship for the "church gathered." Small groups need little structure, but large groups need much more structure to remain orderly. From 1 Corinthians 14:26-40 we find biblical support for a crucial point of attention and reflection. When Paul wrote to the rather carnal church at Corinth, he had to exhort them to do all things in the assembly decently and in order.

This instruction implies that planning is necessary. Paul is not talking about limiting the work of the Spirit of God. In fact, the opposite is true. By limiting chaos, carnality, and subjectivity, one can stop the Spirit from being hindered, quenched, and grieved. Worship done in an orderly manner aids the Spirit's work in our lives and is our responsibility as a community. This responsibility is inherent in Paul's admonition to pay attention to order. Our purposeful initiation and cultivation of worship dynamics will greatly help the gatherings of the church to be fully God-directed.

After reading the introduction to this topic, Pastor Eugene found himself quietly reflecting on the importance and the role that *ordering the service* plays in a healthy and growing church. His thoughts began to motivate him, and he quickly read on to learn more about the advantages and disadvantages of small and large group structures and organization in the life of his church.

Reflecting back to our sports metaphor, a successful soccer team finds time for players to work on their individual skills, small group strategies, and whole team performance. Each of these individual team functions is important in order for a team to be fully prepared to play competitively.

A good soccer coach recognizes the importance of each team function. However, if an unhealthy imbalance occurs in the performance of these team functions, no matter how much a coach tries, the likelihood that the team will be successful is diminished.

An example of an unhealthy team imbalance is a selfish player who wants to receive attention apart from the team concept. This form of imbalance can create a high risk for hurting the performance of a whole team.

Functioning within a church situation can be seen in the same way; there are advantages and disadvantages to individual, small, and large group experiences. Understanding when to use each experience is critical to maximizing the effectiveness of a church's spiritual performance. This topic is designed to help you gain an insight into both the advantages and disadvantages of individual, small, and large group experiences in a church setting.

Reading Assignment

Please read the article titled "Ordering the Service" in the Articles section at the end of this lesson.

QUESTION 20
Planning and ordering the church service limits the work of the Spirit of God. *True or False?*

QUESTION 21
Match the historical context in the left-hand column with the corresponding statement in the right-hand column.

Content	Statement
Martin Luther	Emphasized home gatherings
Moravian revival	Emphasizes small groups with missionary fervor
Fastest growing churches	Sometimes produced heretical doctrines and practices
Danger of small group emphasis	Can lead to institutionalization and ritualism
Over emphasizing large groups	Have small group emphasis

QUESTION 22
Take some time now to evaluate one of the services or gatherings of your church. In evaluating a worship service, you will find it helpful to think through the service as you answer the following questions. Open your Life Notebook and record your answers to the following:

- What is the purpose of this service?
- Write down the traditional order of service currently used for this service in your assembly.
- Now evaluate each element of the service with these questions:
    - What is the purpose of this element of the service?
    - Is this element of the service adequately fulfilling its purpose?
    - How could this element be changed to make it more effective?
    - In what ways does this element of the service celebrate the character or the works of God?
- Are there other elements that should be added to the order of service? Should some be omitted entirely, or perhaps done at a different service?
- Is there a balance between the intellectual, emotional, and volitional elements of worship? Are we out of balance in any area?
- Does the order of service as a whole accomplish the purpose of the service? Would a different order be better?
- In what way are worshipers encouraged to be participants rather than spectators in this service?

Scripture stimulates us to be orderly in our format during meetings. Whether we like it or not, history and culture have determined to a great degree what we are presently using as forms. So as you consider what improvements might be helpful and possible, try to look carefully through both of these lenses at your specific situation.

Topic 5 Key Points:
- Individual, small, and large group experiences are all important to maximize the effectiveness of the church.

- Worship done in an orderly manner aids the Spirit's work in our lives, and it is our responsibility as a community.
- The larger the gathering, the more order and structure it typically requires.

Worship is an integral part of all of church life. It can be expressed corporately in many ways as we gather in large or small groups. It is expressed in the way we edify and multiply ourselves as churches. All of life can become a worship service as Christians realize and experience the all-permeating dynamic of being God-directed in all they do.

Topic 6: Developing Character—Not Arrogant, Not Prone to Anger, Not Violent

In this topic, we continue our focus on developing Christ-like character. The three aspects we look at in this lesson are all negatives. What we are **NOT** to be: arrogant, prone to anger, and violent. Instead, we must be what our leader was: devoted to God's mission for Him, long suffering, and compassionate (Mk 6:34; Heb 10:9-10, 12-13). Developing the character of Christ is not easy, and getting to the root of our problem is often painful, but the resulting peace and improved character is worth it. This is a call to patient endurance!

Peter is often a favorite Bible personality. Before Jesus' resurrection, he is often shown as a hindrance to His ministry. He interrupted Jesus when He sought solitude to pray (Mk 1:35-38), rebuked Jesus for announcing His road to the cross (Mk 8:31-33), and denied even knowing who Jesus was (Mk 14:66-72).

But Peter grew and became a leader in the church who willingly suffered for Jesus, even though he still made mistakes (Acts 12:1-4; Gal 2:11-14). What caused the change? *Peter had eventually integrated Christ's character into his life.* If you are interested in developing this character, this topic was designed to help you.

Not Arrogant

Reading Assignment

Please read the article titled "Not Arrogant" in the Articles section at the end of this lesson.

NOT: Arrogant, Angry or Violent

QUESTION 23

In what situations have you found yourself responding with pride or arrogance? Look at Galatians 5:22-26. What can you do to counteract this response?

Not Prone to Anger

Reading Assignment

Please read the article titled "Not Prone to Anger" in the Articles section at the end of this lesson.

QUESTION 24

Which of the following is Paul concerned about regarding anger? *(Select all that apply.)*

    A. All anger is sinful

    B. Anger coming too quickly

    C. Anger that lasts too long

    D. Anger that is man-centered

QUESTION 25

Help for overcoming a quick temper is to develop a biblical perspective on anger. Open your Life Notebook and number the lines one through three and honestly answer the following questions:

    1. Do I tend to get angry quickly?

    2. Do I find that angry feelings persist and linger?

    3. Do I try to take matters into my own hands and get even?

If you answered yes to any of these, you have a sin problem with handling anger. Confess this to God and claim His forgiveness (1 Jn 1:9). Set specific goals for your life in areas in which you are troubled and record these in your Life Notebook. Ask for God's help in achieving them. Memorize James 1:19-20.

Not Violent

Reading Assignment

Please read the article titled "Not Violent" in the Articles section at the end of this lesson.

QUESTION 26

In both Timothy and Titus, the need for church leaders as "not violent" comes immediately after what exhortation?

    A. NOT a drunkard

    B. Husband of one wife

    C. NOT arrogant

    D. Peaceful

QUESTION 27

Help for overcoming violence. Be sure you have not developed subtle ways to hurt people other than physical attack. Open your Life Notebook and record your answers to the following questions:

    1. How often do I talk about other people's problems?

    2. Whom do I share this information with?

    3. How often do I repeat information about a particular person?

    4. What emotional reaction do I have when I talk about someone else's problems?

If you do these things and enjoy them, you are getting even with a person. Record your plan of action, including personal confession of sin before God.

As Pastor Eugene comes to the end of his study of "Worship Dynamics," he finds himself full of joy. This joy comes from the realization that he more fully understands why worship is the main reason for a congregation to assemble, share, and learn about God. Armed with new understanding of the Scriptures, Pastor Eugene feels he has the knowledge and confidence he needs to achieve his goal of providing his congregation with *meaningful and real* worship experiences.

QUESTION 28

Design at least two different service orders for your situations of "gathering" as a church. Then open your Life Notebook and record them. They should somehow include new insights gained from the study of this lesson.

Lesson 4 Self Check

QUESTION 1
Of worship, edification, and multiplication (the three-fold purpose of the church), which must take priority?

    A. Worship

    B. Edification

    C. Multiplication

    D. All are equal

QUESTION 2
Worship is Christians' recognition of who God is and their response to Him. *True or False?*

QUESTION 3
The problem Saul had with his worship in 1 Samuel 15 was_____.

    A. Idolatry

    B. Disobedience

    C. Witchcraft

    D. Hypocrisy

QUESTION 4
Proper worship is focused on_____.

    A. Biblical forms of expression

    B. Our responses to Christ's sacrifice

    C. Joy, sorrow, and other emotions

    D. The character of God

QUESTION 5
The prayer that the Pharisee said in Luke 18:9-12 is a proper form of worship. *True or False?*

QUESTION 6
Small group ministries are found in the fastest growing churches in the world. *True or False?*

QUESTION 7
Emphasizing large groups sometimes leads to_____.

    A. Missionary fervor

    B. Belief in the priesthood of the believer

    C. Institutionalism and ritualism

    D. Heretical doctrines and practices

QUESTION 8
The arrogant (self-willed) are compared to false teachers in 2 Peter 2, who promise freedom but only offer _____.

QUESTION 9
Paul makes it clear that all anger is sinful. *True or False?*

QUESTION 10

Talking about other people's problems and emotionally enjoying the feeling is a way of getting even with a person. *True or False?*

Lesson 4 Answers to Questions

QUESTION 1:

Verse	Worship Significance
Romans 14:7-9	Our relationship with God is our first priority.
John 15:9-12	Our relationship with God carries over into other relationships.
Philippians. 1:9-11	Worship gives meaning to edification.
Romans 1:1, 5, 9	Worship gives direction for multiplication.

QUESTION 2: True

QUESTION 3:

Verse	Phrase
Acts 4:19-20	Whether it is right before God to obey you rather than God, you decide.
2 Corinthians 4:2	By open proclamation of the truth we commend ourselves to everyone's conscience before God.
2 Corinthians 7:12	I wrote to you to reveal to you your eagerness on our behalf before God.
1 Thessalonians 1:3	We recall in God's presence your endurance of hope in Christ.

QUESTION 4: *Your answer*

QUESTION 5:

C. Adoration

The first aspect of worship as a response to God is adoration. Adoration is the act of giving attention to the Person of God, contemplating who He is, and sitting in wonder and awe before Him.

QUESTION 6:

A. Recognition
C. Response

The fundamental ideas that support worship are recognition and response. We recognize who God is in His splendor and respond in submissive adoration of Him and in active service for Him.

QUESTION 7:

Reference	Worship Form
2 Chronicles 20:18; 1 Kings 8:54; Romans 14:11	Kneeling or bowing down
1 Samuel 1:3; Deuteronomy 12:26-32	Offering sacrifice
Nehemiah 9:3; 1 Kings 8:33-35	Reading the law and confessing
Luke 2:37; Acts 13:2	Fasting and prayer
Psalm 98; Colossians 3:15-17	Praises and singing
Proverbs 3:9; 2 Corinthians 9:6-12	Offerings and gifts

QUESTION 8: *Your answer*
QUESTION 9: True
QUESTION 10: False
QUESTION 11: True
QUESTION 12: False
QUESTION 13: Idolatry
QUESTION 14: Correct answers include:
Disobedience
Rebellion
Presumption

QUESTION 15:

Column A	Column B
God's works	Great and powerful
God's character	Holy and true
God's position	King of the nations

QUESTION 16: True
QUESTION 17: *Your answer*
QUESTION 18:

Scripture	Aspect of Worship
Acts 2:42	Biblical instruction
1 John 1:3	Relational experiences with each other and with God
Philippians 4:6	Praying together
Ephesians 5:19	Singing
Romans 12:13	Giving
1 Corinthians 11:23; Acts 2:46	Meals and the Lord's Supper
1 Thessalonians 1:8	Sharing Christ with non-believers

QUESTION 19: *Your answer*
QUESTION 20: False
QUESTION 21:

Content	Statement
Martin Luther	Emphasized home gatherings
Moravian revival	Emphasizes small groups with missionary fervor
Fastest growing churches	Have small group emphasis
Danger of small group emphasis	Sometimes produced heretical doctrines and practices
Over emphasizing large groups	Can lead to institutionalization and ritualism

QUESTION 22: *Your answer*
QUESTION 23: *Your answer*
QUESTION 24:
B. Anger coming too quickly
C. Anger that lasts too long
D. Anger that is man-centered
All of these problems with anger are characteristic of a lifestyle that Christians must "put aside" (Col 3:8).
QUESTION 25: *Your answer*
QUESTION 26: A. NOT a drunkard
This instruction may seem obvious, as was "husband of one wife," but in the pagan culture in which Christians were previously idolaters, thieves, swindlers, and adulterers, Paul reminded them not to continue those practices as Christians (1 Cor 6:9-11).
QUESTION 27: *Your answer*
QUESTION 28: *Your answer*

Lesson 4 Self Check Answers

QUESTION 1:
A. Worship
QUESTION 2: True
QUESTION 3:
B. Disobedience
QUESTION 4:
D. The character of God
QUESTION 5: False
QUESTION 6: True
QUESTION 7:
C. Institutionalism and ritualism
QUESTION 8: Correct answers include:
Enslavement
Slavery
Bondage
QUESTION 9: False
QUESTION 10: True

Lesson 4 Articles

NOT Arrogant

*"For the overseer must be blameless as one entrusted with God's work, **not arrogant**."* (Tit 1:7, emphasis added)

He must not be stubborn, not always having his own way, and the world must not revolve around him. The arrogant man is his own authority and is greedy and vain.

The only other New Testament use of the word is in 2 Peter 2:10, in which it is translated as insolent. Peter's context is a description of false teachers who follow their sensuality and lust (2 Pet 2:2-3). They despise authority; this attitude dominated those in Sodom and Gomorrah and also characterized Balaam (2 Pet 2:6, 15).

But there are more subtle forms of this trait that affect Christians. For example, the arrogant man runs his home like a dictator, though his family finds shrewd ways to circumvent his authority. The arrogant man only agrees with an idea when it is his own, and will not admit to ever making a mistake.

Some people learn to be this way. Others, over-indulged as children, have always had their way and still expect this as adults. Christians with this trait, though they may be very pious in other areas of their lives, can often be overbearing and insist that others agree with them.

Whatever the cause, the mature Christian must face the problem and overcome it by God's grace.

Note: This material is adapted from Gene A. Getz, *The Measure of a Man*. (Ventura, CA: Regal Books, 1984).

NOT Prone to Anger

*"For the overseer must be blameless as one entrusted with God's work, not arrogant, **not prone to anger**"* (Tit 1:7, emphasis added).

This person does not have a short fuse! But anger itself is not sinful and God also experiences anger (Eph 4:26). Paul is concerned about anger that comes too quickly because the person does not have self-control. He is too easily threatened and too quick to retaliate.

Paul is also concerned about prolonged anger (Eph 4:27). It is subjective and causes someone to lose perspective. It broods, smolders, and seeks revenge (Rom 12:17-21).

This anger is man-centered, taking the law into one's own hand. It is revengeful and impatient (Jas 1:20).

All these problems with anger are characteristic of a lifestyle that Christians must "put aside" (Col 3:8).

There are several causes for anger. It may be learned from associates (Prov 22:24-25), or a child growing up in an angry home learns to respond in anger. Selfishness is another cause. If anyone gets in the way of or crosses a self-centered person, there will be fireworks and "hell to pay."

All people have the capacity for selfishness. But much of it is learned behavior in an attempt to control people. People have allowed this person his/her way because they have not felt like handling the aftermath.

Being insecure and, consequently, easily threatened is another cause. This person's response is often defensiveness and counterattacks. Most causes of this behavior are from unfortunate occurrences in childhood. The person felt put down, rejected, ugly, or somehow felt that he/she did not measure up. Responses vary from withdrawing and becoming a recluse or becoming a specialist in some area of life.

Another cause is restrictive parenting of natural childhood anger to distressful situations. The normal development towards more socially acceptable ways of resolving the distress is blocked.

Whatever the cause, being prone to anger is a mark of immaturity and it must be dealt with.

Note: This material is adapted from Gene A. Getz, *The Measure of a Man*. (Ventura, CA: Regal Books, 1984).

Not Violent

*"For the overseer must be blameless as one entrusted with God's work, not arrogant, not prone to anger, not a drunkard, **not violent**"* (Tit 1:7, emphasis added).

This is anger out of control, not just verbal but physical. In both Timothy and Titus, it follows the exhortation about not getting drunk. Someone who loses his senses may respond violently. This instruction may seem obvious, as was "husband of one wife," but in that pagan culture in which Christians were previously idolaters, thieves, swindlers and adulterers, Paul reminded them not to continue those as Christians (1 Cor 6:9-11). Previously dealing with being prone to anger, Paul now exhorts against violence.

There are several scriptural examples: Cain first responded with violence and murder (Gen 4:1-15). Moses even responded in anger, not waiting for the Lord's timing, by slaying an Egyptian (Acts 7:20-29). He also shattered the first copy of the Ten Commandments in response to Israel's sin (Ex 32:19). God overruled these first two incidents, but Moses' downfall came when he struck the rock twice and he was not allowed to enter the Promised Land (Num 20:1-13).

Peter also suffered from this trait and cut off Malchus' ear the night Jesus was arrested (Jn 18:1-27). Later that night, he also denied his Lord three times.

Jesus' teaching was to not resist evil ones by violence, but to "turn the other cheek" (Mt 5:38-39).

Violence is generally still unacceptable in our culture. But people (even Christians) find other ways of striking out. Verbal abuse can be an even more effective way of hurting others and can come in a "spiritual" guise—such as sharing prayer concerns, though really gossip and malicious talk, for others.

Child discipline is another area where violence is excused "for the good of the child," but it is sometimes is an outlet for anger.

The man of God is not unnecessarily violent either in word or deed, even on those rare occasions when he is angry with proper motives.

Note: This material is adapted from Gene A. Getz, *The Measure of a Man*. (Ventura, CA: Regal Books, 1984).

Ordering the Service

The size of the meeting greatly influences the amount of order needed. The size also affects the organization of the times that we gather together. Some churches are small and do not need much structure. Larger churches need to use one approach with their main worship service and a different approach with their small group gatherings. It is important to note that the larger the church, the greater the need for the church to contribute to the purposefulness of the "scattered" moments.

Let's look at history to better provide us with insight into this topic.

Throughout church history, some churches have organized many smaller gatherings, outside of the main worship services, which have been instrumental in accomplishing the purposes of the church. Prior to the Reformation, the Roman Catholic Church had centralized church life, emotionally and spiritually, completely around large group gatherings. The reformer Martin Luther ("the Scriptures alone," "grace alone," and the "priesthood of all believers") emphasized home gatherings and de-emphasized liturgy.

In the Moravian revival that led to the first worldwide Protestant missionary outreach, churches were divided up into smaller groups of a maximum of fifteen persons per group. Missionary fervor started in these small groups. Similar developments can be pointed out in the German Pietist and the British Methodist revivals, both of which led to much social reform.

It may very well be that the priesthood of all believers and small group emphases go hand in hand. At the present time, the largest and fastest growing churches in the world emphasize small groups meeting together. This phenomenon is not restricted to one country or culture; rather, it is found globally.

We need to stress that this emphasis on small groups is primarily a historical perspective and not a biblical mandate! Balance is an important concern, since small group ministries have not contributed only positive developments to the growth of the church. They have increased worship, edification, and multiplication, but at times they have also provided ground for the spread of heretical doctrines and practices.

On the other hand, we need to see the imbalance of emphasizing only the large group gathering. There are dangers inherent in such an approach. Overemphasizing large group meetings has been instrumental in the institutionalization process, as well as in feeding ritualism.

Balance of approach is very important. Our present biblical concern is to stress the importance of order. Different gatherings have different emphases within the threefold purpose of the "church gathered." The lessons from history can provide us with some insights that we should never overlook!

Private and Family Worship

While worship in the Old Testament became centralized at the tabernacle, private and family worship were already common practice. The law encouraged and commanded the continuation of worship in these personal spheres, emphasizing the important fact that worship in the sanctuary "does not exclude, replace, or weaken the requirement of a broader service of God in fulfillment of the ethical imperatives of the law."[1] This important emphasis on worship as part of private and family life is clearly seen in Deuteronomy 10:12-22. Worship songs in the Psalms, written in the first person, are further evidence of personal worship.

As we noticed in the priesthood metaphor, all of life becomes the territory for the church to worship God. Jesus limited the extent of His words to dissociate true worship from the fulfillment of a given gesture at a given place.

We need to remember, however, that acts of worship, whether private, family, or communal, can also come under judgment. The Old Testament prophets at times protested strongly against the performance of sacrifices, fasts, assemblies, and even prayer, all legitimate means of expressing worship. Two types of problems concerning rituals triggered prophets' voices to turn against these worship practices, and each led to God's judgment of the nation!

Worship practices like those recorded in 1 Kings 18:22 and 1 Samuel 15:22 contain examples of worship problems. The practices like the ones in 1 Kings 18 led to the Assyrian and Babylonian exile, and attitudes like those in 1 Samuel 15 led to the crucifixion of Christ and the Roman exile in AD 70.

Worship as Adoration

The first aspect of worship as response to God is the response of adoration. This is the act of giving attention to the Person of God, contemplating who He is, sitting in wonder and awe before Him.

Exodus 20:5 contains a negative command with two important words central in worship: "You shall not bow down to them nor serve them, for I, the Lord, your God, am a jealous God" (NKJV). In this verse are two Hebrew words, *chawa* and *abad*. *Chawa* means "to bow down" or "prostrate oneself." The word *abad* means "to serve." God commands the Israelites not to bow down before nor serve anything or anyone other than Himself; the combination of these two concepts point to the two aspects of adoration and activity.

In the New Testament, we have the word *proskyneo*, meaning "to bow down." *Proskyneo* is used in John 4:20-24 no less than seven times. Here Jesus speaks to a Samaritan woman coming from a background that the Jews considered to be heretical in its way of worship. He explains to her the true nature of worship. He acknowledges that the worship in the temple of Jerusalem is unique. Yet at the same time our Lord points to a change in which the "bowing down" will be an inward orientation rather than an outward expression.

These various forms of worship may express many different things: humility, need, respect, submission, joy, and adoration, depending on the heart response of the worshiper. In these verses there are activities, such as praying and singing, which are means of expressing our adoration, but there is also an activity which pertains to service for Him, when you leave the throne room, as it were, and live for Him in the world.

The other main Greek word used in the New Testament with regard to worship is *latreia*, meaning "service." In Romans 12:1 Paul uses the word *latreia* for worship. Although the word refers in the Old Testament primarily to service at the altar, and thus is still related to adoration,

---

[1] Geoffrey W. Bromiley, "Worship," in *Zondervan Pictorial Encyclopedia of the Bible*, ed. Merrill C. Tenney, 5 vols. (Grand Rapids, MI: Zondervan, 1975), 5:977.

there is also the suggestion in the word, as well as in a context such as Romans 12:1, that service involves consecrated activity in the world in response to who God is, which embraces the renewal and transformation of life.

This aspect of worship involves a personal lifestyle that brings honor to Him and the specific activities often centered in church life that we do for Him. In effect, the rest of this course is a discussion of this aspect—worshiping Him through activity, or service, for Him.

Whatever words you use, the fundamental idea is recognition and response. We recognize who God is in His splendor and respond in submissive adoration of Him and in active service for Him.

Lesson 5: Edification Dynamics, Part I

Lesson Introduction

Edification: Building up the Church

Worship, edification, and multiplication are the threefold purposes of our church today. In Lesson 4, we learned that "worship" is the main reason for congregations to assemble, share, and learn about God. In this lesson, we will focus on "edification," which is the building up or strengthening of our church. In the eyes of the church, "edification" is the process which builds up the church, helping it to grow strong corporately (1 Cor 14:26; Eph 4:12).

Just as it is your responsibility as a spiritual leader to ensure that *real* worship takes place each time you meet in the name of God, you must also lead your church in growing strong through the process of edification. "Therefore encourage one another and build up each other, just as you are in fact doing "(1 Thess 5:11).

Lesson Outline

Lesson 5: Edification Dynamics, Part I
    Topic 1: Biblical Principles of Edification
    Topic 2: Eight Principles of Edification
    Topic 3: Evaluation of Principles of Edification
    Topic 4: Training Leaders and Teachers
    Topic 5: Church Discipline
    Topic 6: Developing Character—Not contentious, Gentle, Free from the Love of Money

Lesson Objectives

Armed with the knowledge he needs to achieve his goal of providing his congregation with *meaningful* and *real* worship experiences gained from Lesson 4, Pastor Eugene is eager to learn effective ways to encourage and spread the Word of God through the process of edification. *Genuine* growth of a church is not as simple as it may seem; the process of edification requires a spiritual leader to be prepared on a variety of issues. To help Pastor Eugene and you to learn new and exciting ways to encourage *genuine* growth of the church, Lesson 5 will focus on the ability to:

- Identify at least five New Testament principles of edification from selected New Testament passages
- Select at least five principles of edification that can be implemented in your church in order to ensure *genuine* growth
- Develop a plan to implement *genuine* growth in your church based on Christian teaching and learning
- Integrate a leadership training component to ensure that teachers are properly prepared to successfully teach God's people
- Evaluate discipline in your church and develop a lesson on the biblical perspective of discipline, using a three-lens perspective of the edification dynamic of discipline
- Integrate the characteristics of gentleness, freedom from the love of money, and the lack of contentiousness into your life and the life of your church

Topic 1: Biblical Principles of Edification

The New Testament explains how and why Christ wants His body to be fully mature: "We proclaim him by instructing and teaching all [people] with all wisdom so that we may present every [person] mature in Christ" (Col 1:28). He provides sustenance and the ability for each member to make his/her unique contribution (1 Cor 14:12b). Each individual living stone is needed in the qualitative growth of the spiritual building in which God is worshiped (1 Pet 2:5).

Left to themselves, Christians—like sheep—would stray, sometimes with fatal consequences. But when each member ministers to another, they grow together—becoming a pure and blameless bride, ready for the marriage feast of the Lamb! (Rev 21:2, 9)

The examples and directives found in the New Testament help us to recognize characteristics of edification of the church at that time. In this topic, we will examine the edification:

- Characteristics of ministry in local churches found in the New Testament
- Characteristics and activities important for the growth toward maturity in Christ today

Queen Esther was faced with a dilemma: She needed to help her people (the Jews), but going before the king without being summoned was a violation of the law. She had a difficult choice to make (Est 4:16), but her people needed deliverance and she was best suited to intervene for them (Est 4:14). The need to intervene for her people encouraged Queen Esther to make her decision to appear before the king. Make no mistake, God would deliver the Jews in some way, and she recognized and accepted her obligation to help deliver her people.

In the same way, each of us was saved by God to help build His church and each of us has a role to play. As Esther found her role through Mordecai's counsel, we find our role through New Testament principles and teaching.

Admiring Queen Esther's decision to intervene on behalf of her people, Pastor Eugene challenged himself to discover at least five New Testament principles that would help him in his role as a spiritual leader of his church.

QUESTION 1

Match the verse in the left-hand column with the corresponding teaching about edification ministries in the right-hand column.

Verse	Edification Ministries
Matthew 28:19-20	Devotion to teaching, fellowship, breaking bread, and prayer
Acts 2:42-47	Pursue peace and build one another up
Acts 6:1-6	Devotion to prayer and ministering the Word
Acts 20:17, 28-30	Carefully restore sinners and carry one another's burdens
Romans 14:19	Admonish, comfort, help, and pray
Galatians 6:1-2	Shepherd the flock from ravenous wolves
1 Thessalonians 5:12-22	Make disciples, baptize, and teach them

QUESTION 2

Match the verse in the left-hand column with the corresponding teaching about edification ministries in the right-hand column.

Verse	Edification Ministries
2 Thessalonians 3:6-15	Be disciplined and work and admonish those who do not
1 Timothy 5:17	Pray, show hospitality, and use your God-given gifts
2 Timothy 2:2-3	Entrust your teaching to the faithful who will teach others
2 Timothy 3:16	Effective elders work hard in teaching
2 Timothy 4:1-5	Preach the message, reprove, rebuke, and exhort
1 Peter 4:7-11	Teach, reproof, correct, and train in righteousness

The questions above provide the foundations for the following ministry activities you can use within your church to promote the process of edification.

    Providing food for the needy

    Teaching of the Word

    Prayer

    Guarding the believers from false teaching

    Church Discipline

    Encouraging believers

    Evangelizing

    Preaching

Fellowship
Taking meals together

Modeling Fellowship

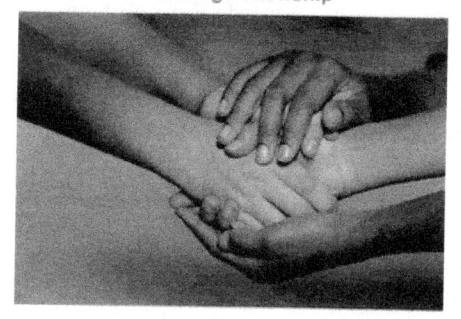

Equipping believers for ministry
Giving financial resources for the support of the ministry
Providing godly examples

Topic 1 Key Points:

The process of edification must be meaningful and effective in all churches in all cultures.

Examples of the principles of edification which apply across cultures are:

- The teaching of the Word of God is an essential element in the edification of believers.
- Leaders must provide models of spiritual maturity for believers to follow.
- Leaders have a responsibility to protect believers in their care from the destructive effects of false teaching.
- Church ministry is to be a shared ministry; leaders are to equip believers for ministry.
- Believers are to be careful to help meet the physical needs of their brothers and sisters in Christ.
- For the health of the church as a whole, leaders have the responsibility to deal with unruly believers.

Topic 2: Eight Principles of Edification

We continue our study of edification by examining eight principles that Getz found as he studied the New Testament. You may wish to supplement these principles with others that you have already found in your personal study. You may disagree with Getz, or you may want to rephrase his principles. We have provided his work to stimulate your thinking. As you formulate edification principles for your congregation, it is important to use Scripture as the foundation of your plan.

Pastor Eugene began to think of how exciting it was in the early church when the apostles went about the countryside to spread the Word of God and model the goodness of life:

> They were devoting themselves to the apostles' teaching and to fellowship, to the breaking of bread and to prayers. Reverential awe came on everyone, and many wonders and miraculous signs came about by the apostles. All who believed were together and held everything in common, and they began selling their property and possessions and distributing the proceeds to everyone, as anyone had need. Every day they continued to gather together by common consent in the temple courts, breaking bread from house to house, sharing their food with glad and humble hearts, praising God and having the good will of all the people. And the Lord was adding to their number every day those who were being saved. (Acts 2:42-47)

To put these ideas into perspective, Pastor Eugene tried to think of a modern day example that would help him clarify his thoughts. He realized that in changing forms to meet the same absolutes for the church, we are really coming to a new solution for an old problem. This idea brought to mind a brain teaser he encountered as a young boy. The challenge of this brain teaser was to connect nine dots arranged in a square with four straight lines without raising your pencil or retracing a line. Please try copying the following graphic and solve the puzzle:

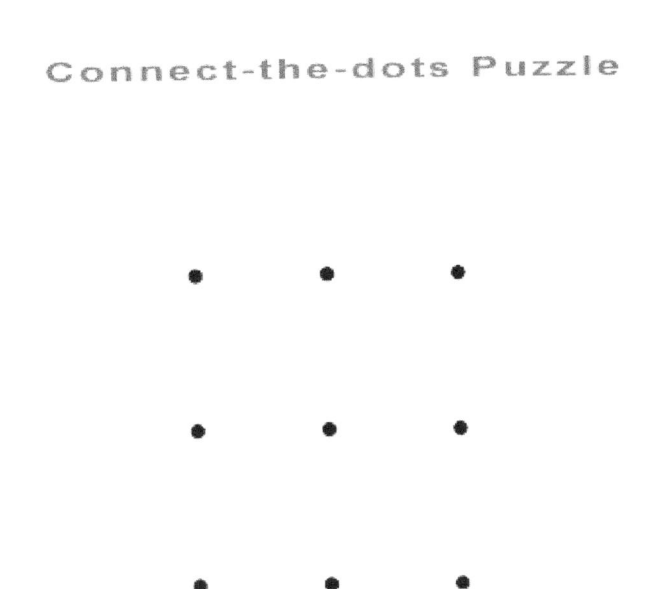

Connect-the-dots Puzzle

• • •

• • •

• • •

Think about this for a while and then check your answer by viewing the Puzzle Solution in the Articles section at the end of this lesson.

If you try to solve this problem without thinking creatively, you may not come to a solution. But, if you realize your straight lines can extend outside the figure, you have the key for arriving at a solution.

To apply several of Getz' principles to your church based upon your individual study of New Testament principles, you must think creatively and consider different opinions.

Reading Assignment

Read "Principles of New Testament Edification" found in Chapter 8 of *Sharpening the Focus of the Church* in the Articles section at the end of this lesson.

QUESTION 3

Paul demonstrated in his own ministry that the way to achieve the goal of a whole and mature universal church was to establish local churches and then to help these churches to become mature entities and independent units. *True or False?*

Lesson 5: Edification Dynamics, Part I

QUESTION 4

Please choose the response that **DOES NOT** support this statement: To provide believers with the sum total of experiences which help them to go beyond the knowledge level, you can offer teaching/learning experiences that:

A. Go beyond mere dissemination of scriptural content and even beyond interaction with that content by those who are being taught

B. Are inclusive of a transmissive-receiving type process only

C. Are in the context of relational Christianity—fellowshipping with God and with one another.

D. Are in the context of dynamic Christian witness and outreach

QUESTION 5

What vital experience(s) do people need to grow into mature Christians? *(Select all that apply.)*

A. Bible teaching that will give them theological and spiritual stability

B. Deep and satisfying relationships, both with each other and with Jesus Christ

C. To hear evangelistic messages strictly from the pulpit

D. Experience seeing people come to Jesus Christ as a result of corporate and individual witness to the non-Christian world

Topic 2 Key Points:

- All believers must be equipped for Christian service.
- Believers must be provided with both a basic and in-depth knowledge of the Word of God.
- Believers must be provided with the sum total of experiences which will help them get beyond the knowledge level—vital learning experiences with the Word, vital relational experiences with one another and with God, and vital witnessing experiences, both individually and corporately.
- Believers must be encouraged and assisted in developing high quality family life.
- The church must develop its own contemporary forms that apply the biblical principles.

Topic 3: Evaluation of Principles of Edification

As we evaluate principles on which to base our ministries, we must understand the nature of principles. We have stressed the importance of biblically formulating principles. We must always be open for any biblical information which we might have overlooked or whose relevance we failed to recognize.

The best approach is continuing in the Word and obedience to God. An excellent biblical example of this is King Josiah. Immediately following the long reign of evil King Manasseh and the brief reign of his son Amon, Josiah commissioned a building project for the Lord's temple (2 Kgs 22:3-7). In the course of that good project, the builders found a copy of the Law, missing for years (2 Kgs 22:8). Josiah continued seeking God's Word and blessed his entire nation because of it, sparing God's judgment and returning them to true worship of Yahweh (2 Kgs 22:13–23:30). God's blessings come to us in similar ways.

Reading Assignment

Please read 2 Kings 22 and 2 Kings 23:1-30 on good King Josiah.

When playing chess, there are certain rules that must be followed to play the game fairly. Each piece has a defined set of moves. For a Christian, these moves correspond to the biblical rules and guidelines God gives us. But within the rules of chess, there are still many different situations that can happen and strategies to use in various situations within each game. The moves you make depend on the strategy you formulate to win the game. Your strategy is based on your evaluation of the effectiveness of your moves, the pieces you have, their position on the board, and the strengths and weaknesses of your opponent. These correspond to the cultural forms you will use to implement these principles to help grow your own church.

Chess: Rules and Strategy

As Pastor Eugene began to recognize the relationship between the principles of edification and the nature of the principles, he began to understand the importance of the biblical rules and guidelines God gives us in order for his congregation to become mature Christians. This new understanding motivated Pastor Eugene to seek out more knowledge on the principles of edification.

Reading Assignment

Please read the article titled "Evaluation of Principles of Edification" in the Articles section at the end of this lesson.

QUESTION 6

The principles Getz proposes are equal to biblical absolutes. *True or False?*

For the following Life Notebook question, the eight principles cited by Getz have been reworded in the form of questions to help you evaluate your own ministry. The "if not, why not" part of the questions is a different way of using the three lenses of Scripture, history, and culture.

Please do not hurry over the questions. Since the author of this course is neither from your culture nor from your church, it is hard to provide you with the right questions that will lead you to discover relevant biblical information. Our main goal is to help you think biblically, historically, and culturally as you try to study and implement the biblical purpose of edification in your particular church.

The process of answering these questions is not intended to encourage a critical spirit against your church, but to promote healthy, scriptural, and relevant self-evaluation, so that you and your church can more effectively fulfill God's purpose in this world. The following questions relate to Getz' principles.

QUESTION 7

Open your Life Notebook, number the lines 1-7, and answer each of the following questions as honestly as you can.

1. Is your local church the primary place where edification takes place for each believer as well as for the whole body of Christians? If it is not, why not?
2. How is your church providing believers with both a **basic** and an **in-depth** knowledge of God's Word? If it is not, why not?
3. How is your church providing believers with opportunities to develop capacities that go beyond knowledge to include wisdom, enlightenment, appreciation, awareness, and sensitivity to the Spirit of God? If it is not, why not?

4. How does your church provide believers with experiences which will help them get beyond the knowledge level? If it does not, why not?
5. How is your church equipping all believers for Christian service? If it is not, why not?
6. How is your church helping believers develop a quality family life? If it is not, why not?
7. How is your church developing contemporary forms for applying the biblical principles? If it is not, why not?

QUESTION 8

Open your Life Notebook and select the five principles most significant for your particular church or ministry situation now. For each one, list several ways it could be implemented. (If it is already in effect, tell how and list some creative variations for your setting.) Write down any questions or comments on this section for discussion in your next group meeting.

Topic 3 Key Points:

- The formulation of principles is a matter of trying to be 100 % biblical, as well as 100% relevant.
- Biblical functions are "absolute" and "universal," but the moment we begin to reformulate them into principles, we take the first step of application.
- These principles are always formulated by someone from a particular cultural context for a particular culture.

Topic 4: Training Leaders and Teachers

Many of the principles discussed above point out the importance of teaching and applying the Scriptures. The church must provide opportunities for all believers to learn the Word of God, and this teaching must meet the present needs of her members.

The church must pay attention to equipping those who lead small groups or children's groups, as well as the development of strong marriages and the rearing of children in the homes. It must also support the continued growth in vision and insight of those with special pastoral responsibilities. Each group must have specialized training from the Word of God. The church must also provide teaching and training for future spiritual leaders in the church. Keep these concerns in mind as you answer the questions in this topic.

As we train a child in God's Word, so we train future leaders: "Train a child in the way that he should go, and when he is old he will not turn from it" (Prov 22:6).

In school we often take tests to evaluate our knowledge *before* we take a class. Or we fill out a form that asked us what we want to learn in a course. These evaluations help the teacher plan what and how to teach.

Evaluating how your own church trains leaders and teachers before making suggestions will help you to more effectively plan for leader and teacher training. To help you evaluate and make your plan, honestly answer the following questions.

QUESTION 9

Which of the following types of leadership and teacher training does your church provide?

1. Basic biblical education
2. In-depth biblical education
3. Marriage and family courses
4. Discipleship training
5. New member classes
6. Other, please list

QUESTION 10

How practical is the leadership and teacher training that your church provides?

Very practical

Somewhat practical

Not very practical

Very impractical

QUESTION 11

Open your Life Notebook and record your answers to the following questions.

- What types of leadership and teacher training programs do you believe your church is lacking? What steps can you take to offer that type of training?
- If you believe that any of your leadership training programs are impractical, what steps can you take to make them more applicable to your congregants?

Topic 4 Key Points:

- The church must provide opportunities for all believers to learn the Word of God.
- Evaluating how your own church trains leaders and teachers before making suggestions help you to more effectively plan for leader and teacher training.

Topic 5: Church Discipline

In addition to providing teaching for our people, we also have the responsibility to provide corrective encouragement. This process has been called "church discipline." The term church discipline is loaded with historical and cultural connotations that many times suggest a negative emotional response. The reason for a negative response may be that our approach to church discipline has not been rooted in Scripture.

There is no victory for God's people when sin is not judged in their midst. We will see an example of this in our reading assignment. The sin of one person led to the defeat of an entire nation.

Paul talks about the personal discipline he needed to achieve his goal (1 Cor 9:23):

> I do all these things because of the gospel, so that I can be a participant in it.

The goal of runners in a race is to successfully complete their race, but only one runner can receive the prize. So they run to win. Each competitor must exercise self-control in everything that deals with a race to improve the chances of winning. Runners compete to win a momentary prize, a prize that is merely put on a shelf and not shared with others.

Christians, just as runners, must exercise self-control in everything that deals with spreading the Word of God. However, as Christians, our reward is far greater. Our reward is alive and ongoing. Our reward is to receive God's grace throughout our lives and proactively pass it on to others.

As Pastor Eugene read this analogy between runners and Christians, he began to think about the self-control it takes to successfully achieve the goals of his church. Pastor Eugene now realizes that he and every member of his congregation must accept their responsibility to act in a disciplined manner as they approach the edification of God's Word to others.

Pastor Eugene realized that it is critical to continuously reflect on and evaluate the "state of discipline" in his own church. In other words, you must be *disciplined* in your approach to discipline in your church. True insight into the needs of your church will allow you to effectively develop a successful edification dynamic of discipline.

Reading Assignments

- Read Joshua 6, Joshua 7, and Joshua 8. Notice Israel's victory is dependent on God's people judging the sin amongst them.
- Please read the article titled "Church Discipline" in the Articles section at the end of this lesson.

Before we examine the Bible, we want to point out two more historical and cultural tendencies that influence attitudes toward discipline. Many people think that discipline is the total responsibility of the ordained church leaders. As you will discover, this is not true! The church carries this responsibility, not just its official leaders. We have seen that "church" means "people," and every member of the church carries the responsibility to actively participate in edification. So whatever your official and unofficial responsibilities may be in the church, the next assignment is for you!

QUESTION 12

What did Joshua want Achan to do to honor the Lord God of Israel and bring Him praise (Josh 7:19-21)?

    A. To return what he had stolen

    B. To submit to judgment

    C. To return to Egypt

    D. To confess his actions

QUESTION 13

Match the verse in the left-hand column with the corresponding teaching on church discipline in the right-hand column.

Verse	Teaching on Discipline
Matthew 18:15-35	When the one disciplined repents, restore him in love.
1 Corinthians 5:1-13	The church judges Christians, not the world.
2 Corinthians 2:1-11	Submit to and learn from the Father's discipline
Hebrews 12:5-11	God's presence promised with two or three witnesses

QUESTION 14

Discipline must always have love as its foundation. *True or False?*

QUESTION 15

Match the teaching from the verse in Matthew 18 in the left-hand column with the corresponding teaching or illustration of the same principle in the right-hand column.

Matthew Verse	Corresponding Verse
Discipline is the responsibility of the brother or sister who knows of a sinning brother or sister (Mt 18:15).	Deuteronomy 19:15
The only occasion for discipline is sin (Mt 18:15).	1 Corinthians 5:11
The goal of discipline is restoration (Mt 18:15).	John 8:7-10
If there has still been no restoration after one or two others have been involved, only then should the matter go before the whole church (Mt 18:16-17).	James 5:19
Anyone who refuses to repent after discipline has been exercised according to biblical principles must be treated as an unbeliever (Mt 18:17).	1 Timothy 5:17-22
According to Mt 18:18-20, God promises to be with us in a special way in disciplinary situations. In these situations, we must call on Him in prayer for wisdom and direction.	Acts 1:21-26

Additional teaching building on Matthew 18:
1. One is not to neglect a brother or sister who needs disciplining or pass the responsibility on to someone else.
2. We must be confident that what we consider sin is clearly delineated in Scripture.
3. The explanation or defense of a brother or sister might change your opinion.
4. The presence of one or two witnesses might provide another perspective on the situation.
5. The purpose of discipline is not punishment but restoration. Make sure that your motive is right. Approach your fellow Christian out of love, honestly wanting to see him/her restored.
6. Bringing the matter before the whole church presents the greatest challenge of discipline. So often problems of fellow Christians get discussed before any direct contact takes place, let alone before any possible private solution and restoration has had a chance to occur. Discipline under biblical guidelines will have a dramatic effect against the flourishing of gossip in the church.

One possible outline of the principles of church discipline, based on the Scriptures given, is:

A. The purposes of discipline are:
  1. To keep the body pure (1 Cor 5)
  2. To lead to repentance (2 Cor 2)
  3. To set an example for others (Acts 5)
  4. To deal with false prophets (Tit 1)
  5. To bring about proper Christian growth as sons of God (Heb 12)

B. Those who might come under discipline are:
  1. Not unbelievers (1 Cor 5)
  2. Any sinning Christian
     Any brother or sister (Mt 18; Gal 6)
     Church leaders (1 Tim 5)
     False teachers (Tit 1)
     Those who are disorderly (2 Thess 3)

C. The stages of discipline should involve: (Mt 18)

QUESTION 16

Discipline should take place in stages or levels. Put the stages of discipline in the correct order by matching the order of the discipline in the left-hand column with the corresponding stage of discipline in the right-hand column.

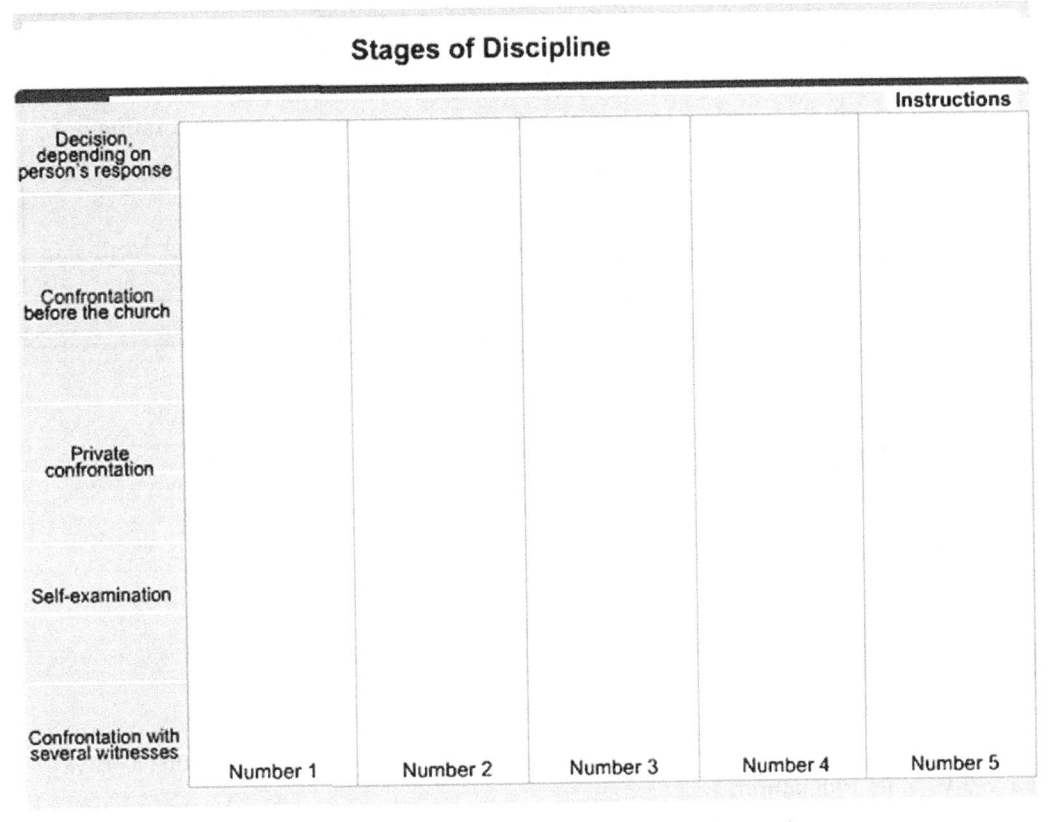

Stages of Discipline

Instructions	Number 1	Number 2	Number 3	Number 4	Number 5
Decision, depending on person's response					
Confrontation before the church					
Private confrontation					
Self-examination					
Confrontation with several witnesses					

The fifth stage as listed in the question above has two possible results:
- Restoration in love (could occur after any of the earlier steps) -or-
- Removal from the fellowship.

D. Discipline may be exercised:

1. In the beginning stages by:
    a. The individual directly involved (Mt 18)
    b. One who is spiritual (Gal 6)

2. At later stages, when there is no repentance, by:
    a. Church leaders (Mt 18; 1 Tim 5)
    b. The whole church (Mt 18)

3. At any stage by the Lord (Acts 5; Heb 12)

E. Discipline should be exercised in the following manner:

Lesson 5: Edification Dynamics, Part I

QUESTION 17

Match the verse in the left-hand column with the corresponding teaching in the right-hand column.

Verse	Teaching
Galatians 6:1	With brotherly admonition
1 Timothy 5:17-22	With gentleness and humility
1 Corinthians 5:1-13; 2 Corinthians 2:1-11	With a forgiving attitude, seeking restoration not judgment
Matthew 18:15-35; 2 Corinthians 2:1-11	With severe reproof, when needed
2 Thessalonians 3:6-15	With sorrow, mourning, and love
Titus 1:10-13	Without bias or partiality

QUESTION 18

Where should a disciplinary situation be discussed with a brother or sister?

    A. In a public, neutral setting

    B. Before the congregation, as soon as possible

    C. In private with your brother or sister

    D. During a Bible study group

Topic 5 Key Points:

- Church discipline should be properly administered when necessary.
- The goal of discipline is to correct, train, and restore a fellow believer; it must always have love at its foundation.
- Discipline is the responsibility of the entire church, *not* just its leaders.
- Discipline should take place in a private setting, with a spirit of humility. Only when a brother or sister does not repent is a situation to be brought before the church.
- God promises to be with us in a special way during disciplinary situations.

Topic 6: Developing Character—Not Contentious, Gentle, No Lover of Money

Edification is a very broad topic! We have made a good beginning by going directly to the Scriptures to observe how edification was carried out in the New Testament churches and by finding principles which can be applied in churches today. We considered the importance of teaching and discipline in the assembly. In the next lesson, we will consider more edification dynamics.

Edification fits in well with developing Christ-like character. We continue our character development by learning not to be contentious, but gentle, and free from the love of money.

- An opposite of contention is seeking unity, which is a great testimony of who Jesus is.

- Another opposite is gentleness, the same type of kindness that God showed towards us by sending His Son to die for us (Tit 3:2-5).
- Those who love money forget God. They show their lack of faith through their attitude, placing money ahead of the needs of others.

Not Contentious

Reading Assignment

Please read the article titled "Not Contentious" in the Articles section at the end of this lesson.

QUESTION 19

Unity among believers helps show Christ's unity with the Father. *True or False?*

Gentle

Reading Assignment

Please read the article titled "Gentle" in the Articles section at the end of this lesson.

QUESTION 20

According to Titus 3:3-5, why does Paul say we must be gentle toward unbelievers? *(Select all that apply.)*

A. They rule in this world.

B. We used to be and act like them.

C. God saved us according to His kindness, love, and mercy.

D. They will be more likely to treat us kindly.

No Lover of Money

Reading Assignment

Please read the article titled "Free from the Love of Money" in the Articles section at the end of this lesson.

QUESTION 21

Explain what happened to Israel after they received the Promised Land and a new generation arrived.

QUESTION 22

Which of these qualities (not contentious, gentle, free from love of money) do you struggle with the most? Why do you think this trait is difficult for you to develop? What steps can you take to further integrate these qualities into your life and your ministry? Record your thoughts in your Life Notebook.

Pastor Eugene now understands the dynamics behind the statement, "Genuine growth of a church is not as simple as it may seem; the process of edification requires a spiritual leader to be prepared in a variety of issues." How to genuinely help his church grow is no longer a question. Due to the teachings in this lesson, Pastor Eugene feels confident in his understanding of:

- The principles of edification
- How to develop and implement a plan to ensure genuine growth of his church
- The need to successfully integrate a strong leader and teacher training initiative into his church structure
- How to reflect and evaluate the discipline in his church
- The need to consciously integrate the character traits of not being contentious, gentleness, and freedom from the love of money into his life and that of his church.

Topic 6 Key Points:

- Edification fits in well with developing Christ-like character.
- An opposite of contention is seeking unity, which is a great testimony of who Jesus is.
- Gentleness is the same type of kindness that God showed towards us by sending His Son for us (Tit 3:2-5).
- Those who love money forget God.

Lesson 5 Self Check

QUESTION 1

Church discipline is classified as an edification ministry. *True or False?*

QUESTION 2

Which of the following was NOT listed as something the early church in Acts 2 devoted themselves to_____.

    A. The apostles teaching

    B. Fellowship

    C. Baptizing

    D. Breaking of bread

QUESTION 3

As part of Getz' Eight Principles of Edification, he says believers need both a basic knowledge and an in-depth knowledge of God's Word. *True or False?*

QUESTION 4

King Josiah turned Israel back to God after his workers found a copy of the _____ while renovating the temple.

    A. Bible

    B. Psalms

    C. Law

    D. Proverbs

QUESTION 5

Who is responsible for church discipline?

    A. Pastors

    B. Church administrators

    C. Bible study leaders

    D. Believers

QUESTION 6

Though Achan sinned and died as a consequence, he brought honor and praise to God by his _____.

QUESTION 7

Anyone who refuses to repent after discipline has been exercised according to biblical principles must be treated as a(n) _____.

QUESTION 8

In studying the characteristic "not-contentious," Getz points out that the unity of believers helps show the _____ of Christ.

QUESTION 9

Paul tells Timothy that an attitude of gentleness toward unbelievers may lead to their repentance. *True or False?*

QUESTION 10

Christian parents should meet their children's needs for food and clothing, but deny them what is common to other children in their society. *True or False?*

Lesson 5 Answers to Questions

QUESTION 1:

Verse	Edification Ministries
Matthew 28:19-20	Make disciples, baptize, and teach them
Acts 2:42-47	Devotion to teaching, fellowship, breaking bread, and prayer
Acts 6:1-6	Devotion to prayer and ministering the Word
Acts 20:17, 28-30	Shepherd the flock from ravenous wolves
Romans 14:19	Pursue peace and build one another up
Galatians 6:1-2	Carefully restore sinners and carry one another's burdens
1 Thessalonians 5:12-22	Admonish, comfort, help, and pray

QUESTION 2:

Verse	Edification Ministries
2 Thessalonians 3:6-15	Be disciplined and work and admonish those who do not
1 Timothy 5:17	Effective elders work hard in teaching
2 Timothy 2:2-3	Entrust your teaching to the faithful who will teach others
2 Timothy 3:16	Teach, reproof, correct, and train in righteousness
2 Timothy 4:1-5	Preach the message, reprove, rebuke, and exhort
1 Peter 4:7-11	Pray, show hospitality, and use your God-given gifts

QUESTION 3: True

QUESTION 4:
B. Are inclusive of a transmissive-receiving type process only.
Teaching-learning experiences must be more inclusive than a transmissive-receiving process. It must go beyond mere dissemination of scriptural content and even beyond interaction with that content by those who are being taught.

QUESTION 5:
A. Bible teaching that will give them theological and spiritual stability
B. Deep and satisfying relationships, both with each other and with Jesus Christ
D. Experience seeing people come to Jesus Christ as a result of corporate and individual witness to the non-Christian world
Believers need all three vital experiences to grow into mature Christians. They need good Bible teaching that will give them theological and spiritual stability; they need deep and satisfying relationships, both with each other and with Jesus Christ; and they need to experience seeing people come to Jesus Christ as a result of corporate and individual witness to the non-Christian world.

QUESTION 6: False

QUESTION 7: *Your answer*

QUESTON 8: *Your answer*

QUESTION 9: Your answer will be specific for your church

QUESTION 10: Your answer will be specific for your church.

QUESTION 11: *Your answer*

QUESTION 12:
D. To confess his actions
If he was not willing to confess that God's choice of him was just, he would in effect be calling God a liar. Though he died in God's judgment anyway, he at least died from God's discipline, at peace with God and, in a way, honoring and praising Him as just before God's people.

QUESTION 13:

Verse	Teaching on Discipline
Matthew 18:15-35	God's presence promised with two or three witnesses
1 Corinthians 5:1-13	The church judges Christians, not the world.
2 Corinthians 2:1-11	When the one disciplined repents, restore him in love.
Hebrews 12:5-11	Submit to and learn from the Father's discipline.

QUESTION 14: True

There is a delicate balance in discipline that corrects and trains a fellow believer with the goal of helping him in his walk with God. We must be sure our motive is for his best interest and not in any way a response to our own self-interest, such as a desire to punish or get even.

QUESTION 15:

Matthew Verse	Corresponding Verse
Discipline is the responsibility of the brother or sister who knows of a sinning brother or sister (Mt 18:15).	John 8:7-10
The only occasion for discipline is sin (Mt 18:15).	1 Timothy 5:17-22
The goal of discipline is restoration (Mt 18:15).	James 5:19
If there has still been no restoration after one or two others have been involved, only then should the matter go before the whole church (Mt 18:16-17).	Deuteronomy 19:15
Anyone who refuses to repent after discipline has been exercised according to biblical principles must be treated as an unbeliever (Mt 18:17).	1 Corinthians 5:11
According to Matthew 18:18-20, God promises to be with us in a special way in disciplinary situations. In these situations, we must call on Him in prayer for wisdom and direction.	Acts 1:21-26

QUESTION 16:

Number	Discipline
1	Self-examination
2	Private confrontation
3	Confrontation with several witnesses
4	Confrontation before the church
5	Decision depending on person's response

QUESTION 17:

Verse	Teaching
Galatians 6:1	With gentleness and humility
1 Timothy 5:17-22	Without bias or partiality
1 Corinthians 5:1-13; 2 Corinthians 2:1-11	With sorrow, mourning, and love
Matthew 18:15-35; 2 Corinthians 2:1-11	With a forgiving attitude, seeking restoration not judgment
2 Thessalonians 3:6-15	With brotherly admonition
Titus 1:10-13	With severe reproof, when needed

QUESTION 18:
C. In private with your brother or sister
Privately meeting to discuss a disciplinary situation with your brother or sister provides a more loving, open, and comfortable setting to confess his/her actions.

QUESTION 19: True
The thought often on the Apostle Paul's mind was to "give you unity with one another in accordance with Christ Jesus" (Rom 12:18, 15:5-6).

QUESTION 20:
B. We used to be and act like them.
C. God saved us according to His kindness, love, and mercy.
God saved us when we were undeserving and He is our example. This attitude may lead to their repentance (2 Tim 2:24-25).

QUESTION 21:
The new generation had not personally experienced God's delivering power, so they abandoned the Lord and worshipped idols. They thought their own power had given them their blessings and conquered their land.

QUESTION 22: *Your answer*

Lesson 5 Self Check Answers

QUESTION 1: True
QUESTION 2:
C. Baptizing
QUESTION 3: True
QUESTION 4:
C. Law
QUESTION 5:
D. Believers
QUESTION 6: Confession
QUESTION 7: Correct answers include:
Unbeliever
Gentile
QUESTION 8: Correct answers include:
Unity
Deity
QUESTION 9: True
QUESTION 10: False

Lesson 5 Articles

Church Discipline

Discipline is one dynamic that churches often seek to avoid because of the difficulty in its application. But to maintain a healthy church, we must be sure that discipline is administered when necessary, and in the proper manner. The maturation of the church can be hindered when discipline is neglected or when it is handled improperly. The basic root of the problem is that, while heartily believing in God's grace, one sinner has to get involved in providing discipline for another sinner. Yet it is exactly this perspective that will provide the right starting point, as well as support, for keeping the proper goal of discipline in focus.

There is a delicate balance in discipline that corrects and trains a fellow believer with the goal of helping him in his walk with God. We must be sure our motive is for his best interest and not in any way a response to our own self-interest, such as a desire to punish or get even. On the other hand, we do not want to be afraid of discipline and avoid it for fear of making someone unhappy. Discipline must always have love as its foundation.

Before we examine the Bible, we want to point out two more historical and cultural tendencies that influence attitudes toward discipline. Many people think that discipline is the total responsibility of the ordained church leaders. As you will discover, this is not true! The church carries this responsibility, not just its official leaders. We have seen that "church" means "people," and every member of the church carries the responsibility to actively participate in edification. So whatever your official and unofficial responsibilities may be in the church, the next assignment is for you!

Evaluation of Principles of Edification

In the identification of biblical principles we must recognize weaknesses in our process. In our definition of the church we tried to be as comprehensive as possible. In the lesson on worship we had to narrow down the quantity of material for our discussion purely for practical reasons. Yet the treatment was complete enough to build a total picture, step by step, from pertinent biblical information.

In a previous exercise you studied just a few of the many available New Testament passages on edification. Then you read Getz' practical principles that were based on his comprehensive study of the New Testament on this topic. By following this procedure, we intended to stimulate your intuitive evaluation of Getz' principles. Now we want to make this intuitive process conscious.

First of all, let's stress that we respect the comprehensive way in which Getz did his study. At the same time, we need to recognize that the formulation of principles is a matter of trying to be 100 percent biblical as well as 100 percent relevant. Biblical functions are "absolute" and "universal." But the moment we begin to reformulate them into principles, we take the first step of application.

Good principles are still very much universally applicable. Though derived from thorough biblical study, these principles are always formulated by someone from a particular cultural context for a particular culture.

To illustrate this observation, let us look at Getz' first principle: keep the local church in focus as the primary means by which edification is to take place. The observation Getz made was about the multiple factors at work in his American culture. One of the factors was television, twenty-four hours a day, with a multitude of channels. It is used by Satan, but it could also be used as a God-given opportunity for many churches to reach people beyond their immediate community with the gospel.

As wonderful as this prospect is, those who become Christians through such broadcasts may never get into their cars to go and be part of a body of believers. Any edification that takes place in their lives is in response to the preacher on television, not in interaction with fellow believers.

No wonder Getz emphasized this as the first principle. It is a clear biblical principle, yet at the same time it is particularly relevant to many situations. You may agree with this principle but might not make it the first one. It might not be as relevant in your situation.

So as Getz presents his principles as "absolute," we have to modify them based on culture. The function of edification is absolutely necessary. The moment you translate "edificational" functions into principles, you have entered into an application process.

We have provided you with several lessons which outline principles formulated by Getz in hopes that they will help you critically evaluate the biblical basis, as well as the relevance, of each principle you formulate for yourself. Some problems of the American church led Getz to formulate his biblical data into certain principles relevant in America. Yet many of these problems are universal and are also present in other parts of the world.

This connection is not true for all of his principles, the priority in which he presents them, or for the exact wording he chooses. When you evaluate his principles and formulate your own, try to be 100 percent relevant—to your own historical and cultural situation.

Free from the Love of Money

"The overseer then must be above reproach, the husband of one wife, temperate, self-controlled, respectable, hospitable, an able teacher, not a drunkard, not violent, but gentle, not contentious, **free from the love of money**" (1 Tim 3:2-3, emphasis added).

Because of the love of money some "have strayed from the faith and stabbed themselves with many pains" (1 Tim 6:10b). But money is not evil; rather, it is "the love of money" that is evil (1 Tim 6:10a). Jesus said it is a man's priorities: "But seek first his kingdom and righteousness, and all these things will be given to you" (Mt 6:33). The lover of money builds treasures on earth (where his heart then resides also) instead of in heaven (Mt 6:19-21; Heb 13:5). We must live as pilgrims in this world with our treasure in heaven.

The human tendency is to forget God when prosperous, as Israel did after conquering the Promised Land (Deut 6:10-12; 8:11, 17): "That entire generation passed away; a new generation came along that had not personally experienced the LORD'S presence or seen what he had done for Israel" (Judg 2:10). A mature Christian keeps the proper perspective toward money.

A quantity of money that meets more than our needs can often be misused as a status symbol. It is used to buy friends, power, status, and security. Christians can run into problems with a desire for excess wealth if they were deprived or felt deprived as children. The balance must be sought and

Christian parents should not deprive their children of what is "normal" in their society. If they do, they may create an insatiable desire for those goods in their children.

Christian leaders face particular temptations with money and are warned against dishonest gain (Tit 1:7, 10-11; 1 Pet 5:2). However, they should receive pay for their work in the Lord (1 Cor 9:14; 1 Tim 5:17).

Note: This material is adapted from Gene A. Getz, *The Measure of a Man*. (Ventura, CA: Regal Books, 1984).

Gentle

*"The overseer then must be above reproach, the husband of one wife, temperate, self-controlled, respectable, hospitable, an able teacher, not a drunkard, not violent, but **gentle**"* (1 Tim 3:2-3, emphasis added).

Jesus' words teaching the multitudes were: "Blessed are the meek (gentle), because they will inherit the earth" (Mt 5:5). This person reflects qualities opposite of the undesirable characteristics we have just studied. Paul tells us a gentle person is NOT prone to anger, violent, or contentious. Rather, he is meek, forbearing, and kind.

We must be gentle not only to believers but also to non-believers: "Be peaceable, gentle, showing complete courtesy to all people" (Tit 3:2). The next verse tells us why: "For we too were once foolish, disobedient, misled, enslaved to various passions and desires, spending our lives in evil and envy, hateful and hating one another" (Tit 3:3). But in spite of what we were, God saved us because of His kindness, love, and mercy (Tit 3:4-5). So, our Lord must be our example in gentleness also. This attitude may lead to their salvation. Perhaps God will grant them repentance and then knowledge of the truth (2 Tim 2:24-25).

Paul held himself up as an example of how he behaved toward the Thessalonians: "Although we could have imposed our weight as apostles of Christ. But we were little children among you—like a nursing mother caring for her own children" (1 Thess 2:7). In Christianity, there is no contradiction between being a man's man and being a gentle man. For women, Peter exhorts them to win over a disobedient husband with the "beauty of a gentle and tranquil spirit" (1 Pet 3:4).

Believers must correct carnal Christians with "a spirit of gentleness" (Gal 6:1; 2 Cor 10:1). That is also the attitude Christians must have toward each other, always (Eph 4:3; Col 3:12-13).

Note: This material is adapted from Gene A. Getz, *The Measure of a Man*. (Ventura, CA: Regal Books, 1984).

Not Contentious

*"The overseer then must be above reproach, the husband of one wife, temperate, self-controlled, respectable, hospitable, an able teacher, not a drunkard, not violent, but gentle, **not contentious**"* (1 Tim 3:2-3, emphasis added).

The Greek word for contentious, *amachos*, is used only twice in the New Testament, here and in Titus 3:2. Another good substitute word is quarrelsome, or its opposite, peaceable. In Titus, Paul's exhortation applies to all Christians and they must act peaceably toward all men.

A contentious person struggles against others, competes and debates, trying to lead on his own. He/she insists on his/her own way and is unable to compromise. This is the opposite of Christ's teaching that the greatest must also be a servant (Mk 10:45). In the church, there are leaders within a team concept—one among equals.

No concept is more important for functioning within the body of Christ than unity. In His high priestly prayer, Jesus prayed for the unity of His followers (Jn 17:20-23). Unity among believers shows the world the deity of Christ—His unity with the Father (2 Cor 5:19). "Blessed are the peacemakers" (Mt 5:9; see also Rom 12:18). The thought often on the apostle Paul's mind was "give you unity with one another in accordance with Christ Jesus" (Rom 12:18; 15:5-6).

Note: This material is adapted from Gene A. Getz, *The Measure of a Man*. (Ventura, CA: Regal Books, 1984).

Chapter 8: Principles of New Testament Edification

In order for a local church to become a mature body of believers reflecting faith, hope, and love, there are certain New Testament principles that must be applied. These principles grow naturally out of our study of the activities and functions of New Testament Christians and the directives that were given to them in the Epistles.

The Whole Body, A Mature Organism

First, keep the local church in focus as the primary means by which edification is to take place. Paul's ultimate concern was that the whole body—the universal church—become a mature organism (Eph 4:11-13), but he demonstrated unequivocally in his own ministry that the way to achieve this goal was to establish local churches and then to help these "microcosms" of the universal church to become mature entities and independent units. He, with his coworkers, made disciples, taught and encouraged them, and helped each group to become a dynamic *koinonia*.

Part of his teaching, of course, was to help them recognize their relationship to the universal church—that they were part of the whole. This was even more difficult to achieve in New Testament times, since these local groups were much more geographically cut off from one another. Their primary means of relationship with other local bodies of believers was through oral reports. Despite limited means of communication, it is obvious that strong ties and relationships developed between local groups, even when they had never met personally (2 Cor 8:1-6).

The Bible clearly states that there should eventually be qualified leaders,[1] and a form of discipline for those who claim to be believers but who violate scriptural teachings regarding living the Christian life. Certainly there must also be teaching of the Word, prayer, practice of baptism, and sharing of the Lord's Supper. All of these factors point to a church that has the potential for

---

[1] Note in Acts 14:21-23 that the text seems to indicate that elders were appointed in Lystra, Iconium, and Antioch after the groups of believers were designated as churches. In other words, it was not necessary to have elders before a group of believers were called a church. It is my personal opinion that there were no elders in the Corinthian church, particularly when Paul wrote his first letter, because there was not a man mature enough to be one (see 1 Cor 6:5).

maturity. But it must be strongly emphasized that many of these practices can be present and still there may be a dead, sterile, immature church. It takes true life and vitality to give meaning to these experiences. It is God's plan that, as these norms are established, they contribute to edification.

In conclusion then, this first New Testament principle for edification must be reemphasized and amplified. It is simply this: Any of us who wish to have spiritual success in our ministries and have the full blessing of God upon our efforts must work toward either the establishment of local churches as new converts are won to Christ, or, if we are serving with a parachurch agency, we must channel new Christians into an already established church. It is there that they can be nurtured into full-grown Christians as they become a part of a local body of believers, drawing strength from other members of the body as well as contributing to the growth of the church.

One of my most encouraging experiences in sharing principles of New Testament church life in a transcultural setting took place in Brazil. There I met with a number of national Christian leaders who had come to Christ through the ministry of The Navigators.

Jim Pederson, Latin American director, invited me to share with this dynamic group what the Bible teaches regarding the process of edification. Jim recognizes that if the people they are reaching for Christ are to grow spiritually, they must have the experiences God ordained in the context of a local church.

These Christian leaders have a problem, however. There are no traditional local churches that can absorb these new believers. For one thing, it would interfere with their unique strategy to continue reaching people like themselves—people who are totally secularized. Therefore, they must face this problem creatively, which they have! Suffice it to say at this juncture, Jim agrees with this New Testament principle. The local church must be kept in focus as a primary means whereby edification is to take place.

Get Believers into the Word

Second, provide believers with a basic knowledge of the Word of God. This is why Paul spent an entire year in Antioch teaching the disciples and why Paul and Barnabas returned to Lystra and Iconium and Antioch "strengthening the souls of the disciples, encouraging them to continue in the faith." He also spent a year and a half in Corinth and three years in Ephesus teaching and admonishing believers.

Paul also went beyond a personal ministry among his converts. While in Athens, he sent Timothy back to Thessalonica to strengthen and encourage the believers in their faith (1 Thess 3:2). Likewise, Paul sent Timothy back to Corinth to teach them the doctrines that he was teaching "everywhere in every church" (1 Cor 4:17). Titus remained in Crete to "speak the things which are fitting for sound doctrine" (Tit 2:1). Beyond doubt, Paul was vitally concerned that believers be instructed in basic doctrine.

It is the Word of God that is foundational to spiritual growth. "Like newborn babes," said Peter, "long for the pure milk of the Word, that by it you may grow in respect to salvation" (1 Pet 2:2, NASB). Unfortunately, there are individuals in today's church who have been Christians for years but who have never been taught even the most elementary Bible doctrines. It is here we must begin in the edification process, whether we are ministering to "new babes" or mature believers.

Provide In-Depth Teaching

Third, provide believers with an in-depth knowledge of the Word of God. Teaching his new converts face to face and sending others to instruct and lead them was not sufficient follow-up in

Paul's opinion. His next step involved correspondence—letters to the Thessalonians, the Corinthians, the Galatians, the Ephesians, and the Philippians. All of these epistles were written to provide the believers, not just with a basic knowledge of the Word of God, but with a deeper knowledge of God's truth. And of no little significance, he put this instruction in permanent form, so that it could be read again and again, studied, and circulated among other churches. On occasions they wrote back to him about what he meant, and he, in turn, wrote another letter to elaborate on his previous correspondence (for example, 1 and 2 Corinthians.) Ultimately, of course, he was providing us with a large portion of the written Word of God, which we have at our disposal today to use in the same way it was intended to be used in the first century—to provide Christians with a comprehensive knowledge of God's message to man.

Develop Capacities Beyond Knowledge

Fourth, provide believers with opportunities to develop capacities that go beyond knowledge—to include wisdom, enlightenment, appreciation, and an awareness and sensitivity to the Spirit of God. That is why Paul prayed for the Ephesians the way he did!

Probably no other Christians had the opportunity to be exposed to Paul's teaching as did those in Ephesus. They had the wonderful privilege of listening to him teach month after month. Remember, too, that it was in Ephesus that Paul lectured daily for two years in the school of Tyrannus. This helps to explain the depth of the Ephesian letter. These people were beyond the infant stage!

But notice what Paul prays for these well-fed Christians: that they may gain a "spirit of wisdom," that the eyes of their "heart may be enlightened," that they may truly know what it means to be called, that they may really know how rich they are, and how much power was demonstrated toward them in saving their souls.

Paul wanted them to know the love of Christ which goes beyond knowledge! The greatest danger today in the edification process is that Christians learn the deep truths of the Word of God but never move to the level of behavior that demonstrates wisdom, appreciation, deep awareness, and sensitivity to their position in Christ.

We must lead Christians beyond the realm of knowing in a merely superficial sense. Experience has demonstrated beyond doubt that knowing does not automatically lead to doing. A Christian can know many things about God without sensing His greatness, His power, His riches, and His grace, without being moved by the marvel and wonder of it all. It is possible to know every jot and title in the Scriptures and still lack the conviction and motivation to live out one iota of its truth.

We have established that knowledge, however, is basic to arriving at maturity. What, then, is the means by which Christians go beyond the knowledge level? The answer lies in another New Testament principle.

Provide Beyond Knowledge—Experience

Fifth, provide believers with the sum total of experiences which will help them get beyond the knowledge level.

This begins with teaching-learning experiences, but it is far more inclusive than a transmissive-receiving type process. It must go beyond mere dissemination of scriptural content and even beyond interaction with that content by those who are being taught.

This learning process must be in the context of relational Christianity—fellowshipping with God and with one another. It must also be in the context of dynamic Christian witness and outreach.

If believers are merely recipients of truth without the opportunity to truly worship God, minister to one another, and win others to Christ, they will not get beyond the knowledge level. The great problem in many evangelical churches has been in maintaining a balance in all three vital New Testament experiences. In fact, churches can almost be classified by these emphases.

There is the church that has a strong emphasis on Christian witness. Most of the time, believers hear evangelistic messages from the pulpit, and the Bible teaching they get is often superficial.

For those who are sensitive to the Lord, they yearn for solid Bible teaching and good exposition. Many who become dissatisfied eventually leave and find a good Bible-teaching church. Here the Word is faithfully taught every Sunday morning and every Sunday night and several times during the week. For a while, their hearts are thrilled and their souls are fed. But eventually the excitement of hearing the Word taught begins to disappear. Taking notes and underscoring scriptural truths in their Bibles becomes purely an academic routine. Again, those who are sensitive to the Lord begin asking the question, "What's wrong with my Christian life?"

Then there are those who are starved for fellowship and long for intimate relationships within the body of Christ. They seek out a church where there is sharing, discussion, informality, and warm fellowship. They have small-group involvement and an emphasis on honesty and openness. Individual members of the church function effectively. For a while the vacuum is filled in their lives. They are excited and thrilled with their new relationships. But gradually these experiences seem to become mechanical and routine, and even superficial. In some cases, relationships are spawned that degenerate into behavior that is questionable and have led, at times, even to immoral activities.

What is the problem? Believers need all three vital experiences to grow into mature Christians. They need good Bible teaching that will give them theological and spiritual stability; they need deep and satisfying relationships, both with each other and with Jesus Christ; and they need to experience seeing people come to Jesus Christ as a result of corporate and individual witness to the non-Christian world.

And they need all three! Not just one or two will do. Any combination other than the three in proper balance will not produce New Testament results. It is therefore the task of every church leader to determine and plan a structure for the twentieth-century church that will allow Christians to have these vital experiences which were also the experiences of the first-century Christians.

Equip For Service

Sixth, equip believers for Christian service. Note again: this involves all believers.

This is the primary thrust of Ephesians 4:

> *And He gave some as apostles and some as prophets, and some as evangelists, and some as pastors and teachers, for the equipping of the saints for the work of service, to the building up of the body of Christ ... but speaking the truth in love, we are to grow up in all aspects into Him, who is the head, even Christ, from whom the whole body, being fitted and held together by that which every joint supplies, according to the proper working of each individual part, causes the growth of the body for the building up of itself in love* (Eph 4:11-12, 15-16, NASB).

The church is a unique organism. It is edified and becomes mature as every member functions. God never intended for members of the body of Christ to depend on one leader to do the work of the ministry. As will be shown in more detail later, God did not even intend for several leaders to do the work of the ministry.

Rather, He intended for the *whole* church to do this work. It is a responsibility of church leaders to "equip the saints" to serve one another. Then—and only then—can a local body of believers grow and develop into a mature church.

Develop Family Life

Seventh, help believers develop qualitative family life. The family unit has a central place in the Bible. It antedates the church, being a basic unit throughout the Old Testament. And in the New Testament it is to form the building blocks of the church. Strong Christian families make strong churches, both in terms of evangelism and edification. And in turn, strong churches create strong families. In fact, the New Testament presents the family as the church in miniature.

Deuteronomy 6:6-9 is a classic biblical example of how a home should function according to God's pattern. This message was delivered to the children of Israel before they entered the Promised Land. They had been wandering in the wilderness as a result of their disobedience. Now as they are ready to take the final step securing for themselves the land God had promised, they were given these instructions: "
These words, which I am commanding you today, shall be on your heart. You shall teach them diligently to your sons and shall talk of them when you sit in your house and when you walk by the way and when you lie down and when you rise up" (Deut 6:6-7, NASB).

These instructions were followed by a warning. Be careful, Moses said, for when you get into the land your tendency will be to "forget the Lord." When you inherit "houses full of good things" and "cisterns" and "vineyards and olive trees," then "watch yourself lest you forget the LORD who brought you from the land of Egypt, out of the house of slavery" (Deut 6:11-12, NASB).

Unfortunately, when they arrived in the land they did forget God. When they had "eaten" and were "satisfied," when their "herds" and their "flocks" and their "silver and gold" multiplied (Deut 8:12-13, NASB), they said in their hearts, "My power and the strength of my hand made me this wealth" (Deut 8:17, NASB).

Most tragic of all, they forgot to instruct and teach their children by precept and example. The instructions in Deuteronomy 6 became only a memory, so far removed from their consciousness that they were no doubt unaware of their existence. The result was pitiful! Consequently, "there arose another generation after them who did not know the Lord, nor yet the work which He had done for Israel" (Judg 2:10, NASB).

The rest of the story can be simply told. The family unit failed and so did the nation, for a strong nation is no stronger than its family units. The same is true of the Christian community or the church. Then we must assist families to develop in their mutual life, and churches must help fathers and mothers rear their children in the discipline and instruction of the Lord. We must help them develop qualitative Christian families that will serve as solid building blocks within the local church and also serve as dynamic examples in their individual communities.[2]

---

[2] See Gene A. Getz, *The Measure of a Marriage*, Regal Books; see also *The Measure of a Family*.

Develop Contemporary Forms and Structures

Eighth, the twenty-first-century church must develop its own contemporary forms and structures for applying the biblical principles just outlined.

One thing is clear from a careful study of the New Testament: Forms and structures in Scriptures are presented as a means to biblical ends. In themselves they are not absolute. This is a danger area for evangelicals because we think in terms of absolutes. We believe in a God who has spoken through the inspired Word and who has given us propositional truth that is absolute and never changing. We believe in a God who is eternal and a Savior who is the same "yesterday and today and forever" (Heb 13:8). Consequently, it is easy for us to allow forms and patterns and ways of doing things to become just as sacred as our theology.

The twenty-first-century church must be creative in the areas where God intended it to be free. For example, the Bible does not dictate how frequently believers should meet together, nor does it dictate when. We are not told what kinds of meetings to have, nor are we locked into certain formats or patterns which should characterize these meetings. Furthermore, the Bible doesn't dictate where we should meet. Actually, the Bible doesn't even lock us in to nomenclature in describing the church. All of these are areas of freedom.

Back to my experience in Brazil. As stated earlier in this chapter, the Christian leaders I ministered to face unusual challenges. The vast majority have come to Christ out of a totally secular society. They are doctors, lawyers, dentists, architects, teachers, and other professional people. They grew up secularized, having rejected the institutional church as they know it in their culture.

Though they as Christians now understand more fully that the church as they experienced it in their preconversion days is not a true reflection of the church as God designed it to be, they are still concerned about reaching others who are still like they were— totally turned off to any mention of the church and its leadership.

Therefore, understanding freedom in form, they meet in groups to be edified. But they do not call themselves a "Church." Rather, they use the word *turma*, which means "group" in Portuguese.

They do not use the word pastor. Rather, they use the word master, which means "teacher." And they have not built church buildings since this too creates a barrier to those they are trying to reach. In summary, these Brazilian Christians are applying New Testament principles of church life, but they are using the freedom God has given them to do His work in their cultural situation.

In conclusion, the important fact is that whatever terminology we use, and whatever structures we develop, we must make sure they are helping Christians become a mature body of believers, and they are not causing us to violate the biblical principles for edification just outlined. And above all, whatever forms and structures the twenty-first-century church develops, and in whatever culture, they must never be allowed to become absolute or an end in themselves. If we do, we will fall into the same subtle trap that the church has fallen into again and again throughout church history.

Summary

1. The local church must be kept in focus as the primary means by which edification is to take place.
2. Believers must be provided with a basic knowledge of the Word of God.
3. Believers must be provided with an in-depth knowledge of the Word of God.
4. Believers must be provided with opportunities to develop capacities that go

beyond knowledge.
5. Believers must be provided with the sum total of experiences which will help them get beyond the knowledge level— vital learning experiences with the Word, vital relational experiences with one another and with God, and vital witnessing experiences, both individually and corporately.
6. All believers must be equipped for Christian service.
7. Believers must be encouraged and assisted in developing high quality family life.
8. The twenty-first-century church must develop its own contemporary forms and structures for applying the biblical principles.

Puzzle Solution

Puzzle Solution

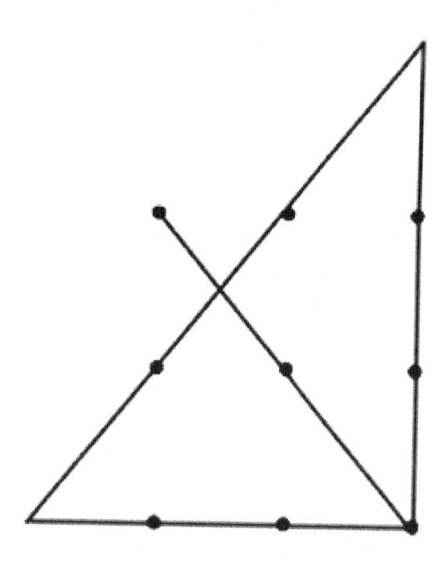

Lesson 6: Edification Dynamics, Part II

Lesson Introduction

In Lesson 1, we began our spiritual journey by studying different metaphors of the church, such as body, bride, building, priesthood, and flock. The embodiment of these earthly metaphors serves as an important bridge to the understanding of our spiritual role associated with the fulfillment of worship, edification, and multiplication in our church today. Our roles as spiritual leaders are supported in 1 Peter 2:9: "But you are *a chosen race, a royal priesthood, a holy nation, a people of his own,* so that you may *proclaim the virtues* of the one who called you out of darkness into his marvelous light."

As we pursue the goals of a spiritual leader, we must understand and maintain the unity between the leaders and the other church members. In Lesson 6, we will study ways in which the functions of the spiritual leaders and those of the other church members complement one another.

> God has blended together the body, giving greater honor to the lesser member so that there may be no division in the body, but the members may have mutual concern for one another. If one member suffers, every other member suffers with it. If a member is honored, all rejoice with it. Now you are Christ's body, and each of you is a member of it (1 Cor 12:24b-27).

Lesson Outline

Lesson 6: Edification Dynamics, Part II
- Topic 1: Who Are the Ministers in the Church?
- Topic 2: Unity, Diversity, and Interdependence
- Topic 3: Spiritual Gifts
  - What Is a Spiritual Gift?
  - Characteristics of Spiritual Gifts
  - Descriptions of Spiritual Gifts
  - Discovering Your Spiritual Gift
  - An Important Qualification
- Topic 4: Body Life and Small Meetings
  - The Biblical Basis for Small Groups
  - The Functions of Small Groups
  - Types of Small Groups
  - Characteristics of Small Groups
- Topic 5: Character Development—Household Management, Reputation, Devotion to Goodness

Lesson Objectives

Pastor Eugene now faces the difficult challenge of unifying his congregation into a blended body of one, as envisioned by God. This will take careful attention and work to ensure that all the unique segments of his congregation feel honored and have mutual concern for one another. To successfully blend Pastor Eugene's and your congregation into a body of one, Lesson 6 will provide you with teaching that will help you to:

- Identify those responsible for doing God's work in the church, supporting your answer with Scripture
- Value the need for diversity in individuals and gifts, while maintaining the need for the unity of the body of Christ
- Explain the individual gifts every believer receives and the purpose of each gift
- Evaluate your local "body" to see if it is functioning according to scriptural principles drawn from the body analogy
- Suggest forms that would encourage edification in your local body and integrate Christ's character in its life

Topic 1: Who Are the Ministers in the Church?

Maturity in a church does not just happen. The godly leader must apply the biblical principles of edification to encourage the development of faith, hope, and love in his people. But the responsibility for edification is not his alone; each member of the body should be involved in building the church. As noted in the text, one significant principle of edification is to equip **believers** for service. The goal of this lesson is to examine how God wants believers involved in edification.

> It was he who gave some as apostles, some as prophets, some as evangelists, and some to be pastors and teachers, to equip the saints for the work of ministry, that is, to build up the body of Christ, until we all attain to the unity of the faith and of the knowledge of the Son of God—a mature person, attaining to the measure of Christ's full stature. The purpose of this is to no longer be children, tossed back and forth by waves and carried about by every wind of teaching by the trickery of people who with craftiness carry out their deceitful schemes. But practicing the truth in love, we will in all things grow up into Christ, who is the head. From him the whole body grows, fitted and held together through every supporting ligament. As each one does its part, the body grows in love (Eph 4:11-16).

If you were Jesus, who would you assign to run your church—your team—in your physical absence? Would you want one person—a superstar—performing all the major duties while the overwhelming majority of your team members slacked off or performed menial tasks? Or would you want a "responsible" person—a coach—delegating duties to other gifted individuals who use their giftedness and share in the tasks and outcome? Would you make all team members vital contributors or only the one (1 Cor 12:12-31a)?

Delegating to Others

As a Christian, what the Bible says about these questions should interest you. To whom has Jesus entrusted the work of ministry? If you have ever wondered about this, please read on to find what the Bible says about your role on Jesus' "team."

QUESTION 1

Why does God want to equip His saints for work of the ministry?

- A. In order for all God's people to provide for themselves in this world
- B. To ensure that there were enough ministers in the church
- C. To ensure that His followers are believers of the truth
- D. To build up, or edify, the body of Christ
- E. In order for the body of Christ to have hope for the future

God wants to equip His saints to build up, or edify, the body of Christ until we all attain to the unity of the faith and of the knowledge of the Son of God.

QUESTION 2

In Ephesians 4:11 some gifted men are mentioned. Are they the leaders in the church? (Look through both the lens of Scripture and the lens of culture.) *True or False?*

QUESTION 3

The responsibility of the leaders, as described in Ephesians 4:12, is to equip the _____.

QUESTION 4

In what ways is equipping the saints for service different from the usual view of the responsibility of church leaders?

QUESTION 5

What happens when God's people are equipped to do the work of the church (see Eph 4:13-16)? Match the verse in the left-hand column with the result of when God's people are equipped to do the work of the church in the right-hand column.

Verse	Result of Equipping
Ephesians 4:13a	Growth of the body in love
Ephesians 4:13b	Ability to discern true and false teaching
Ephesians 4:13c	Knowledge of Christ
Ephesians 4:14	Unity in the faith
Ephesians 4:15	Speaking truth with love
Ephesians 4:16	Greater maturity and Christ-likeness

QUESTION 6

"From him the whole body grows, fitted and held together through every supporting ligament. As each one does its part, the body grows in _____."

Topic 1 Key Points:
- All Christians are responsible for equipping believers to do the work of the church.
- God designed the church so that growth occurs when all believers work together to edify each other.

Topic 2: Unity, Diversity, and Interdependence

Togetherness: The Power of We

As a spiritual leader, "togetherness" of Christians is an exciting concept for Pastor Eugene because he can *feel* the power of "we." The definition of the *church*, as Pastor Eugene has discovered, involves using metaphors that strengthen the emphasis on "togetherness" of Christians. He joyfully embraces the belief that "togetherness" occurs in all situations where two or more are gathered in God's name.

"Togetherness" should occur during church meetings, celebrations, or whenever a feeling of closeness occurs in being with others. The key concept of church points to a corporate relationship—in addition to an individual relationship—between Christians and God.

Paul uses the metaphor of the body extensively, emphasizing how Christians respond to the uniqueness of one another. This is a powerful example of how vivid a metaphor can be. The major emphasis in the body metaphor is the dependency of the members of the body on the head.

Yet the wholeness of the body in no way implies uniformity or anonymity of the members. Each member has its Christ-coordinated unique contribution to make. From Ephesians 4 we conclude that human leaders must be instruments in Christ's hands to equip the members and help them contribute for the growth of the body to maturity.

The question Pastor Eugene and you must answer is: Does "togetherness" truly exist in his/your church? If it does not, how can you equip your members to contribute to the growth of the body of Christ?

Feeling Synergy

The ability to maintain the unity of the body of Christ while supporting the ability to value diversity in individual gifts is an important trait of a spiritual leader. In this topic, we will examine the need to value diversity.

Have you ever observed or been part of a winning team? If you have, you know that sometimes good teams develop a *synergy* that raises the team's performance beyond their expectations to reach a level of greatness. This synergy often

---

Lesson 6: Edification Dynamics, Part II

takes place as result of the "mental energy" a group uses to focus on a unified goal. The power of "togetherness," or synergy, can accomplish greatness! Correctly focused, synergy can create an incredibly strong and powerful force to achieve goals once thought unattainable. To members of a winning team, moving beyond their expectations to a level of greatness becomes so much fun, so rewarding, that few experiences in life can match it. A winning team realizes that their success comes from members selflessly playing their roles so the team has the best chance to succeed. A good example of this church is the church of Philadelphia (Rev 3:7-12).

If you are interested in having this experience with your role in the church, you will enjoy studying our next topic on Unity, Diversity, and Interdependence.

Reading Assignment

Please read the article titled "Unity, Diversity, and Interdependence" in the Articles section at the end of this lesson.

QUESTION 7

Match the verse in the left-hand column with Paul's teaching about how the body must function in the right-hand column.

Verse	Body Teaching
1 Corinthians 12:12-13	Different and distinctive members are necessary for a fully functioning body.
1 Corinthians 12:14-19	For the body to function properly, it must be unified.
1 Corinthians 12:20-27	All members are dependent on one another and cannot exist or function alone.

This treatment of the body in both 1 Corinthians 12 and Ephesians 4 tells us how each member contributes toward making the church function corporately. In the biblical text, the unique function of each member has a direct relationship to the spiritual gift(s) of each member of the body. The manifestation of these gifts helps the body function properly.

QUESTION 8

The church places a high value on the diversity of its members. *True or False?*

QUESTION 9

The definition of "unity" is having everyone in the church believe and behave in the same manner. *True or False?*

Topic 2 Key Points:

- We are all one body, united by the Holy Spirit.
- Each member of the church is important and can provide a unique contribution.
- The members of the church are dependent upon each other for encouragement, sustenance, and growth.

Topic 3: Spiritual Gifts

As we begin our study of spiritual gifts and their purpose in the church, it should be pointed out that this topic is difficult. There are many different opinions about spiritual gifts, and their manifestation and use, but their purpose should not be lost in the discussion. God gifts each believer with a particular ability for a significant ministry contribution to the body of believers.

This ability is a gift from an all-sovereign God equipping His children with power and purpose. It is a gracious blessing from Him and is evidence of His love for us. A proper understanding and practice of spiritual gifts in the life of each believer is critical for developing the concept of shared ministry in the body of Christ. Knowing your giftedness encourages everyone to minister.

What Is a Spiritual Gift?

The feeling of team synergy is like no other and, if correctly focused, can take a team to greatness. This high level can also be felt by individuals. For example, a person with talent, such as a musician, who works hard to develop his or her talent through years of hard work, reaches toward greatness. The discipline and practice required to achieve higher levels of success are truly gratifying in and of themselves. Paul understood the importance of discipline and practice to achieve a "prize," or goal, as seen in his experiences in 1 Corinthians 9:24-27 and 2 Timothy 2:5.

Pastor Eugene understood the feeling of synergy, but wanted to learn more about how to aid and support others in developing spiritual talents. He wanted his whole congregation to experience a synergy that would lead them to a level of greatness in the edification of the body of Christ unlike his church has ever felt before—a feeling of true love for one another.

To learn more about how to develop God-given spiritual talents, Pastor Eugene eagerly read on to learn more about the topic on Spiritual Gifts.

Reading Assignments

- Please read the article titled "What is a Spiritual Gift? Part I" in the Articles section at the end of this lesson.
- Please read Getz' approach to spiritual gifts in Chapter 11 titled "The Functioning Body" in the Articles section at the end of this lesson.
- Please read 1 Corinthians 12 for Paul's illustration of the human body to show the functioning church, the body of Christ.
- Please read Getz' approach to spiritual gifts in the article summary from Chapter 1 "Building Up One Another" in the Articles section at the end of this lesson.

QUESTION 10

What danger(s) does Getz observe in some people who search for their personal spiritual gifts? *(Select all that apply.)*

A. Frustration at not being able to determine one's gift, which may result in giving up any thought of serving through the exercise of one's spiritual gift

B. Quick fixation on what a person thinks is his spiritual gift, leading to rationalizing one's failure to fulfill other biblical responsibilities

C. Frustration that God does not answer their prayer for their gift, leading to efforts to increase their faith

D. Self-deception, thinking that one has a certain spiritual gift when, in fact, one does not possess that gift

QUESTION 11

According to Paul, if a person desires to be a spiritual leader in the church, what should be his/her primary concern?

    A. To identify spiritual gifts in others
    B. To identify spiritual gifts in oneself
    C. To manifest New Testament maturity
    D. To manifest oneself as a true spiritual leader

Reading Assignment

Please read the article titled "What is a Spiritual Gift, Part II" in the Articles section at the end of this lesson.

QUESTION 12

Which of the following best identifies something as a "spiritual gift"?

    A. A natural talent given by God
    B. A fruit of the Holy Spirit
    C. A talent given by God with a power and a blessing
    D. An office in the church, such as deacon or elder

QUESTION 13

A spiritual gift is a divine endowment of a special ability for service upon a member of the body of Christ: an ability to function effectively and significantly in a particular service as a member of Christ's body, the church. *True or False?*

Characteristics of Spiritual Gifts

Reading Assignment

Please read the article titled "Characteristics of Spiritual Gifts" in the Articles section at the end of this lesson.

QUESTION 14

Fill in the columns with a pen or pencil by matching the option on the left to the verses in the bottom rows.

1 Corinthian 12

Options								
Each believer receives a spiritual gift								
Gifts are given for the common good								
There are many different gifts, each of which may be exercised in different ways with differing results								
The Spirit gives the gifts according to His will								
A multiplicity of gifts is needed								
Spiritual gifts are given by the Holy Spirit								
Multiple gifts function to unify the body								
Each person does not have the same gift	1 Cor. 12 4-6	1 Cor. 12 7, 11	1 Cor. 12 7, 11	1 Cor. 12 7	1 Cor. 12 8-10	1 Cor. 12 11	1 Cor. 12 19-25	1 Cor. 12 24-25

Lesson 6: Edification Dynamics, Part II

QUESTION 15

Fill in the columns with a pen or pencil by matching the option on the left to the verses in the bottom rows.

Emphasis of Passages on Spiritual Gifts

	Romans 12:3-8	1 Corinthians 12:7-12	1 Corinthians 12:27-31	Ephesians 4:7-16	1 Peter 4:10-11
use gifts to serve to God's glory					
desire corporately the greater gifts					
Christ's spiritual gifts lead to maturity					
gifts are for the benefit of all					
humbly exercise the gifts					

Instructions

QUESTION 16

Read the following passages which deal with spiritual gifts, and make a list of the gifts mentioned in each passage. Then generalize the list into 2-5 categories and list each gift in the appropriate category.

1. Romans 12:3-8—humbly exercise the gifts
2. 1 Corinthians 12:7-12—gifts are for the benefit of all
3. 1 Corinthians 12:27-31—desire corporately the greater gifts
4. Ephesians 4:7-16—Christ's spiritual gifts lead to maturity
5. 1 Peter 4:10-11—use gifts to serve to God's glory

This list is divided according to the categories of gifts in 1 Peter 4:10-11:	
Speaking Gifts	*Serving Gifts*
Apostles	Giving
Prophets	Administration
Evangelists	Mercy
Pastor-Teachings	Faith

Lesson 6: Edification Dynamics, Part II

Teaching	Healings
Exhortation	Miracles
Word of Wisdom	Helps
Word of Knowledge	
Tongues	
Interpretation	

Descriptions of Spiritual Gifts

Reading Assignment

Please read the article titled "Descriptions of Spiritual Gifts" in the Articles section at the end of this lesson.

QUESTION 17

Which of the following are correct concerning spiritual gifts, according to the article "Descriptions of Spiritual Gifts"? *(Select all that apply.)*

    A. A person can be gifted as a pastor without having the gift of teaching.

    B. A person can be gifted as a teacher without having the gift of a pastor.

    C. A woman may have the gift of pastor-teacher.

    D. Normally, there will only be one person with the gift of pastor-teacher in a church.

QUESTION 18

Match the person with the gift in the left-hand column with the corresponding gift in the right-hand column.

Person/Verse	*Spiritual Gift*
Phoebe in Romans 16:1	Service (helping)
Pricilla and Aquila in Acts 18:26	Giving
Paul in 1 Thessalonians 4:1	Teaching
Dorcas in Acts 9:36	Mercy
Titus in Titus 1:5	Exhortation
Corrie ten Boom	Administration
Stephen in Acts 6:10	Word of Wisdom

QUESTION 19

All spiritual Christians are expected to speak in tongues (1 Cor 12:30). *True or False?*

Discovering Your Spiritual Gift

Reading Assignments

- Please read Romans 12, 1 Corinthians 12, Ephesians 4, and 1 Peter 4. These four chapters all discuss spiritual gifts.
- Please read the article titled "Discovering Your Spiritual Gift" in the Articles section at the end of this lesson.

The following may help you have a better idea of your gift:

QUESTION 20

Open your Life Notebook and number the lines 1-7. Then record your answers to the following questions:
1. What do you or would you enjoy doing in the church? What forms of ministry have given you a sense of joy and fulfillment?
2. What are you doing now to serve in the church?
3. In what areas of ministry have mature members of the body confirmed or encouraged your participation?
4. In what areas of ministry has God provided opportunities for you to serve?
5. In what areas of ministry have you personally seen fruit or experienced God's blessing?
6. Based on your answers to the above questions, what do you feel is your gift, or gifts? If you are doing some things you dislike but are doing them because no one else will, do you think you are operating in your area of giftedness? Why or why not?
7. Recall that Paul said that the whole body builds itself up as each individual part supplies its unique contribution to the body as a whole (Eph 4:16). The church functions best when each believer ministers through his or her spiritual gift. What kind of things can your church do to help members discover and use their spiritual gifts?

The confirmation of others can be a great help in discovering your own optimal functioning in the body. We are not encouraging long and deep introspection to discover it. The best way is serving and letting the process of interaction with others guide you. Spiritual gifts are not unique traits of isolated individuals, but manifestations of the Spirit as each member functions.

An Important Qualification

God gives spiritual gifts to enable us to minister effectively to build up the church. Remember, though, that all believers are commanded to minister in several areas, whether gifted in that area or not. For example, all believers should evangelize whether they have the gift or not. This means believers cannot use their lack of giftedness to excuse their lack of involvement in that area of God's command.

Topic 3 Key Points:

- God gifts each believer with a particular ability for a significant ministry contribution to the body of believers.
- The Bible describes spiritual gifts in conjunction with body function and mutual edification.
- The best way to discover your spiritual gift is through serving and letting the process of interaction with others guide you. Spiritual gifts are not unique traits of isolated individuals, but manifestations of the Spirit as each member functions.

Topic 4: Body Life and Small Meetings

In Lesson 5, we looked at several passages that dealt with edification. For example, Paul's prayer in Colossians 1:9-10 serves as a model for us to pray for the spiritual growth of one another. In 1 Peter 4:8-10, hospitality is promoted among the brethren. Galatians 6:1-2 speaks of forgiveness and bearing one another's burdens. Other passages encourage edification as believers are asked to serve (1 Pet 4:10), encourage (1 Thess 5:11), accept (Rom 15:7), and love one another (1 Jn 4:11).

As Pastor Eugene reads through this material, he wonders how he can practically provide opportunities for edification in his church. Although we have established "freedom of form" for each church as it interprets its various functions, does the Bible provide an example of how the church can best carry out edification?

The example in the Bible involves small meetings to fill this need. Smaller groups within large ones give people the chance to share with one another and develop relationships.[1] Of course, a church with less than one hundred members already has an intimate atmosphere for sharing. Regardless of size, the body life is enhanced when the needs of church members are addressed. Small groups provide more opportunities for expressing needs. As people get familiar, they better understand how the other person needs prayer and encouragement. Let us look at the biblical basis for small groups in the church body.

The Biblical Basis for Small Groups

Since most of you are church leaders, you must know that helping others contribute fully to their role on a team can be more rewarding than winning individual rewards. For a team to perform at its best, sometimes it needs its less visible contributors, like assistant coaches, to work on specialized skills or to give individual attention to some performers.

The "assistant coaches" in the church are the small group leaders. To find out how they bring out the best "performance" in a church, please continue reading this topic (see how Titus 2:1-10 *breaks members down into categories of people for specialized teaching*).

Reading Assignment

Please read the article titled "Biblical Basis for Small Groups" in the Articles section at the end of this lesson.

QUESTION 21

Match the verse in the left-hand column with the teaching about small group meetings in the early church in the right-hand column.

Verse	Teaching on Small Groups
Acts 2:42	Paul lived in Rome and proclaimed Christ with boldness with no restrictions.
Acts 5:42	Every day from house to house they proclaimed Jesus as the Christ.
Acts 20:20	They proclaimed what is helpful from house to house.
Acts 28:30-31	They were devoted to teaching, fellowship, breaking of bread, and prayer.

From the verses in the question above, we are impressed that the meetings in the homes were regular and purposeful, and that Christ was taught and preached in large and small settings. While the house meetings varied in size, it is clear that these meetings emphasized times of fellowship, prayer, and breaking bread together (which are generally small group type activities), as well as teaching (which may be done in any size group).

---

[1] Ron Jenson and Jim Stevens, *Dynamics of Church Growth* (Grand Rapids, MI: Baker, 1981), p. 147.

It is crucial to note in Scripture the reasons for what they did. Following the model of the Lord Jesus and the need to express body life and the priesthood of all believers, they initiated forms, regularly meeting in homes, as well as in larger, more formal gatherings. In some cases, they kept meetings small in response to cultural persecutions. But it also purposefully provided a setting for necessary functions of the church. For us today, we need to keep the functions in mind as we learn from the models in the New Testament.

QUESTION 22

Review the article on the *Biblical Basis for Small Groups* and use Jesus' example to write a list of principles that can be followed in your own small groups.

The Functions of Small Groups

Reading Assignments

Please read the article titled "Functions of Small Groups" in the Articles section at the end of this lesson.

Please read 1 Thessalonians 3 in which Paul expresses his love for his brothers in Christ.

QUESTION 23

Match the verses in the left-hand column with the three functions of small groups, plus one inspiration from keeping Christ in the center, as listed in the left-hand column.

Verses	Functions and Inspiration
Philippians 2:1-2	Inspiration
Proverbs 27:17	Spiritual intimacy
Hebrews 10:23-25	Accountability
Matthew 28:20	Encouragement

Reading Assignment

Before moving on, take a moment to read the "one another" principles at the end of Chapter 11 "The Functioning Body" in Getz' book *Sharpening the Focus of the Church* in the Articles section at the end of this lesson.

Types of Small Groups

Reading Assignment

Please read the article titled "Types of Small Groups" in the Articles section at the end of this lesson.

Characteristics of Small Groups

Although each of these groups may have different functions, there are several characteristics that should be true for every group. The verses in the next two matching questions point to characteristics that should be part of every church small group. Although these characteristics should be part of the nature of the church, a small group provides increased opportunity to put these priorities in focus.

QUESTION 24

Look up each set of references and decide what goal is to be pursued. Then match the verse(s) in the left-hand column to the corresponding goal in the right-hand column.

Verse	Goal to Pursue
John 13:35; 1 Corinthians 13:13	Building up one another to reach maturity
Acts 4:32; Romans 12:5	Ministering through one's gifts for the good of the body as a whole
Romans 14:19; Ephesians 2:19-22	Caring for one another, sharing of resources to meet personal needs, fellowship, and unity
Romans 12:6-8	Loving one another

QUESTION 25

In talking about spiritual gifts in 1 Peter 4:8-11, how do verses 8-9 provide a contextual setting for their functioning? Record your response in your Life Notebook.

Each group is different according to the personalities and backgrounds of the members. If you maintain an open atmosphere of sharing, then each members' needs can be addressed. When people share with one another, they build relationships and the basis of edification is built.

QUESTION 26

Now open your Life Notebook and write your answers to the following: Considering Scripture (trying to determine the reasons in the methods of the New Testament examples), your cultural situation (especially new opportunities you may have), and your church's history, list one or two different types of groups that you would like to try to start within your congregation and what you would like to accomplish with these groups.

Topic 4 Key Points:

- Our own need for and use of groups is a logical extension of the fact that God exists within the divine form of a small group.
- The best biblical example of a small group is Jesus and His disciples.
- There are many different types of small groups, and the groups should be designed to meet the needs of its members.
- Small groups provide strength as they build relationships, encourage personal growth, and supply leadership training.
- As the group members are edified, the church body grows stronger, as well.

Topic 5: Developing Character—Household Management, Good Reputation, Devoted to Goodness

This lesson ends the study on edification in the New Testament. We have studied the Scriptures, our primary authority. We have also provided you with materials which may open the doors for you to discover God's will in your life. This study has required much work on your part, but it is bound to have borne much fruit as a result.

We will now continue developing a Christ-like character by learning to be one who manages his own household well, because that is the test of whether we are capable of running God's household. A leader is also one who is well thought of and devoted to what is good.

A team, whether it's a sports or chess team, is made up of a group of individuals who have a distinctive set of qualities. These distinctive qualities range from a defined skill set to a person's general mindset, nature, integrity, or feelings. Qualities such as a person's nature, integrity, or feelings are often referred to as a person's "character." A team's character is made up of the sum of its members and is a key component of success. Can you think of teams that have not been successful because of a lack of character? When members of a team have character breakdowns, their behavior can negatively impact the team's chemistry and synergy. This character imbalance affects all aspects of teamwork and, if not dealt with, can cause a team to break apart.

As Pastor Eugene thought about this, he easily made the connection between a functional team and a functional church. Just as a team is the sum total of its members, so is the church. In this topic, Pastor Eugene looked forward to learning more about how to develop "character" from a personal and leadership point of view.

The information in this topic will help you develop your personal character as part of God's team. From Paul's description in 1 Thessalonians 1:1-10 *the Thessalonian believers had developed that character and achieved great results!*

Managing One's Household

Reading Assignment

Please read the article titled "He Must Manage His Own Household Well" in the Articles section at the end of this lesson.

QUESTION 27

Recognize that respect and love cannot be forced, but come by example and maturity. Open your Life Notebook and record the answer to the following questions about how well you manage your household:

1. Do I manage my household well? Is it a place filled with love and peace? Do I get along well with those who live with me?
2. If you are married, how can I become a better spouse? What are my strengths and weaknesses?
3. If you have children, how can I become a better parent? What are my strengths and weaknesses?

Set up specific goals for having a well-ordered household from actual needs that have surfaced through this study. Record your goals in your life-notebook.

Good Reputation

Reading Assignment

Please read the article titled "Of Good Reputation" in the Articles section at the end of this lesson.

QUESTION 28

Paul says a Christian leader must be "well thought of." To qualify as a leader, this person must never be reproached for his/her lifestyle. *True or False?*

Reproach should come for a godly lifestyle but never for ungodly behavior.

Devoted to Good

Reading Assignment

Please read the article titled "Devoted to Goodness" in the Articles section at the end of this lesson.

QUESTION 29

Match the reference in the left-hand column with the corresponding teaching about "devoted to what is good" in the right-hand column.

Reference	Teaching
Romans 12:21	He offers his body as a living sacrifice.
Philippians 4:8	He is purified from the inside out.
Romans 7:19	He thinks pure and excellent thoughts.
Titus 1:15-16	He overcomes evil with good.
Romans 12:1-2	He does NOT win the battle in the flesh.
2 Timothy 3:14-17	He has received spiritual wisdom.
Colossians 1:9-10	His walk is based on knowing God's Word.

As Pastor Eugene comes to the end of Lesson 6, his new knowledge about edification dynamics has given him the confidence to meet the many challenges of unifying his congregation into a blended body of one, as is envisioned by God. Through his studies, he has learned the importance of paying careful attention to all the unique talents and abilities of his congregation in order to ensure his members feel honored and have mutual concern for one another. The areas in which he feels most confident and knowledgeable are his abilities to:

- Identify those responsible for doing God's work in the church, supporting his choices with Scripture
- Value the need for diversity in individuals and gifts while maintaining the unity of the body of Christ
- Explain the individual gifts every believer receives and the purpose of each gift
- Evaluate the local "body" to see if it is functioning according to scriptural principles drawn from the body analogy
- Suggest forms that would encourage edification in the local body and integrate Christ's character into each life

QUESTION 30

Consider your work in Lesson 6 as you complete the following assignment. Write your philosophy of gifts and how they function in the body, including what they are, their purpose, and their manifestations.

Then evaluate your own church by answering the following:

1. Are the gifts given to believers by the Holy Spirit used in your church to edify?
2. If yes, how? If no, what needs to be done so that this will take place?
3. Is each member of your church involved in an aspect of edification? If not, why not?

Lesson 6 Self Check

QUESTION 1

In the church body, who is supposed to do the work of the church (service)?

    A. The saints

    B. The leaders

    C. The pastor/teacher

    D. The elders

QUESTION 2

In the body metaphor that Paul uses extensively, the wholeness of the body implies that the individual members are anonymous. *True or False?*

QUESTION 3

Which of the following is NOT a proper scriptural emphasis for the purpose of spiritual gifts in the church?

    A. Desiring corporately the greater gifts

    B. Using the gifts to God's glory

    C. Using gifts for self-edification

    D. Using the gifts in humility

QUESTION 4

Every believer receives a spiritual gift from God at the moment of her/his salvation. *True or False?*

QUESTION 5

Paul instructs a person desiring to be a spiritual leader to have this as the primary concern:

    A. To assist others in finding their gifts

    B. To first identify one's own spiritual gift

    C. To show oneself as a true spiritual leader

    D. To show spiritual maturity

QUESTION 6

The best biblical example of a small group is Jesus' relationship with His _____.

QUESTION 7

The basis for edification in small groups is in building relationships. *True or False?*

QUESTION 8

It is inevitable that the Christian will be reproached by unbelievers just for being a Christian, but he should never be reproached for_____.

    A. Ungodly behavior

    B. Widespread evangelism

    C. Harsh language

    D. Being counter-cultural

QUESTION 9

Which of the following is NOT true about the man devoted to good?
- A. He overcomes evil with good.
- B. He overcomes evil in the flesh.
- C. He offers his body as a living sacrifice.
- D. He is purified from the inside out.

QUESTION 10

Each member of the church should be involved in an aspect of edification. *True or False?*

Unit 2 Exam: Church Dynamics

QUESTION 1
Of worship, edification, and multiplication (the threefold purpose of the church), the one that must take priority is _____.

QUESTION 2
It is a scriptural principle that edification takes priority over multiplication relationships. *True or False?*

QUESTION 3
The fundamental idea behind worship is recognition and response. *True or False?*

QUESTION 4
Which of the following is a biblical example of proper worship?

    A. Making God's house a den of robbers (Mk 12:38-40)

    B. The widow's offering (Mk 12:41-44)

    C. The disciples' reaction to Mary anointing Jesus (Mk 14:4-5)

    D. The pretentious Jewish leaders (Mk 12:38-40)

QUESTION 5
Emphasizing large groups sometimes leads to _____.

    A. Institutionalism and rituals

    B. Missionary fervor

    C. The priesthood of the believer

    D. Heretical doctrines

QUESTION 6
From 1 Corinthians 11:22-26 we see that the lenses of culture and history may enhance worship, but should never interfere with the worship itself. *True or False?*

QUESTION 7
According to 2 Peter 2, following false teachers leads to _____, even though they offer freedom.

QUESTION 8
According to Scripture, all anger is sinful. *True or False?*

QUESTION 9
Church discipline is classified as an edification ministry. *True or False?*

QUESTION 10
What was the key to King Josiah's reforms that brought Israel back to God?

    A. Removing idols from the land

    B. Reinstating the sacrifices in the temple

    C. Letting the land rest every seventh year

    D. Finding a copy of God's law

QUESTION 11

Biblical functions are "absolute" and "universal." But the moment we begin to reformulate them into principles, we take the first step of application. *True or False?*

QUESTION 12

Training for various groups in the church should be specialized to meet their needs. *True or False?*

QUESTION 13

Church discipline should happen in progressive steps. Which of the following is properly the next step after self-examination and private confrontation?

    A. Decision, depending on person's response

    B. Confrontation with several witnesses

    C. Removal from or restoration to fellowship

    D. Confrontation before the church

QUESTION 14

Paul tells Timothy that the following Christ-like attitude toward unbelievers may lead to their repentance:

    A. Gentleness

    B. Respectable

    C. Hospitable

    D. NOT contentious

QUESTION 15

According to Getz, within their budget, Christian parents should allow their children most of the same material provisions common to their society. *True or False?*

QUESTION 16

Biblically, the church _____ are meant to do the work of ministry.

    A. Elders

    B. Leaders

    C. Teachers

    D. Members

QUESTION 17

Any individuality within the body of Christ inhibits the body from functioning correctly. *True or False?*

QUESTION 18

Paul's exhortation in 1 Corinthians 12:31 to "be eager for the greater gifts" is mainly directed toward_____.

    A. Each individual believer

    B. Church leaders

    C. Every person everywhere

    D. The church corporately

QUESTION 19

Spiritual gifts can properly be unique traits of isolated individuals. *True or False?*

QUESTION 20

This course taught that the best way to discover your spiritual gift is by serving other believers. *True or False?*

QUESTION 21

Why will the full expression of the church as body and priesthood tend to be meager when a given church only has large gatherings?

    A. Most people will not get opportunities to exercise their spiritual gifts.

    B. There will be a lack of gifted people.

    C. It is more difficult to picture the universal church.

    D. There is usually a lack of variety in programs to meet believers' needs.

QUESTION 22

The key to enhancing individual and collective church growth is to keep Christ at the center of our focus. *True or False?*

QUESTION 23

The three functions of small groups are spiritual intimacy, encouragement, and _____.

QUESTION 24

To be biblically "well thought of," a Christian leader may be reproached by unbelievers for being a Christian. *True or False?*

QUESTION 25

Which of the following is NOT true about the man devoted to good?

    A. He overcomes evil with good.

    B. He offers his body as a living sacrifice.

    C. He overcomes evil in the flesh.

    D. He is purified from the inside out.

Lesson 6 Answers to Questions

QUESTION 1:
D. To build up, or edify, the body of Christ

QUESTION 2: True

These apostles, prophets, evangelists, and pastor-teachers certainly are leaders in the New Testament churches. From these categories, the minimal conclusion follows that each leader has their special area of giftedness. God gives to the universal church and to the local church a broad spectrum of leadership as ministers.

QUESTION 3: Correct answers include:
Saints
Believers
Body

According to Ephesians 4:12, the gifted men are to equip the saints for service and building up the body of Christ.

QUESTION 4:

The usual (incorrect) view is that the main church leader (e.g., the pastor) does the "work of service," or the entire ministry, while the congregation is ministered to (except for a few menial tasks). The biblical role of the leaders is to equip the believers (saints) for the ministry, according to their gifts and training.

QUESTION 5:

Verse	Result of equipping
Ephesians 4:13a	Unity in the faith
Ephesians 4:13b	Knowledge of Christ
Ephesians 4:13c	Greater maturity and Christ-likeness
Ephesians 4:14	Ability to discern true and false teaching
Ephesians 4:15	Speaking truth with love
Ephesians 4:16	Growth of the body in love

QUESTION 6: Love

QUESTION 7:

Verse	Body teaching
1 Corinthians 12:12-13	For the body to function properly, it must be unified.
1 Corinthians 12:14-19	Different and distinctive members are necessary for a fully functioning body.
1 Corinthians 12:20-27	All members are dependent on one another and cannot exist or function alone.

QUESTION 8: True

QUESTION 9: False

Unity involves functioning together as a whole toward the same purpose. Diverse members can perform different functions (behaviors) to contribute toward achieving that purpose and still be unified.

QUESTION 10:

A. Frustration at not being able to determine one's gift, which may result in giving up any thought of serving through the exercise of one's spiritual gift

B. Quick fixation on what a person thinks is his spiritual gift, leading to rationalizing one's failure to fulfill other biblical responsibilities

D. Self-deception, thinking that one has a certain spiritual gift when, in fact, one does not possess that gift

QUESTION 11:
C. To manifest New Testament maturity

If a person desires to be a spiritual leader in the church, his/her primary concern should be to manifest the qualifications of maturity specified in the New Testament.

QUESTION 12:
C. A talent given by God with a power and blessing

The following is a good definition of a spiritual gift: a divine endowment of a special ability for service upon a member of the body of Christ; an ability to function effectively and significantly in a particular service as a member of Christ's body, the church.

QUESTION 13: True

QUESTION 14:

Scripture	Characteristic of Spiritual Gifts
1 Corinthians 12:4-6	There are many different gifts, each of which may be exercised in different ways with differing results.
1 Corinthians 12:7, 11	Spiritual gifts are given by the Holy Spirit.
1 Corinthians 12:7, 11	Each believer receives a spiritual gift.
1 Corinthians 12:7	Gifts are given for the common good.
1 Corinthians 12:8-10	Each person does not have the same gift.
1 Corinthians 12:11	The Spirit gives the gifts according to His will.
1 Corinthians 12:19-25	A multiplicity of gifts is needed.
1 Corinthians 12:24-25	Multiple gifts function to unify the body.

QUESTION 15:

Scripture	Emphasis on Spiritual Gifts
Romans 12:3-8	Humbly exercise the gifts.
1 Corinthians 12:7-12	Gifts are for the benefit of all.
1 Corinthians 12:27-31	Desire corporately the greater gifts.
Ephesians 4:7-16	Christ's spiritual gifts lead to maturity.
1 Peter 4:10-11	Use gifts to serve to God's glory.

QUESTION 16: *Your answer*

QUESTION 17:
B. A person can be gifted as a teacher without having the gift of a pastor.

C. A woman may have the gift of pastor-teacher.

QUESTION 18:

Person/Verse	Spiritual Gift
Phoebe in Romans 16:1	Service (helping)
Pricilla and Aquila in Acts 18:26	Teaching
Paul in 1 Thessalonians 4:1	Exhortation
Dorcas in Acts 9:36	Giving
Titus in Titus 1:5	Administration
Corrie ten Boom	Mercy
Stephen in Acts 6:10	Word of Wisdom

QUESTION 19: False
QUESTION 20: *Your answer*

QUESTION 21:

Verse	Teaching on Small Groups
Acts 2:42	They were devoted to teaching, fellowship, breaking of bread, and prayer.
Acts 5:42	Every day from house to house they proclaimed Jesus as the Christ.
Acts 20:20	They proclaimed what is helpful from house to house.
Acts 28:30-31	Paul lived in Rome and proclaimed Christ with boldness with no restrictions.

QUESTION 22: *Your answer*

QUESTION 23:

Verse	Functions and Inspiration
Philippians 2:1-2	Spiritual intimacy
Proverbs 27:17	Accountability
Hebrews 10:23-25	Encouragement
Matthew 28:20	Inspiration

QUESTION 24:

Verse	Goal to Pursue
John 13:35; 1 Corinthians 13:13	Loving one another
Acts 4:32; Romans 12:5	Caring for one another, sharing of resources to meet personal needs, fellowship, and unity
Romans 14:19; Ephesians 2:19-22	Building up one another to reach maturity
Romans 12:6-8	Ministering through one's gifts for the good of the body as a whole

QUESTION 25:

Love (v. 8) and hospitality (v. 9) provide a secure environment in which to exercise gifts to serve one another. Hospitality, in particular, usually occurs in a small group setting, which provides the opportunity for many people in the body to exercise their spiritual gifts.

QUESTION 26: *Your answer*

QUESTION 27: *Your answer*

QUESTION 28: False

It is also inevitable that the Christian, just for being a Christian, will be reproached by unbelievers (Matthew 5:11; 2 Timothy 3:12; 1 Peter 4:14). Since they hated Jesus they will also hate us (John 15:18-20). How then can these concepts be reconciled? Reproach should come for a godly lifestyle but never for ungodly behavior.

QUESTION 29:

Reference	Teaching
Romans 12:21	He overcomes evil with good.
Philippians 4:8	He thinks pure and excellent thoughts.
Romans 7:19	He does NOT win the battle in the flesh.
Titus 1:15-16	He is purified from the inside out.
Romans 12:1-2	He offers his body as a living sacrifice.
2 Timothy 3:14-17	His walk is based on knowing God's Word.
Colossians 1:9-10	He has received spiritual wisdom.

QUESTION 30: *Your answer*

Lesson 6 Self Check Answers

QUESTION 1:
A. The saints
QUESTION 2: False
QUESTION 3:
C. Using gifts for self-edification
QUESTION 4: True
QUESTION 5:
D. To show spiritual maturity
QUESTION 6: Disciples
QUESTION 7: True
QUESTION 8:
A. Ungodly behavior
QUESTION 9:
B. He overcomes evil in the flesh.
QUESTION 10: True

Unit Two Exam Answers

QUESTION 1: Worship
QUESTION 2: True
QUESTION 3: True
QUESTION 4:
B. The widow's offering (Mk 12:41-44)
QUESTION 5:
A. Institutionalism and rituals
QUESTION 6: True
QUESTION 7: Correct answers include:
Slavery
Bondage
QUESTION 8: False
QUESTION 9: True
QUESTION 10:
D. Finding a copy of God's law
QUESTION 11: True
QUESTION 12: True
QUESTION 13:
B. Confrontation with several witnesses
QUESTION 14:
A. Gentleness
QUESTION 15: True
QUESTION 16:
D. Members
QUESTION 17: False
QUESTION 18:
D. The church corporately
QUESTION 19: False
QUESTION 20: True
QUESTION 21:
A. Most people will not get opportunities to exercise their spiritual gifts.
QUESTION 22: True
QUESTION 23: Accountability
QUESTION 24: True
QUESTION 25:
C. He overcomes evil in the flesh.

Lesson 6 Articles

Biblical Basis for Small Groups

In thinking about the biblical basis for small groups, consider first the nature of the Holy Trinity. The Trinity is a union of three Persons: the Father, the Son, and the Holy Spirit. This union represents the positive force of relationship. In his book *How to Lead Small Groups,* Neal McBride states, "Our own need for and use of groups is a logical extension of the fact that God exists within the divine form of a small group."[1]

A further look into the biblical basis of small groups brings us to the Israelites. In the Old Testament, the Jewish people were a special race with whom God chose to have a unique relationship. These Israelites were made up of even smaller groups—namely, tribes, families, and households.[2] As God revealed Himself, His promises, and salvation through His Son, Jesus, He did it within the context of this special group of people.

The best example of the benefits of a small group setting is within Jesus' ministry on earth. He chose twelve men to form His inner circle of friends and disciples. What can be learned from this example? Neal McBride summarizes how Jesus fulfilled His ministry, including the call for edification, through His role as a small group leader. The following five points are a paraphrase of McBride's presentation[3]:

1. One of Jesus' first acts as part of His ministry was to create a small circle of disciples as His foundation (Mt 10:2-4).

2. The time Jesus spent with His small group, His disciples, was an investment in relationships, not in any sort of organization. He became involved in their lives and showed them how to love one another by example and command (Jn 15:12-13).

3. Due to the fact that Jesus had built relationships with His disciples, He was able to share with them the "mysteries of the kingdom of God" (Lk 8:10).

4. As the crucial hour of His crucifixion came nearer, Jesus withdrew from the crowds more often to spend His last few hours with His disciples.

5. Just as you are learning leadership skills through participation in a small group, Jesus chose this setting to train the future leaders of the early church. Their daily travels, conversations, lessons, and experiences became the education for these men who were later described as having "upset the world" (Acts 17:6).

---

[1] Neal F. McBride, *How to Lead Small Groups* (Colorado Springs, CO: NavPress, 1990), p. 14.

[2] Ibid.

[3] Ibid., pp. 16–18.

Building up One Another (Chapter 1 Summary)

A functioning body is absolutely essential for growth and maturity to take place in any given church. The very nature of the body of Christ makes it important for every member to function and contribute to the process of edification. Christians cannot grow effectively in isolation. They need to experience each other. In fact, the words to *edify* and *edification* are used most frequently in the context of the functioning body.

It is also true that the Bible describes spiritual gifts in conjunction with body function and mutual edification. However, the Scriptures do not emphasize searching for or trying to discover one's spiritual gifts. Rather, they emphasize again and again the importance of becoming mature in Christ, both as individual believers and as a corporate body. Furthermore, New Testament Christians were not given the choice of whether or not they wanted to function. As we've seen from our study of the "one another" injunctions, they were told to help "one another" in many ways.

This process was not dependent on whether or not they were gifted in these areas.

Furthermore, if a person desired to be a spiritual leader in the church—"Which," wrote Paul, "is a fine work"—he should be primarily concerned about manifesting the qualifications of maturity specified in the New Testament, rather than being able to identify his own spiritual gifts.

Characteristics of Spiritual Gifts

1 Corinthians 12 introduces us to spiritual gifts. Remember this as you study the passage: The context of 1 Corinthians 12 concerning the gifts of believers is within Paul's discussion of the church, the body of Christ. Also, remember spiritual gifts are to edify the church body. Studying the characteristics of these gifts helps us to understand how they fulfill their purpose in edifying the body.

In verses 4-25, we learn the following facts about spiritual gifts:
1. There are many different gifts, each of which may be exercised in different ways with differing results (vv. 4-6).
2. Spiritual gifts are given by the Holy Spirit (vv. 7, 11).
3. Each believer receives a spiritual gift (vv. 7, 11).
4. Gifts are given for the common good (v. 7).
5. Each person does not have the same gift (vv. 8-10).
6. The Spirit gives the gifts according to His will (v. 11).
7. A multiplicity of gifts is needed (vv. 19-25).
8. The multiplicity of gifts is intended to function for the unity of the body, not for the division of the body (vv. 24-25).

The truths above lead to practical conclusions concerning gifts.

First, **it is not necessary to seek to obtain a gift** since the Holy Spirit has already given each believer at least one gift (1 Cor 12:7, 11; see also 1 Pet 4:10). This assures him or her that every Christian has an important part in the life of the body.

Second, **the gift given is the Holy Spirit's choice**. He knows what is best for each person and for his place in the body. This fact can give us great peace because God is sovereign, so believers need not question their gift. The Holy Spirit empowers each person within the pattern of God's design as we acknowledge God's purpose in our lives.

Third, **the gift given is for building up the body**. Consider the metaphor of the church as the body of Christ and think how a body copes with a nonfunctioning member. A blind body can manage, but with more difficulty. The responsibility falls on other members to make up for the weakness. For example, the sightless often develop a keener sense of hearing to partially compensate. Thus, when a member of Christ's body does not fulfill its purpose, the body continues functioning, but it feels the loss of the member and must compensate in some way.

Fourth, **each gift is valuable and needed in the church**. Thus, each person's contribution is valuable and necessary. It is wrong to depreciate any gift. Some receive more public recognition (the speaking gifts, for example), but all are valuable, and none unnecessary. Indeed, Paul reminds us that sometimes the less visible gift is more important (1 Cor 12:22-25). It is through exercising one's gift that others are edified. The more a person applies his gift for the church, the more he strengthens them.[4]

Finally, **each person must use his gift**. God entrusts us with special abilities to contribute to developing His kingdom, and we must use these abilities and privileges accordingly.[5]

Descriptions of Spiritual Gifts

The following descriptions of spiritual gifts have been taken from William J. McRae, *The Dynamics of Spiritual Gifts*.[6] To help you know what your gift might be, read the descriptions below and see if you can identify with them.

Some people believe that the lists of spiritual gifts given in Scripture are not exhaustive. It should be noted that Paul's purpose in the three passages in which he deals with spiritual gifts (Rom 12:3-6; 1 Cor 12-14; Eph 4:4-16) is not to give a complete list of spiritual gifts, or even a systematic theology of spiritual gifts. His point in each passage is to show that the Holy Spirit manifests Himself in the lives of believers in various ways, and does so always for the purpose of building up the body of Christ as a whole (1 Cor 12:7). What follows, therefore, is more of a list of some ways in which the Spirit manifests Himself rather than a fixed list of what have

---

[4] Win Arn, *The Pastor's Manual for Effective Ministry*, (Monrovia, CA: Church Growth Incorporated, 1988). p. 34.

[5] Ibid., p. 20.

Ibid., p. 20.

80. The definitions in this section are either exact or adapted quotes from McRae's book. The explanations that follow are a paraphrase of his comments, with occasional additional explanatory comments included. Also bear in mind that this presentation represents an understanding of the gifts from a twentieth-century Western perspective.

Lesson 6 Articles

commonly come to be called "spiritual gifts."[7] The usual practice of discussing these manifestations as "spiritual gifts" will be used simply because it is so common.

In interpreting the gifts mentioned, remember to stay close to the text of Scripture. The great temptation in dealing with spiritual gifts is to interpret the gifts according to one's experience.

For example, a believer may sense a strong impression to pray for a missionary or another believer. Sometime later he discovers that the person he prayed for was—at the very time he prayed—in great danger or engaging in significant spiritual ministry. Some have interpreted the believer's impression to pray as a revelation and the announcement to the church of that impression as the exercise of the gift of prophecy.[8] It seems better to simply accept that God gives impressions to pray without using this experience to define prophecy.

Ministry Gifts

This list of gifts includes those whose exercise throughout church history is generally agreed upon.

Evangelism: The supernatural ability to present the Hospel message with exceptional clarity and overwhelming conviction

Of course, every believer has the privilege and responsibility to share Christ with unbelievers. It is part of Christ's final instruction to us to be witnesses for Him throughout the world. Yet the person with the gift of evangelism has four distinguishing characteristics:

> He has an overwhelming desire to see people saved.
>
> His understanding of the Gospel is comprehensive.
>
> He is able to present the Gospel so that unbelievers understand it.
>
> The gift brings great joy to the person who has it as Jesus is shared.

An excellent example of this gift is found in Philip the evangelist (Acts 8:5-13; 8:26-40). Philip was gifted both in speaking to large crowds, as he did with the Samaritans in Acts 8, and also to individuals, as he witnessed to the eunuch later in this same chapter. This chapter, incidentally, also contains many excellent precepts for sharing with unbelievers.

Pastor-Teacher: This expression in Ephesians 4:11 is actually "and pastors and teachers." The construction of the Greek text indicates that these terms describe two aspects of one gift.[9]

As a pastor, this person has the capacity to shepherd the flock of God. As a teacher, he is divinely equipped to prepare and serve a balanced diet of nutritious spiritual [food] that produces growth

---

[7] For a good discussion of these ideas, see Gordon D. Fee, gen. ed., *The New International Commentary on the New Testament*, 15 vols. to date (Grand Rapids, MI: Eerdmans, 1959—), vol. 7: *The First Epistle to the Corinthians*, by Gordon D. Fee, pp. 582–89.

[8] See, for example, Wayne Grudem, "Why Christians Can Still Prophesy," *Christianity Today*, September 16, 1988, p. 34.

[9] T. K. Abbott, *A Critical and Exegetical Commentary on the Epistles to the Ephesians and to the Colossians*, The International Critical Commentary (Edinburgh: T. & T. Clark, 1968), p. 118. So also John Eadie, *A Commentary on the Greek Text of the Epistle of Paul to the Ephesians* (reprint ed.; Grand Rapids, MI: Baker, 1979), p. 304.

and maturity in Christians. One may be a gifted teacher without being a pastor (Rom 12:7; 1 Cor 12:28-29), but one may not be a pastor without being a teacher.[10]

The gift of pastor-teacher is prevalent in every church; it is not held solely by the man designated "pastor." In fact, the position of pastor of a local church is not presented as an official office of the local church in the New Testament.

The word "pastor" comes from the Greek verb "to shepherd." The passages that use this verb are directed toward the elders of the church. Read Acts 20:28-31 and 1 Peter 5:1-5 to see how the elders were responsible for the church as a shepherd is for a flock. The shepherd assists the flock in three ways: he feeds them, leads them, and guards them from dangers. A person with the gift of pastor-teacher has the capability to serve the flock in this manner.

One way a man could exercise his gift of pastor-teacher is by leading a men's Bible study or by becoming an elder. The qualifications for elder include shepherding the flock (Acts 20:28; 1 Pet 5:1-4) and being able to teach (1 Tim 3:2). There are other qualifications in addition to these (1 Tim 3:1-7), but an elder is more effective if he possesses this gift.

The Bible never indicates that the gift of pastor-teacher is reserved for men only. As soon as churches recognize that multiple persons in a local church may have this gift, the local church will begin to receive the ministry benefit of the multiple expressions of this important gift.

Service (Helping): A person with the gift of service has a supernatural capacity to serve faithfully behind the scenes, in practical ways, to assist in the work of the Lord and encourage and strengthen others spiritually.

Exercising this indispensable gift enables a ministry to run smoothly, consequently reaching more people with the Gospel. Consider the numerous examples of this gift in the Bible: Romans 12 discusses the function of church members and emphasizes the importance of the gift of service. Romans 16:1 lists Phoebe as having this gift and she is praised by Paul for her assistance. Acts 20:35 mentions a specific command to "help the weak" and points to the Christlike quality of their service.

Some specific examples of gifted service include: assisting with the church service, making sure enough chairs are available for the members each week, helping with the tape ministry, distributing books or materials to those without, and meeting transportation needs.

An important expression of this gift is prayer. James 5:16b says, "The prayer of a righteous person has great effectiveness." As friends and coworkers of this ministry carry the Gospel into various countries like yours, those with the gift gladly assist at home through supportive prayer.

Teaching: A person with the gift of teaching is marked by two distinct characteristics. He will have a keen interest in personally studying the Word and in the disciplines involved in studying Scripture. Also, he will communicate clearly the truths and applications of the Word so others may learn and profit. After you have heard a "teacher" teach, your response should be, "I see what he means."

This gift of teaching is clearly important because it is mentioned in three New Testament lists: Romans 12:7, 1 Corinthians 12:28-29, and Ephesians 4:11. This gift prompts spiritual growth and blessing, while the natural talent can only communicate factual material. It must be understood that the gifted teacher explains only the truth that the Spirit has revealed to him. It is impossible to teach the truths of God's Word without depending on the Spirit to first teach us (Jn 16:13).

---

[10] McRae, pp. 59–60.

The gift of teaching is seen in several people in the Bible. For example, Paul, in Acts 18:11, exhibited this gift while living in Corinth for a year and a half. He welcomed the opportunity to teach God's Word to the people there. Priscilla and Aquila were apparently gifted teachers who exercised this gift by explaining "the way of God... more accurately" to a fellow believer (Acts 18:26).

Exhortation: This gift empowers a believer to exhort ("I urge you," Rom 12:1), encourage ("Encourage one another," 1 Thess 5:11), or comfort ("Comfort one another," 1 Thess 4:18) his fellow believers.

When one exhorts another, he "drives home spiritual truth and fires men to action" in the Lord's power. The exhorter works together with the gifted teacher who explains the spiritual truth. Paul is a primary example of an exhorter. Every one of his thirteen letters is filled with loving exhortations. He consistently exhorts the obedient to even greater devotion (1 Thess 4:1) and the disobedient into obedient action (Eph 4:28).

Barnabas, on the other hand, exemplifies the encouragement side of this gift. In fact, his name, which means "son of encouragement," comes from the others who clearly saw this gift demonstrated in him (Acts 4:36). Several times Barnabas put his gift to use by loyally ministering to people who needed help. When Paul was a new Christian, Barnabas took him in and convinced the other believers that he was no longer hostile toward the church (Acts 9:27). Indeed, had Barnabas not been Paul's source of encouragement from the beginning, perhaps his many letters would not have been written.

Later, Barnabas encouraged Mark by choosing him as his traveling companion after Paul refused to travel with him (Acts 15:39). The fruit of this effort is seen in 2 Timothy 4:11 when Paul specifically asks that Mark be brought to him because his ministry was helpful to Paul.

Giving: The supernatural capacity to give of his substance to the work of the Lord or to the people of God consistently, liberally, sacrificially, and with such wisdom and cheerfulness that others are encouraged and blessed.

People without a spiritual gift for giving still make a difference in meeting people's needs. The gifted giver, however, meets needs and brings God's special blessing as well. Consider Philippians 4:10-16 and 2 Corinthians 8, in which Paul was powerfully blessed through people's gifts. It was more important to Paul to see his friends' spiritual growth through their gifts than to have them meet his needs. He says, "Not that I seek the gift itself, but I seek for the profit which increases to your account" and explains, "I can do all things through Him who strengthens me" (Phil 4:17, also 13, NASB).

Dorcas in Acts 9:36 is a woman with a gift for giving. She is praised for her generosity and sincerity of heart. The gifted giver will practice giving cheerfully (2 Cor 9:7) as a member of the body of Christ (Rom 12:8).

Men and women with the gift of giving carry God's blessing, not only through the amount of the gift, but also through the attitude of the giver.

Administration: The believer with the gift of administration has a God-given capacity to organize and administer with such efficiency and spirituality that not only is the project brought to a satisfactory conclusion, but it is done harmoniously and with evident blessing.

There is a great need for gifted Christian leaders today. Consider Jesus' example when He says, "And whoever wishes to be first among you shall be your slave; just as the Son of Man did not come to be served, but to serve, and to give His life a ransom for many" (Mt 20:27-28 NASB). A spiritual leader is not one who forces his direction on the people, but he is one who leads them in their spiritual growth with "vision and direction."

The biblical examples of such people are Joseph, Daniel, and Nehemiah in the Old Testament. In the New Testament, Titus was given the responsibility by Paul to "set in order what remains and appoint elders in every city as I directed you" (Tit 1:5, NASB). This command to set things in order indicates the area where the spiritual gift lies; he is able to organize things for the good of the people. As Paul says in 1 Corinthians 14:33 (NASB), "For God is not a God of confusion but of peace, as in all the churches of the saints." A gifted leader is able to apply God's Word in such a way that it provides order and leadership for the people.

Mercy: Mercy is undeserved aid. Christians who have the gift of mercy have a special capacity for receiving and aiding those who need help, especially the undeserving. They are willing and eager to share themselves with these people, such as an orphan, an alcoholic, a retarded person, a widow, a poor person, or even a former persecutor.

One of the best examples of showing mercy was Barnabas toward Saul. Saul deserved no help from the Christians, since he had caused them pain and persecution for so long. Yet it was mercy that Barnabas shared with Saul when he took him in and encouraged him. God wants us to show mercy to our enemies, as well.

A woman who had a great gift of mercy was Corrie ten Boom. Corrie and her family are known as war heroes for their efforts to save the lives of Jews in Holland during World War II. Yet before she was a "war hero," Corrie taught a Bible study to retarded children. Her family raised many foster children in their house. During the war her family was arrested for hiding Jews in their home, and Corrie's father, brother, and sister died as a result of their imprisonment.

Yet after the war Corrie set up a house to receive those who had been wounded by the war. Corrie realized that the wounded included not only the victims of persecution but also the Nazi soldiers and the Dutch collaborators, the men and women who had betrayed their country.

The house was intended to bring together the victims and their persecutors to give them a chance to experience forgiveness. This kindness extended to the men who had killed her family. It was an extreme act of mercy on Corrie's part, an example of the tremendous healing and blessing that a person with the gift of mercy can share.

Word of Wisdom: A believer with the gift of a word of wisdom has a special faculty for receiving, knowing, and especially presenting the wisdom of God. This gift is mentioned only once, in 1 Corinthians 12:8. It is characterized by the description in 1 Corinthians 2:6-12 as it concerns the wisdom of the mystery of God.

The person with the gift of a word of wisdom differs from the person addressed in James 1:5 ("But if any of you lacks wisdom, let him ask of God, who gives to all men generously and without reproach, and it will be given to him" NASB) and the man mentioned in Proverbs 2:6-7 ("For the LORD gives wisdom; from His mouth come knowledge and understanding. He stores up sound wisdom for the upright; He is a shield to those who walk in integrity" NASB). These passages are directed toward every believer who seeks God's guidance and direction in making decisions. God's wisdom is available to all who ask.

The person with the gift of a word of wisdom, however, is set apart from other believers in that he has a special capacity for receiving the revealed wisdom of God directly and presenting it authoritatively to the people. His expressions of wisdom are contrary to the foolish wisdom of the world and the useless wisdom of this age (1 Cor 1:20; 3:18-20). The wisdom of the gifted believer constantly points men to God in the midst of their everyday circumstances. As the Spirit reveals God's wisdom to the gifted believer, other men encounter God through his words.

For example, the men who were listening to Stephen could not overlook the power and wisdom in his words: "And yet they were unable to cope with the wisdom and the Spirit with which he was speaking" (Acts 6:10, NASB). The believer with the gift of a word of wisdom will be recognized for his gift. His judgments will be consistent with James' description of wisdom in James 3:17 (NASB): "But the wisdom from above is first pure, then peaceable, gentle, reasonable, full of mercy and good fruits, unwavering, without hypocrisy."[11]

Word of Knowledge: This is the ability to understand correctly and to proclaim clearly the spiritual truth of God revealed in the Scriptures. The emphasis here, as in the gift of a word of wisdom, is on the communication of the message. Beyond this we cannot be dogmatic about the meaning or use of this gift.

Faith: The gift of faith is the faith which manifests itself in unusual deeds of trust. This person has the capacity to see something that needs doing and to believe God will do it through him even though it looks impossible. He is a man of vision with firm conviction that God will bring it to pass.

Sign Gifts

The following gifts are so controversial that they will not be discussed in detail in this course. These may, in general, be considered "sign gifts" because their exercise was normally a sign to authenticate the person or revelation which the person was giving (Heb 2:4).

One of these gifts, tongues, is specifically called a sign in 1 Corinthians 14:22 (note that this verse also implies that prophecy is a sign). Healings and miracles were generally used as authenticating signs in the ministry of Christ and the apostles (for example, Acts 4:29-30, in which healing, signs, and wonders were connected to the speaking of God's Word). Paul calls signs, wonders, and miracles the "signs of a true apostle" (2 Cor 12:12 NASB).

Whether these gifts are still active in the church is a matter of interpretation. While it is certainly true that God can give any of the gifts to the church today, the question is whether He is actually doing so and whether it is His purpose to do so. For example, there is no question that God still heals miraculously today and that He still does other miraculous things. The question is whether God still gives believers the gifts of healings and miracles today. The question may be phrased in another way: Does God intend that the exercise of these sign gifts be **normal** for the church today?

Healings: The ability to heal diseases, any and all diseases, miraculously is possessed by the person with the gift of healings.

Miracles: This gift seems more comprehensive than the gift of healings. Literally, it is the ability to do "works of powers." This person has the capacity to do miracles in general.

In studying this gift you should note the kinds of miracles done and the purpose of miracles. In general, miracles authenticated a message or the messenger himself.

Tongues: The gift of tongues is the supernatural ability to speak in an existing human language which the speaker has not learned but it is known to those who hear.

The subject of speaking in tongues has become very complex because of the powerful impact of experience on our understanding of the text of Scripture. In your interpretation, it is important to adhere closely to the Scriptures, to interpret them correctly, and to refuse to "exceed what is written" (1 Cor. 4:6 NASB).

---

[11] Rick Yohn, *Discover Your Spiritual Gift and Use It* (Wheaton, IL: Tyndale, 1974), pp. 95–96.

Interpretation: The person with this gift has the supernatural ability to understand and proclaim what was hidden in the tongue or language spoken. He can interpret or translate into his own language the foreign language which he has never learned. This accompanies the gift of tongues as a confirmatory gift.

Devoted to Goodness

*"The overseer must be blameless as one entrusted with God's work, not arrogant, not prone to anger, not a drunkard, not violent, not greedy for gain. Instead he must be hospitable, **devoted to what is good**"* (Tit 1:7-8, emphasis added).

This is a man who overcomes evil with good (Rom 12:21). Paul summarized this concept well: "Finally, brothers and sisters, whatever is true, whatever is worthy of respect, whatever is just, whatever is pure, whatever is lovely, whatever is commendable, if something is excellent or praiseworthy, think about these things" (Phil 4:8).

Paul found this battle was not won in the flesh, but only through Christ (Rom 7:19). Titus 1:15-16 summarizes how the Christian wins the battle of good and evil: "All is pure to those who are pure. But to those who are corrupt and unbelieving, nothing is pure, but both their mind and conscience are corrupted. They profess to know God but with their deeds they deny him, since they are detestable, disobedient, and unfit for any good deed."

This victory comes more often to the mature, those becoming more like Christ, by presenting your body as a living sacrifice based upon God's mercy toward us in sending Jesus as an acceptable sacrifice (Rom 12:1-2).

This man walks consistently in God's will. His walk is based on knowledge of God's Word and the desire to walk in it (2 Tim 3:14-17). Besides knowledge of God's Word, this takes wisdom: "We . . . have not ceased praying for you and asking God to fill you with the knowledge of his will in all spiritual wisdom and understanding, so that you may live worthily of the Lord and please him in all respects: bearing fruit in every good deed, growing in the knowledge of God" (Col 1:9-11). James tells us this wisdom is there for the asking: "But if anyone is deficient in wisdom, he should ask God, who gives to all generously and without reprimand, and it will be given to him" (Jas 1:5).

Note: This material is adapted from Gene A. Getz, *The Measure of a Man*. (Ventura, CA: Regal Books, 1984).

Discovering Your Spiritual Gift

Now that you have a better understanding of what each gift is, you can begin to examine what your own gift may be. How does a person discover his or her spiritual gift? We have some suggestions to help you. Read through the following process of discovery.[12] Let this process guide you in your search as you apply it to your life.

---

[12] McRae, pp. 111–19. These six concepts and the related discussion are based on this book.

Focused Prayer

Before doing anything else, take some time to pray about your gift. God is the one who gave it to you. Let Him know you are thankful and desire to find out more about this gift. Let this discovery draw you closer to Him (Phil 4:6-7).

Careful Study

There are two areas on which you should focus your attention. The first is Scripture. Make note of the four chapters in Scripture where spiritual gifts are addressed at length: Romans 12, 1 Corinthians 12, Ephesians 4, and 1 Peter 4.

Study these passages and keep in mind that your understanding of the gifts should be rooted in the Word of God before you consider modern-day explanations. The second area where you must pay attention is to the people of God. God has provided countless examples of spiritual gifts through the lives of His people. Search the Bible for evidence of these people's gifts, and consider also the Christians whom you know today. The believers around you are saints of God. They are gifted individuals. Who do you know who is an exhorter? Evangelist? Pastor-teacher? Teacher? Helper? Administrator? Let these two areas, the Word of God and His people, minister to you as you discover your gift.

Personal Desire

Another thing to consider as you search for your spiritual gift is your own personal desire. What sorts of things interest you? Does a particular ministry intrigue you? For example, have you ever wanted to teach? Often God may lead us through our desires. Think about what you desire to do as you study His Word and "delight in His will." See if He leads you in this way. If it is not His direction, this next point will tell you so.

Demonstrated Ability

If you think you know God's spiritual gift in your life, act on it. Get involved in an activity in that area. Try a new experience. Let people know that you are available to be involved in a ministry activity. If it is the direction God has chosen for you, He will confirm it by giving you the capability. Give yourself time, of course, as it may not be immediately apparent that you have the gift. The ability may become evident with practice. Remember that giving you the competency to do something is often God's means of showing affirmation. Try several kinds of ministries to discover where you have ability.

Evident Blessing

Another means of discovering God's spiritual gift is by seeing if your work is accompanied by God's blessing. If your work is done to the glory of the Lord, He will bless you through His Holy Spirit. McRae suggests some ways that you might see this blessing: "It may simply be the joy of our overflowing hearts. It may be the salvation of souls, the edification of believers, the encouragement of a broken heart, the recovery of a backslider or the successful completion of a project. God's blessing will accompany it."

Affirmation of the Body

The recognition of your gift should take place as a function of the body of Christ. Do not rely on yourself as the final judge of whether or not you have a certain gift. Since the gifts are intended for building up the body, other members will be a primary source of encouragement as they observe your gift exercised in ministry. You will certainly want the wise counsel of the elders in your church, since they are responsible for overseeing the growth of the members. Additionally, you should seek out the opinions of other faithful Christian friends.

Functions of Small Groups

We have just discussed the biblical basis for small groups in the church. Now we will establish some practical guidelines for a group's formation. These guidelines include setting biblical goals and opening communication between the members. Before we move on to these practicalities, however, we will look at the purpose of the small group in light of church growth. The lesson title, "Edification Dynamics," shows the small group is meant to bring to the church opportunities for edification. But how does this happen? How does the church body grow through what takes place in its small groups?

According to the authors of *Dynamics of Church Growth*, the small groups in a church perform three functions that all build the body of the church. These functions are **spiritual intimacy**, **accountability, stimulation, and encouragement**.[13] The authors stress that small groups should not be self-contained and limiting. The key to enhancing corporate and individual growth is to keep the Lord as the center. As relationships are cultivated through spiritual intimacy, accountability, and encouragement, these relationships will be the attraction that draws people to the congregation of a church.

Spiritual Intimacy

One of the first advantages offered by a small group is spiritual intimacy. Christians are capable of sharing this closeness because they are united by the Holy Spirit. In Philippians 2:1-2, Paul encourages his believing friends by reminding them of who they are in Christ: "Therefore, if there is any encouragement in Christ, any comfort provided by love, any fellowship in the Spirit, any affection or mercy, complete my joy and be of the same mind, by having the same love, being united in spirit, and having one purpose."

Paul wants his friends enjoying the uncommon fellowship possible as fellow believers. Now read 1 Thessalonians 3. This chapter expresses Paul's love for his brothers in Christ. This is the spiritual intimacy that God hopes that we will share. How can your group begin to form this close bond?

Built on the Word of God. Spiritual intimacy is built on sharing the Word and praying for one another. This means that as the members of the group relate experiences in their lives, they are put in the context of Scripture. The leader must direct the members to the Word as they share. This direction prevents the conversation from dissolving into gossip, but instead throws light on the application of God's Word.

As a group leader, how can you put the experiences of your group members in the "context of Scripture"? Perhaps these next few questions will help.

    1. In what area of his life is the group member being challenged?

---

[13] This section on the functions of the small group is based on Jenson and Stevens, *Dynamics*, pp. 151–53.

2. Is his experience reflected by a specific example in the Bible? Remember, the Bible is made up of the stories of men and women who are part of God's plan in sharing His Gospel.

3. Does the group member's problem or praise seem similar to one of these personal accounts?

4. What did the person in the Bible learn about God?

5. Is the group member gaining a similar insight?

6. How do the lessons of Christ pertain to this member's experience?

Asking questions like these can bring Scripture into the lives of the group members. As members share how God has been present in their experiences, the believers become united by the Holy Spirit.

Built on prayer. In addition to sharing the Word, spiritual intimacy is built on prayer. As Christians pray for one another, they become involved in one another's lives. Requests can be shared without people feeling obligated to divulge personal information. Let trust be built in the group over time. Once the group feels comfortable about sharing prayer requests, it can be an exciting and encouraging experience to listen to the answers God has given.

The purpose of praying for our fellow Christians is to invest in their lives. When a person invests himself in anything, that item becomes more precious. As we become involved in prayer for others, then God's answers to them are answers for us as well. This investment brings us closer—closer to one another and closer to God. Spiritual intimacy is a natural outgrowth from this caring. Consequently, if small groups have spiritual intimacy, then the church's spiritual life is strengthened.

Accountability

The church body is also strengthened by developing accountability between group members. Proverbs 27:17 says, "As iron sharpens iron, so a person sharpens his friend." Accountability is the tool a person uses to help another achieve a goal.

For example, a person may wish to memorize more Scripture, but does not have the discipline to do it alone. When a group of friends try to achieve this same goal, they can keep each other faithful. The goal may even be breaking a bad habit, such as losing control of one's temper. Knowing that the group members will ask about his progress at each meeting helps the person control his anger throughout the week. When the person holding you accountable also shares Scripture with you and genuinely prays for your welfare, then the correction will be in love and the insight positive.

The small group setting is perfect for members to keep one another accountable. As the group shares and becomes closer, the members learn where the others need accountability. These needs are best met in a small setting where each person can reveal where he needs correction. As members stay faithful through accountability in small groups, then again the church body is strengthened.

Encouragement

In addition to spiritual intimacy and accountability, a small group offers encouragement to its members. Hebrews 10:23-25 says, "And let us hold unwaveringly to the hope that we confess, for the one who made the promise is trustworthy. And let us take thought of how to spur one another on to love and good works, not abandoning our own meetings, as some are in the habit of doing, but encouraging each other, and even more so because you see the day drawing near."

This passage alerts us to stimulating and encouraging one another as we assemble. "Something about being together with those who share a relationship to Christ is uniquely stimulating and encouraging."

What is it about meeting that is so inspiring? We are assured by Christ that He is present with us at all times (Mt 28:20). That is the essence of our encouragement and why we feel impelled toward love and good deeds when we are together. Our Lord is right there with us. As Christians gather, they are reminded of why they feel a common bond: Each person has a relationship with the Lord Jesus Christ. This common relationship is both stimulating and encouraging.

The encouragement felt as Christians meet in small groups is deepened by sharing with one another. Comfort comes from sharing similar experiences, and other Christians can often find the words to strengthen and motivate a person to faithfulness in his or her walk with God. It reinforces us to know that other Christians claim Christ's victory over struggles as well.

In conclusion, edification within a small group invests in the strength of the church body. Small groups provide strength as they build relationships, encourage personal growth, and supply leadership training. As the group members are edified, the church body grows stronger as well.

He Must Manage His Own Household Well

"The overseer then must be above reproach, the husband of one wife, temperate, self-controlled, respectable, hospitable, an apt teacher, not a drunkard, not violent, but gentle, not contentious, free from the love of money. **He must manage his own household well**" (1 Tim 3:2-4, emphasis added).

- *Paul is not saying that a man must have children to be a mature man or leader in the church.* He is not even saying an elder must be married. But if he has a family, he must measure up to this standard.

- *Paul is not referring to small children when he talks about keeping his children under control with all dignity.* The word Paul uses and the way he uses it seems to refer to grown children. Paul further defines the expected behavior for children in Titus 1:6: "With faithful children who cannot be charged with dissipation or rebellion." Eli is a good example of someone who disqualified himself from God's leadership position because of his son's behavior (1 Sam 2:12, 17; 3:13).

- *Paul is not referring to normal stages of a child's development.* Also, children should not be disciplined for the sake of one's own reputation, and a leader's children should not be held to a superior standard. If they are they will resent it.

- *Paul is not saying that a man must have a perfect family,* because all are in a process of growth.

- *Paul is not referring primarily to how successful someone is in business.*

- *Paul is not talking about how well a person can do church work.* Even highly successful Christian "leaders" may disqualify themselves at home.

He is looking for an entire household dedicated to Jesus Christ, a wife dedicated to her husband, and grown children who respect and love their parents. The members of a family draw much of their image of what God is like from the parents.

Note: This material is adapted from Gene A. Getz, *The Measure of a Man*. (Ventura, CA: Regal Books, 1984).

Of Good Reputation

"And he must be well thought of by those outside the faith, so that he may not fall into disgrace and be caught by the devil's trap" (1 Tim 3:7).

This is another significant spiritual mark of maturity. Other verses teach the same concept for all believers. They teach us to behave properly toward outsiders, conduct ourselves with wisdom toward outsiders, give no offense toward any man, and keep our behavior excellent among the Gentiles (1 Thess 4:11-12; Col 4: 5-6; 1 Cor 10:31-33; 1 Pet 2:12). It is clearly God's will that the Christian leader have a good reputation among outsiders.

But it is also inevitable that the Christian, just for being a Christian, will be reproached by unbelievers (Mt 5:11; 2 Tim 3:12; 1 Pet 4:14). Since they hated Jesus they will also hate us (Jn 15: 18-20). How then can these concepts be reconciled?

Reproach should come for a godly lifestyle but never for ungodly behavior. Peter teaches the difference: "But let none of you suffer as a murderer or thief or criminal or as a troublemaker. But if you suffer as a Christian, do not be ashamed, but glorify God that you bear such a name" (1 Pet 4:15-16).

One danger of appointing this person is that he will fall into the snare and reproach of the devil (1 Tim 3:7). This seems to mean the shame the person feels for the reproach he suffers and this leads to emotional problems (2 Cor 2:7; 1 Cor 5:1). Even Paul suffered from fear and emotional conflict—for godly behavior—when reproached verbally and physically by unsympathetic people (2 Cor 7:5-6). Believers are encouraged to persevere when doing the will of God (Heb 10:36). Those suffering for ungodly behavior are even more vulnerable.

Other dangers to avoid are anger and retaliation, which are the natural reaction of the immature, and only make the situation worse.

Note: This material is adapted from Gene A. Getz, *The Measure of a Man*. (Ventura, CA: Regal Books, 1984).

Paul's "One Another" Profile

Paul's letter to the Romans includes the most extensive "one another" profile. There are seven basic "one another" statements in chapters 12 to 16—the part of this letter that we call the practical section. The first 11 chapters are doctrinal and outline great truths of salvation. Chapters 12 to 16 outline how Christians are to live in view of their position in Christ.

The seven "one another" statements (based on NASB) are as follows:
- We are "members of one another" (Rom 12:5).
- We are to "be devoted to one another in brotherly love" (Rom 12:10a).
- We are to "give preference to one another in honor" (Rom 12:10c).
- We are to "be of the same mind with one another" (Rom 12:16a).

- We are to "accept one another, just as Christ also accepted us" (Rom 15:7).
- We are to "admonish one another" (Rom 15:14).
- We are to "greet one another" (Rom 16:16).

Several other New Testament letters include some unique "one anothers," (NASB) though somewhat similar in meaning to those in Romans. They are as follows:

- "Serve one another" (Gal 5:13).
- "Bear one another's burdens" (Gal 6:2).
- Show "forbearance to one another" (Eph 4:2).
- Be "subject to one another" (Eph 5:21).
- Encourage one another (1 Thess 5:11).[14]

As you study the "one another" injunctions just outlined and compare them with the total number of "one another" injunctions listed in the New Testament (approximately sixty), you will note the following:

1. The first seven "one anothers" which appear in Paul's letter to the Romans form a basic profile which in essence includes all of the other "one another" injunctions in the New Testament.

This is not surprising when we understand the basic purpose and content of the Roman letter. It is a very comprehensive epistle.

The first 11 chapters include all of the major doctrines of Christianity. And chapters 12 to 16 (where the "one anothers" appear), include all the major concepts regarding how members of the body of Christ should live and function.

2. These "one another" functions are to be carried out by all members of the body of Christ—not just by Christians who are specially gifted. This means that all believers are to be devoted to one another, to honor one another, to accept one another, to teach and admonish one another, to greet one another, to serve one another, to bear one another's burdens, to submit to one another, and to encourage one another.

These principles are biblical examples of ways to encourage fellow believers.

Now that we have moved beyond the history of small groups and their function in the church body, it is time to determine some practical goals for the groups in your church.

The Functioning Body

We cannot formulate leadership principles without looking carefully at another important dimension of New Testament churches total body function. The church is a unique entity. Even in its local expression, it is much more than an organization. Every localized group of believers is

---

[14] For an in-depth study of the "one another" injunctions in the New Testament, see the following books written by Gene A. Getz and published by Victor Books: *Building Up One Another, Loving One Another, Encouraging One Another, Praying for One Another,* and *Serving One Another.*

composed of individual members who are to function and be a part of the whole. The church is to be a dynamic organism.

There are several figures of speech used to describe the church but none so graphic as the term *soma* or "body."[15] Though exclusively a Pauline analogy, the word appears approximately thirty times to illustrate and describe the functioning body of Christ.

Approximately half the time Paul used the word literally to refer to the physical body. The rest of the times he applied the word to the "church" and called God's people the body of Christ. He described the church as being many members yet one body. However, all the members did not have the same function (Rom 12:4). All had gifts that differed according to the grace given by Christ (Rom 12:6). One member of the body could not say to the other, "I do not need you" (1 Cor 12:21). Since the church was "many members but one body" (12:20), all members were to contribute to the growth of the body. Anything that interfered with the functioning body interfered with the process of edification. This means, first and foremost, that every member of the body of Christ is important! In a sense, every member is a leader, called of God to help other members of the body to grow and mature.

Every "joint" must function and every individual part is to make its contribution to the life of the church. When this happens, the body of Christ will build itself up in love (Eph 4:16).

Spiritual Gifts

In studying the concepts of the functioning body in the New Testament, you cannot bypass references to spiritual gifts. Furthermore, there is a renewed interest on this subject in the twenty-first-century church. This is understandable, for the evangelical church in general has for years neglected the importance of body function and relational Christianity. We have come to rely on the "preacher" and the "pastor" to do the "work of the ministry."

What does the Bible actually teach about spiritual gifts? Many have attempted to answer this question. For years some evangelical Christians have taught that all of the gifts are present in the church today. They form a large segment of the body of Christ and identify themselves as "charismatic" Christians.[16] There's also a large segment of Christians who classify themselves as "noncharismatic." In turn, some noncharasmatics believe that some gifts are present but not all. Generally speaking, they contend that there were "sign gifts" which have ceased—such as the gift of tongues, prophesy, healing, etc. On the other hand, they believe that there are nonsign gifts which continue to be present in the church—such as the gifts of pastoring, teaching, evangelism, administration, etc.

There is a third category of evangelical Christians who believe that all gifts have ceased. They teach that the original gifts were all sign gifts to demonstrate the validity of the gospel and were also given to assist the body of Christ in functioning until a body of Christian truth was revealed to enable Christians to function in the body of Christ.

---

[15] Following are some additional metaphors and figures of speech used by scriptural writers to describe the church: The household of God (Eph 2:19); the building of God (1 Cor 3:9; Eph 2:20-22); the flock of God (Acts 20:28; 1 Pet 5:2); the bride of Christ (2 Cor 11:2; Eph 5:22-32); the temple of God (1 Cor 3:16-17; Eph 2:20-22).

[16] The word *charismatic* is derived from the Greek word *charisma* which was used frequently to refer to the gifts of the Holy Spirit.

It should be added that within each of these general viewpoints are varied opinions regarding what these gifts are, their purposes, how they should be used in the church, and how Christians discover their gifts.

In view of so many different viewpoints, is it possible to discover what the Bible actually teaches on this subject? Several years ago I decided to face that question as objectively as possible. As much as it was humanly possible, I attempted to lay aside my own presuppositions regarding this subject and once again study through the New Testament noting every reference to spiritual gifts and the context in which they appeared, in order to try to discover what scriptural writers were actually saying. As a result of this process I made the following observations:

1. **The number and kinds of gifts varied significantly from church to church in the New Testament world.**

This observation is based on the list of gifts mentioned in the letters written to various churches. Note the following:

The Letter to the Corinthians

(1 Cor 12:8-10)
- Word of wisdom
- Word of knowledge
- Faith
- Healing
- Miracles
- Prophecy
- Distinguishing of spirits
- Tongues
- Interpretation of tongues

(1 Cor 12:23)
- Apostles
- Prophets
- Teachers
- Miracles
- Healing
- Helps
- Administrations
- Tongues

The Letter to the Romans

(Rom 12:6-8)
- Prophesies
- Serving
- Teaching
- Exhortation

Lesson 6 Articles

- Giving
- Leading
- Mercy

The Letter to the Ephesians

(Eph 4:11)
- Apostles
- Prophets
- Evangelists
- Pastors
- Teachers

Peter's Letter to Various Churches

(1 Peter 4:11)
- Speaking
- Serving

Why is this variation significant? The Corinthian church had more gifts manifested than any other New Testament church.

Paul affirmed this in his introductory remarks in his first letter when he wrote that they were gifted "in all speech and all knowledge ... not lacking in any gift" (1 Cor 1:5, 7, NASB).

The Roman church was also a gifted church. But note that only two of the gifts mentioned in the Roman list (prophecy and teaching) are mentioned in the Corinthian list. Likewise, the Ephesian list, though shorter, includes two additional gifts (evangelists and pastors) not included in the Corinthian letters or the Roman list.

What this seems to indicate is that there was a significant difference in the kinds of gifts manifested from church to church in the New Testament. Furthermore, some of them had many gifts; others had fewer. Therefore, as twenty-first-century Christians, we must be careful not to total the gift list in the New Testament and conclude that it is God's will and plan for this total list to be present in every twenty-first-century church. If it were not so in the New Testament churches, it is only logical it would not be true in churches today.

2. **The passages where gifts are referred to most extensively are written to correct the improper use of spiritual gifts.**

The Corinthian Church

The Corinthians, who represent the most gifted church mentioned in the New Testament, were definitely misusing their gifts. It was not a matter of knowing what their gifts were. Rather, they were using their gifts inappropriately.

First, some were evidently using their gifts to build themselves up while putting others down. They were guilty of spiritual pride. If not, why would Paul spend most of chapter 12 emphasizing that "one part of the body" should not say to "another part of the body" that it had no need for the other? (1 Cor 12:21) Note the following key statements that emphasize this point:

- "If the foot should say, 'Because I'm not a hand, I'm not a part of the body' it is not for this reason any the less a part of the body."

- "And if the ear should say, 'Because I'm not an eye, I'm not part of the body,' it is not for this reason any the less a part of the body."
- "If the whole body were an eye, where would the hearing be? If the whole were hearing, where would the sense of smell be?" (1 Cor 12:17, NASB)
- "And if they were all the same member, where would the body be?" (1 Cor 12:19).
- "And the eye cannot say to the hand, 'I have no need of you'; or again the head to the feet, 'I have no need of you'" (1 Cor 12:21, NASB).
- "On the contrary, those members that seem to be weaker are essential; and those members we consider less honorable, we clothe with greater honor, and our unpresentable members are clothed with dignity, but our presentable members do not need this. Instead God has blended together the body giving greater honor to the lesser member, so that there may be no division in the body, but the members may have mutual concern for one another" (1 Cor 12:22-25).

Second, the Corinthians were giving attention to the "lesser gifts" while neglecting the "greater gifts."

Paul clearly stated what the greater gifts were "first, apostles; second, prophets; third, teachers." He then listed the lesser gifts: miracles and gifts of healing, helps, administrations, various kinds of tongues (1 Cor 12:28). He then made his point. The Corinthians should "be eager for the greater gifts" (1 Cor 12:31). The context clearly indicates that they were giving attention primarily to the lesser gifts (see chapter 14).

Third, the Corinthians were not only giving priority to the lesser gifts, but they were misusing them in the church. (Again, carefully read chapter 14.) There was disorder and confusion.

Thus, Paul ended chapter 14 with this exhortation: "But let all things be done properly and in an orderly manner" (1 Cor 14:40, NASB).

The Roman Church

The Roman church evidently did not have as many problems as the Corinthians relative to the way in which they were using their spiritual gifts. However, one problem seems to be the same—the presence of spiritual pride. This is the context in which Paul discussed their gifts and emphasized humility. Thus, before listing the gifts, he wrote: "For just as we have many members in one body and all the members do not have the same function, so we, who are many are one body in Christ and individually members one of another" (Rom 12:4-5, NASB).

Furthermore, before emphasizing unity in the body, and prior to listing the gifts he warned against pride and emphasized humility. Thus we read: "For through the grace given to me, I say to everyone among you not to think more highly of himself than he ought to think; but to think so as to have sound judgment, as God has allotted to each a measure of faith" (Rom 12:3, NASB).

The Ephesian Church

We see the same emphasis in the Ephesian letter. Before listing the gifts, he wrote: " Live worthily of the calling with which you have been called, with all humility. . . making every effort to keep the unity of the Spirit in the bond of peace. . . . But to each one of us grace was given according to the measure of the gift of Christ" (Eph 4:1-3, 7).

These are important observations. Frequently, we use these passages to teach the importance of gifts and that every believer should try to discover his gift or gifts. This is not Paul's point in these three letters. If anything, Paul was trying to temper the use of gifts and, most important, he was exhorting all believers not to use their gifts to elevate themselves in the local assembly and thus destroy unity in the church. Striving for oneness and unity through humility is the primary theme in all of the spiritual gift passages in Scripture.[17]

3. **Nowhere in the Bible does it say we are, as individuals, to search for or to try to discover our spiritual gifts.**

This is also an important observation—one that I personally found difficult to acknowledge and accept. The reason is that I had been emphasizing the opposite, just as many Christians today emphasize looking for and discovering gifts. Furthermore, we use the passages just outlined in the previous section to make that point. As just illustrated, that is definitely not the thrust of these passages. These people clearly knew what their gifts were. They weren't searching for them. Rather, they were misusing the gifts that were so obvious among them.

What about 1 Corinthians 12:31 and 1 Corinthians 14:13? This is a very legitimate question. We need to look at these verses which may appear to contradict this third observation. After Paul outlined the greater and lesser gifts in the Corinthian letter (1 Cor 12:28-30), he then exhorted, "But be eager for the greater gifts" (1 Cor 12:31).

And then at the beginning of chapter 14, he wrote, "Be eager for the spiritual gifts" (1 Cor 14:1).

A careful evaluation of these specific texts, as well as the contexts, demonstrates that Paul was not encouraging individual Christians in Corinth to seek to be apostles, prophets, and teachers (the greater gifts—1 Cor 12:28). Rather, he was exhorting these Christians to give priority to those with these greater gifts. Thus he used the second person plural in the Greek text. We can legitimately paraphrase his statement in 1 Corinthians 12:31 as follows: "But, you as a church, desire that the greater gifts be manifested rather than the lesser gifts." In 1 Corinthians 14:1 he broadened his statement. Again we can paraphrase: "As a body of believers pursue love, yet as a body desire earnestly that spiritual gifts be manifested, but give particular attention to the prophets rather than the tongue-speakers" (see 1 Cor 14:2-4).

We see a similar emphasis when Paul wrote to the Romans and told them he longed to see them so that he might impart some spiritual gift to them (Rom 1:11). When we realize that Paul had never been to Rome and when we look at the context of this statement in verse 11, we can see more clearly what Paul meant.

The gift he wanted to impart was his own unique contribution to their spiritual growth. Since Paul possessed all of the greater gifts (1 Tim 2:7; Acts 13:1), he would be able to help them in a special way. Furthermore, he wanted to be ministered to by them through a mutual relationship (Rom 1:12).

Thus we must conclude from the whole of Scripture that individual Christians are never instructed to search for or to try to discover spiritual gifts. To do so would be to emphasize something that the Bible doesn't emphasize. Paul particularly implied that if a person is gifted in some special way, that individual will know it and other Christians will know it too. It has nothing to do with human effort, for God has chosen to sovereignly bestow these gifts apart from any searching or even asking (Acts 2:1-4; 10:44-48; 1 Cor 1:4-7; 2 Tim 1:6). Thus we read in the Hebrew letter that God bore witness to the message of the gospel, "both by signs and wonders and by various miracles and by gifts of the Holy Spirit according to His own will" (Heb 2:4).

---

[17] Note that the same is true in the context of 1 Peter 4:11.

4. **The Scriptures emphasize that there is a more excellent way than an emphasis on the gifts of the Spirit.**

We've already seen this to be true in our study of what the Bible defines as a mature church. After Paul told the Corinthians to earnestly desire the greater gifts rather than the lesser gifts (1 Cor 12:28-31a), he went on to say, "And I show you a still more excellent way" (1 Cor 12:31b, NASB). Paul then made it clear that a Christian may have the gift of tongues (1 Cor 13:1), the gifts of prophecy, knowledge, and faith (1 Cor 13:2), as well as the gift of giving (1 Cor 13:3), and yet lack love, the most important quality in Christian living.

If so, we are "nothing" (1 Cor 13:2); all of these gifts profit nothing (1 Cor 13:3).

The Corinthians lacked love, and yet again as far as we know they were the most gifted church in the New Testament. And because they were carnal and immature, Paul urged them to do away with "childish ways" (1 Cor 13:11). Though he did not forbid them to desire that spiritual gifts be used (1 Cor 14:1), he exhorted them to make it a priority to pursue love, for without this quality, all of their gifts were basically meaningless.

5. **When local church leaders were to be appointed, Paul did not instruct Timothy and Titus to look for spiritual gifts; rather, he instructed them to look for spiritual qualifications and maturity.**

This is one of the most significant observations regarding spiritual gifts. When I noticed this, several questions went through my mind. Why didn't Paul tell Timothy and Titus to look for the gifts of administration and leading? After all, these men were to manage the church (1 Tim 5:17). Why didn't Paul instruct them to look for the gift of pastor? Of teacher? Again, this was to be their responsibility (1 Pet 5:2; Acts 20:28; Tit 1:9). And since they were to pray for the sick (Jas 5:14), wouldn't they need the gift of healing?

Though these elder functions were definitely outlined in Scripture, Paul said nothing about selecting these men on the basis of the spiritual gifts that related to these functions. Again, the question is why?

We see the same approach in the appointment of deacons and deaconesses. Since these people were to be involved in serving roles, why didn't Paul specify that they were to be selected if they had the gift of serving? And what about the gifts of helps, and mercy? And certainly their cultural responsibilities would require that they be good organizers. And yet there is nothing stated about the gift of administration and leading. And again, we must ask why?

Some have pointed out that Paul does mention the requirement to "be able to teach" (1 Tim 3:2, NASB). Is this not the gift of teaching?

First of all, it would be strange that Paul would refer to this gift and say nothing about the gifts of managing and pastoring when these were to be the primary functions of an elder. The facts are that Paul is very pragmatic about the ability to manage, using the family as a basic criteria in determining a man's ability in this area. Thus, he said, "If someone does not know how to manage his own household, how will he care for the church of God?" (1 Tim 3:5). With this requirement, Paul was implying that every Christian father was responsible to be a good manager of his household. He could not use the excuse that he was not especially gifted in this area.

Regarding being "able to teach," Paul illustrates beautifully what this concept means in his second letter to Timothy. Here Paul used this quality in the context of a number of other spiritual characteristics. Writing to Timothy, he said, "And the Lord's bond-servant must not be quarrelsome, but be kind to all, able to teach, patient when wronged, with gentleness correcting those who are in opposition, if perhaps God may grant them repentance leading to the knowledge of the truth" (2 Tim 2:24-25. NASB).

Notice the cluster of words surrounding the quality of being "able to teach." It is clear from these characteristics that Paul is dealing with a quality of life that demonstrates an even temper, kindness, patience, and gentleness. In essence, Paul was saying that when a spiritual leader faces people who oppose what he is teaching, if he is "able to teach" he will respond in a nondefensive and nonthreatening way. Though he will be firm in what he believes, he will not respond in a quarrelsome, negative, and insensitive way. This, Paul was saying, is very important in being able to communicate with those who are initially unresponsive to the Word of God.

It is difficult to explain satisfactorily why Paul bypassed any reference to the gifts of the Spirit when he listed the qualifications for spiritual leaders. However, it is not necessary to have a clear-cut answer when we realize that this observation correlates with an earlier observation; that is, that nowhere in the Bible does it say we are as individuals to search for or try to discover our spiritual gifts before we can function in the body of Christ. And this leads us to a final observation, which is perhaps the most interesting of all.

6. **Body function is not dependent on spiritual gifts, but rather on biblical teaching and a love and concern for one another.**

The Greek word *allelon* frequently translated "one another" is used approximately sixty times in the New Testament, excluding the Gospels. Paul leads the list for frequency, having used the word forty times. And just as basic doctrines are repeated from letter to letter in the New Testament, so are many of these "one another" injunctions. This is understandable, since these letters were originally designed to be self-contained for particular churches.

Types of Small Groups

There are several types of small groups that can be helpful in your church. This list is not inclusive, but it provides foundational ideas that you can use to establish groups that meet the needs of your congregation.

Fellowship Groups:

These groups have a goal to develop fellowship relationships with each other. Fellowship groups are the least structured of the various groups because the goal is simply giving people an opportunity to know others in a more personal way. This gives time for people to find out about each other and start closer friendships. Fellowship groups are helpful when a church has grown large enough that believers cannot easily get to know others in the church.

Bible Study Groups:

The purpose is to study the Scriptures in a more personal setting. Bible study in a small group context allows believers to learn from each other and to mutually encourage each other to apply the Scripture they study.

Growth Groups:

These use Scripture as a catalyst to study or discuss topics such as marriage, singleness, child rearing, and relating to one's work as a Christian.

Lesson 6 Articles

Target Groups:

These are ministry oriented groups in which a small group of believers meets together to minister to specific people. For example, they may meet together to plan and carry out ministry to older people, hospitalized people, or children.

Accountability Groups:

These people enter into a mutual commitment to each other to deal with personal issues in their lives. They commit to pray for each other and to deal honestly and openly with what they see in each other's lives as they meet and share. They depend upon a willingness of each believer to be open about his or her own life and the spiritual and personal issues he or she deals with.

Unity, Diversity, and Interdependence

Notice how Paul in 1 Corinthians 12:12-27 compares the life of the church to the relationships and functions of the human body. In this passage, we can learn three key things that will help the church to function according to God's design. Remember that they are dependent upon one another:

1. **Unity**—1 Corinthians 12:12-13. Paul points out that there is only one body but many members. Even though there are many members, they make one body. We are all united together by the one Spirit. We are unified by the Spirit of God. This means that we are to function together as a whole.

2. **Diversity**—1 Corinthians 12:14–19. We are taught that though there is one body, it is made up of many different members. Each member is important. You could not have a body if all the members were the same.

3. **Interdependence**—1 Corinthians 12:20–27. Each member of the body is dependent on the other. If a member is not functioning properly, it hurts the function of the body as a whole. In the church everyone is needed! We need each other to function as we should.

The church fulfills its purpose on earth only when it functions as God designed it. In order for this to happen, we must believe and apply the principles that we studied above from 1 Corinthians.

First, for the body to function properly, it must be unified. All members must work together for the good of the whole.

Second, we must recognize that different members are necessary. We must appreciate one another for our distinctiveness and our different contributions to the building up of the body of Christ. Each member of the body should be enabled to make his or her unique contribution by being encouraged and empowered to serve using his or her area of giftedness.

Third, we must remember that we are dependent upon one another. In a physical bod, each part is dependent on the others and cannot exist or function alone. In the body of Christ, none of us, no matter what our gift, can function well alone. We are reminded not to think of ourselves as separate or independent, but as needing each other.

What is a Spiritual Gift? Part I

In the Bible, one of the words translated "spiritual gift" is the word **charisma**. It signifies the gift of salvation through God's grace, and also the special ability God gives each believer to function in the church.[18] **Charisma** has been translated also to mean "grace gift."

The significance of these gifts makes it important for us to discover what our particular spiritual gift is so that we may put it to effective use. Some scholars, including the author of our text, Gene Getz, believe that God does not intend for Christians to search out their gift. They believe that it will be made manifest over time and practice.

Getz has formed this opinion based on an inference from Paul's discussion of spiritual gifts. His interpretation is that Paul's purpose in most of his references to spiritual gifts is to correct their improper use. Paul wrote to people who became proud because of their gifts, maintaining that love and humility should accompany their use.

Getz also believes that Paul's exhortations to desire spiritual gifts are not directed to individuals at all, but to the church as a body. He encourages them to give priority to love and the greater gifts, and not focus on the use (misuse) of the lesser gifts. Getz also notes that Paul emphasizes personal and corporate maturity. Thus, for Getz, focusing on love and the greater gifts brings a church to maturity.

What is a Spiritual Gift? Part II

While we agree with Getz that the Bible does not teach that believers must search for and discover their spiritual gift **before** they can function as members in Christ's body,[19] we believe that a thoughtful search for one's gift brings greater opportunity for service in His body. Even if, as Getz correctly says, 1 Corinthians 14:1 means that the church **body** should desire that spiritual gifts be manifested, it is important to remember that spiritual gifts are manifested by **individuals**, not by the body corporately.

Therefore, knowledge of one's gift is helpful to its manifestation in the body. In fact, one of the primary arguments for discovering one's spiritual gift is that Paul indicates gifts are necessary for the proper functioning of the body (1 Cor 12; Eph 4). Getz is correct in placing the emphasis on the maturity of the body and of the individual believer, but we should not forget that the exercise of individual spiritual gifts is a means of building up the body of Christ to maturity (1 Cor 12:7; 14:12; Eph 4:11-13).

The search for one's spiritual gift, or even the exercise of one's spiritual gift, is never the primary goal of the Christian life. Rather, it is one important aspect of serving Jesus Christ. Our purpose is not to glorify the believer who possesses the gift, but to enable him to glorify God by his unique contribution through the exercise of his spiritual gift. For this reason, we will discuss later how a person may recognize his gift.

First of all, however, let us begin by defining the term "spiritual gift." We will start by examining what a spiritual gift is **not**. A spiritual gift is neither a natural talent, a fruit of the Spirit, nor an

---

[18] J. G. S. S. Thomson and Walter A. Elwell, "Spiritual Gifts," in *Evangelical Dictionary of Theology* (Grand Rapids, MI: Baker, 1984), p. 1042.

[19] Gene A. Getz, *Building Up One Another* (Wheaton, IL: Victor, 1979), p. 13.

office of the church.[20]

A natural talent is similar to a spiritual gift in that it is given by God, but the two are not the same. One reason is that talents are often inherited through family, while a spiritual gift is not related to heredity. In addition, while a person may be talented in a particular area, such as teaching, this talent does not necessarily signify one's spiritual gift. A person may be an excellent teacher but not have the **gift** of teaching. The difference is that God's gift of teaching has a "power and blessing" that is absent from the natural talent.[21] Often a spiritual gift may be related to natural talent (which, of course, is also a gift from God) in that the Holy Spirit manifests Himself in the believer's life in a special way through that talent.

A spiritual gift is also not one of the fruits of the Spirit as listed in Galatians 5:22-23. These character qualities are what the Spirit wishes to cultivate in our lives, but they are not spiritual gifts.

In addition, an office in the church is not a spiritual gift. Many churches have elders (1 Tim 3:1-7) and deacons (1 Tim 3:8-13), but these offices are not to be confused with a spiritual gift.[22] The men who fill these offices should be gifted in such a way that they are able to function in their office, but the gift is not the same thing as the office.

What, then, is the definition of a spiritual gift? According to McRae, a good definition is the following:[23]

> A divine endowment of a special ability for service upon a member of the body of Christ; an ability to function effectively and significantly in a particular service as a member of Christ's body, the church.

---

[20] William J. McRae, *The Dynamics of Spiritual Gifts* (Grand Rapids, MI: Zondervan, 1976), pp. 17–18.

[21] Ibid., pp. 20–21.

[22] Ibid., p. 18.

[23] Ibid.

Unit Three: Applying the Three Lenses, Part II

We applied the three lenses of Scripture, history, and culture to the subjects of worship and edification in the previous unit. We discovered that individual members, as well as their leaders, have ministry responsibilities. All worship their Lord corporately and help edify each other in their Christian faith.

In Unit Three, we continue applying the three lenses as **we** look at multiplication and leadership. For the Church to grow and edify, the churches must reach out to their communities with the Gospel. As individuals open their hearts and souls to Christ, it is imperative that we have strong church leaders to shepherd and support the new followers of Christ as they grow in the Christian faith.

Pastor Eugene now finds himself even more curious about multiplication and leadership and his role as a church leader. He recognizes that his new-found knowledge discovered in Units One and Two of this course are only part of the puzzle of becoming a godly and successful church leader. This enlightenment has ignited a new desire to seek out more information of multiplication and church leadership.

To support Pastor Eugene, and you, in your spiritual journey as a church leader, Unit Three presents relevant information from three distinct perspectives. Lesson 7 examines personal, corporate, and expansion evangelism in relation to church leadership. Lesson 8 deals with the study of who the leaders of the church are and what their responsibilities are, as found in the New Testament. And finally, Lesson 9 rounds out the learning experience by presenting the qualifications and development of well-prepared church leaders.

Unit 3 Outline: Applying the Three Lenses, Part II

Lesson 7: Multiplication Dynamics
Lesson 8: Leadership Dynamics, Part I
Lesson 9: Leadership Dynamics, Part II

Lesson 7: Multiplication Dynamics

Lesson Introduction

At the beginning of this course, we stated that the church is an organism—alive and growing. In the previous lessons, we considered those dynamics which help the church experience meaningful worship and the members mature in their Christian walk. In Lesson 7, we will examine the issues associated with the numerical growth of our church. To achieve this goal, the church must grow spiritually as the size of its flock increases. Remember, both spiritual and numeric growth of a church magnifies God's glory.

Multiplication emphasizes the church's need to grow in size and to disciple new converts. In this lesson, you will examine Scripture passages pertaining to the evangelistic mission of the church, as well as two assigned readings by Getz titled "Making Disciples" and "Principles of New Testament Evangelism." The goal is to further refine your thinking on this topic to develop more effective strategies for multiplication in the ministry the Lord has entrusted to you.

Lesson Outline

Lesson 7: Multiplication Dynamics
    Topic 1: The Great Commission
    Topic 1: Personal and Corporate Evangelism
    Topic 2: New Testament Principles of Evangelism
    Topic 3: Developing Character—Upright, Devout, Not a Recent Convert

Lesson Objectives

At the completion of Lesson 7, you will be able to:

- Define at least five New Testament principles of evangelism and the reasons for your choices based on your own study of selected New Testament passages
- List and briefly define seven principles of New Testament evangelism, as described in the chapter "Principles of New Testament Evangelism"
- Integrate the characteristics of uprightness, devotion to Christ, and spiritual maturity into your life and your leadership selection process.

Topic 1: The Great Commission

Just prior to His earthly departure, the Lord Jesus Christ summarized for the disciples the ministry He had prepared for them in the Great Commission (Mt. 28:19-20a):

> *Therefore go and make disciples of all nations, baptizing them in the name of the Father and the Son and the Holy Spirit, teaching them to obey everything I have commanded you*

Looking carefully at the original text in these passages, Pastor Eugene clearly understands that the actions

Jesus' Ascension

Christ has identified are expressed as commands. Christ tells us to "go and make disciples," "baptizing them," and "teaching them." His words are plain and achievable; they urge *action*! As church leaders, our duty is to go forth and teach the Word of God to "make disciples."

Jesus' great commission is like the speech a general gives before entering an important battle. Sir Winston Churchill, leader of Britain during WWII, was famous for giving inspirational speeches. One was titled "This Was Their Finest Hour." He spoke this phrase while encouraging his people to perform their duties in such a way that others would comment: "This was their finest hour."

Jesus' battle is to win souls, and He sends each of us on a mission to spread the Gospel. To find the inspiration and teaching needed for success, we must search God's Word for principles of evangelism or, stated in another way, the equivalent of our marching orders. These orders apply both to individual believers and to the church corporately. To find the marching orders for the evangelizing believer, please continue working through this topic.

QUESTION 1
Carefully study this important passage: Matthew 28:18-20. To help with this study, open your Life Notebook and number the lines 1-7. Then record your answers to the following questions:

1. Who is speaking and who is addressed?
2. How is verse 18 connected to verses 19 and 20?
3. What is a disciple?
4. How does one go about making a disciple?
5. What is the meaning of "all the nations"?
6. Why is "baptizing" mentioned in this passage? What does it contribute to the discipling process?
7. What role does "teaching" play in disciple-making? What should be taught?

Reading Assignment

When you have finished answering Question 1, compare your thoughts with the considerations from the article titled "The Great Commission" in the Articles section at the end of this lesson.

Topic 1 Key Points:

- A healthy church must emphasize winning men and women to Christ and teaching them to become His lifelong disciples.
- Christ tells us to "go and make disciples," "baptizing them" and "teaching them."
- We must evangelize and train the flock of God to do likewise.

Topic 2: Personal and Corporate Evangelism

From the previous topic, Pastor Eugene realized that while evangelism and disciple-making is the responsibility of each Christian, it is also the purpose of the entire local church. He realized that his local church must consider how they can impact their community. Please continue reading through this topic to learn more about principles for personal and corporate evangelism.

Getz emphasizes this in his chapters "Making Disciples" and "Principles of New Testament Evangelism." He believes people must, wherever they are and in whatever culture, creatively apply biblical principles to develop their own ministry forms and to become a corporate witness.

QUESTION 2

Match the passage in the left-hand column with the corresponding clues given for evangelistic ministry in the right-hand column.

Passage	Teaching
Mark 16:15	Go in the Holy Spirit's power to the ends of the earth.
John 13:34-35; 17:21-22	Preach the Gospel so men might hear and believe.
Acts 1:8	Proclaim the Gospel to everyone.
Acts 11:19-21	Christians love one another with the unity of the Godhead.
Romans 10:14-15	Go into the world and preach the Gospel to everyone.

QUESTION 3

Match the passage in the left-hand column with the corresponding clues given for evangelistic ministry in the right-hand column.

Passage	Teaching
2 Corinthians 5:17-21	The Lord wants all to come to repentance.
1 Thessalonians 1:8	Fulfill your ministry by doing an evangelist's work.
2 Timothy 4:5	We must spread the Lord's message.
1 Peter 3:15	Always be ready to testify about our hope.
2 Peter 3:9	We are ambassadors of Christ's salvation from sin.

Reading Assignment

Please read the textbook chapter titled "Chapter 4: Making Disciples" in *Sharpening the Focus of the Church* in the Articles section at the end of this lesson.

QUESTION 4

There is very little direct instruction in the Epistles regarding evangelism. *True or False?*

QUESTION 5

The following includes some areas of the Christian lifestyle that the Epistles mention as being important for evangelism. For each area, record in your life notebook how Christians in your culture could demonstrate their Christian lifestyle:

1. Business life
2. Social life
3. Home life
4. Church life
5. Life in general

Topic 2 Key Points:

- At the end of the three-and-a-half years, Jesus had basically accomplished two major goals in terms of strategy: He had saturated the minds of the multitudes with His teachings, and prepared a small group of men (disciples) in depth to enter into His labors and bring in the harvest.

- Emphasis on "verbal presentation" of the Gospel was subordinated to "maintaining a dynamic relationship within the church" and "maintaining a loving, exemplary relationship" with those in the world.
- As recounted across the Epistles, early Christians used many different types of communication to spread the Gospel message. Communication methods were varied by the cultures to whom they spoke and the accepted communication practices in those cultures.

Topic 3: New Testament Principles of Evangelism

As we have repeatedly seen throughout this course, we must have established principles by which to formulate relevant evangelism plans. Let us take a few moments, then, to talk about some principles of evangelism.

It's interesting to look at the first recorded push of evangelism in the early church. It was not triggered by the believers' great desire to fulfill the Great Commission, as we humanly might expect (Mt 28:18-20). Believers were exhorted by Jesus to go to all the nations and were promised the power to fulfill this commission. But instead of spreading out and carrying out their mandate, they all remained in Jerusalem. It took the persecution that arose after Stephen's martyrdom to scatter the believers, and, as they scattered, the Holy Spirit worked through them to preach the Gospel and gain converts (Acts 8). Salvation is truly a work of God, but we must faithfully fulfill our roles (Rom 10:14-15).

Jesus' command to the church was to go out into the world and preach the Gospel, not stay in Jerusalem and remain isolated (Mt 28:18-20). In this case, persecution by non-believers scattered Jesus' followers and caused them to carry His message out into the world (Acts 8:1-40). Regardless of whether this scattering was the result of God's plan or was God's response to the evil that men do, the ultimate result, as always, was that God's command to spread the Gospel was carried out.

As church leaders, it is our honor, responsibility, and duty to freely follow the command that Jesus issued to us. Pastor Eugene firmly believes that freely following the commands of Jesus is an honor and his responsibility as a church leader; therefore, he is eager to learn more about New Testament principles of evangelism.

Reading Assignment

Please read the textbook chapter titled "Chapter 5: Principles of New Testament Evangelism" in the Articles section at the end of this lesson.

QUESTION 6

Short-term mission trips for church members increase a church's desire for evangelism and missions. *True or False?*

QUESTION 7

Who should be the primary target for evangelism? *(Select all that apply.)*
- A. Children
- B. Adults
- C. Households
- D. Infants

Topic 3 Key Points:

The following New Testament principles will guide you in carrying out the Great Commission:
- Every body of believers must be responsible for its own community first.
- Corporate evangelism forms the foundation for personal evangelism.
- When possible, presenting the Gospel to the unsaved is to take place against the backdrop of a loving and unified body of Christians.
- The primary target for evangelism should be adults and, consequently, whole households.
- The church is responsible to identify those who have a desire to carry the Good News in a special way out into the community and beyond the immediate community, even to "the remotest part of the earth."
- New believers, as soon as possible, should be integrated into the life of the church.
- The church must develop its own contemporary forms and approaches to evangelism using the principles and purposes just stated as biblical guidelines.

QUESTION 8

Open your Life Notebook and review the principles in the Topic 3 Key Points.
- Choose one or two principles that are well executed in your church and write about some of your best practices in this area.
- Choose one or two principles that could be implemented better in your congregation and write an action plan for the improvements you'd like to see.

Topic 4: Developing Character—Upright, Devout, Not a Recent Convert

Our work on developing Christ's character in ourselves continues with our study on the leadership qualities of being upright, devout, and not a recent convert.

Who will fight the military battle when the situation is darkest? There are many stories of heroism in battle we could use to illustrate. Biblically, at a maturing stage as a believer, Peter denied the Lord rather than suffer with Him (Mk 14:66-72). Later, he lived a faithful life and endured persecution (Jn 21:1-19; Acts 4:1-21; Acts 5:17-42). What caused the change in Peter's behavior? Peter's character developed in the power of the Holy Spirit, and he was an effective leader of God's people (Jn 21:15-19).

Upright

Reading Assignment

Please read the article titled "Upright" in the Articles section at the end of this lesson.

QUESTION 9

Two things must be true for a man to become wise and just. He must be_____ and_____.

   A. Spiritually and psychologically mature

   B. Excited and full of joy for the Lord

   C. Wise and knowledgeable about the Bible

   D. An exceptional non-Christian and psychologically mature

QUESTION 10

Match the passage in the left-hand column with teaching from the reading about being **upright** in the right-hand column.

Passage	Teaching
Romans 1:17	The believer's positional righteousness
Acts 10:22	Setting your mind to please and serve God
Hebrews 5:11-14	Cornelius's practical righteousness
1 Kings 3:5-9	Solomon humbly asks God for wisdom
Daniel 1:8	No one wise enough in this church to settle disputes
1 Corinthians 6:1-5	Believers not maturing by practicing righteousness

Devout

Reading Assignment

Please read the article titled "Devout" in the Articles section at the end of this lesson.

QUESTION 11

Match the passage in the left-hand column with teaching from the reading about being **devout** in the right-hand column.

Passage	Teaching
Ephesians 4:1	We can only avoid immoral people by going out of the world.
Hebrews 7: 26	Paul exhorts us to walk worthy of our calling.
Matthew 9:9-12	Jesus was questioned about mingling with sinners.
1 Corinthians 5:9-10	Believers could imitate Paul as he imitated Christ.
Matthew 5:13-16	We must be salt and light in the world.
1 Thessalonians 2:10	Paul's behavior was holy and righteous and blameless before the church .
1 Corinthians 11:1	Jesus was innocent, undefiled, and separated—not isolated—from sinners.

Not a Recent Convert

Reading Assignment

Please read the article titled "Not a Recent Convert" in the Articles section at the end of this lesson.

QUESTION 12

Match the passage in the left-hand column from the reading on "Not a Recent Convert" with the description of the person filled with pride in the right-hand column.

Passage	Person
Isaiah 14:12-14	Being saved by grace eliminates pride.
1 Timothy 6:3-4	The conceit of false teachers
Ephesians 2:8-9	King Hezekiah is judged for his pride.
James 4:6	Satan fell because of pride.
2 Chronicles 32:26-33	God opposes the proud.

QUESTION 13

Give some thought to how your church can reach out to the people in your community. Open your Life Notebook and write down your observations and ideas. The following thoughts may help:

- It is best to have a clear idea of those to whom you desire to direct your evangelistic efforts. Can you identify some logical "target groups" for evangelism? Consider the following:
  1. Are there different ethnic groups that live near your church?
  2. What special groups are in the area of your church?
     University students
     Business people
     Government workers
     Military
     Homeless people
     Medical personnel

- When you have identified some "target groups" to whom you might reach out, identify some ways that you might make contact with them. Look for the following:
  1. Points of **stress**

     Are people in economic stress? Families feeling relational stress? Marriages struggling?

     What does the Gospel offer to meet these stresses?

  2. Points of **need**

     What are the particular personal needs of the people in the target group? Is there a need for counseling? for food? for information? for housing?

     How can you minister to those points of need in order to gain a hearing for the Gospel?

  3. Points of **interest**

What are the people in the target group interested in? What do they think about most often? What do they want to talk about?

How can you get involved in the things they are interested in so that the Gospel may be lived out and proclaimed to them?

QUESTION 14

In this lesson, you have looked through the lens of Scripture and read from Getz regarding disciple-making and principles of evangelism. Open your Life Notebook and **write a strategy for evangelism for your church**. Your strategy should include the following:

1. 5-8 principles of evangelism that are biblical and relevant to your current cultural context
2. Goals for corporate and personal evangelism (include short-term and long-term goals)
3. Teaching and/or preaching plans to inform and motivate members of your congregation in the area of evangelism
4. New ideas for evangelism methods and approaches that take into consideration contemporary circumstances and opportunities
5. A plan to train individuals in techniques of personal evangelism
6. Based on your strategy, **identify 3-5 definite actions** that can be taken, arrange them in order of priority, and determine when they will be done. Be prepared to share parts or all of your strategy and action plan.

Your work for this lesson is now complete! Now you must implement what you have learned. It is one thing to study and think about evangelism; it is another to actually do it. Reaching the lost is one of the three primary functions of the church. Because it is so high on God's priority list, it must not be neglected to concentrate on fellowship or edification needs.

Practically, you should believe that growing churches are strongly committed to evangelizing the lost and to planting churches. Without this commitment, an essential dynamic is absent from churches who focus only on their current members.

Leading your church to develop and implement a strategy of evangelism is a vital task. Cultural changes mean old methods of church evangelism are not working as they did in days past. The pressing need is for leaders to develop contemporary strategies to bring the changeless truth of the Gospel to people today.

Lesson 7 has strengthened Pastor Eugene's biblical perspective on multiplication dynamics, as well as provided him with practical biblical strategies to help him focus on the growth and multiplication of his church. Key areas he found helpful are:

- New Testament principles of evangelism
- The seven principles of New Testament evangelism described in the chapter "Principles of New Testament Evangelism"

Topic 4 Key Points:
- A man must be spiritually and psychologically mature to become wise and just.
- We must walk in a way worthy of our calling and be the salt and light of the world.
- Older Christians should be leaders because they have more experiences and are less likely to become prideful.

Lesson 7 Self Check

QUESTION 1
A healthy church must emphasize winning men and women to Christ and teaching them to become His lifelong disciples. *True or False?*

QUESTION 2
For effective evangelism, what do the New Testament epistles emphasize?

    A. The oral message

    B. Having the gift of evangelism

    C. Showing unity and love

    D. Having altar calls

QUESTION 3
Evangelism is both an individual responsibility and the purpose of the entire church. *True or False?*

QUESTION 4
What caused the first recorded push of evangelism in the early church?

    A. Obedience to the Great Commission

    B. Peter's release from prison

    C. Persecution after Stephen's martyrdom

    D. The conversion of Saul (Paul)

QUESTION 5
The local church's priority in missions is foreign missions. *True or False?*

QUESTION 6
To best evangelize a group, a church should find out as much as possible about the group. *True or False?*

QUESTION 7
The church must give priority to its current members' needs over evangelism. *True or False?*

QUESTION 8
As an example of uprightness, what did Daniel do in Daniel 1?

    A. He set his mind to please and serve God.

    B. He asked God for wisdom to judge His people.

    C. He asked God for positional righteousness.

    D. He asked God to fulfill His promise.

QUESTION 9
In connection with being devout, according to 1 Corinthians 5:9-10, we can only avoid immoral people by going out of the _____.

QUESTION 10
Spiritual maturity is a biblical requirement for a church leader. *True or False?*

Lesson 7 Answers to Questions

QUESTION 1: *Your answer*

QUESTION 2:

Passage	Teaching
Mark 16:15	Go into the world and preach the Gospel to everyone.
John 13:34-35; 17:21-22	Christians love one another with the unity of the Godhead.
Acts 1:8	Go in the Holy Spirit's power to the ends of the earth.
Acts 11:19-21	Proclaim the Gospel to everyone.
Romans 10:14-15	Preach the Gospel so men might hear and believe.

QUESTION 3:

Passage	Teaching
2 Corinthians 5:17-21	We are ambassadors of Christ's salvation from sin.
1 Thessalonians 1:8	We must spread the Lord's message.
2 Timothy 4:5	Fulfill your ministry by doing an evangelist's work.
1 Peter 3:15	Always be ready to testify about our hope.
2 Peter 3:9	The Lord wants all to come to repentance.

QUESTION 4: True

QUESTION 5: *Your answer*

QUESTION 6: False

QUESTION 7:

B. Adults

C. Households

Only churches built out of basic social units have the true health and the potential of rapid growth and steady expansion. The decisive question is this: How many families form the foundation of the church? Churches founded by families have the potential to flourish (but this does not mean children should not be reached before parents)

QUESTION 8: *Your answer*

QUESTION 9:

A. Spiritually and psychologically mature

Two things must be true for a man to become wise and just: He must be spiritually and psychologically mature.

QUESTION 10:

Passage	Teaching
Romans 1:17	The believer's positional righteousness
Acts 10:22	Cornelius's practical righteousness
Hebrews 5:11-14	Believers not maturing by practicing righteousness
1 Kings 3:5-9	Solomon humbly asks God for wisdom
Daniel 1:8	Setting your mind to please and serve God
1 Corinthians 6:1-5	No one wise enough in this church to settle disputes

QUESTION 11:

Passage	Teaching
Ephesians 4:1	Paul exhorts us to walk worthy of our calling.
Hebrews 7:26	Jesus was innocent, undefiled, and separated—not isolated—from sinners.
Matthew 9:9-12	Jesus was questioned about mingling with sinners.
1 Corinthians 5:9-10	We can only avoid immoral people by going out of the world.
Matthew 5:13-16	We must be salt and light in the world.
1 Thessalonians 2:10	Paul's behavior was holy and righteous and blameless before the church.
1 Corinthians 11:1	Believers could imitate Paul as he imitated Christ.

QUESTION 12:

Passage	Person
Isaiah 14:12-14	Satan fell because of pride.
1 Timothy 6:3-4	The conceit of false teachers
Ephesians 2:8-9	Being saved by grace eliminates pride.
James 4:6	God opposes the proud.
2 Chronicles 32:26-33	King Hezekiah is judged for his pride.

QUESTION 13: *Your answer*
QUESTION 14: *Your answer*

Lesson 7 Self Check Answers

QUESTION 1: True
QUESTION 2:
C. Showing unity and love
QUESTION 3: True
QUESTION 4:
C. Persecution after Stephen's martyrdom
QUESTION 5: False
QUESTION 6: True
QUESTION 7: False
QUESTION 8:
A. He set his mind to please and serve God.
QUESTION 9: World
QUESTION 10: True

Lesson 7 Articles

Devout

*"For the overseer must be blameless as one entrusted with God's work, not arrogant, not prone to anger, not a drunkard, not violent, not greedy for gain. Instead he must be hospitable, devoted to what is good, sensible, upright, **devout**"* (Tit 1:7–8, emphasis added).

The Greek word *hosios* refers to practical holiness and means to be free of sin and wickedness. All Christians are positionally holy but not all are practically holy. Paul exhorts us to walk worthy of our calling (Eph 4:1). Practical holiness (being devout) is developed and worked out in human behavior, becoming more like Christ in practice and in practical ways.

This word is used of Jesus and His practical holiness (Heb 7:26). He was innocent, undefiled, and separated— not isolated— from sinners. For Christ often was questioned about mingling with sinners (Mt 9:9–12). He is our example of how to live a devout life in the midst of sinners, for we can only avoid immoral people by going out of this world (1 Cor 5:9–10). We must be salt and light in the middle of this world and not be a lamp placed under cover (Mt 5:13–16).

Paul also had practical holiness as he behaved "holy and righteous and blameless" before believers (1 Thess 2:10). Paul could exhort other believers to imitate him because he imitated Christ (1 Cor 11:1). He had "put on the new man who has been created in God's image – in righteousness and holiness that comes from truth (Eph 4:24). He had learned that we must stop living as unbelievers and practically live devoutly, like Jesus, developing His character (Eph 4:17–23).

Note: This material is adapted from Gene A. Getz, *The Measure of a Man*. (Ventura, CA: Regal Books, 1984).

Chapter 4: Making Disciples

A Panoramic View

Jesus Christ spent three and a half years ministering on this earth. He went everywhere preaching the kingdom of God to the multitudes, teaching people who He was and demonstrating His deity by working miracles (Jn 20:30-31).

But He also spent much of His time with twelve men He had carefully selected and then trained, not in a formal educational setting, but in a field-type, real-life learning situation. They associated with Him in His ministry, and they saw Him demonstrate with His own life how to do God's work. He eventually sent them out on their own and then carefully helped them learn from their successes and failures.[1]

At the end of the three and a half years, Jesus had basically accomplished two major goals in terms of strategy: He had saturated the minds of the multitudes with His teachings, and prepared a small group of men in depth to enter into His labors and bring in the harvest (Jn 4:35-38). After

---

[1] For an excellent study of how Jesus worked with the Twelve, see Robert E. Coleman, *The Master Plan of Evangelism*, Fleming Revell.

His death and resurrection (His primary purpose in coming into this world), He gave His followers a great evangelistic commission—"Make disciples!"

They did! They built immediately upon the foundations which Jesus had laid. They began in Jerusalem where He had taught, died, and rose again. They went everywhere—in the temple, from house to house, before the Jewish council, in the synagogues, and on the streets.

Hearts were prepared. The Holy Spirit worked in power! The harvest was great—so great the Jewish leaders were threatened and responded with hatred and counteraction.

But this response only served to fulfill the ultimate plan of God, for believers were scattered everywhere throughout Judea and Samaria and to the uttermost parts of the then-known world. Everywhere they carried the message of Christ's death and resurrection and that He truly was the promised Messiah—not only for the Jews but also the One spoken of to Abraham so many years before—the One in whom "all the families of the earth" would "be blessed" (Gen 12:3). "And I have other sheep," Jesus said, "that do not come from this sheepfold. I must bring them too, and they will listen to my voice so that there will be one flock and one Shepherd" (Jn 10:16). Both Jews and Gentiles entered the family of God after the church expanded its outreach and its impact upon the world.

As a result a new phenomenon came into being—something which had not existed while Christ was on earth. It began in Jerusalem after Christ's ascension and then spread throughout the New Testament world. Wherever believers made disciples, local churches came into being. People who lived in various communities and cultures were brought together to form new relationships. They became brothers and sisters in Christ—members of the family of God. A new force was established, not to form as a traveling group but as a people settled in a community, where they lived, worked and carried on the other routine responsibilities in life. And as they were taught and edified, they soon discovered that they had two basic responsibilities—one "to the world" and the other "to each other."

The Power of Love

Interestingly, the Epistles contain few instructions regarding direct evangelism as it was practiced by those who traveled in the book of Acts. Great emphasis was placed on corporate responsibility. Emphasis on verbal presentation of the gospel was subordinated to maintaining a dynamic relationship within the church and maintaining a loving, exemplary relationship with those in the world.

Opportunities to present the gospel of Christ verbally were to grow naturally out of relationships in the community that reflected love and concern for all men. Lifestyles were to be so different and dramatically changed by Christ that unbelievers could not help but notice and inquire what made the difference.

Above all, the love that existed among the local group of believers was to be so dynamic that unbelievers would notice the uniqueness of disciples of Jesus Christ. Further, they would become convinced that Jesus truly was who He said He was.

As Christ was approaching the time of His crucifixion, He remarked to His disciples one day, "A new commandment I give to you, that you love one another, even as I have loved you, that you also love one another." Notice the objective which follows this directive from the Lord Jesus: "By this all men will know that you are My disciples, if you have love for one another" (Jn 13:34-35, NASB).

Community evangelism was to be preceded by a corporate example of love among believers. It would be proof positive that the disciples of Christ reside there. And without its existence, evangelistic efforts would be thwarted.

The Power of Unity

But there is another factor here that is basic to community evangelism. It is actually a reflection of love. Jesus spoke of it in John 17:21, 23 while praying for His disciples. He asked the Father "that they may all be one; even as You, Father, are in Me and I in You, that they also may be in Us, so that the world may believe that You sent Me .... I in them and You in Me, that they may be perfected in unity, so that the world may know that You sent Me, and loved them, even as You have loved Me." (NASB)

Here Christ speaks of the results of love—that is, unity and oneness. By seeing these results, non-Christians would be drawn to the followers of Jesus Christ.

But by observing unity and oneness they would become convinced of who Christ really was—that He came from God—that He was truly the Son of God, the Savior of the world.

In the book of Acts this phenomenon was demonstrated forcefully. It was the love and unity among Christians in Jerusalem that provided the base for effective witness. And this idea is reinforced again and again throughout the Epistles.

A Closer Look—Evangelistic Communication in the Book of Acts

Though a number of words are used to recount the evangelistic activities and functions of first-century believers, Luke used several basic words to describe the process of communication with non-Christians.

Those which follow appear most frequently, and although similar in meaning, each, as used in context, contributes to our understanding of how the unsaved world was reached with the gospel of Christ in the first century.

They Spoke

One of the most common words is the one translated "speaking" or "spoke." The word *laleo* simply means "to talk" or "to tell." We read that Peter and John were in the temple "speaking to the people" (Acts 4:1). Later as the congregation of the disciples was filled with the Holy Spirit, they all "began to speak the Word of God with boldness" (Acts 4:31, NASB).[2]

Though this word (*laleo*) is the most common one used in describing the way the message of Christianity was presented, we can learn several lessons about the process from the context in which the word was used. Frequently, we are told they "spoke the word" (their message); they spoke "in the name of Jesus" (their authority); and they spoke with "boldness" (their manner). They were to speak "the whole message of this Life"; and they spoke "in such a manner that a great multitude believed."

---

[2] See also Acts 5:20, 40; 11:19-20; 14:1, 25; 16:13, 32.

They Evangelized

This word is frequently translated that the followers of Christ "preached the gospel" or "told the good news." Unlike the word "to speak," this word (*evangelidzo*) is a "content" word in itself. It refers to the message that was being given as well as the process of communication. In Acts 5:42 (NASB), Luke recorded that "every day, in the temple and from house to house, they kept right on … preaching Jesus as the Christ".

This process of communication was carried on by both groups and individuals. It was carried out by all believers; it took place in the temple, from house to house, from village to village, from city to city, on a desert road, and its outreach was constantly expanded to regions beyond. They went everywhere telling the good news.

They Taught

Though *didasko* (meaning to teach) is one of the most common words in the New Testament used to describe edification, it is also used to describe evangelism. In this latter sense, the word appears most frequently, in the opening chapters of the book of Acts and on several occasions was used in a context of displeasure and unhappiness on the part of the Jews. They were "angry because they [Peter and John] were teaching the people" (Acts 4:2).[3]

Following the apostles' secret release from jail, they all entered the "temple courts about daybreak and began teaching" (Acts 5:21). Surprised by their appearance, someone rushed off to tell the chief priest that the men they had locked in prison the day before were "standing in the temple courts and teaching the people" (Acts 5:25). The apostles were immediately taken into custody again, and in consternation the high priest said, "We gave you strict orders not to continue to teach in this name. Look, you have filled Jerusalem with your teaching"[4] (Acts 5:28).

Perhaps the most significant observation regarding the teaching process with non–Christians in the early days of the church is that it was used primarily by the apostles. This may imply that it is a more sophisticated process than just "speaking" or "evangelizing," calling for greater skill and knowledge. Obviously, it involved more than just presenting the gospel of Christ but rather included the presentation of the total message of Scriptures (see Acts 5:21-22). The apostles, of course, were in a unique position to communicate this message, having spent three and a half years being trained by the greatest Teacher who ever lived. It is significant that the rulers and scribes "observed the confidence of Peter and John, and understood that they were uneducated and untrained men." Consequently, "they were marveling, and began to recognize them as having been with Jesus" (Acts 4:13, NASB).

Note too that the apostles' teaching among non-Christians brought both positive and negative results. The positive results were conversions, first among the Jewish lay people. Consequently, the negative results came from their religious leaders. Here was one group of religious leaders against another group of religious leaders, false teachers reacting to true teachers. The apostles were presenting the truth, which laid bare the sins and false views of the priests and leaders of Israel. They became jealous and angry and fought back.

But, interestingly, we read in the chapter following this persecution that when the apostles resolved the material problems in Acts 6 and were able to maintain their priorities in teaching the Scriptures, many of the priests also responded to the gospel (Acts 6:7).

---

[3] See also Acts 5:41-42; 28:30-31.

[4] Frequently translated "doctrine."

Here we see the true test of effective teaching among non–Christians. The apostles not only won lay people to Christ but eventually won many religious leaders as well.

They Proclaimed or Preached

The word *kerusso* means "to cry or proclaim as a herald." "Philip went down to the city of Samaria and began proclaiming Christ to them. And the crowds with one accord were giving attention to what was said by Philip" (Acts 8:5-6, NASB).[5]

The word "proclaim" is used primarily in conjunction with the activities of certain key people in the book of Acts, specifically, Philip the evangelist, the apostle Peter and the apostle Paul.

Again, like "teaching," this activity among non-Christians seemed to be the responsibility of certain gifted individuals who had been chosen by God to proclaim in a special way the gospel of Christ (see Acts 10:40-42). All Christians, of course, spoke about Christ and witnessed for Him, but not all proclaimed Christ in a formal way.

They Announced

A word closely related to *kerusso* is the word *katangello*, meaning "to announce publicly," or "to proclaim and tell thoroughly." Like *kerusso*, it is used in Acts in describing the communication of apostolic leaders, particularly the ministry of Paul.[6]

In most cases this word was used to describe communication in the various Jewish synagogues. Here in these religious centers of learning and worship Paul "thoroughly announced" and "proclaimed" the Word of God.

They Solemnly Testified

A common word for testify is *martureo*, meaning "to bear witness" (Acts 1:8). However, throughout the book of Acts some form of the verb *diamarturomai* was also used to describe the evangelistic process and is frequently translated "solemnly testified." It means to "earnestly charge and attest," and has both strong intellectual and emotional overtones. The Word of God was being presented seriously, carefully, and with determination. If *martureo* means "to bear witness," *diamarturomai* means "to bear a thorough witness."

This concept first appeared in Acts in Peter's sermon on the Day of Pentecost, when "with many other words he testified and exhorted them, saying, 'Save yourselves from this perverse generation!'" (Acts 2:40). And it appeared finally in the last chapter of Acts, where we find Paul in Rome. When he arrived he was allowed to "stay by himself, with the soldier who was guarding him" (Acts 28:16). Paul called together the Jewish leaders and rehearsed the events from Jerusalem onward. The Jews appointed a day for Paul to present his total case. And on that day, "they came to him at his lodging in large numbers; and he was explaining to them by solemnly testifying about the kingdom of God, and trying to persuade them concerning Jesus, from both the Law of Moses and from the Prophets, from morning until evening" (Acts 28:23, NASB).[7]

As you trace this word through the book of Acts, it takes on a strong "apologetic" syndrome. Both Peter and Paul, the two apostles whose communication was described by this word, were

---

[5] See also Acts 9:20; 10:39, 42; 20:25; 28:30-31.
[6] See Acts 4:2; 13:5, 38; 15:36; 17:3.

[7] See also Acts 10:42; 18:5; 20:24; 23:11.

attempting to convince their hearers that Jesus Christ was truly the Messiah promised in the Old Testament. They were not simply presenting the gospel but were attesting and giving evidence from the Old Testament as well as from their own personal experience that Jesus was the Christ.

They Reasoned

The word *dialegomai*, meaning to "to reason, to discourse with, or to discuss," is used only of Paul's communication with the non-Christian world. And, also, the word does not appear in the Acts until Paul arrived in Thessalonica. Here we find him going into the synagogue and "for three Sabbaths, reasoned with them from the Scriptures, explaining and giving evidence that the Christ had to suffer and rise again from the dead" (Acts 17:2-3, NASB).[8]

As you look at the communication process that took place in this new dimension involving extensive dialogue and interaction, note that Paul's ministry was increasingly taking him into a pagan environment permeated with Greek and Roman thought and culture.

Notice too that Luke began recording time factors in the context where this word was used. For example, Paul stayed on in Corinth for a year and a half (Acts 18:11) and in Ephesus for two years. Taking into consideration the mentality of these people, their cultural backgrounds, their total ignorance regarding Christianity as well as the method of communication they were used to, the implication is obvious. Paul adopted an evangelistic methodology that could more effectively reach these people. Consequently, he settled into these strategic communities, got to know the thinking of these people, and taught the Scriptures in depth on their mental and emotional wave lengths.

Evangelistic Communication in the Epistles

As you trace through the communication process in the book of Acts, the emphasis is naturally upon the activities and functions of first–century Christians as they *spoke* about Christ, *told* the good news, *taught, proclaimed, testified,* and *reasoned* with unbelievers. But as you move to a study of the Epistles, activities become directives. This, of course, is what we would expect. Throughout the first century, Christian slaves regularly won their unsaved masters to Christ as well as winning their freedom. To do the opposite in those days would have brought instant persecution and perhaps even death. But most of all, it would have interfered with the cause of Christ.

Regarding Paul's approach to the problem of slavery, Merrill Tenney succinctly observes: "Nowhere in its pages is the institution attacked or is it defended. According to Paul's letters to the Asian churches, there were both slaves and slaveholders who were Christians. Slaves were enjoined to obey their masters, and the masters were commanded not to be cruel to them. Such was the power of Christian fellowship, however, that the institution of slavery gradually weakened under its impact and finally disappeared."[9]

Social Life

To live in a community day after day and week after week necessitates maintaining relationships. Many of the believers of the New Testament were converted out of a society that involved a

---

[8] See also Acts 17:17; 18:4, 19; 19:8-10; 24:24-25.
[9] Merrill C. Tenney, *New Testament Survey*, rev. ed. Eerdmans, p. 50, 51.

lifestyle unbecoming to a Christian. With their unsaved friends in view, Paul admonished Christians to give no offense either to Jews or to Greeks in their social life. "Whether, then, you eat or drink or whatever you do, do all to the glory of God," in order, said Paul, "that they may be saved" (1 Cor 10:31-33).

With the pagan Corinthian culture in view, these words are not hard to understand. The way to win people to Christ was not to tell them about Jesus Christ and then to participate in their immoral and anti-Christian activities either within the church or outside in the community. To do so would only offend the unbeliever and create disillusionment with the true message of Christianity.

"Keep your behavior excellent among the Gentiles," wrote Peter, "so that ... they may ... glorify God in the day of visitation" (1 Pet 2:12, NASB). Also, he said, "Keep a good conscience so that ... those who revile your good behavior in Christ may be put to shame" (1 Pet 3:16, NASB).

Peter was not saying that all would respond to the gospel. But he was saying that when the Holy Spirit begins His work in the heart of a man, he needs the backdrop of a Christian lifestyle to be able to evaluate objectively the claims of Christianity. Furthermore, Peter was saying that those who do not respond will be "put to shame" or silenced.

Home Life

There were those in New Testament days who were married to unbelievers. Their marital partners had not yet come to Christ, particularly husbands.

Were these Christian wives to verbally bombard their unsaved husbands with the gospel? Were they to hound them to come out to church and hear the pastor or visiting evangelist? Were they to talk about the virtues of other Christian men, particularly the leaders of the church?

Not at all! "Be submissive to your own husbands," wrote Peter, "so that even if any of them are disobedient to the Word they may be won without a word by the behavior of their wives" (1 Pet 3:1, NASB).

The apostle was stating a profound truth! It is not the piling up of words that convinces unsaved spouses that they need Christ, but rather the impact of a continuous Christ-like lifestyle that reflects the reality of the indwelling Holy Spirit (1 Pet 3:2-7).

Church Life

Very little is said in the New Testament about preaching gospel messages when believers gathered to be edified.

Rather, Christians were to devote themselves to the apostles' teaching; that is, to learning the Word of God. They were to devote themselves to fellowship with one another and with God. And in the process they were to have favor with all the people; that is, with the unsaved world. We see this model in the first church—the church in Jerusalem (Acts 2:42-47). And as will be demonstrated later, we see this emphasis throughout the Epistles.

The Corinthian church stands out as a negative example. The church meetings were chaotic. People spoke in tongues—one after the other—with no interpreter. No doubt more than one spoke at the same time, and women were obviously doing much of the talking. "If... unbelievers or uninformed people enter, won't they say that you are crazy?" queried Paul (1 Cor 14:23).

This is why he put an emphasis on speaking the Word of God clearly and in an orderly manner. Unbelievers must understand the Word in order to be saved (1 Cor 14:25).

The church was also to engage in another very important evangelistic ministry—that of prayer. They were to pray for all men that they may be saved (1 Tim 2:1-4). They were also to pray for those who were called especially to preach the gospel to regions beyond their own communities. On several occasions, Paul requested prayers for his own evangelistic ministry, "that the Word of the Lord may spread rapidly and be glorified" (2 Thess 3:1).

Life in General

Though the Epistles pinpoint special situations and environments in which Christians were to maintain a good testimony, they also speak to life in general. "You are our letter ... known and read by everyone," Paul said to the Corinthians (2 Cor 3:2). "Love your neighbor as yourself," he wrote to the Romans (Rom 13:9). "Conduct yourself with wisdom toward outsiders, making the most of the opportunities," he admonished the Colossians. "Let your speech always be gracious, seasoned with salt, so that you may know how you should answer everyone" (Col 4:5-6). To this Peter adds: "Being ready to make a defense to every one who asks you to give an account for the hope that is in you" (1 Pet 3:15, NASB). The Philippians were told to conduct themselves "in a manner worthy of the gospel" (Phil 1:27).

Summary

The book of Acts and the New Testament correspondence leave no doubt that the great evangelistic impact of a group of believers in a given community was based first of all upon an individual and corporate testimony before the unsaved world, reflecting love, unity, and godly living. This was to become the backdrop against which a vital verbal witness was to be shared with those who were influenced daily, as Christians carried on their business in the community, associated with the unsaved through social and community activities, and lived a dynamic Christian life, both in what was said, and in what was done.

Not a Recent Convert

*"He must not be **a recent convert** or he may become arrogant and fall into the punishment that the devil will exact"* (1 Tim 3:6, emphasis added).

A man chosen to be a Christian leader should not be a new Christian. No matter how zealous or sincere, he will not have the experience necessary to be an elder in the church. He must be a mature man of God. Paul says the danger to him is "arrogance," falling into the devil's punishment (1 Tim 3:6–7). Arrogance is pride that causes someone to lose perspective. This person imitates the fall of Satan, who fell because of pride (Isa 14:12–14).

It takes time to develop the leadership qualities necessary for the church: prudence, apt to teach, not contentious and respectability. It also takes time to learn the Scriptures and how to walk with God.

The broader application is not giving too much of any kind of responsibility to any new Christian. The emphasis must not be merely on time itself, but to someone maturing in the faith, not remaining a babe in Christ. This was apparently true for every candidate in the Corinthian church (1 Cor 3: 1–3). They had many marks of immaturity, could not be taught truth, and even doubted the resurrection without which true Christianity cannot exist (1 Cor 15).

Paul uses a similar word—conceited—to describe false teachers (1 Tim 6:3–4). It was also the reason King Uzziah was criticized by God and King Hezekiah judged by God (2 Chr 26:16;

32:26–33). Once someone changes and becomes humble again, he can receive God's blessing (Dan 4; Jas 4:6). A Christian— saved by grace— with pride is a man out of place (Eph 2:8–9).

Note: This material is adapted from Gene A. Getz, *The Measure of a Man*. (Ventura, CA: Regal Books, 1984).

Chapter 5: Principles of New Testament Evangelism

What does a study of first-century evangelism say to the twenty-first-century church, wherever it may be? What overarching principles can we glean from the study, which in turn can be established as purposes for the church today, in any culture or subculture?

Following are seven key principles which grow naturally out of the study of the evangelistic activities and functions described in the book of Acts and the directives stated in the Epistles.

Create a Basis for Evangelism

First, every local body of believers is responsible to saturate its community with love and to demonstrate a unity and oneness that provide the basis for verbal communication; to demonstrate a Christian lifestyle in all human relationships, in order to create a basis on which to discuss the life-changing Christ.

This principle is clear from the activities of New Testament Christians and the directives given to local groups of believers in the Epistles. They began in Jerusalem, and then, as churches were established in other communities and countries, Christians were instructed to live like Jesus Christ to be able to share the gospel.

Frequently, local churches neglect their own communities. A virile foreign missions program becomes a substitute for local outreach. Missionary budgets replace across-the-street evangelism. Overseas missionaries supported by the church become a substitute for engaging in local outreach.

This should not be! We must not neglect our own "Jerusalem." The field is the world—of course—but the world begins in our own backyard, our own hometown, our own community. This was the story of New Testament believers. They set the example for foreign missions— true—but they had a proper worldview. It included "Jerusalem," "Judea," "Samaria," and then "the farthest parts of the earth" (Acts 1:8).

True, one of the greatest accomplishments of evangelical Christianity has been its foreign missionary thrust. It is commendable! And it should be continued and expanded.

It is important to underscore again that when Jesus Christ was on earth, people saw and heard Him; His miracles and lifestyle became the means by which unbelievers could evaluate His claims (Jn 20:20-31). But when He returned to heaven, His body, the church, became the visible means by which people could evaluate the message of Christ. (Read again Jn 13:13-35; 17:19-23.) One of the challenges facing us in our ministry in the Dallas Metroplex is how to apply this principle. First, we work hard at creating an atmosphere of warmth and love when the church meets corporately. The people leading and participating in any given service are encouraged to view the place we meet as a large, comfortable living room. This, in turn, affects our manner and approach from the platform and also influences the attitude of our people toward others— particularly newcomers. We want people to sense that we are real, that we care about one another and we care about them, though they may be new.

Corporate Evangelism Basic

This leads us to a second New Testament principle: *corporate evangelism is basic to personal evangelism.*

In the New Testament, the functioning body of Christ set the stage for individual witness. This is why Jesus said, "Love one another" so that "all men will know that you are My disciples" (Jn 13:34-35, NASB). This is why Paul said, "Love your neighbor as yourself" (Rom 13:9), and why Peter exhorted believers to keep their "behavior excellent among the Gentiles" (1 Pet 2:12, NASB). Personal evangelism takes on unusual significance against the backdrop of a mature body of local believers—Christians who are making an impact in their communities because of their integrity (1 Thess 4:11-12), their unselfish behavior (Rom 13:7); their orderly conduct (1 Cor 6:1); their humility (1 Pet 2:18); and yet, their forthright testimony for Jesus Christ (1 Pet 3:15).

It is difficult to witness in isolation. It is often necessary, but God's general plan is that community evangelism be carried out in the context of dynamic Christianity and "body life."

Applying this principle calls for unique church practices. Most traditional forms do not provide the best opportunities to demonstrate love in action. True, we can create a warm, accepting atmosphere when the church meets corporately, but as the congregation grows, body life quickly becomes difficult to maintain.

Furthermore, many unsaved people who need to see the body functioning in love and unity will not enter a church building.

However, many will come to a meeting in a home. In that sense, we can take the functioning body to the world—through evangelistic home Bible studies, nonthreatening discussion meetings, and what we call in our own ministry "mini-churches." There is great potential in this kind of form for applying the New Testament principles just stated. Personally, I feel we have not even begun to implement this principle in this kind of home setting.

Evangelize in Love

Third, when possible, presenting the gospel to the unsaved is to take place against the backdrop of a loving and unified body of Christians.

The Scriptures do not suggest that non-Christians should be excluded from the "church gathered." Rather, the Bible teaches that unbelievers should be exposed to the church gathered as an orderly and unified body.

This was the problem in Corinth. Unbelievers who might enter would misinterpret what was happening because of the lack of orderliness. But Paul also spoke of non-Christians who might enter and fall under conviction and come to Christ (1 Cor 14:23-25).[10]

Notice in this passage that the unbeliever will be "convicted by all" and will be "called to account by all" (1 Cor 14:24). Here is a clear-cut reference to body evangelism. It was the whole church functioning that was to be used by the Holy Spirit to win this person to Christ. Note, too, that he would not come to Christ because of a special evangelistic message preached from the pulpit by a

---

[10] Note that this is the only specific illustration in the New Testament of evangelism "in the church."

pastor, geared to the unsaved in the audience; rather, he would be impressed by the believers themselves, their behavior, and the process of mutual edification.[11]

I am reminded of a non-Christian businessman who was attending a new church I was pastoring in its initial days. He asked if he might talk with me about his spiritual condition. Later, when he walked into my office, he told me how impressed he was with the love and concern expressed among the members of this new church. "I have been in many churches," he said, "and served on a number of boards—but have never experienced the kind of Christianity I have seen in this new church."

He then stated openly that he was sure he didn't know Christ personally. Interestingly, he did not tell me how impressed he was with my sermons, though I knew he appreciated the messages. Rather, he was impressed with the "body." Yes, I had the privilege of leading him to Christ, but it was the local body of functioning believers who were used by God to bring conviction to the man.

The New Testament then presents the "church gathered" as a context in which non-Christians can view and experience the realities of Christianity—love, unity, and Christlike living. And, within this context, the Holy Spirit is able to bring conviction and a desire to worship the same God and to know the same Savior.

Evangelism in the New Testament also took place, not only as the "church gathered," but as the church was scattered into the world—at work, in the communities where the believers lived, in their homes. In fact, it appears that it was in this context that non-Christians most frequently heard the gospel of Jesus Christ.

Aim For Adults/Families

Fourth, the primary target for evangelism should be adults and consequently, whole households.

Nowhere in the New Testament are examples given of "child evangelism" as we frequently practice it today; that is, to win children to Christ out in the community apart from the family setting. But don't misunderstand. This does not mean there is not emphasis on the importance of child life and child conversion.

Jesus Christ Himself set the supreme example in His attitude toward children. Paul also wrote to Timothy reminding him of his religious heritage, "From childhood you have known the sacred writings which are able to give you the wisdom that leads to salvation through faith which is in Christ Jesus" (2 Tim 3:15, NASB).

New Testament evidence is also buttressed by the tremendous Old Testament examples of child nurture. In fact, when the family is discussed in Scripture, more seems to be said about children—their needs and their importance—than any other aspects of family life.[12]

---

[11] This does not mean it is "wrong" to preach an evangelistic message in a church service. God has used and continues to use this approach. It does mean, however, that the New Testament does not model this approach for carrying out local church evangelism.

[12] See Gene A. Getz, *The Measure of a Family*, Regal Books.

The New Testament pattern is clear! The target for conversion was adults. Jesus chose twelve grown men—not children. He spoke to the multitudes (children were no doubt included in the crowds), but His remarks were directed at the adults.

Similarly, in the book of Acts, the apostles won adults to Christ first of all. They did not go after children as their primary target, hoping to use this as a means to get to parents, nor did they go after children because they were more pliable or easier to reach for Christ. No, they reversed the process. They went after adults—knowing that parental conversion meant reaching the whole household.

Dr. George Peters goes so far as to say in his excellent book *Saturation Evangelism* that "household evangelism and household salvation are the biblical ideal and norm in evangelism and salvation."[13] By this he does not mean that children become Christians because their parents believe. Nor does he mean a "covenant idea" which teaches that children of believing parents experience regeneration through "infant baptism," or that through this rite the child is related to God in some unique way that makes him a potential and actual candidate for conversion later in life.[14]

Conversion is not automatic for any human being. It is an individual matter based on an intelligent and responsible decision—receiving Christ as personal Savior.

Household salvation, however, refers to first reaching parents and consequently reaching the whole family for Christ. The New Testament gives several outstanding illustrations of this process.

In Philippi, Paul first spoke to Lydia at the riverside. She was converted, and consequently her whole household came to Christ (Acts 16:15). Later in the same city, the Philippian jailer believed in Christ, and as a result his whole household was converted. (Acts 16:31-34).

Other examples in the New Testament include Zaccheus, and the nobleman in the Gospels (Lk 19:9; Jn 4:53). In Acts and the Epistles we see Cornelius (Acts 10), Crispus (Acts 18:8), Stephanas (1 Cor 1:16), Onesiphorus (2 Tim 1:16), and Philemon (Phm 1).

In fact, the household churches referred to frequently both in the book of Acts and in the Epistles were no doubt the results of the conversion of whole families.

There are some very practical advantages in reaching adults for Christ and consequently, the whole family. First, it is often psychologically frustrating for a small child to become a Christian apart from the understanding and blessing of his father and mother and other members of the family. In fact, the basic need of a child is acceptance and love within the family setting, and to experience this kind of rejection can be psychologically demoralizing. A child is ordinarily emotionally incapable of tolerating this kind of family persecution.

Second, parents who are also Christians become the primary means for the child's spiritual growth following conversion. If adults need nurture and help following conversion (and they do), so much more do children. The family is a natural spiritual womb for spiritual growth and development.

Third, a total family reached for Christ can create a tremendous impact in a community. Each member of the household in turn becomes an influence for Christ in winning other households.

---

[13] George W. Peters, *Saturation Evangelism*, Zondervan, p. 160. Dr. Peters, Professor Emeritus of World Missions at Dallas Theological Seminary, discusses this idea in depth in his book on pages 147–167.

[14] Ibid, pp. 148–149.

Fourth, family units are the building blocks for a healthy church. Again, Dr. Peters reminds us:

> Only churches that are built out of basic social units have the true health and the potential of rapid growth and steady expansion. The decisive question in founding a church is not how many people are interested in the project but rather how many families form the foundation of the church. Churches founded by families have the potential to flourish.[15]

Let me say in conclusion, however, that this does not mean that children should not be reached for Christ before parents are reached.

Though biblical examples do not support the sequence, it certainly does not eliminate this approach. The Lord is concerned about children and that they come to know Him personally.

But what the biblical examples do say is that when the child is reached for Christ through an individual Christian or through an agency of the church, every attempt should be made to reach the parents for Christ as well, and in the process to seek to keep from interfering with the family's unity and harmony. It may also mean that the church must provide in some way a father or mother substitute in cases where non-Christian parents are unresponsive and particularly if they are antagonistic.

Finally, it means that Christians must not allow the difficulty of reaching adults and the fear of rejection themselves to cause them to put all of their efforts into winning children because they are more responsive and it is easier to "secure decisions."

One reason statistics show that more children come to Christ is that we are not efficiently winning adults. Statistics simply reflect our failure. If whole families could be reached for Christ in the first-century pagan community, we can reach whole families in the twenty-first century. The task before us is to develop the right strategy and approach that will work in pagan America.

We must realize, however, that the American culture particularly and the Western culture generally is very much different from the New Testament culture. When a father and mother come to Christ, it does not mean the children will automatically become believers, particularly if the children are older. Furthermore, if a husband comes to Christ, it does not mean the wife will respond as well—or vice versa.

I saw this cultural difference illustrated dramatically on one occasion when a Vietnamese family came to the States and came in contact with one of the members of our church. The father became a believer, told his wife, and she immediately wanted to accept Christ as well. And then all of his children who were old enough to understand automatically did the same. Here, we saw the "biblical" or "Eastern" culture at work in our Western society that so often fosters individualistic rather than corporate decisions.

Nevertheless, adult influence is far greater on children than child influence on adults—even in the Western culture. The biblical emphasis is still normative and transcends culture.

Identify Missionaries

Fifth, the church is responsible to identify those who have a desire to carry the good news in a special way out into the community and beyond the immediate community—even to "the farthest parts of the earth."

---

[15] Ibid, p. 155.

As emphasized earlier, the unique nature of the church, with its potential for mutual love and unity, gives unlimited opportunities for an "apologetic" ministry among the unsaved. But within the body are certain people who sense a special burden for evangelistic work. These people must be encouraged to use their talents and represent the local body in a special ministry of evangelism.

Yet they must not become substitutes for the other members of the body but rather function as those who are able in a special way to present Christ to various individuals and groups. We see this principle demonstrated clearly in the book of Acts. Many believers "spoke" the message of Christ, and all believers seemed to have a part in telling the good news, but it was the apostles especially who engaged in evangelistic teaching and preaching. It was Peter and particularly Paul who engaged in an evangelistic ministry characterized by "solemnly testifying" and "reasoning" with unbelievers.

The church is further responsible to pray God's blessing upon those individuals and in some cases to support them financially as they engage in a part-time or full-time ministry of evangelism and missionary work. This principle is illustrated by the church at Antioch when it set apart Barnabas and Saul and commissioned them for an evangelistic ministry (Acts 13:1-2).

But the church must be careful at this point! Its tendency is to look beyond its immediate community and overlook those within the whole group of believers who are not led to leave the community and sail the seven seas. There are those who should be encouraged, trained, and used in a special way to reach out into the community surrounding the church and to lead people to Christ.

One way we have discovered which creates a desire for evangelism and missions is to encourage Christians (church members) to participate in overseas ministries, particularly on a short-term basis. Short-term mission trips provide a life-changing opportunity for members of the church.

Integrate New Believers

Sixth, new believers, as soon as possible, should be integrated into the life of the local church.

What it means to be a part of the church will be discussed in more detail later, but at this juncture it is important to emphasize—and to emphasize strongly—that outside of the context of the church and the experience of drawing upon other members of the body, a new babe in Christ will not grow into a mature responsible disciple of Jesus Christ. He cannot, for he is not involved in basic experiences which God has designed as absolutely essential for spiritual growth.

There are some who will interpret these ideas as criticisms of para–church organizations and agencies. Let me clarify! I believe God has raised up many organizations, first, to supplement the work of the local church, and, second, to do what, in many cases, the churches have failed to do. But I firmly believe that these organizations must not ignore biblical examples and principles; for if they do, God's richest blessings will not rest on them ultimately. The most obvious example and principle is that God ordained the local church as the primary place where believers are to be nurtured and edified. Each new Christian needs the body of Christ in order to be built up in the Christian life.

Every parachurch organization should seriously consider its relationship to the local church. It must teach this biblical doctrine, promote it as basic to Christian nurture, and strive in a loving and tactful way to correct both the church's theological and functional errors. It must not become a substitute for the local church nor antagonistic to the local church. It must in every way cooperate in furthering the ministry and outreach of this God ordained plan.

Develop New Methods

Seventh, the twenty-first-century church must develop its own contemporary forms and approaches to evangelism, using the principles just stated as biblical guidelines.

One thing becomes clear from the study of the functions of the New Testament church. *What* they said is consistent; the *way* they said it and *how* they went about evangelizing varies from situation to situation. They considered the directives as *absolute*. But their methods were *relative* and merely served as means to accomplish divine ends.

This is the genius of the Scriptures. They set men free to create unique approaches and devise methods that are workable in any culture and at any time in history.

Whether you study the structure of Peter's sermons, or follow Paul as he moved out from the Jewish community into the Gentile world, one thing is certain! These men were not locked into one approach or a single way of presenting the divine message.

They varied their methodology, depending on the circumstances. As a result, as we have noted, as Paul entered the pagan world and moved farther and farther away from the environment that had been previously saturated with the teachings of Jesus Christ, he changed his methods of communication. What had been previously a proclaiming-type approach became one that was characterized by dialogue and interaction. In Paul's initial work, he could at least assume a basic belief in God and divine revelation, but in the pagan world he could assume neither. It called for a distinct, apologetic approach to evangelism.

Thus the new culture, the new mentality, the difference in awareness—all of these things—served to help Paul determine what methods he should use to reach these people with the gospel of Christ. True, he always communicated the simple gospel and did so with humility, but this has to do with message and attitude, not methods.

We have allowed purely human patterns and forms which have been developed in the last fifty to one hundred years to become absolute. We actually believe some of the ways we do things now are biblical norms.

A typical example of allowing a purely human approach to become absolute is our thinking regarding the Sunday night evangelistic service (or for that matter any other evangelistic service in the church). Many believers actually believe this is the way the church in the New Testament functioned, whereas we don't have a single example of this approach, nor is it alluded to. In fact, as already pointed out, all church meetings illustrated in the New Testament were designed to build up believers, not to preach at unbelievers.

Is it wrong, then, to have a Sunday night evangelistic service? Of course not. The New Testament certainly allows this freedom. But let's remember that this approach was developed in America around the turn of the century, and it worked effectively because of a completely different cultural situation and religious mentality. In many places in America today, the Sunday night evangelistic service is a total failure, for unbelievers no longer come out to church. And yet, some pastors keep preaching their Sunday night evangelistic sermons to a crowd of believers and actually feel guilty if they even consider changing the format and thrust of the service.

The evangelical church cannot and must not allow itself to get locked into forms and patterns—either first century or twenty-first century—that have been designed as a means to biblical ends.

Every church in every culture and subculture needs to develop its own unique approaches to community evangelism. Under the creative leadership of the Holy Spirit, and using all of the human resources available, we need to develop dynamic churches that are creating contemporary evangelistic strategies that are built on New Testament principles and guidelines.

Summary

Why the church exists in the world is clear! God is calling out a people to be His very own. Someday Christ will return to take the church to be with Himself.

But why has He not returned? This question was asked even by the skeptics in the first century (2 Pet 3:4). Notice Peter's answer! "The Lord is not slow about His promise, as some regard slowness, but is being patient toward you because he does not wish for any to perish but for all to come to repentance" (2 Pet 3:9).

How well is your church reaching people for Jesus Christ—first in your "own Jerusalem" and then in "all Judea and Samaria, and even to the farthest parts of the earth"?

The Great Commission

The risen Jesus talks to the disciples on an unspecified mountain in Galilee. Only the eleven are mentioned, but some writers believe that the uniqueness of the occasion suggests that other followers of Jesus were included. It is the concluding address of the Lord before His ascension. In this most Jewish of the gospels, Matthew deals with several themes from the Old Testament covenants. This passage has a form that resembles the covenantal promises of the Old Testament, as well as some of the Old Testament passages in which one of God's servants was commissioned for his particular ministry (see, for example, Gen 12:1-4; Ex 3:1-12; Isa 6; Jer 1:1-10).[16]

The Lord's authority makes it legitimate for Him to deliver this commission. He certainly has the authority to command His followers to make disciples and to expect His command to be carried out. His power over heaven and earth also ensures that He can enable His followers to fulfill His commands. It is clear that the main purpose of the command is to *make disciples*.

The command "Go" implies "do this." It is as if the Lord had said to the disciples, "This is what I want you to do: make disciples." Therefore, it is not a direct command to go out into the world, but a command to be fulfilled by the church wherever it is located.

The meaning of "make disciples" refers either to evangelism alone or to the whole program of evangelism and growth in the Christian life. Thus, your definition of what a disciple is will either be a believer or a mature believer.

If you believe that "make disciples" is primarily evangelism, then you will probably see "baptizing" and "teaching to obey" as that which follows initial belief in Christ. If you believe that "make disciples" speaks of the whole program of the Christian life from conversion to maturity, then "baptizing" and "teaching to obey" will probably be the components of disciple-making, with "baptizing" representing evangelism and "teaching to obey" representing growth to maturity.

It is important to note that "all the nations" refers to all people throughout the world. Earlier, the followers of Jesus had been commanded to restrict their ministry to the "lost sheep of the house of Israel" and avoid the Gentiles and Samaritans (Mt 10:5-6). The focus of the ministry is now broadened to include all people. Simply put, "all the nations" refers to all people everywhere,

---

[16] The comments on the form of the Great Commission are based on Peter T. O'Brien, "The Great Commission or Matthew 28:18-20—A Missionary Mandate or Not?" *Evangelical Review of Theology* 2 (October 1978): 256–59.

though in this Jewish context there was probably the implication that Gentiles were particularly in view.

Minimally, baptism is a public recognition and testimony of belief in Christ as Savior. "Baptizing" and "teaching to obey" are related to the command to make disciples either as the content of making disciples or as the consequences of making disciples.

Note especially that the goal of teaching is not simply communicating truth. The goal of teaching is to change the life of the learner so that he becomes obedient to the truth that he learns. A disciple is not measured by the truth he knows but by the truth he obeys. "Teaching to obey" plays a highly significant role in disciple-making. Believers are to be taught the truths of Scripture with the goal of obeying them. The assumption is that a believer wants to please his Lord by obedience. Thus, he needs to know the definition of biblical obedience.

The last statement in verse 20 at least gives the disciples encouragement that the Lord will be with them in the disciple-making process. The promise "I will be with you" has been a source of encouragement and strength to God's people throughout the ages (see, for example, Ex 3:12; 4:12; Deut 31:23; Josh 1:5-9; Jer 1:8). The statement also suggests that the command applies until the end of the age.

It must mean that your church is to be involved in making disciples, baptizing, and teaching to obey.

While there may be some variations on these thoughts, these suggestions include the primary alternative views on this command. In light of these alternatives, we understand the Great Commission to mean that the church, of which the disciples present when Jesus spoke were the earthly founders, has been given the task of penetrating the entire world for the purpose of making disciples among all peoples. A disciple is a believer who has grown to be thoroughly committed to Jesus Christ and to His Word. Disciples are produced by the two-stage process of evangelism, signified here by the term "baptizing" and "edification," described here in terms of teaching that leads to an obedient life.

Summary: Whether you agree with our understanding, and even if there are some fine points about these verses we may never completely understand, it is clear that we are to go out to unbelievers in the world, present the Gospel to them, lead them to Christ, have them baptized to confirm and give public witness to this decision, and then lead them in a lifelong process of Christian growth.

Upright

*"For the overseer must be blameless as one entrusted with God's work, not arrogant, not prone to anger, not a drunkard, not violent, not greedy for gain. Instead he must be hospitable, devoted to what is good, sensible, **upright**"* (Tit 1:7–8, emphasis added).

The Greek word translated "upright," *dikaios*, can refer to the positional righteousness of believers (Rom 1:17) or to the practical righteousness of men (Joseph, Mt 1:19 and Cornelius, Acts 10:22). But the more specific application of Scripture is that the upright man is also wise and discerning and able to make mature judgments in his relationships with others.

The negative example of this is the Corinthian church, where Paul chided them for having no one mature enough to settle their dispute (1 Cor 6:1–5; Heb 5:11–14). The positive example is Solomon, who humbly asked the Lord for wisdom to judge God's people (1 Kgs 3:5–9). Another positive example is Daniel. Daniel's life was exemplary toward God from beginning to end because he had set his mind to please and serve God (Dan 1:8). His attitudes toward prayer and worship are an unparalleled example of his unbending commitment and devotion to God despite the fact that his commitment put his life in danger (Dan 6).

Two things must be true for a man to become wise and just: He must have both spiritual and psychological maturity. An exceptional non–Christian man can be psychologically mature and make fair decisions. But the unbeliever can never be spiritually mature and *both* types of maturity are required in the church. A person can be in fellowship and be immature psychologically and spiritually.

Note: This material is adapted from Gene A. Getz, *The Measure of a Man*. (Ventura, CA: Regal Books, 1984).

Lesson 8: Leadership Dynamics, Part I

Lesson Introduction

What constitutes capable local church leadership? This lesson teaches God's plan for local church leadership and its responsibilities. While the New Testament describes leaders' responsibilities, it also gives much freedom in how they are carried out. This lesson presents principles to guide you in carrying out your leadership role, and to help you select and develop other leaders within the church.

Moses found the task of judging the entire nation of Israel too difficult as the people stood around him "from morning until evening" (Ex 18:14b). "Moses' father-in-law said to him, 'The thing that you are doing is not good! You will surely wear out, both you and this people who are with you, for this is too heavy for you; you are not able to do it by yourself'" (Ex 18: 17-18).

The same is true of the burden of the church if the pastor or someone else must do it all. Here is Jethro's advice to Moses:

> But choose from the people capable men, God-fearers, men of truth, haters of bribes, and put them over them as rulers of thousands, and rulers of hundreds, and rulers of fifties, and rulers of tens. And they will judge the people all the time, but every great issue they will bring to you, but every small issue they themselves will judge, so that you may make it easier for yourself, and they will bear the burden with you. If you do this thing, and God so commands you, then you will be able to endure, and all these people will be able to go to their place satisfied (Ex 18:21-23)

Lesson Outline

Lesson 8: Leadership Dynamics, Part I
    Topic 1: The Beginnings of Church Leadership, Leaders Defined
    Topic 2: The Beginnings of Church Leadership, Leaders' Job Descriptions
    Topic 3: Developing Character—Building up, Devoted To, Honoring Each Other

Lesson Objectives

Pastor Eugene's problem is to identify and develop capable church leaders. He wants to know what God's plan is for this. He notices the New Testament describes leaders' responsibilities, but also gives much freedom in how they carry out their functions. He is also impressed by how much the Bible emphasizes character qualities over abilities.

During this lesson, to help Pastor Eugene and ourselves, we will:
- Define the terms elder, deacon, and deaconess as they are used in the New Testament.
- Explain how local church leaders should manage and shepherd their people.
- Explain how local church leaders should be selected.
- Build up, honor, and devote ourselves to others.

Topic 1: The Beginnings of Church Leadership, Leaders Defined

As you read the following passage, notice that Paul and Barnabas won converts and established churches in various cities. Later, they returned to those churches to encourage the new believers and to appoint leaders.

> After they had proclaimed the good news in that city and made many disciples, they returned to Lystra, to Iconium, and to Antioch. They strengthened the souls of the disciples and encouraged them to continue in the faith, saying, "We must enter the kingdom of God through many persecutions." When they had appointed elders for them in the various churches, with prayer and fasting they entrusted them to the protection of the Lord in whom they had believed (Acts 14:21-23)

The pattern of Paul and Barnabas was to go, make disciples, teach them, and then provide for the leadership of the new church. The individual churches then provided ongoing worship, edification, and evangelistic ministries in their communities. The beginning of this process can also be observed in Paul's letter to Titus, in which he explains, "The reason I left you in Crete was to set in order the remaining matters and to appoint elders in every town, as I directed you" (Tit 1:5).

Acts 14 and Titus 1 show that local churches were always organized. Organization in the church is related to *function*. Because the church has the function of worshiping God, edifying believers, and evangelizing the lost, it must be organized to effectively fulfill its function.

Organization is also related to the size of a local church; for as a church grows in size, it must also grow in organizational complexity. It is not possible to lead a church of 1200 people with the same structure it had when there were 100.

God chooses to increase the purposefulness in the gathering, as well as in the scattering movements of the church, by appointing church leaders.

Sample: Church Org Chart

```
              Pastor
              Eugene
            /        \
           ↓          ↓
       Elder(s)    Deacon(s)
           ↓
      Congregation
```

Pastor Eugene needs to look to New Testament Scripture for a definition of the church's leadership positions before he can identify individuals in his growing church that can fill them.

Take some time to do your own study by completing the following exercise.

QUESTION 1

Open your Life Notebook and list the following passages at the beginning of the line. All of the primary New Testament passages related directly to the functions of elders are included. Read and reflect on each passage, then describe in your Life Notebook the specific elder functions identified in that passage: Acts 20:17, 28, 35; 1 Thessalonians 5:12; 1 Timothy 3:2, 5; 1 Timothy 5:17; Titus 1:7-9; Hebrews 13:17; James 5:14-15; 1 Peter 5:1-4.

QUESTION 2

After you have noted the various functions of elders in the previous question, organize them into a logical presentation of the functions of an elder. Write this in your Life Notebook.

Reading Assignments

- Please read the textbook chapter entitled "Chapter 10: Leadership in the New Testament Church, Phase Two" from Getz' *Sharpening the Focus of the Church* in the Articles section at the end of this lesson.
- Please read the article titled "Leadership Defined" in the Articles section at the end of this lesson.

Based on New Testament data, Getz described the major local church leadership offices.

Interact carefully with the biblical text by using the insights Getz provides and by answering the following questions.

QUESTION 3

Based on 1 Timothy 3:4-5 and 1 Peter 5:1-3, what two words does Getz use to describe the primary role of an elder?

    A. Organizing and preaching

    B. Managing and shepherding

    C. Evangelizing and coordinating

    D. Ruling and serving

QUESTION 4

Wherever possible, churches should have multiple leaders. *True or False?*

QUESTION 5

According to Acts 6:1-7, why was the office of deacon inaugurated?

    A. The apostles needed a rest

    B. To train them as future pastors

    C. Church member needs were not being met

    D. The members of the church wanted to do more for the church

QUESTION 6

What is the primary role of deacons and deaconesses in the Church today?

    A. To distribute food to widows and orphans

    B. To make sure the church building is maintained

    C. To help lead the church

    D. Their responsibilities are open ended

QUESTION 7

How does Getz' list of items from Psalm 23 compare with your list in Question 2? Open your Life Notebook and record your observations.

QUESTION 8

Look at the areas of responsibility you identified (Question 2) and those in Getz's list (Question 7). Consider your church and your own role(s) in relation to these areas of responsibility. Then open your Life Notebook as you respond to the following:

1. Summarize this combined list of responsibilities into 4-8 categories of responsibility
2. Define each of these areas according to your understanding.
3. Explain in writing how you or others in your church are presently fulfilling these duties.
4. Do your present responsibilities allow you the time and freedom to fulfill these tasks? Consider the same for other leaders in your church. If not, why?
5. What would help the leadership of your church be the most effective in fulfilling these responsibilities?

Topic 1 Key Points:

- Elders are appointed to manage the church and pastor the flock.
- Scripture supports the concept of multiple eldership.
- Deacons and deaconesses assist church members as needs arise.
- All church leaders should be spiritually and psychologically qualified to lead.

Topic 2: The Beginnings of Church Leadership, Leaders' Job Descriptions

It is not enough to simply appoint leaders in the church. Pastor Eugene must now find out more about the responsibilities that these men and women fulfill and how to select them. Again, Pastor Eugene turns to New Testament Scripture for help.

However, not all details for elder and deacon roles are described in Scripture. For example, the New Testament does not say how many leaders to appoint for a single church, how long these leaders should serve, or the specific ways in which these leaders should carry out their functions. Furthermore, the Bible does not say who should take the primary leadership when there is more than one spiritual leader. These are all "form" questions to answer according to the context of a given local church in a particular cultural context at a certain point in time.

In Getz's chapter "Principles of New Testament Leadership" (Chapter 12 of *Sharpening the Focus of the Church*), he makes some observations to help church leaders increase their effectiveness. His observations regarding leadership in the local church lead to some principles which every modern church can put into practice. They can help you evaluate your own philosophy and practice in church leadership.

Reading Assignment
- Please read the textbook chapter entitled "Chapter 12: Principles of New Testament Leadership" from Getz' book *Sharpening the Focus of the Church* in the Articles section at the end of this lesson.
- Please read the article titled "Leaders' Job Descriptions" in the Articles section at the end of this lesson.

QUESTION 9
Based on 1 Timothy 3:1-7, when appointing elders the most important selection criterion is_____.
- A. Organizational skills
- B. Ability to manage finances
- C. Joyful and calm demeanor
- D. Spiritual qualifications

QUESTION 10
What does 1 Timothy 5:17-18 indicate about pay of elders?
- A. All elders should receive wages for their service.
- B. Elders that preach and teach should receive adequate wages
- C. To prevent the desire for "sordid gain" no elders should be paid.
- D. Whatever is customary in our society and time

QUESTION 11
To maximize efficiency and avoid conflict, a church is best managed by a committee of elders with equal authority. *True or False?*

QUESTION 12
Do you observe in your church any tasks that are being performed by elders that could be delegated to deacons or deaconesses? If so, list them in your Life Notebook.

QUESTION 13
In your Life Notebook, number the lines 2-7, for principles two through seven, as formulated by Getz. Next to each number, write how your church could apply the principle more effectively.

Topic 2 Key Points:
- Qualified leaders must be selected on the basis of spiritual qualifications.
- Cultural responsibilities can be delegated.
- Staff leaders must be adequately paid.
- When there are multiple leaders, a primary leader must exist.

Topic 3: Developing Character—Building Up, Devoted To, Honoring Each Other

A true concern for others is a critical requirement of leadership. As a leader, you must develop this character quality in yourself first to help develop other leaders and members of your church.

In the remaining topic for this lesson, we will discuss the character traits of building up, being devoted to, and honoring each other.

When God had Samuel help Him choose a new king, He gave him instructions: "Don't regard his appearance or his height, for I have rejected him. It's not the way that man sees, for man looks on what the eyes can see, but the LORD looks on the heart" (1 Sam 16:7b). Though Saul was more impressive physically, God looked at David's character and told Samuel not to look at outward appearance (1 Sam 10:23-24).

Building Up One Another

Reading Assignment

Please read the article titled "Members Who Belong to One Another" in the Articles section at the end of this lesson.

QUESTION 14

The individual Christian can function effectively alone. *True or False?*

The following questions (15-19) are designed to help you function more effectively within Christ's body. In your position of Christian leadership, check yourself in the following areas to make sure you are helping others become participating members in Christ's body. Please read through the following questions.

QUESTION 15

I'm doing all I can to help other believers become mature in Christ—measured according to the qualities specified in 1 Timothy 3 and Titus 1. *True or False?*

QUESTION 16

I look for as many opportunities as possible to encourage other mature Christians to participate in teaching the Scriptures, praying, helping others, counseling, etc. *True or False?*

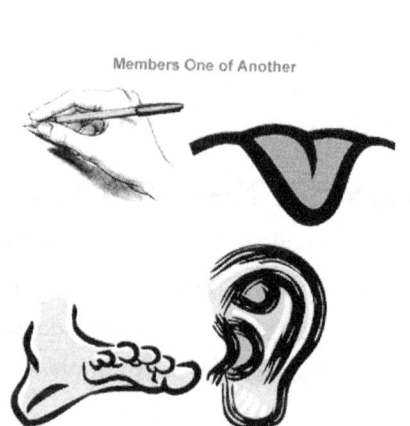

QUESTION 17

I realize that God can use other members of the body of Christ, even though they may not have had as much training as I have. *True or False?*

QUESTION 18

I have a subtle sense of pride, which keeps telling me I am the only one capable of effectively ministering to other people. *True or False?*

QUESTION 19

I have difficulty trusting other members of Christ's body—either because I have not viewed other Christians properly, or I am threatened by the fact that they might be able to do things better than I can. *True or False?*

QUESTION 20

Go back through questions 15-19 above. For every question you answered incorrectly, write a brief plan for improving in that area.

Then continue by helping one person in your church function better in the body of Christ.

Devoted to One Another

Reading Assignment

Please read the article titled "Devoted to One Another" in the Articles section at the end of this lesson.

QUESTION 21

Paul uses the illustration of the body to show how the church functions; he uses the illustration of the family to illustrate the _____ dimension.

QUESTION 22

This question is designed to help you increase your family love for other Christians.

Fill in the columns with a pen or pencil by matching the option on the left to the verses in the bottom rows.

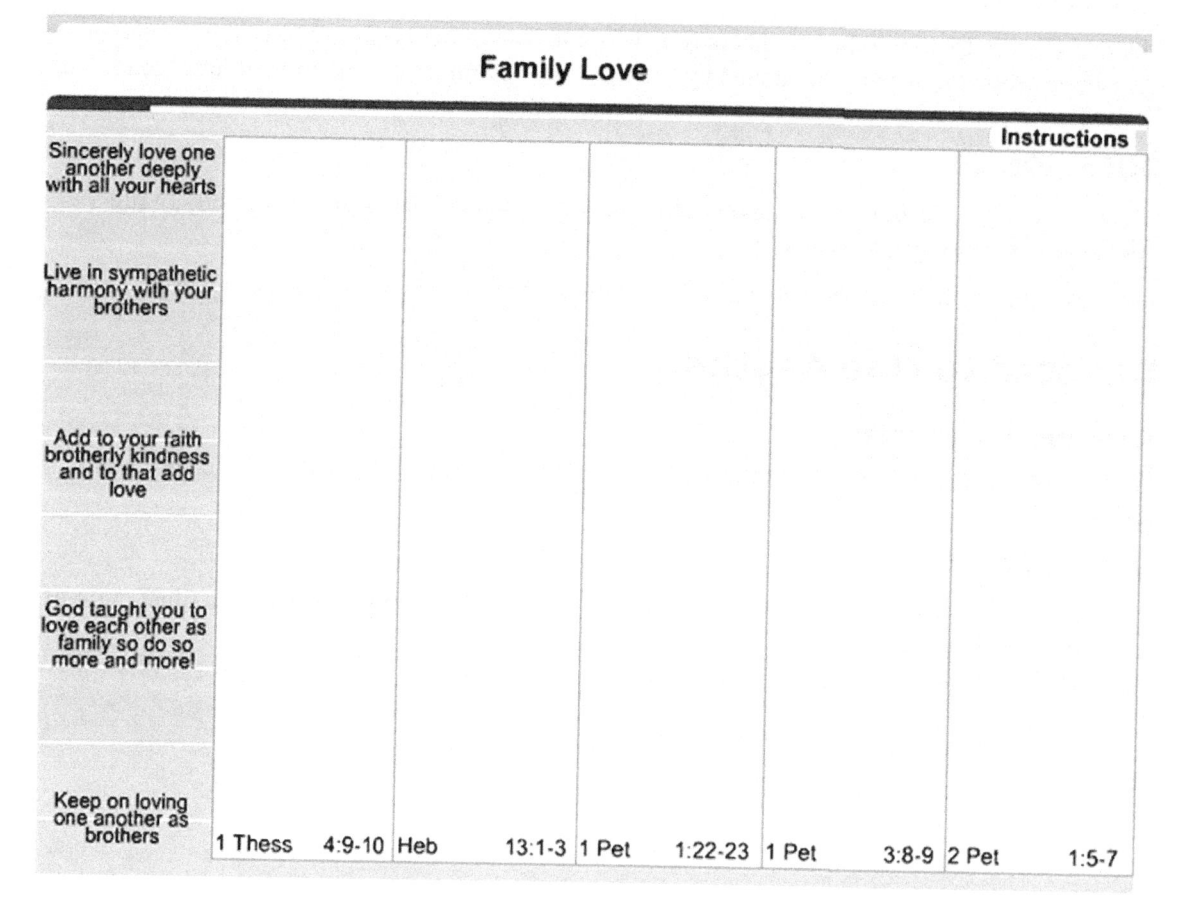

Family Love

Instructions				
Sincerely love one another deeply with all your hearts				
Live in sympathetic harmony with your brothers				
Add to your faith brotherly kindness and to that add love				
God taught you to love each other as family so do so more and more!				
Keep on loving one another as brothers				
	1 Thess 4:9-10	Heb 13:1-3	1 Pet 1:22-23	1 Pet 3:8-9	2 Pet 1:5-7

Honoring One Another

Reading Assignment

Please read the article titled "Honoring One Another" in the Articles section at the end of this lesson.

QUESTION 23

In the article "Honoring One Another," Jesus' attitude of serving in Mark 10:43-45 is contrasted with the attitude of_____.

    A. Judas

    B. The Jewish leaders

    C. Nicodemus

    D. The Philippians

QUESTION 24

This question is designed to help you learn to honor other Christians. How many situations can you recall where you purposely attempted to honor someone above yourself? In what way did you reflect sincere appreciation for the other person? *Note: This does not mean doing so expecting to get something back yourself!* Record your answer in your Life Notebook.

QUESTION 25

Open your Life Notebook and write a job description for each of the offices of an elder and a deacon. Include their primary areas of responsibility and their specific duties. Since such a job description will vary with the leader's major area of responsibility—such as teaching, music, and evangelism—you only need to write one for each office. One of these should be your own. When you do this project, carefully distinguish biblical and cultural elements.

Lesson 8 Self Check

QUESTION 1

Which biblical character appointed elders to help him judge the multitudes of Israel?

- A. David
- B. Samuel
- C. Moses
- D. Joshua

QUESTION 2

Paul and Barnabas established new churches by first appointing church leaders. *True or False?*

QUESTION 3

Paul usually used the term "elder" as the name of the office of elder. He used the term bishop (overseer) to better communicate his meaning within a specific _____.

QUESTION 4

Which of the following organizational structures is most highly recommended?

- A. Female elders
- B. Non-shepherding elders
- C. Multiple, equal elders
- D. Multiple elders with one head elder

QUESTION 5

What was the first need that led to the creation of the office of deacon?

- A. Distribution of food
- B. Widows' need for prayer
- C. Serving the communion table
- D. Cleaning up the church

QUESTION 6

Biblically, elders should be paid whatever is customary in our culture and time. *True or False?*

QUESTION 7

The main tasks of spiritual leaders are managing and _____.

QUESTION 8

According to Mark 10:45, which of the following is NOT a reason the Son of Man came?

- A. To be served
- B. To serve
- C. To give His life
- D. To ransom many

QUESTION 9

The "family" analogy illustrates the _____ dimension of church function, while the "body" analogy shows the overall picture of how the church functions.

QUESTION 10

To honor someone is to act in his or her best interest. *True or False?*

Lesson 8 Answers to Questions

QUESTION 1: *Your answer*
QUESTION 2: *Your answer*
QUESTION 3:
B. Managing and shepherding
Christians will always need managing and pastoring to learn the Word of God from qualified teachers and to be ministered to in other spiritual ways.
QUESTION 4: True
QUESTION 5:
C. Church member needs were not being met
The apostles could not neglect the ministry of the Word of God to attend to the needs of the Hellenic widows who were being overlooked in the daily distribution of food.
QUESTION 6:
D. Their responsibilities are open-ended.
The Bible clearly delineates the qualifications for this office, but the functions are open-ended. As opposed to the biblically defined role of elder, the role of deacon varies considerably depending on the cultural needs of the church.
QUESTION 7: *Your answer*
QUESTION 8: *Your answer*
QUESTION 9:
D. Spiritual qualifications
QUESTION 10:
B. Elders that preach and teach should receive adequate wages.
This principle is clear in Scripture. A "The worker deserves his pay" (1 Tim. 5:18). Teaching pastors should receive adequate wages so that they can concentrate their efforts on these responsibilities. Unfortunately, many pastors and other Christian workers are not paid adequately. There are some Christians who believe that full-time Christian workers should live more sacrificially than themselves. This creates hardship for the children of Christian leaders, leading to negative feelings and even rebellion against spiritual things.
QUESTION 11: False
QUESTION 12: *Your answer*
QUESTION 13: *Your answer*
QUESTION 14: False
QUESTION 15: True
QUESTION 16: True
QUESTION 17: True
QUESTION 18: False
QUESTION 19: False
QUESTION 20: *Your answer*
QUESTION 21: Correct answers include:
Emotional
Psychological
The family analogy adds the necessary emotional dimension of warmth, tenderness, concern, and loyalty. The body illustrates every member's need to participate while the family illustrates the psychological aspects of relational Christianity.

QUESTION 22:

Scripture	Family Love
1 Thessalonians 4:9-10	God taught you to love each other as family, so do more and more!
Hebrews 13:1-3	Keep on loving one another as brothers.
1 Peter 1:22-23	Sincerely love one another deeply with all your hearts.
1 Peter 3:8-9	Live in sympathetic harmony with your brothers.
2 Peter 1:5-7	Add to your faith brotherly kindness and to that add love.

QUESTION 23:
B. The Jewish Leaders
"For even the Son of Man did not come to be served but to serve, and to give his life a ransom for many" (Mark 10:45).

QUESTION 24: *Your answer*

QUESTION 25: *Your answer*

Lesson 8 Self Check Answers

QUESTION 1:
C. Moses
QUESTION 2: False
QUESTION 3: Correct answers include:
Culture
City
Region
QUESTION 4:
D. Multiple elders with one head elder
QUESTION 5:
A. Distribution of food
QUESTION 6: False
QUESTION 7: Correct answers include:
Shepherding
Pastoring
QUESTION 8:
A. To be served
QUESTION 9: Correct answers include:
Emotional
Psychological
QUESTION 10: True

Lesson 8 Articles

Devoted to One Another

*"Be **devoted to one another** with mutual (brotherly) love, showing eagerness in honoring one another"* (Rom 12:10, emphasis added).

This concept is illustrated by family ties. In most families, even though the siblings may fight with each other, they close ranks when attacked from the outside. This attitude is what Paul expected of those in the body of Christ because they are also brothers and sisters in Christ. The analogy of the body is limited to illustrating how the church functions, so the family analogy adds the necessary emotional dimension of warmth, tenderness, concern, and loyalty. The body illustrates every member's need to participate, while the family illustrates the psychological aspects of relational Christianity.

The Greek word *adelphos,* or mutual, literally means "from the same womb"—blood-brothers in Christ (Eph 1:7)! We are all born again in God's forever family, and the fact that we are family is even the basis of God's discipline of us (1 Pet 4:17). Devotion literally refers to the mutual love of parents, children, husbands, and wives—willing to die for one another.

We naturally begin as babes in Christ and go through various stages of development. But we must not remain there in immaturity and selfish behavior. "Each of you should be concerned not only about your own interests, but about the interests of others as well" (Phil 2:4).

Note: This material is adapted from Gene A. Getz, *The Measure of a Man.* (Ventura, CA: Regal Books, 1984).

Honoring One Another

*"Be devoted to one another with mutual love, showing eagerness in **honoring one another**"* (Rom 12:10, emphasis added).

To illustrate this concept, picture a great musician who seeks to enhance the performance of others without drawing attention to them, or the accompanist who brings out the best in others and rejoices when they are honored. Our desire should be to make the other members of the body look and sound good and rejoice at their success.

Jesus again is the prime example, honoring others above Himself, saying: "You know that those who are recognized as rulers of the Gentiles lord it over them, and those in high positions use their authority over them. But it is not this way among you. But whoever wants to be great among you must be your servant, and whoever wants to be first among you must be the slave of all. **For even the Son of Man did not come to be served but to serve, and to give his life as a ransom for many**" (Mk 10:42-45, emphasis added).

The opposite is illustrated in His rebuke of the Jewish leaders: "Watch out for the experts in the law. They like to walk around in long robes and be greeted in the marketplaces, and to have the prominent seats in the synagogues and the places of honor at banquets. They devour widows' property, and as a show make long prayers. These men will receive a more severe punishment" (Mk 12:38-40).

We are exhorted to have the same attitude toward one another that Christ did. He did not think of His own best interest, but of ours (Phil 2:5-11). He was not honored during His earthly life, but endured shame and even death on a cross. We must follow His example as other heroes of the faith did who "were tortured, not accepting release, to obtain resurrection to a better life" (Heb 11:35b).

Acts 6:1-7:

> Now in these days, when the disciples were growing in number, a complaint arose on the part of the Greek–speaking Jews against the native Hebraic Jews, because their widows were being overlooked in the daily distribution of food. So the twelve called the whole group of the disciples together and said, "It is not right for us to neglect the word of God to wait on tables. But carefully select from among you, brothers, seven men who are well-attested, full of the Spirit and of wisdom, whom we may put in charge of this necessary task. But we will devote ourselves to prayer and to the ministry of the word." The proposal pleased the entire group, so they chose Stephen, a man full of faith and of the Holy Spirit, with Philip, Prochorus, Nicanor, Timon, Parmenas, and Nicolas, a Gentile convert to Judaism from Antioch. They stood these men before the apostles, who prayed and placed their hands on them. The word of God continued to spread, the number of disciples in Jerusalem increased greatly, and a large group of priests became obedient to the faith.

Note: This material is adapted from Gene A. Getz, *The Measure of a Man*. (Ventura, CA: Regal Books, 1984).

Leader's Job Descriptions

"Managing" and "shepherding" in the New Testament are words that overlap in meaning. They are not exclusive tasks but concepts that portray the same truth from different angles. "Managing" is the more technical term, while "shepherding" is the more personal term. Note also that in the only two passages in the New Testament where elders are directly addressed regarding their responsibilities, they are commanded to "shepherd the flock" (Acts 20:28; 1Pet 5:2).

The two words together provide a sense of balance to the ministry of elders. The personal emphasis of the term "shepherd" helps prevent elders from becoming impersonal managers of the church, while "manager" emphasizes that there is organization necessary to give structure and direction to the personal ministry of the church. Therefore, we must understand what is included in the two concepts.

The flock metaphor contributes great insight to our understanding of the role of leaders in the church. It is clear from the other metaphors of the church that all church members, not just recognized leaders, must minister to one another. Leaders should come from the most mature members proven capable to fulfill this task.

Chapter 10: Leadership in the New Testament Church, Phase Two

New Testament church leaders faced some unusual problems during the early years of the church's existence. They had no inspired literature from which to teach doctrine which was distinctly New Testament. It is conceivable that some Christians even at the end of the first century had not yet been exposed to all of the Gospels, Paul's letters, and the other Epistles.[1]

God had a plan, however, which enabled the apostles, prophets, evangelists, pastors, and teachers to "equip the saints for the work of service"—even apart from having the New Testament literature. He bestowed upon these individuals supernatural capacities and abilities—involving both knowledge and skill to enable them to edify the church (Eph 4:7-12).[2] But as churches were founded and established in the faith, a new plan for church leadership unfolded—one which, for practical reasons, is designated as phase two.

Local Church Leadership

The book of Acts as well as some material in the Epistles clearly demonstrates that, in the most part, those individuals who possessed the greater gifts—that of apostle, prophet, evangelist, pastor, and teacher—had a ministry at large. They made disciples, founded churches, and moved from one group of believers to another, helping them become established in the faith.

The primary responsibility of the first-century pastor-teacher was to help the new and struggling church to get organized and to grow spiritually. As mentioned previously, Timothy was one of the most prominent pastor-teachers in the New Testament. When the church at Corinth was struggling in its carnality and immaturity, Paul sent Timothy to teach them (1 Cor 4:17). Paul also indicated his plans to send him to Philippi to have a ministry among the Christians there (Phil 2:19-20). He left him in Ephesus to instruct and guide the believers (1 Tim 1:3). On his second missionary journey, he left Timothy in Berea along with Silas (Acts 17:14), apparently to help establish the church. On the same journey, after starting the church in Thessalonica, Paul sent Timothy back to this church to strengthen and encourage them (1 Thess 3:1-2).

Timothy and other men like him, such as Titus, served the New Testament church as God's plan for church leadership moved from phase one to phase two. They instituted the second phase as soon as there were believers in the local congregation who were mature enough to be appointed as elders. Paul and Barnabas demonstrated this as they retraced their steps and went back to the cities in which they had previously "made many disciples" and then "appointed elders... in every church" (Acts 14:21-23, NASB).

Elders or Bishops?

Following are several important observations regarding this process:

1. These local church leaders are identified in Scripture with two basic titles.

The two words used to describe these spiritual leaders were "Bishop" (*episkopos*) and "elder"

---

[1] 1. Regarding the canon of the New Testament, Tenney notes: "It is evident that not all of the present books of the New Testament were known or accepted by all the churches in the east and in the west during the first four centuries of the Christian era." (Merrill C. Tenney, *New Testament Survey*, p. 411.)

[2] 2. All members of Christ's body were recipients of spiritual gifts. However, as we've seen in the previous chapter, the "greater gifts" were important in God's plan "to prepare God's people for works of service" and their expression was to be given priority in local churches.

(*presbuteros*). It is commonly understood that the terms were used inter-changeably, particularly by Paul.[3]

The word *bishop* actually means "an overseer." This word was used as an official title among the Greeks. Synonyms for the word bishop might be overseer, curator, guardian, or superintendent.[4]

The word *elder*, though used in the literature of many societies, is found most frequently in the writings which describe the activities of God's chosen people. Moreover, the word elder appears in the New Testament more frequently than the word bishop, and especially in the book of Acts. Reference to being a bishop appears only once in Acts, and that is where Paul is addressing the Ephesian elders (Acts 20:28). The rest of the time it appears in the Pauline epistles, and as just mentioned, is used interchangeably with the word elder.

Some have suggested that the term bishop is used to refer to the office and the word elder has to do with the man or person. It seems there is a more accurate explanation. Since Paul had a special ministry to the Gentiles, and since he used the word bishop more frequently than other New Testament writers, it appears he did so to communicate more effectively to the mixture of converted Jews and Gentiles in the New Testament church. If this is true, it indicates Paul's sensitivity to culture and how important it is to communicate in the language of the people.

So whether we call them elders (a term well known to Jews) or bishops (a term well known to Greeks), it matters not, implied Paul. The important issue is what characterized their lives and what they did. The title was commonly understood to be secondary, and their qualifications and functions were primary.[5]

2. These spiritual leaders were to manage and shepherd God's people.

There are also two words used to describe the overall responsibility of elders. They were to manage and to pastor or shepherd.[6] "Managing" is the more technical term, whereas "pastoring" and "shepherding" are more colorful and illustrative concepts.

Managing the Church

First, Paul used the word "manage" in his writings when listing the qualifications for elders. Note that he did so by referring to the role of the father in a family setting. An elder "must be one who manages his own household well," wrote Paul, (1 Tim 3:4). He then correlated this observation

---

[3] 3. Compare Acts 20:17, 28; Titus 1:5, 7; 1 Tim 3:1-2, and 1 Tim 5:17, 19.

[4] 4. J.P. Lightfoot, Saint Paul: *The Epistle to the Philippians*, McMillan, p. 95.

[5] The only other author of Scripture who recorded the word "bishop" interchangeably with the word "elder" was Luke. Significantly, he used the term to describe the spiritual leaders in Ephesus (Acts 20:17), and then quoted Paul who addressed these leaders as "bishops"(Acts 20:28). It is also interesting to note that Luke was a Gentile convert and would understand this cultural adaptation.

[6] Since the title "elder" is used more frequently in our culture, hereafter it will be used in this book to describe spiritual leaders in the local church. In actuality the term bishop is often used differently from what it was in the New Testament.

Today it often refers to an individual who has the oversight of a group of churches and/or pastors. The word "elder," however, has continued to be used in similar ways as it was used in the New Testament. Consequently, elder is more acceptable to many evangelical Christians.

with leadership in a local church. "If a man does not know how to manage his own household, how will he take care of the church of God?" (1 Tim 3:5). This is a very significant observation. First, it demonstrates a relationship in Paul's thinking between a family unit and the local church. A single household was often the church in miniature. The father was to lead his family just as elders were to lead the church.

Second, it is important to note that Paul's illustration gives us a functional definition of the word "manage." It is an all-inclusive concept. There is nothing that is not included in this task. It involves total and complete oversight of the family or the church.

Put another way, God holds the father responsible for the overall leadership in a home, and He holds the elders responsible for the overall leadership in a church. God has ordained the same set of principles for the church and for the family.

The same can be said regarding the husband-wife relationship as well as how an individual believer orders his life within the body of Christ.

Third, this family-church relationship as described by Paul leads to a very practical question. It is clear from Scripture that God never intended the home to function with more than one primary leader—the husband and father. Does this imply, particularly in Paul's reference to family and church management, that local churches also need one primary leader? We need to address this question particularly in view of the various opinions that exist on this subject in contemporary churches. But first, we need more biblical data.

Pastoring the Flock

The words "pastoring" and "shepherding" are used more frequently in Scripture to describe the overall leadership responsibility of an elder than the words "manage" and "rule".[7] This concept would be meaningful to first-century Christians who understood experientially a relationship between a shepherd and his sheep. Unfortunately, many twenty-first-century Christians do not grasp the full meaning of this kind of analogy, as pointed out by Phillip Keller in his delightful and informative book *A Shepherd Looks at Psalm 23*:[8] [This is taken from p. 9 of this book]

> Many who either read or study the Scriptures in the twenty-first century come from an urban man-made environment. City people, especially, are often unfamiliar with such subjects as livestock, crops, land, food, or wildlife. They miss much of the truth taught in God's Word because they are not familiar with such things as sheep, wheat, soil, or grapes.

The apostle Peter used this analogy more graphically than any other New Testament writer. In his first epistle, he exhorted the elders to "shepherd the flock of God" (I Pet 5:2). They were to do it with freedom (not under compulsion) and with pure motives (not for sordid gain). Furthermore, they were not to approach this task in an authoritarian manner, lording it over those allotted to their charge. Rather, they were to "be examples to the flock" (1 Peter 5:1-3). Peter then ended this paragraph on pastoral leadership by referring to the greatest Shepherd who ever walked the face of the earth—Jesus Christ Himself. "And when the Chief Shepherd appears," he wrote, "you will receive the crown of glory that never fades away" (1 Pet 5:4).

---

[7] The word "rule" which comes from the same basic Greek word translated "manage" is also used in Paul's letter to Timothy to describe those elders who are paid financially for their efforts (1 Tim. 5:17).

As with the term "manage," "shepherding" is an all-inclusive term.

A shepherd is responsible for the total welfare of his sheep. He is to guard them from savage wolves—false teachers (Acts 20:28, 29). He is to feed them by declaring and teaching the whole purpose of God (Acts 20:27; Tit 1:9). He is to care for them and pray for them when they are ill (Jas 5:14).

Psalm 23 illustrates the shepherding responsibility more completely than any other passage of Scripture. David's description of God's care for him personally provides a powerful model for men who serve as shepherds of God's people:

Psalm 23 (NASB)

"I shall not want."

"He makes me lie down in green pastures."

"He leads me beside quiet waters."

"He restores my soul."

"He guides me in the paths of righteousness."

"Even though I walk through the valley of the shadow of death, I fear no evil, for Thou art with me."

"Thy rod and Thy staff, they comfort me."

"Thou dost prepare a table before me in the presence of my enemies."

"Thou hast anointed my head with oil."

Just so, an elder shepherds and manages his people by:
- Meeting their spiritual needs
- Making them feel secure and restful
- Caring for their spiritual thirst
- Building them up when they fail and are discouraged

"Managing" and "shepherding" then describe synonymous functions. They are overarching concepts which include more specific functions, such as exemplifying Christlikeness, preaching the gospel, exhorting and warning Christians against inappropriate behavior, teaching the truth of God, and praying for those who are sick. This is what is meant by the observation—these leaders were to manage or shepherd God's people.

3. Some of these leaders were to be paid for their ministry.

Paul made specific reference to this congregational responsibility in his first letter to Timothy. He wrote that "the elders who rule well be considered worthy of double honor, especially those who work hard at preaching and teaching" (1 Tim 5:17, NASB). This is clear from the context.

This is the biblical basis for spiritual leaders who are identified today as staff pastors. When an individual gives a large portion of time to the ministry, that person usually doesn't have time left over to work at a regular job in order to provide for his family.

If a body of believers encourages and accepts this kind of effort, then that church is responsible to remunerate that person for his efforts.

Paul is saying that there will be those elders—when they carry out their "ruling" or "managing" role—who will work particularly hard in the areas of "preaching and teaching." Anyone who has served as a staff pastor with these primary responsibilities can verify that these are the most time-consuming aspects of managing or shepherding—that is, if preaching and teaching are to be done in a qualitative manner.

4. New Testament churches evidently had more than one elder or bishop.

At this juncture the New Testament record becomes somewhat unclear. Unless we understand their structures, it is difficult to state dogmatically how elders carried out their functions.

Multiple Eldership

What can we say for sure relative to multiple eldership in a given church?

First, it is true that the Bible always speaks of the "elders" of the church; that is, the term is pluralized. The only exception is when an individual elder is referred to (see 1 Tim 3:1-2), but again this kind of reference is always in the context of plurality.

Second, the term church, as it is used to speak of local churches in specific geographical settings, was used by scriptural writers to refer to all the believers in a particular area, whether they met together regularly or not. For example, Luke referred to the "church in Jerusalem" (Acts 8:1). But we know from the biblical record that believers were not able to continue to meet in one place.

There was not a building large enough, nor would they have been allowed to do so if there had been. The fact is that they initially met in the temple (Acts 2:46a). On one occasion shortly after the church was founded, they gathered in the portico of Solomon to hear Peter preach. As a result, both Peter and John were arrested (Acts 3:11; Acts 4:1-3). Eventually, the persecution spread to the whole church and Luke recorded that "they were all scattered throughout the region of Judea and Samaria, except the apostles" (Acts 8:1). Until that happened, the normal meeting place in Jerusalem was in homes. They met "from house to house" (Acts 1:46b).

The church in Ephesus gives us another illustration. Luke referred to "the elders of the church" in that city (Acts 20:17). Here the term elder is pluralized in conjunction with the single, local church, just as it was in Jerusalem (Acts 21:18). But again, this does not refer to the fact that the church had a permanent or even a temporary meeting place as we usually do in our twenty-first-century American culture.

True, Paul met with believers (and probably unbelievers) daily in the school of Tyrannus for a period of two years (Acts 19:9-10). But it is clear from the context that this was not the regular meeting place for the church to fellowship, worship, and be taught. Rather, they also, no doubt, met in homes.

We cannot find any record of church buildings as we think of them in terms of our culture until sometime in the third century. In fact, one of the first buildings used primarily as a regular place for Christian meetings was discovered by archeologists in the ruins of the ancient city Dura-Europus in the Syrian desert. It was used as a private home by a well-to-do person. The date of construction was the year AD 232–233.[9]

Before drawing any firm conclusions, consider one more New Testament example. Paul left Titus in Crete to help these new churches get organized. The process was to "appoint elders in every town" (Tit 1:5). Again, we have the term elder pluralized.

---

[9] "Jack Finegan, *Light From the Ancient Past*, vol. 2, Princeton University Press, pp. 495–499.

But we also have reference to more than one city. Therefore, we can conclude only one thing: Titus was to appoint more than one elder in each city.

Assuming that "house churches" were the normative meeting place for the churches in Crete as they were in other places in the New Testament world, we can now raise some interesting questions.

1. Was there one elder for every house church? If so, this would in no way be in contradiction to the previous reference to plurality of elders in Jerusalem or Ephesus. It would simply mean there was more than one house church in each city.

2. Was there more than one elder in each house church? Perhaps, but probably not unless the house church was unusually large. This is a possibility, however, since they have discovered homes that were used for the church to meet in that had rooms that could seat up to 500 people. Practically speaking, it would probably take more than one elder to adequately manage and shepherd this size church.

But beyond this we cannot go. There is not sufficient biblical data regarding church structure to explain more fully the concept of plurality of elders and how this actually worked out in a given locality. There are, however, some pragmatic considerations we can bring to bear up on the observation that New Testament churches seemingly had more than one elder or bishop. But more about that later.

5. These spiritual leaders were to delegate responsibility to other qualified men and women to care for the cultural needs of the church.

Elders were not the only leaders appointed in New Testament days to direct the affairs of the local church. The Bible also refers to deacons and deaconesses.

In Paul's letter to Timothy, who was stationed at the time in Ephesus, he specified, first of all, the qualifications for elders (1 Tim 3:1-7). He then specified the qualifications for deacons, men in serving roles (1 Tim 3:8-10, 12), and deaconesses, women in serving roles (1 Tim 3:11). [10]:

Functions of Deacons and Deaconesses

What were these people supposed to do in the church? To some it may be surprising that biblical writers did not specify functions for these church leaders as they did for elders. Rather, the Scriptures specify qualifications for both positions, but they leave the deacons' and deaconesses' roles open-ended.

---

[10] Though there is some ambiguity regarding the role of deaconesses, it appears that the women Paul referred to in 1 Timothy 3:11 were those who served as deaconesses (1 Tim 3:8). It seems Paul was outlining the qualifications for men and then very naturally inserted the statement that "women [who are in a serving role] must likewise" have certain qualifications. Otherwise, the flow of Paul's thoughts is interrupted with a totally different idea—the "qualifications of Christian women in general." If this is true, and in view of the context, it is legitimate to ask, "Qualifications for what position?" The only logical answer to this question seems to be "deaconesses." It should be noted that some believe Paul was referring to "deacons' wives." But, if so, why didn't Paul specify qualifications for "elders' wives"? In view of an elder's function in the church, it would seem more important to include qualifications for their wives, or at least to include them too.

Lesson 8 Articles

Why is this true? Once again, we see the importance of understanding culture. The role of elders is a biblical absolute. No matter what their societal background, Christians will always need to be managed, pastored, taught the Word of God, and ministered to in other spiritual ways. On the other hand, cultural needs vary from society to society and from time to time even in the same community.

This is illustrated in the church in Jerusalem. When the Hellenistic widows were being neglected in the daily distribution of food (Acts 6:1-7), the apostles appointed seven men to make sure the women's needs were cared for. Though they were not directly identified as deacons, it is commonly understood that they were functioning as deacons should.[11] Later, when the church was scattered, these men no longer were needed for this task. In fact, we know that at least two, Stephen and Philip, became evangelists (Acts 7–8).

Note one other observation. When Paul instructed Titus to "appoint elders in every town" in Crete (Tit 1:5), he said nothing about deacons. However, when Timothy was in Ephesus, he gave instructions regarding elders, plus deacons as well as deaconesses. The question is why? From a study of all passages that deal with local church leadership, the reason seems to be related to cultural needs. The church in Ephesus had already become established and operative for some time. As the church grew, cultural needs had developed over the process of time. However, the churches in Crete were new. The first step was to appoint elders to meet spiritual needs, just as Paul and Barnabas had done in Lystra, Iconium, and Pisidian Antioch (Acts 14:21-23). The implication is clear. Deacons were to be appointed in Crete when the need arose.

6. These spiritual leaders were to be appointed on the basis of spiritual qualification.

There are two passages that specify elder qualifications (1 Tim 3:1-13; Tit 1:5-9). Paul's letter to Timothy includes qualifications for elders, deacons, and deaconesses. His letter to Titus includes only qualifications for elders.

Though each maturity profile for elders is self-contained and in essence is qualitatively the same as the other, it is helpful to combine them for a more thorough perspective on what God expects spiritual leaders to reflect with their lives. This combined list is as follows.

1. Above reproach (1 Tim 3:2; Tit 2:7)
2. Husband of one wife (1 Tim 3:2; Tit 1:6)
3. Temperate (1 Tim 3:2; Tit 1:8)
4. Prudent (1 Tim 3:2; Tit 1:8)
5. Respectable (1 Tim 3:2)
6. Hospitable (1 Tim 3:2; Tit 1:8)
7. Able to teach (1 Tim. 3:2; Tit 1:9)
8. Not addicted to wine (1 Tim. 3:3; Tit 1:7)
9. Not pugnacious but gentle (1 Tim 3:3; Tit 1:7)
10. Uncontentious (1 Tim 3:3)
11. Free from the love of money (1 Tim 3:3; Tit 1:7; 1 Pet 5:2)

---

[11] These men were appointed to "serve tables" and the word deacon comes from the word serve. In this sense we can legitimately call these men "deacons."

12. One who manages his own household well, keeping his children under control with all dignity (1 Tim 3:4; Tit 1:6)
13. Not a new convert (1 Tim. 3:6)
14. Of good reputation with those outside the church (1 Tim 3:7)
15. Not self–willed (Tit 1:7)
16. Not quick tempered (Tit 1:7)
17. Love what is good (Tit 1:8)
18. Just (Tit 1:8)
19. Devout (Tit 1:8)
20. Hold fast the faithful word (Tit 1:9)

Note we did not cover these traits in depth here because they are discussed in articles accompanying each lesson.

Paul also included a list of qualities for deacons and deaconesses in 1 Timothy 3. Notice the similarity to the qualifications for elders.

Deacons

1. Men of dignity (1 Tim 3:8)
2. Not double tongued (1 Tim 3:8)
3. Not addicted to much wine (1 Tim 3:8)
4. Not fond of sordid gain (1 Tim 3:8)
5. Holding to the mystery of the faith with a clear conscience (1 Tim 3:9)
3. Beyond reproach (1 Tim 3:10)
4. Husbands of only one wife (1 Tim 3:12)
5. Good managers of their children and their own households (1 Tim 3:12)

Deaconesses

1. Dignified (1 Tim 3:11)
2. Not malicious gossips (1 Tim 3:11)
3. Temperate (1 Tim 3:11)
4. Faithful in all things (1 Tim 3:11)

When it comes to describing how spiritual leaders (elders particularly) did their work, we are told less by Scripture writers than any other area of New Testament church life. For example, elders' functions are clear and the qualities that are to grace their daily lifestyles are spelled out in detail. But the following "form questions" are not answered in the Bible:

1. How old should these leaders be?
2. How should these leaders be selected?
3. How many leaders should there be in a single church?
4. How long should these leaders serve?
5. What is the best way for these leaders to carry out their functions?
6. When there is more than one spiritual leader, who takes primary leadership?

Summary

What have we learned about phase two in God's plan for leadership in the New Testament church?

1. God does not lock us into specific titles for our spiritual leaders in the church.
2. Spiritual leaders should manage and shepherd the people of God.
3. Spiritual leaders who spend a lot of time in the ministry should be cared for financially.
4. When possible, churches should have more than one spiritual leader to serve as godly models.
5. When necessary, spiritual leaders should delegate responsibility to other qualified leaders to care for cultural needs.
6. All church leaders should be spiritually and psychologically qualified to lead.
7. Adequate forms should be developed in particular cultures for church leaders to carry out their functions in the best possible way.

Leadership Defined

What emerges from a study of the New Testament is that very early in its life the church was organized. In this regard, we often drift to two extremes in our thinking. Some say that "the best organization is **no** organization" and that "the church is an **organism**, not an **organization**." On the surface these assertions sound spiritual. After all, if God the Holy Spirit indwells each believer and guides us, why do we need any human organization? Human organization often (some say 'always') becomes very worldly in its operation.

Others promote a very strong, even authoritarian, leadership structure whereby the church is highly organized. Their basic argument is that God has gifted some with skills to manage the church and appointed them to the position of elder. These few men hold all authority in the church because other believers are not mature enough to lead the church.

In reality, Acts 14 and Titus 1 show that local churches were always organized. Organization in the church is related to function. Because the church has the function of worshiping God, edifying believers, and evangelizing the lost, it must be organized to effectively fulfill its function.

Organization is also related to the size of a local church, for as a church grows in size it must also grow in organizational complexity. It is not possible to lead a church of 1,200 people with the same structure it used when there were 100 members.

From the flock metaphor, we saw how essential leadership is for the church. God chooses to increase the purposefulness in the gathering, as well as in the scattering movements of the church, by appointing church leaders. Knowing the total picture of the church from the New Testament tells us a lot about the nature of this leadership.

Several details of church organization remain unspecified. As we noted before, the manner of church leader's service and submission receive extra attention; whereas many other things about the functioning of leaders remains unspecified.

Members Who Belong to One Another

*"So we who are many are one body in Christ, and individually we are **members who belong to one another**"* (Rom 12:5, emphasis added).

Biblically, Christians are members who belong to one another. This concept is similar in many ways to Paul's analogy of the human body and the body of Christ, the church (1 Cor 12:27).

First, Paul teaches that no individual Christian can function effectively alone.

Second, no member of Christ's body should feel more important than another member. No one can legitimately say, as some of the Corinthian believers were, that they do not need—or are more important than— someone else (Rom 12:3). Paul emphasizes humility, patience, and gentleness for functioning within the body (Eph 4:2). One person may have a more responsible position, but even the person whose contribution is unnoticed is equally important to God (1 Cor 12:22-23).

Third, Christians should work hard at creating unity in the body of Christ. It is a unit made up of many parts, and we must agree with one another and be perfectly united without divisions (1 Cor 1:10; 12:12).

The biblical emphasis is on maturing in Christ—no longer thinking or acting like children—through love, the most significant key to unity and effective body function.

Note: This material is adapted from Gene A. Getz, *The Measure of a Man*. (Ventura, CA: Regal Books, 1984).

Chapter 12: Principles of New Testament Leadership

A study of leadership in the New Testament yields some clear-cut principles for the twenty-first-century church. These principles can serve as guidelines and objectives for starting new churches in our contemporary culture—wherever that might be—and can also provide established churches with a criteria for evaluating their own philosophy and practice of church leadership.

Distinguish Between Leadership Phases

First, in discerning and practicing God's plan for leadership in the church today, we must carefully distinguish between the two leadership phases in the New Testament, but yet understand the applicability of both an "apostolic" ministry and a local church ministry in carrying out the Great Commission in the twenty-first-century world.

Even a brief study and casual reflection regarding the context in which the church came into existence reveals some unique problems we do not face today. First, the Jewish religious world into which Christ came had become thoroughly institutionalized.

Its leaders had become self-serving and manipulative. They had twisted God's laws to benefit themselves. Jesus' strongest barbs were directed at the leaders in Israel. "Woe to you, scribes and Pharisees, hypocrites!" He said. "For you are like whitewashed tombs which on the outside appear beautiful, but inside they are full of dead men's bones and all uncleanness" (Mt 23:27, NASB). Jesus then applied this illustration more specifically. "Even so," He continued, "you, too, outwardly appear righteous to men, but inwardly you are full of hypocrisy and lawlessness" (Mt 23:28, NASB).

Second, Jesus came to launch the church, a completely new phenomenon. Though Israel represented the people of God on earth, the church was to be uniquely different. It would be composed of both Jews and Gentiles, born-again people indwelt by the Holy Spirit. Paul summarized it well when he wrote to the Ephesians speaking specifically to the Gentiles and reminded them that they were "no longer strangers and aliens, but ... fellow citizens with the saints." They were "of God's household, having been built upon the foundation of the apostles and prophets, Christ Jesus Himself being the cornerstone, in whom the whole building, being fitted together is growing into a holy temple in the Lord, in whom," Paul said, "you also are being built together into a dwelling of God in the Spirit" (Eph 2:19-22, NASB).

Third, when Jesus returned to heaven, His followers had no body of literature to guide them in this new mission. Though the Old Testament recorded the laws of God and the history of Israel, it did not contain the doctrines and teachings they would need to equip the members of Christ's body for ministry.

Fourth, the world Christ's followers faced was hostile. The message of Christ itself challenged the Jewish leaders who rejected His messiahship. And the pagan world viewed Christianity as another fanatical religion that deserved little attention.

The first challenge facing the apostles particularly was to launch this new movement in spite of the problems just outlined. Armed with Christ's promise that He would guide them into all truth and teach them what to say by means of the indwelling Holy Spirit (Jn 14-16), they did just that. The church was born. Furthermore, God bore witness to their message, "with signs and wonders and various miracles and gifts of the Holy Spirit distributed according to his will" (Heb 2:4). Through this process, local churches came into existence, which led first to the appointment of elders and later to deacons and deaconesses. The truth revealed primarily to the apostles by direct revelation and inspiration of the Holy Spirit was transmitted to local church leaders who in turn taught others. Thus Paul wrote to Timothy, "And the things which you have heard from me in the presence of many witnesses, these entrust to faithful men, who will be able to teach others also" (2 Tim 2:2, NASB).

Today we face a similar world. However, we have at our disposal the written Word of God in its entirety. The apostles and a few selected individuals first spoke the message under the leadership of the Holy Spirit but eventually recorded it for us as sacred Scripture. Armed with God's truth, we can face both a hostile religious culture and a pagan world. Led by the Holy Spirit who dwells within us, we can speak God's truth with divine authority. Furthermore, we can demonstrate the reality of Christianity by means of visible local churches. And when those churches are unified in love, it provides the evidence that verifies that the message of Christ is true (Jn 13:34-35; 17:20-23).

God's two leadership phases are still necessary today. There's a need for those who will fulfill apostolic, prophetic, and teaching ministries by evangelizing the unsaved and establishing churches—just as Paul, Barnabas, Silas, Timothy, and Titus did in New Testament days. Though God's power may be revealed differently, these spiritual pioneers still have the same divine message, but in completed form and the same basic authority that was given by Christ when He uttered the Great Commission.[12] Phase two in God's leadership plan is directly ongoing and has been since New Testament days. Men must be equipped to be elders and appointed to manage and shepherd local churches.

---

[12] It is an enlightening study to trace in the book of Acts the way the apostles used the Old Testament in winning people to Christ.

This leads us to a second New Testament principle of leadership.

Appoint Qualified Leaders

The first step in assisting local churches in their spiritual growth is to appoint spiritually qualified people to lead these churches.

These leaders must be first of all selected on the basis of spiritual qualifications—not gifts, talents, and abilities.

Qualities Vs. Abilities

Out of the twenty specific qualifications listed by Paul in 1 Timothy 3 and Titus 1, almost all of them have to do with a man's reputation, ethics, morality, temperament, habits, and spiritual and psychological maturity. Today we need to refocus our thinking in this area. People become qualified for a local church ministry by measuring up to the criteria set forth in the New Testament. Unfortunately, we frequently look at the obvious abilities, talents, and gifts and not at the more basic and fundamental qualities.

Once you get to know a person well, the qualifications for eldership listed by Paul are clearly discernible. This does not mean that this individual is perfect. Far from it. It does mean that the direction of his life is clear.

However, it must, be noted that you cannot make accurate judgments regarding a person's qualifications without some careful, long-range evaluation by those who have lived in close proximity to that individual. This is why a church who calls a "pastor" on the basis of hearing him preach may make some serious errors in judgment. The person may be able to sway the people with his oratory and yet be extremely lacking in the qualifications spelled out so clearly in the New Testament.

Furthermore, in today's churches, we often appoint members to church boards who are successful in business. They have built large organizations in the secular world. In these instances we, at times, make judgments based on financial acumen and administrative abilities. In the selection process, these talents may take precedence over the basic qualifications listed by Paul. For example, many men are successful in the business world but fail woefully as managers of their own households. If we overlook this very important qualification for spiritual leadership, the church is headed for serious trouble. It is easy to hide spiritual weaknesses in our lives, especially if we are talented with unusual intellectual abilities and social graces.

Age and Experience

Another factor that is significant in selecting elders who are qualified is age and experience. It is not accidental that the word elder in itself refers to age.

This poses problems, however, for several reasons. First, the Bible does not give a specific age for elders. Second, being an older person does not guarantee maturity. Third, some younger men are mature for their age—more so than some older individuals.

However, the fact remains that there are only certain things that can be learned over the process of time. Age and experience produce wisdom in Christians who are truly seeking to follow the will of God. All of us can learn as much from our mistakes as our successes.

As a person involved in church planting, I have concluded that most major problems in the churches I've helped start were caused by the appointment of men to leadership who were too young both as staff pastors and non-staff pastors. They lacked experience and wisdom. Furthermore, some were threatened by older, more experienced leaders.

On the other hand, there are younger Christians who excel in major leadership positions in the church. Usually, however, they succeed because they have a good self-image, are teachable, and seek to learn from older and more experienced spiritual leaders. They do not react defensively to those who may disagree with them but attempt to learn in the process.

Timothy, of course, stands out as a unique example of a young man who had a heavy leadership responsibility. He was not only responsible to help establish churches but to appoint elders to lead those churches. In most instances these men were probably older than Timothy.

We must realize, however, that Timothy was probably at least thirty years old when he began his ministry. In that sense he was older and more experienced than many men who become leaders in our churches today. Furthermore, he brought himself under the authority of the apostle Paul, who was able to guide him and lead him through the difficult aspects of the ministry. When he was discouraged, Paul encouraged him. Furthermore, Paul built bridges for Timothy. He not only encouraged Timothy to live a life that would win respect, but he encouraged Christians in various churches to accept Timothy even though he was young (1 Cor 16:10-11).

In this sense, Timothy serves as an excellent role model for younger men who are entering the ministry.

I often face the question regarding "age" since many men graduate from seminary in their mid-twenties. Are they qualified to lead a church? This is a difficult question since the answer depends on several factors. How mature is the person in spite of his chronological age? How large is the church? What is the expectation level in the community and in the church?

Generally, I recommend that young men (particularly under thirty) seek an associate position for several years, assisting an older and more experienced spiritual leader. This can be done even though you may not agree totally with a particular leader's philosophy of ministry. However, the object must be to learn not to change the senior pastor and the direction of the church.

Though this may be a difficult assignment, it can yield unusual opportunities to mature and grow spiritually, psychologically, and in many areas involving management skills.

Managers and Pastors

Spiritual leaders must function as managers and pastors and not merely as administrators and decision makers.

Unfortunately, many church leaders have superimposed a modern-day definition of management on the biblical concept of being a manager of God's people. As is noted in our study of New Testament leadership in a previous chapter, "Elder Management" is functionally synonymous with the concept of "pastoring." Thus, a man who serves as an elder must be a shepherd. The greatest example of a shepherd is the Lord Jesus Christ Himself. On one occasion, He said:

> *I am the good shepherd; the good shepherd lays down His life for the sheep. He who is a hired hand and not a shepherd, who is not the owner of the sheep, sees the wolf coming, and leaves the sheep and flees, and the wolf snatches them and scatters them. He flees because he is a hired hand, and is not concerned about the sheep. I am the good shepherd; and I know My own, and My own know Me, even as the Father knows Me and I know the Father; and I lay down My life for the sheep* (Jn 10:11-14, NASB).

How illustrative of a man with a true pastoral or shepherd heart! He is willing to give himself to the members of the body of Christ that inhabit his fold. He stands by them no matter what the cost. He knows his sheep. He calls them by name! And the sheep know him; they know his voice.

There is no way to escape the implication of what it means to be a true elder. He must be with his people—not separate from them. He must know them personally—their needs, their concerns, their problems! He must be willing to leave the ninety and nine in the fold, and go out into the darkness of the night to find the straying lamb who has wandered away from the safety of the flock, and has been caught up in the thicket of disillusionment and sin (Mt 18:12-13).

His door must be open to the flock. No good shepherd excludes a single sheep from the fold. He must be available—not in word only, but truly available! His personality must say in no uncertain way, "I love you, I care about you, and I'm here beside you; you can talk with me anytime, anywhere and about anything you wish. I won't condemn you! I won't hurt you! I will help you become the person you really want to become—a mature member of the body of Christ."

This concept of shepherding is true for both staff and non-staff elders. For the elder "worthy of double honor"—the elder "who works hard at his preaching and teaching" and who receives wages (1 Tim 5:17-18, NASB)—must in no way circumvent people. The sacred desk must not become a barrier between shepherd and flock.

Non-staff elders should also be shepherds. To function biblically, they must not merely be members of a board that meets to make administrative decisions. True, this is part of managing God's people. But it is only one aspect of being a good pastor. In fact, elders who are only decision makers and administrators will not make adequate decisions because they are out of touch with people's needs. They don't really "know the sheep."

Managing and pastoring also involve teaching (1 Tim 3:2; Tit 1:9). This means that an elder must know the Word of God and be loyal to it. He must be able to share its dynamic truth with members of the body of Christ. This is a charge to both staff and non-staff elders.

Obviously, the staff pastor will have a ministry that is more public than the non-staff elder. He is the one who is working hard at preaching and teaching (1 Tim 5:17). But the Scripture teaches that all elders must be involved in the teaching process. To understand the biblical process, we must go back and look at the biblical examples. Jesus Christ, of course, becomes the supreme example in carrying out this process.

As we travel through the Gospels, following the Man of Galilee, we see a Teacher reflecting many varied characteristics. He taught individuals, small groups, large groups—and even several different groups at the same time (Lk 15:1-7:11, NASB). He was not limited to a classroom, but rather taught anywhere He saw people in need—on a hillside, in an upper room, in the synagogue, by a well, on a rooftop, on a boat in the middle of a lake, on a mountaintop, and even as He hung between two thieves on a cross. Sometimes they came to Him; other times He went to them. At times He delivered a discourse and at other times He asked questions.

Sometimes He told stories. Frequently, He visualized His words by referring to the fowls of the air, the water in the well, the sower on the hillside, or even to the people themselves. He was never stereotyped; never rigid; never without the right words. He was always meeting the needs of listeners, getting them intellectually and emotionally involved, and always penetrating to the deepest recesses of their personality. He was indeed the Master Teacher!

How different from our stereotyped approach to teaching in the church today, particularly among those of us who are staff pastors.

We often mount our platforms and deliver our sermons, which we hope are homiletically perfect. We seldom go to the people; they come to us and to the usual place, where they settle into their comfortable pews and wait to be stimulated. There is seldom opportunity for response, very little variation in the process, and experiential learning is rarely used. Furthermore, with this limited definition of teaching, we eliminate those opportunities for teaching that are personal, one on one—and which can be carried out effectively by non-staff elders.

Don't misunderstand. I am not suggesting that we cannot be effective unless we go back to the exact pattern of Jesus' example of teaching. We are living in a different culture, a different world.

But may I suggest that in many instances we are not even coming close to applying New Testament principles? We assume our present forms and structures are adequate to create a dynamic learning experience. We glorify the scholar who knows the content of the Bible, while we ignore the body of Christ and its many members who also have something to contribute to the ministry and the building up of the body.

Do we want a dynamic church? A dynamic ministry? Then I suggest that we must develop a philosophy of leadership that grows out of the Scriptures. We need spiritual leaders who are shepherds—men who teach God's people in an intimate and personal way. Furthermore, we need structures that permit these men to be and do what God intended them to be and do.

Priorities and Delegation

Spiritual leaders should maintain their priorities and delegate cultural responsibilities to other qualified men and women.

The apostles of old, when confronted with the problems in Jerusalem, said to the people, "It is not desirable for us to neglect the Word of God in order to serve tables." They solved the problem by delegating, by having seven men appointed to handle this matter, while they continued to give themselves "to prayer and to the ministry of the Word" (Acts 6:2, 4). Not that these matters were unimportant, nor were they matters that did not call for leaders with spiritual qualifications (Acts 6:5), but they were matters that could have taken the apostles away from their primary work.

Local church elders, too, are given priorities. They are to effectively manage the flock of God, which means shepherding, teaching, and praying for people. Their primary responsibility is to meet the spiritual needs of people.

Therefore, God has established a plan for delegation. Thus, we see the role of the deacon and deaconess as important. Their responsibilities and functions are basically cultural, as pointed out in an earlier chapter. Though their qualifications are pointed out in Scripture, their functions are open-ended.

Failing to maintain priorities and delegate responsibilities is one explanation as to why elders often become typical administrators and decision makers. Their time is totally used up attending board and committee meetings, making administrative decisions, and handling other routine details. When this happens, elders are not functioning as God intended them to function.

Personal contacts with the members of the body of Christ are limited to large group meetings where, separated from people by a pulpit, they expound the Word.

As a church grows large, this is why multiple leadership is so important. No one staff pastor, or even several pastors, can meet the needs of all the people in the body. There are unique and creative ways for staff leaders to utilize non-staff elders to help them minister to people's spiritual needs.

In many of the churches which I've helped establish, all of our elders are required to minister to people in small groups, which we call mini-churches. In addition, we have a large group of church leaders who serve as pastors, though they are not identified as elders.

But they too are ministering under the guidance and leadership of the elders and other staff pastors. In this way, the staff pastors are able to concentrate on ministering to the elders, other spiritual leaders in the church, and to concentrate on effective teaching and preaching to the body at large.

It is important to realize that in our culture, which is permeated by large centers of population, churches are going to grow in numbers. This obviously calls for strong spiritual leaders to serve as staff pastors. God needs multitalented Christian leaders who can lead these large dynamic churches. But we must remember that God also designed a multitalented body—a body made up of people who all contribute in a special way to the building up of the church.

At this juncture, I must add a word of warning. One of the most tragic things happening in our culture today is that highly gifted leaders are attempting to train ordinary leaders to be like themselves.

Unfortunately, these ordinary leaders (who make up the majority of us) have neither the capacity nor the ability to become this kind of leader. The result is frustration. Or even more tragic, these ordinary leaders attempt to imitate the life of a multitalented man and end up a total failure—hurting the body of Christ, and sometimes leaving the ministry.

Does this mean a highly gifted pastor shouldn't train others to be pastors? Not at all! But in training them, he must recognize they may not all be able to do what he is capable of doing. It is possible to get a person "in over his head," thinking he can function in all respects as his mentor. When he cannot, he is doomed to failure.

Strong leaders must be careful, then, not to think unrealistically. At the same time they must inspire others to rise to the highest level of achievement possible, but not to set their goals based on another man's capabilities.

Appoint and Reward

Churches should appoint certain spiritual leaders to serve in staff positions and adequately pay them for their efforts.

This principle is clear in Scripture. "The worker deserves his pay" (1 Tim 5:18). Unfortunately, many pastors and other Christian workers are not paid adequately. There are some Christians who believe that full-time Christian workers should live more sacrificially than themselves. Unfortunately, this often leads to discouragement. Also, it creates hardship for the children of Christian leaders, leading to negative feelings and even rebellion against spiritual things. It is far better to be on the "high side" in caring for spiritual leaders financially than on the "low side." God will honor this generosity.

A good rule of thumb is that a pastor and other Christian leaders should be cared for financially based on the average income of families in the congregation. The person's age, tenure, experience, education, and capabilities should all be considered, just as is true in any well-managed business organization. Furthermore, special attention should be given to benefits (insurance, retirement plan, etc.), just as is also true among the average people in the congregation.

Yet we must realize that there are times that spiritual leaders must give up rights because they are in the ministry. The apostle Paul illustrated this often. But on the other hand, Christians should not take advantage of their spiritual leaders. If they do, God's ultimate blessing will not be upon that ministry.

Primary Leader

When feasible, churches should be led by more than one spiritual leader, but it is important to designate one spiritual leader as the primary leader.

The Bible definitely teaches multiple leadership. In fact, the more godly leaders we have in a given local church who measure up to the qualities of 1 Timothy 3 and Titus 1, the greater impact on the members at large. A group of godly elders and pastors serve as a multiple model of Christlikeness.

However, there are those who teach that a church should be led by a committee. No one is to be designated to be the primary leader. Generally, this has resulted in recent years in non-staff elders being appointed as if they are the leaders of the church. And, indeed they are, but not the primary leader. The staff pastor should emerge as an elder to the elders, a pastor to the pastors. And when an additional staff pastor is added, it is very important that that person be responsible to the senior spiritual leader. He cannot be equal in authority, for if he is, it usually leads to inefficiency and eventual conflict.

Take for example one practical consideration. Who determines salary structures in a church where there are no lines of authority among the paid staff? It is impossible for men who are on staff to meet together to determine their own salary structures. Someone has to be the primary leader who recommends salary increases because of an obvious awareness of those who are on staff. Non-staff elders do not have enough exposure to the day-to-day operations of a church to be able to make wise judgments regarding who is and who is not responding well to his tasks.

But it is important to underscore that the more authority and the more position a spiritual leader is given, the more he is to be a servant. He is not to lord it over those who are to respond to his leadership. It is possible to be a senior pastor and yet to be a servant to the total paid staff, to the non-staff leadership, as well as to the body of Christ at large. Jesus demonstrated this principle in His own life when He taught that he who was greatest is to be servant of all.

Freedom to Develop

Churches should be free to develop creative forms and structures to apply the functions and principles just outlined.

There are many "form" questions that are not answered specifically in Scripture when it comes to leadership. Some of those questions are as follows:

1. How old should spiritual leaders be?
2. How should these leaders be selected?
3. How many leaders should there be in a specific church?
4. How long should these leaders serve?
5. What is the best way for these leaders to carry out their functions?
6. When there is more than one spiritual leader, who takes primary leadership?
7. What titles should we give to these spiritual leaders?

Though there are not specific answers to these questions, the Scriptures do give specific principles and the lenses of history and culture yield additional guidelines. They are as follows:

1. Spiritual leaders should be chosen from among those who've learned from years of experience, making them wise and discerning.
2. A system of selection should be developed that discovers and appoints qualified leaders who are highly respected by the people of the church. In our own church,

elders are selected from men who have successfully ministered to a small group of Christians for a substantial period of time. Furthermore, he must be approved by the small group as being qualified to serve as an elder. After all, it is the people who have been ministered to who know this person best.

3. The board of elders should be small enough to make decisions quickly, yet wisely. In my own experience, I have seen the result of a board getting too large. When it does, attendance patterns vary at board meetings. Communication begins to break down. Eventually, it is difficult to maintain unity in decisions and when you do, the process becomes long, laborious, repetitious, and inefficient.

4. If the church board size is limited for effective decision making, then a system should be developed to allow leaders to rotate off the board in order to make room for other qualified leaders to serve. Otherwise, the board becomes "ingrown."

5. A plan should be developed to allow spiritual leaders to carry out their functions effectively as pastors. If we do not, they will become administrators only, which leads to decisions that are out of touch with people's needs.

6. Finally, it is logical and practical for the local church elders to designate the primary leadership role in the church to the senior staff pastor or elder. It is doubly important to establish lines of authority when more than one elder is added to the paid staff, so these people are responsible to the primary staff pastor.

Lesson 9: Leadership Dynamics, Part II

Lesson Introduction

When Moses, the servant of the Lord, died in the land of Moab, the children of Israel mourned for him for thirty days. They lost their great leader and few, if any, of their leaders would ever measure up again (Heb 3:3). Thankfully, Moses had developed Joshua as a leader for forty years (Ex 17:9; Deut 31). Though Moses could not fully be replaced, Joshua was a capable leader as the Israelites entered the Promised Land (Ex 33:11; 34:29-35; Josh 1:1-9).

As a strong and intuitive leader, Moses keenly realized his human limitations and that he alone could not complete the work of God. Therefore, he carefully chose and mentored Joshua to support him in God's work, and to assume the leadership position for the children of Israel after he had gone to be with the Lord.

Leadership is the ability to guide, direct, or influence people. A critical element of leadership that faces Pastor Eugene, and you as a church leader, is the development of future church leaders that have the qualifications listed in the New Testament. It is the responsibility of the church's present leaders to accomplish this task. Paul made this clear to Timothy when he wrote:

> And what you heard me say in the presence of many others as witnesses entrust to faithful people who will be competent to teach others as well (2 Tim. 2:2)

In Lesson 8, we looked at the New Testament leadership offices and their responsibilities. Now we want to focus in on the qualities essential for church leaders to be respected and successful. A critical question to reflect upon as a church leader is: *How can I develop the leadership skills required to successfully lead my church and to carefully choose and mentor capable church members as future church leaders?*

Lesson Outline

Lesson 9: Leadership Dynamics, Part II
    Topic 1: Leadership Qualities—Self Assessment
    Topic 2: Developing Church Leaders
    Topic 3: Issues in Developing Church Leaders
    Topic 4: Developing Character: Unity, Diversity, Instruction
        Unity
        Diversity
        Instruction

Lesson Objectives

At the completion of Lesson 9, you will be able to:
- Assess your own strengths and weaknesses as a church leader
- Develop the framework for a leadership training process for your church
- Evaluate potential church leaders and properly choose, develop, and support them

Topic 1: Leadership Qualities—Self Assessment

Pastor Eugene is excited to learn more about the various aspects of church leadership. The knowledge he has gained through this course has given him the spiritual confidence to recognize the importance of periodically reflecting on one's personal leadership qualities. Careful self-reflection will help Pastor Eugene to not only identify his leadership gaps, but to remind himself of his areas of strengths. Armed with a clear and honest view of his own leadership capabilities, he can effectively use his spiritual strengths to help build up others in his congregation, while openly accepting support from members who possess the spiritual gifts and insights needed to effectively close his leadership gaps.

How can a leadership assessment help you avoid dangers in your own life? It is like looking into a mirror and correcting the problems with our appearance.

King Joash was very young when he became king of Judah. He succeeded as long as he had a good mentor: "Joash did what the LORD approved, throughout the lifetime of Jehoiada the priest," but he never developed his own character and he never realized his deficiency (2 Chr 24:1-2, 14-27). So after Jehoiada the priest died, Joash was less effective as God's leader because he had not matured as an individual man of God.

Joash made a major mistake: He never took the time to assess his personal leadership qualities. Honestly assessing your leadership qualities on a periodic basis provides you with a clear and current understanding of both your leadership gaps and strengths. It is essential that we reflect on our personal leadership qualities. The information in Topic 1 has been designed to help you avoid Joash's mistake.

Reading Assignment
Please read 2 Chronicles 24 on King Joash.

QUESTION 1
What mistake did Joash make early in his life that led to problems later?

QUESTION 2

Why was the smaller Syrian army able to defeat the larger Judean army?

    A. The Syrian army had better training and out-smarted the Judean army.

    B. The "Lord" allowed the Syrian army to defeat the larger Judean army.

    C. The Judean army was over-confident.

    D. The Syrian army was better armed.

QUESTION 3

Open your Life Notebook and make a summary list of your own strengths and weaknesses as one of the Lord's servants entrusted with leadership responsibilities. Note the leadership qualities you feel you must give immediate attention to, along with ideas/actions and a timeline for improving these areas.

Topic 1 Key Points:

- It is important to periodically examine your leadership skills to ensure that you are an effective and genuine leader.
- Self-reflection helps you become a stronger and intuitive church leader, just as Moses was for the children of Israel.

Topic 2: Developing Church Leaders

Although there are many strategies to foster the development of leadership qualities, one recommended method is to form leadership study groups. These groups should meet specifically to study leadership qualities and to help group members develop, or enhance, leadership qualities in their lives.

As a member of a leadership group, it is your responsibility to be open, honest, and trustworthy. Without these qualities, the group will not be effective and will not meet the standards of God's Word.

How can you as a church leader bring revival?

To examine this question, let's look back in history and review how our predecessors brought revival to their nation.

Old Testament revivals often came by studying the Law. The revival under King Hezekiah came in accordance with the Word of the Lord (2 Chr 29:15b). It resulted in the reinstitution of the Temple rituals and sacrifices (2 Chr 29). The Israelites also observed the first Passover celebration, "for they had not observed it on a nationwide scale as prescribed in the law" in years (2 Chr 30:5b).

As church leaders, it is critical that Pastor Eugene understands the importance of obeying God's Word. Favor and blessings are bestowed on those who freely observe and honor God's Word: "The LORD responded favorably to them as *their prayers reached his holy dwelling place in heaven* (2 Chr 30:27b, emphasis added)."

If you covet God's blessing on your leadership training process, the information in Topic 2 will help you reach your goal.

Reading Assignment

Please read 2 Chronicles 29 and 2 Chronicles 30 on King Hezekiah's reforms.

QUESTION 4

A church leader must hold firmly to God's message and His commands. *True or False?*

QUESTION 5

The leadership qualities Paul outlined in 1 Timothy 3:1-7 and Titus 1:6-9 set the standards for becoming a church leader. Which of the following leadership qualities are important for church leaders? *(Select all that apply.)*

    A. They must be respected by people outside the church.

    B. They must have one wife, be self-controlled, and orderly.

    C. They must be able to manage their own family.

    D. They must welcome strangers into their house.

    E. They must be gentle and peaceful, not violent.

Reading Assignment

Please read the article titled "Developing Church Leadership" in the Articles section at the end of this lesson.

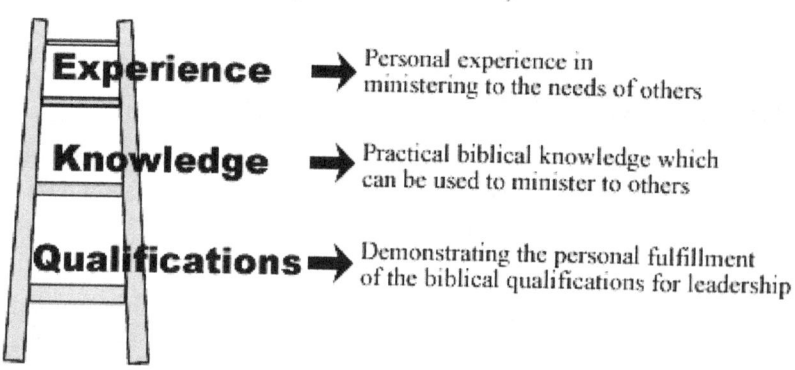

Spiritual Leadership

- **Experience** → Personal experience in ministering to the needs of others
- **Knowledge** → Practical biblical knowledge which can be used to minister to others
- **Qualifications** → Demonstrating the personal fulfillment of the biblical qualifications for leadership

QUESTION 6

In light of the preceding thoughts on the qualifications for church leadership, open your Life Notebook and design an outline of a training process that you would employ in your church to help qualified men and women develop in the areas of practical biblical knowledge and personal ministry experience.

The following represents one church's plan for helping a person become a church leader. The entire process from conversion to leadership in the church is covered by various training plans appropriate to the person's level of maturity and involvement.

One Church's Leadership Plan

Leader

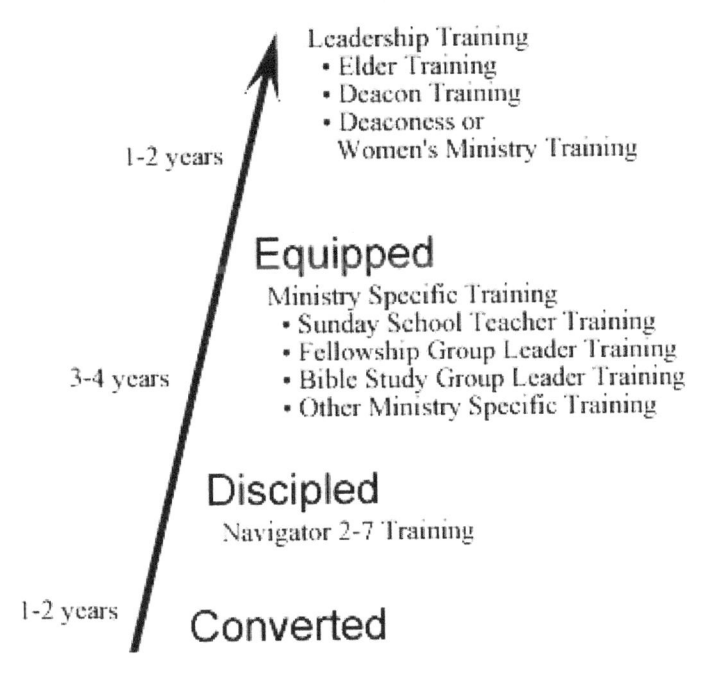

Leadership Training
- Elder Training
- Deacon Training
- Deaconess or Women's Ministry Training

1-2 years

Equipped

Ministry Specific Training
- Sunday School Teacher Training
- Fellowship Group Leader Training
- Bible Study Group Leader Training
- Other Ministry Specific Training

3-4 years

Discipled

Navigator 2-7 Training

1-2 years

Converted

Topic 2 Key Points:

- It is critical to understand the importance of obedience to God's Word. Favor and blessings are bestowed on those who freely observe and honor His Word.
- The twenty characteristics and qualities of maturity specified by the apostle Paul in 1 Timothy 3:1-7 and Titus 1:6-9 provide the qualities of a good church leader.
- Since the primary task of elders is to shepherd the people (the church), they need to relate to people with integrity, gentleness, selflessness, personal warmth, and concern.
- Active, personal ministry and practical knowledge of the Scriptures should be the prerequisite to leadership in the church.

Topic 3: Issues in Developing Church Leaders

Further Issues to Think About

Before we leave the area of leadership training in the church, there are some important issues that you must think about. These issues will often surface when a church seriously considers leadership development; therefore, they are important to consider as you choose and mentor future church leaders.

- Are leaders born or made?
- What is the balance between choosing someone for doctrinal correctness and for the ability to minister to people?
- How do you support your church leaders so that they do not burn out?
- What criteria are used to fairly select candidates for church leadership?

Addressing these questions before they are asked will help you be prepared when they come up.

What difference does the process of choosing church leaders really make? How does it affect me as a church leader? Believe it or not, even God had to deal with this issue: Aaron and Miriam both challenged Moses' leadership (Num 12) as did Korah in his rebellion (Num 16–17; Jude 1:11b). The choice of someone as a leader has a human aspect based upon the assessment of character qualities and actions (1 Tim 3:1-7), but ultimately it is (and should be seen as) a human confirmation of someone God has already chosen (Mt 16:19; Acts 1:15-26).

Choosing God's Leaders

If you are concerned about properly choosing, developing, and supporting church leaders, you will find help by working through the information in Topic 3.

Reading Assignments

- Please read Numbers 12 on Miriam and Aaron and Numbers 16–17 on the rebellion of Korah.
- Please read the article titled "Principles Organized" in the Articles section at the end of this lesson.

QUESTION 7

What justification did God give to punish Miriam with leprosy for seven days even after Moses' appeal to heal her immediately?

    A. She rebelled for seven days so she must be disgraced for seven days.

    B. Lepers remain unclean for seven days after they are healed.

    C. If her father had only spit in her face she would have been disgraced for even days.

    D. Seven is the number of perfect judgment.

QUESTION 8

What was/were the basis/bases of Korah's objection to Moses' leadership? *(Select all that apply.)*

    A. Moses was taking too long to get to the Promised Land.

    B. Moses was exalting himself.

    C. Moses married an Egyptian wife.

    D. The entire congregation is equally holy.

QUESTION 9

Some of your current leaders may have a strongly entrenched belief that leaders are born. Those with inherent leadership abilities will naturally surface and be able to handle a leadership position in most any area of the church ministry without extra training. Their view is: "God will send us leaders; we can't build them." How will you answer this objection? Please open your Life Notebook and record your answer.

QUESTION 10

At times, the attitude communicated—intentionally or unintentionally—by some of the leaders of the church is that only certain types of very mature, doctrinally oriented people are suitable to be leaders. Specifics of correct doctrine (usually less important doctrines) are emphasized; while the ability to relate to people and a demonstrated desire to minister to people on a personal level are neglected. How will you handle this overemphasis on doctrinal correctness coupled with an unwillingness to minister to people on a personal level? Please open your Life Notebook and record your answer.

QUESTION 11

The demands on people in church leadership positions are heavy. There is always more to do in a church, and there are always more needs to meet. In order to avoid "burnout" in leaders, they need some kind of support system. How do you plan to minister to your leaders to help them avoid the consequences of overwork and wrong priorities? Please open your Life Notebook and record your answer.

QUESTION 12

Selection for leadership training is often a difficult process. How will you identify people who should receive training for leadership in the church? What characteristics will you look for? How will you avoid the charge of "favoritism" when some are selected and others are not? Please open your Life Notebook and record your answer.

Topic 3 Key Points:

- Aaron and Miriam both challenged Moses' leadership (Num 12), as did Korah in his rebellion (Num 16-17, Jude 1:11b). Their sin of rebellion shows their lack of leadership qualities necessary in a church leader.

- The choice of a church leader is an important assignment and is a key element of a successful church.
- The process of choosing the right church leaders is an important decision because it directly and intimately affects the spiritual growth of the church and its people.

Topic 4: Developing Character—Unity, Diversity, Instruction

In this unit, you have studied multiplication, the third element in the threefold purpose of the church. You have also investigated the leadership offices of the church and considered their responsibilities and qualifications. In the next unit, you will look at how to integrate all the topics you have studied so far.

Christian Unity Proclaims the Gospel

Meanwhile, we will continue developing the character of Christ. In this topic, we learn to have unity with one another, receive one another, and instruct (admonish) one another.

Jesus prayed for believers that we may be one just as He and the Father are one (Jn 17:11); that through our unity, the world may believe that the Father sent Him and that the Father's love would be in us (Jn 17:21-26). Christian unity somehow testifies to the heart of the Gospel message! To find out how you can fulfill your part in this testimony, please continue reading in this topic.

Unity

Reading Assignment

Please read the article titled "Unity with One Another" in the Articles section at the end of this lesson.

QUESTION 13

Christian unity is a testimony to the truth of the Gospel. *True or False?*

QUESTION 14

There are two factors in maintaining unity: (1) the supernatural factor that Christ prayed for us and (2) for us to make every effort to not allow human factors to create irritations that bring about misunderstandings that divide us. Open your Life Notebook and list three things that should divide us as churches and three things that do but should not.

Diversity

Reading Assignment

Please read the article titled "Receive One Another" in the Articles section at the end of this lesson.

QUESTION 15

Historically, there are two areas that Christians have violated the exhortation to receive one another: by legalism and by showing _____.

Instruction

Reading Assignment

Please read the article titled "Instruct (Admonish) One Another" in the Articles section at the end of this lesson.

QUESTION 16

According to the reading in this topic, what is the proper goal of admonishing a fellow Christian?

    A. To cleanse the church of sin

    B. To help them become mature in Christ

    C. To set the proper example for others

    D. To make sure Christians are united

QUESTION 17

Building Up One Another—Instruct (Admonish) One Another

Open your Life Notebook and record your answers to the following questions (if you are a parent, you may want to answer the questions from that perspective).

1. When I exhort or admonish another Christian, do I reflect deep love and concern or do I come across as harsh and angry (2 Tim 2:24-25)?
2. Do I admonish in a private setting rather than appearing to speak to everyone? Do I use the crowd to cover up my speaking to only one person?
3. Am I persistent in my admonishment without being obnoxious and overbearing?
4. Do I admonish others to build them up to become mature in Christ?
5. Does our church structure make it natural and easy for all members of Christ's body to be involved in mutual exhortation or is only the pastor involved?

Topic 4 Key Points:

- We need to have unity with one another, receive one another and instruct (admonish) one another.
- In order to be a properly functioning church, a church must be a unified church that reaches out to its own with compassion and caring concern for the well-being and admonishment of all its followers.

You have learned to:

- Assess your own strengths and weaknesses as a church leader
- Develop the framework for a leadership training process for your church
- Evaluate potential church leaders and properly choose, develop, and support them

As Pastor Eugene finishes this lesson, he recognizes his deeper understanding of the complexities of church leadership. He now realizes that leadership requires a genuine commitment and ability to guide, direct, and influence people for the sake of spiritual and church growth. Pastor Eugene also learned that the task of choosing and developing church leaders according to New Testament principles is a major responsibility for all church leaders.

Lesson 9 Self Check

QUESTION 1
Why was King Joash so successful early in his reign as king?

    A. He found a copy of the Law and followed it closely.

    B. He observed the Passover Feast as God commanded.

    C. He worked hard developing his own personal character.

    D. He had a godly mentor in the priest Jehoiada.

QUESTION 2
Leaders should be chosen based on their adherence to God's Word. *True or False?*

QUESTION 3
The character qualities listed in 1 Timothy 3:1-7 are for Christians who aspire to leadership and are not expected of Christians in general. *True or False?*

QUESTION 4
The person who challenged Moses' leadership by saying the whole congregation of Israel is holy was _____.

QUESTION 5
Training a new convert to be a church leader should take several years. *True or False?*

QUESTION 6
Mature, doctrinally oriented candidates are preferred as leaders over people who have the ability and desire to minister to people. *True or False?*

QUESTION 7
Historically there are two areas that Christians have violated the exhortation to receive one another: by showing prejudice and by _____.

    A. Disunity

    B. Legalism

    C. Denominationalism

    D. Grace

QUESTION 8
The Bible writer that specifically calls prejudice sin is _____.

QUESTION 9
Admonishment must be done with the proper goal of helping brothers and sisters in Christ become more mature. *True or False?*

QUESTION 10
It is better to admonish the entire congregation in a general way than to confront someone individually to avoid hurt feelings. *True or False?*

Unit Three Exam: Church Dynamics

QUESTION 1

Which of the following is the primary command within the Great Commission?

- A. Go
- B. Make disciples
- C. Baptizing them
- D. Teaching them to obey

QUESTION 2

The word "go" in the Great Commission can be understood to mean "do this." *True or False?*

QUESTION 3

What caused the first recorded push of evangelism in the early church?

- A. Obedience to the Great Commission
- B. The conversion of Saul (Paul)
- C. Paul's imprisonment in Rome
- D. Persecution after Stephen's martyrdom

QUESTION 4

The Bible book that has been referred to as the "History of the Expansion of the Church" is _____.

- A. Acts
- B. John
- C. Romans
- D. Revelation

QUESTION 5

The local church's priority in missions is within their local community. *True or False?*

QUESTION 6

Evangelizing the lost is an equal priority with meeting current member needs in a church. *True or False?*

QUESTION 7

Part of being devout is holy isolation from the world. *True or False?*

QUESTION 8

As an example of uprightness, what did Daniel do in Daniel 1?

- A. He asked God for wisdom to judge His people.
- B. He asked God for positional righteousness.
- C. He set his mind to please and serve God.
- D. He asked God to fulfill His promise.

QUESTION 9

What is the primary role of deacons and deaconesses in the Church today?

    A. To distribute food to widows and orphans

    B. To make sure the church building is maintained

    C. Their responsibilities are open-ended

    D. To help lead the church

QUESTION 10

Paul usually used the term "elder" as the name of the office of elder. He used the term "overseer" to better communicate his meaning to _____.

    A. Political leaders

    B. New converts

    C. The Jews

    D. The Greeks (Gentiles)

QUESTION 11

Wherever possible, churches should have multiple leaders. *True or False?*

QUESTION 12

Two words that overlap in meaning describe New Testament leadership: The more technical term is "manage"; while the more personal term is _____.

    A. Pastor

    B. Father

    C. Shepherd

    D. Teacher

QUESTION 13

What was the first need that led to the creation of the office of deacon?

    A. Widows' need for prayer

    B. Serving the communion table

    C. Cleaning up the church

    D. Distribution of food

QUESTION 14

If there are multiple pastors in a church, they should all be equal in authority. *True or False?*

QUESTION 15

Active, personal ministry and practical knowledge of the Scriptures should be THE prerequisite to leadership in the church. *True or False?*

QUESTION 16

The individual Christian can function effectively alone. *True or False?*

QUESTION 17

The "family" analogy illustrates the emotional dimension of church function; while the analogy that shows how the church functions is the _____.

   A. Shepherd
   B. Body
   C. Vine
   D. Bread

QUESTION 18

Why was King Joash so successful early in his reign as king?

   A. He found a copy of the Law and followed it closely.
   B. He observed the Passover Feast, as God commanded.
   C. He worked hard developing his own personal character.
   D. He had a godly mentor in the priest Jehoiada.

QUESTION 19

What was the special blessing that came because of King Hezekiah's revival?

   A. Israel defeated its enemy at war.
   B. The sun went backward in its orbit.
   C. There was rain sent from heaven.
   D. His prayers reached unto God in heaven.

QUESTION 20

The man who challenged Moses' leadership by saying the whole congregation of Israel is holy was _____.

   A. Joshua
   B. Aaron
   C. Korah
   D. Pharaoh

QUESTION 21

Which of the following leadership qualities is LEAST important for church leaders?

   A. They must provide proven leadership in their employment.
   B. They must be respected by people outside the church.
   C. They must be able to manage their own family.
   D. They must welcome strangers into their house.

QUESTION 22

People who have the ability and desire to minister to people are preferred as leaders over mature, doctrinally oriented candidates. *True or False?*

QUESTION 23

Christian unity is a testimony to_____.

    A. God's love for us

    B. The truth of the Gospel

    C. Our unity in diversity

    D. The accuracy of Scripture

QUESTION 24

According to the reading in this topic, what is the proper goal of admonishing a fellow Christian?

    A. To cleanse the church of sin

    B. To set the proper example for others

    C. To help them become mature in Christ

    D. To make sure Christians are united

QUESTION 25

It is better to confront someone individually than admonish the entire congregation in a general way. *True or False?*

Lesson 9 Answers to Questions

QUESTION 1:
He depended on a good, godly advisor in the priest Jehoiada, but ran into problems because he did not develop his own character and maturity in the Lord.

QUESTION 2:
B. The "Lord" allowed the Syrian army to defeat the larger Judean army.
The "Lord" allowed the smaller Syrian army to defeat the larger Judean army because the Judean people had abandoned him and disobeyed his commands.

QUESTION 3: *Your answer*

QUESTION 4: True
By holding firmly to these ideals, he/she will be able to encourage others with the true teaching and also to show the error of those who are opposed to it.

QUESTION 5:
A. They must be respected by people outside the church.
B. They must have one wife, be self-controlled, and orderly.
C. They must be able to manage their own family.
D. They must welcome strangers into their house.
E. They must be gentle and peaceful, not violent.
If a man is eager to be a church leader, he desires excellence in every aspect of his life. All the leadership qualities stated above are important for church leaders to possess.

QUESTION 6: *Your answer*

QUESTION 7:
C. If her father had only spit in her face, she would have been disgraced for seven days.
God supports His leaders. Notice that Moses endured rebellion through no fault of his own, for we are told: "Now the man Moses was very humble, more so than any man on the face of the earth" (Num 12:3).

QUESTION 8:
A. Moses was taking too long to get to the Promised Land.
B. Moses was exalting himself.
D. That the entire congregation is equally holy
Again, God supports his properly chosen leadership. He expects churches to appoint leaders according to His guidelines. Korah's rebellion is used as a classic example of the sin of rebellion in the New Testament (Jude 1:11b).

QUESTION 9: *Your answer*
QUESTION 10: *Your answer*
QUESTION 11: *Your answer*
QUESTION 12: *Your answer*
QUESTION 13: True
QUESTION 14: *Your answer*
QUESTION 15: Correct answers include:
Partiality
Favoritism
Prejudice
Prejudice destroys the unity of the body! James clearly says that "if you show prejudice, you are committing sin" (Jas 2:9a).

QUESTION 16:
B. To help them become mature in Christ

QUESTION 17: *Your answer*

Lesson 9 Self Check Answers

QUESTION 1:
D. He had a godly mentor in the priest Jehoiada.
QUESTION 2: True
QUESTION 3: False
QUESTION 4: Korah
QUESTION 5: True
QUESTION 6: False
QUESTION 7:
B. Legalism
QUESTION 8: James
QUESTION 9: True
QUESTION 10: False

Unit 3 Exam Answers

QUESTION 1:
B. Make disciples

QUESTION 2: True

QUESTION 3:
D. Persecution after Stephen's martyrdom

QUESTION 4:
A. Acts

QUESTION 5: True

QUESTION 6: True

QUESTION 7: False

QUESTION 8:
C. He set his mind to please and serve God.

QUESTION 9:
C. Their responsibilities are open-ended.

QUESTION 10:
D. The Greeks (Gentiles)

QUESTION 11: True

QUESTION 12:
C. Shepherd

QUESTION 13:
D. Distribution of food

QUESTION 14: False

QUESTION 15: False

QUESTION 16: False

QUESTION 17:
B. Body

QUESTION 18:
D. He had a godly mentor in the priest Jehoiada.

QUESTION 19:
D. His prayers reached unto God in heaven.

QUESTION 20:
C. Korah

QUESTION 21:
A. They must provide proven leadership in their employment.

QUESTION 22: True

QUESTION 23:
B. The truth of the Gospel

QUESTION 24:
C. To help them become mature in Christ

QUESTION 25: True

Lesson 9 Articles

Developing Church Leadership

Consider the example given by Dr. Getz. He planned a series of study sessions using *The Measure of a Man* with a group of men from his church. On twenty successive Thursday mornings, he met with the group for one hour before they went to work for the day. Their goal was to discover from Scripture and from each other how they could become more mature men of God.

The twenty characteristics and qualities of maturity specified by the apostle Paul in 1 Timothy 3:1-7 and Titus 1:6-9 formed the basis for this study. Getz began the course and led the first few studies. Then each week thereafter a different man took about thirty minutes to share what the Scripture had to say about one of the qualities. This was followed by approximately thirty minutes of discussion and personal sharing. Each week the group tried to focus on how the members of the group could better develop the quality they were discussing in their lives. Dr. Getz' project with these men was a good example of how a group of people committed to growing in the Lord can make a difference in one another's lives through Scripture and fellowship.

Plan to take the time necessary for this project soon! Not only will you be challenged to grow spiritually, but you will also reap rich benefits as you see God using you to train others for leadership in the church. It will take time and effort in the beginning, but whatever you invest now will be richly repaid to you. It will be rewarding to see those you trained as they help bear the burdens and responsibilities of the ministry.

The focus of the book *The Measure of a Man* and the exercises relating to it was on a study of the **qualifications** for church leaders based on the biblical qualifications of an elder. These qualifications deal primarily with the areas of personal and spiritual maturity. It is almost impossible to overemphasize the importance of these qualifications in choosing church leaders. When you look carefully at the biblical responsibilities of an elder, pastor, or church official, you can see that these spiritual and personal qualifications are essential to the successful fulfillment of their ministry.

Since the primary task of elders is to shepherd the people (the church), they need to relate to people with integrity, gentleness, unselfish personal warmth, and concern. A contentious or self-willed man will not make a good shepherd. In addition, since elders manage and lead the church as part of a group of elders, a quick-tempered elder or an elder who always has to have his way will be painfully destructive in meetings of the elders and divisive among the people of the church. These qualities, therefore, form the essential foundation for church leadership. It is far better to have fewer qualified leaders than more leaders, many of whom are not qualified.

There are other areas of preparation for leadership that are important in addition to the qualifications for leadership. Before one is accepted as a leader in a local church, he should demonstrate some accepted level of **practical biblical knowledge** and **ministry experience**. Your leadership training process should also provide opportunities to develop in these areas.

Even if a man is generally qualified, he needs the time and opportunity to develop his knowledge and experience. There is great wisdom in not allowing a new convert to become an elder, even if he has most of the personal qualities listed in the biblical qualifications. He needs time to develop his practical knowledge of the Scripture to use it effectively to teach, counsel, and encourage others. And he needs the opportunity to gain experience ministering to people.

Remember, the elders are not the only ones who should be involved in ministry. Our earlier study of Ephesians 4:11-17 demonstrates that biblically all the believers in a church should minister at some level. Active, personal ministry should be the prerequisite to leadership in the church. Personal ministry gives the opportunity to demonstrate that a person has the shepherding heart essential to spiritual leadership.

Instruct (Admonish) One Another

*"But I myself am fully convinced about you, my brothers and sisters, that you yourselves are full of goodness, filled with all knowledge, and able to **instruct one another**"* (Rom 15:14, emphasis added).

The Greek word *noutheteo,* or "instruct," does not refer to casual communication or normal teaching, but it implies a definite exhortation, correction, and warning. In 1 Thessalonians 5:14 this same word is translated "admonish" and in Acts 20:31 and 1 Corinthians 4:14 as "warn."

They were competent to admonish because they were "full of goodness." They generally lived Christian lives and could "remove the beam" from their brother's eye because they had cleaned up their own lives (Mt 7:3-5).

They were also "filled with all knowledge." This is knowledge of God's Word and not just their opinion of what they think other Christians should do (2 Tim 2:15). Biblical absolutes and non–absolutes are not confused. Any admonishment must be based on the true teachings of Scripture.

Other important points:

- Admonishment must be done with deep concern and love. Paul had never stopped warning (admonishing) the Ephesian elders with tears, and they knew he loved them (Acts 20:31).
- To be effective, admonishment must sometimes be personal. It should not be individual admonishment directed generally at the entire church (1 Thess 2:11-12).
- It also must be persistent when necessary, not stopping after one brief encounter (Acts 20:31).
- Admonishment must be done from pure motives as Paul did, warning the Corinthians as his dear children (1 Cor 4:14).
- It must be done with the proper goal of helping them become more mature in Christ (Col 1:28-29).
- It must also be the natural outgrowth of proper body functioning, and it must be not only corrective (after the fact) but also preventive (Col 3:16).

Note: This material is adapted from Gene A. Getz, *The Measure of a Man.* (Ventura, CA: Regal Books, 1984).

Principles Organized

What contributions do tradition and culture make to the organization of your church?

The textbook outlined four principles of organization which emerge from four biblical case studies. They are as follows:

> Organize to apply New Testament principles and to reach New Testament purposes
>
> Organize to meet needs
>
> Keep organization simple
>
> Keep organization flexible

The following is a broad perspective on tendencies that are true in many different countries of the world.

For instance, in some cultures people tend to over organize. In other cultures, there is a substantial lack of organization. In both cases, this has its effect on church structures. Over organization is recognized by bureaucratic mentalities in church, as reflected in our discussion on institutionalization. On the other hand, lack of emphasis on organization can often be recognized in the habits of leaders having too much direct personal control over things. In this case, the structure provided is not "organizational" but rather "personal."

From tradition, two organizational phenomena present themselves to churches in many countries which are not optional for us and which are hardly open to any change. The first is denominational ties between local churches. Oftentimes this relationship is limited to doctrinal and organizational binding agreements. The Bible is silent on this matter, and any biblical evaluation must come from the threefold purpose of the church.

A second organizational factor history gives the church is the relationship she has with the status quo government. The New Testament only provides us with situational, antagonistic examples of such a relationship, and little can be learned from that in terms of positive structuring of this relationship. A prophetic perspective from the Old Testament is helpful in this, but it is virtually impossible to draw "organizational" principles from a totally theocratic context for use in the political context of today.

Receive One Another

"*Receive one another*, then, just as Christ also received you, to God's glory" (Rom 15:7, emphasis added).

Churches often mistakenly receive one another based on what someone does or does not do. The list of their rules is not biblical but is an extra-biblical list that is cultural, (aka modern legalism!). These rules shatter true unity among Christians. They attempt to define a person's relationship to Jesus Christ, creating judgmental attitudes and guilt, as well as destroying a person's freedom to relate to God. They also stymie true spiritual maturity. There are behavioral expectations for Christians, but the Bible condemns external judgments beyond these scriptural statements. Receiving fellow Christians is a key to Christian unity (Rom 15:5-7). In two specific areas, Christians have historically violated the exhortation to receive one another:

- By judging (legalism)
- By showing partiality (prejudice)

Each is condemned to sin.

In Romans, some Christians had personal problems even while engaging in legitimate activities (like eating meat sacrificed to idols) because of previous sinful associations with those activities (Rom 14:14; 1 Cor 8:4, 7-8). Paul dealt with the judgment issue in this way and by speaking to both the weak and strong brother: "The one who eats everything must not despise the one who does not, and the one who abstains must not judge the one who eats everything, for God has accepted him. Who are you to pass judgment on another's servant?" (Rom 14:3–4b).

Likewise, Romans 12:16 deals with partiality: "Live in harmony with one another; do not be haughty but associate with the lowly. Do not be conceited" (see also Jas 2:1). James clearly says, "If you show prejudice, you are committing sin" (Jas 2:9a). Prejudice destroys the unity of the body!

Note: This material is adapted from Gene A. Getz, *The Measure of a Man*. (Ventura, CA: Regal Books, 1984).

Unity with One Another

*"Now may the God of endurance and comfort **give you unity with one another** in accordance with Christ Jesus"* (Rom 15:5, emphasis added).

Church history teaches one outstanding lesson: Satan's primary strategy involves destroying unity among Christians. According to the Bible, one soon discovers the power of one-mindedness that defeats his strategy: unity.

Central in Jesus' High Priestly Prayer in John 17 is that Christians in all times experience unity with one another (Jn 17:11, 20-23). His concern is for a visible unity that reveals the very essence of the Gospel. Unbelievers crave the type of love that creates unity among Christians.

That is why Satan targets Christian unity—in order to destroy the witness of the Gospel. Humanity cannot be saved apart from coming to know Jesus as Savior (Jn 20:30-31). It is no accident that Jesus prays for believer's protection from Satan (Jn 17:15).

The unity of the church immediately after Pentecost was profound (Acts 2:46; 4:32). The results of this unity are revealing: They had "the good will of all the people. And the Lord was adding to their number every day those who were being saved" (Acts 2:47b). Continuing in one mind also led the apostles to testify with great power and grace (Acts 4:33). There is a direct correlation between the unity of Christians and the result of that unity in non-Christians' lives (also Acts 6:1–7).

Of course, Paul's concern for unity was expressed multiple times (Rom 12:16; 14:19; Eph 4:3; Phil 1:27, et al).

In conclusion, a functioning church must be a unified church. In fact, they are a reciprocal dynamic! The reflection of this oneness is the heart of the Gospel.

Note: This material is adapted from Gene A. Getz, *The Measure of a Man*. (Ventura, CA: Regal Books, 1984).

Unit Four: Growing Toward Maturity in Christ

Maturing in Christ is not an easy or simple process. It requires an open, honest, and committed pursuit through the Word of God. Our goal is to provide you with a solid understanding of the nature of spiritual growth, and how to use biblical criteria to estimate the spiritual growth of your congregation. The tactics and strategies presented in each lesson are carefully designed to help you understand and grow a Bible-based church rich in God's love and confidence. As you walk this road to spiritual maturity with your congregation, you will feel the cleansing and strengthening effects of spiritual growth within your church.

In Unit Four, you will discover a practical overview that shows how the different topics studied—worship, edification, evangelism, leadership, administration, and organization—are interrelated. This knowledge provides you with criteria to evaluate the spiritual health of your church and to help your church grow, or continue growing, toward maturity in Christ. A key to maturing spiritually is personally acknowledging one's dependence upon the wisdom, direction, strength, and grace of the Lord Jesus Christ.

Unit 4 Outline: Growing Toward Maturity in Christ

Lesson 10: Administration and Organization Dynamics
Lesson 11: Testing the Dynamics
Lesson 12: Your Biblical Philosophy of Ministry

Lesson 10: Administration and Organization Dynamics

Lesson Introduction

Godly leaders have the privilege and responsibility of serving God's people. Unfortunately, being godly does not necessarily mean that all leaders within a church are skilled at administration and organization.

A disorganized pastor often leaves important actions undone, and many good opportunities to serve the church are left untouched. Sometimes problems linger unnecessarily. This is true for any poorly organized leader in the church. Even a person with deep awareness of why the church and its organizations exist is hindered by poor organization or administration.

Disorder = Ineffectiveness

Pastor Eugene pondered this thought and began to evaluate his personal administrative and organizational abilities. As he examined his ongoing actions, he began to think about areas in his life that were not as orderly as they could be. He often said to himself, "I'll get to it later," but "later" rarely occurred. He found that he was good at making excuses about why some things just did not get done! Now Pastor Eugene found himself having to face these issues and to make adjustments to his leadership style and personal work habits. The topics in Unit Four clearly identify leadership gaps in administration and organization so we can effectively close those gaps.

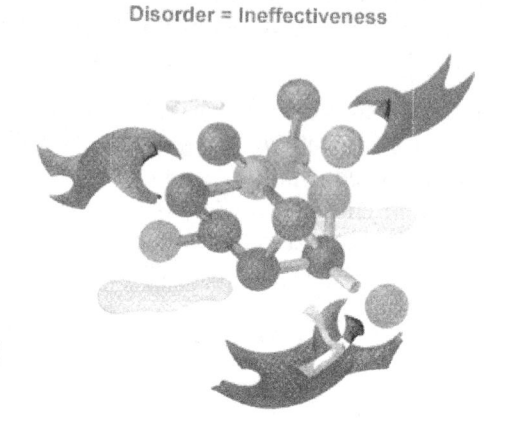

Lesson 10 considers two dynamics of church life: administration and organization. All church leaders should develop perspective and skills in these areas. Whenever people work together, they need clear perspectives and mature abilities in administration and organization. This is true for both Christian and non-Christian endeavors. For the church, however, accomplishing her eternal purpose with relevance to the local context, while being hindered by the sinful tides of antagonism, stubbornness, or apathy, puts high demands on those serving in leadership roles. The privilege and task for those serving in their church with God-given passion is to look at their organizational responsibilities and actions through clearly focused lenses!

Lesson Outline

Lesson 10: Administration and Organization Dynamics
    Topic 1: Biblical Examples of Administration and Organization
    Topic 2: Principles of Administration
    Topic 3: Principles of Organization
    Topic 4: Developing Character—Greet, Serve, Carry One Another's Burdens
        Greet
        Serve
        Carry One Another's Burdens

Lesson Objectives

At the completion of Lesson 10, you will be able to:

- Recognize the organizational and administrative problems faced by leaders in at least two selected Bible passages, in addition to understanding their solutions and the consequences of their decisions
- Identify biblical principles to apply to administrative and organizational needs in any area of the church today
- Develop the Christian character traits of greeting, serving, and carrying one another's burdens

Topic 1: Biblical Examples of Administration and Organization

People who excel in church leadership, like Getz, find it easy to identify teachings in the Bible that address administration and organization. Many examples of administration and organization in the Bible are integrated into other teachings and may be overlooked by less mature Christians. It is crucial for Church leaders to become mature Christians possessing the knowledge, skills, and experience necessary to identify and interpret the multiple meanings of the teachings found in the Bible.

Pastor Eugene recognizes the importance of the administration and organization skills inherent in strong leaders and is very interested in learning more about this topic. He eagerly wants to identify and interpret the multiple meanings of Bible teachings, especially the strategies and techniques for becoming a stronger administrator and organizer as he matures in Christ.

Daniel: Administrator *Exrtaordinaire*

Lesson 10 begins by examining several passages from the Old and New Testaments pertaining to administration and organization.

Daniel is the administrator *extraordinaire* in the Bible. King Darius appointed him as one of three supervisors over 120 satraps (governors) in the kingdom (Dan 6:2-3). The king intended to put Daniel in charge of the entire kingdom because he distinguished himself with his extraordinary spirit (Dan 6:4). The other supervisors were jealous of him and tried to find some pretext to charge him before the king (Dan 6:5). Yet they could not because he was completely trustworthy (Dan 6:5). What a testimony! They could only charge him in connection with keeping the law of his God (Dan 6:6).

In this topic, we explore other Bible passages with organizational and administrative problems, along with the solutions and consequences of the decisions. To learn about these solutions—and to become more like Daniel—please read on.

Reading Assignment

Please read Daniel 6 on Daniel and his experience as an administrator.

QUESTION 1

King Darius unwillingly punished Daniel for his disobedience to the king's edict. *True or False?*

QUESTION 2

In Daniel 6, King Darius trusted Daniel with a high administrative position because he had extraordinary _____.

    A. Strength

    B. Speaking skills

    C. Spirit

    D. Popularity

QUESTION 3

Fill in the columns with a pen or pencil by matching the option on the left to the verses in the bottom rows.

OT Principles of Administration

Principle	Gen 41:33-49	Ex 18:13-27	Ruth 4:1-12	1 Kings 5:1-6	Ezra 7:25-26	Haggai 1:1-15	Neh 2:1-10
Administrators have a heart for God's work							
Administrators can reason with the people from God's word							
Administrators appoint proven men to help them							
Everything done by procedure and with witnesses							
Administration is best done by someone not fighting battles							
Choose capable, God-fearing, truthful men							
Pharaoh looked for a wise and discerning man							

QUESTION 4

Fill in the columns with a pen or pencil by matching the option on the left to the verses in the bottom rows.

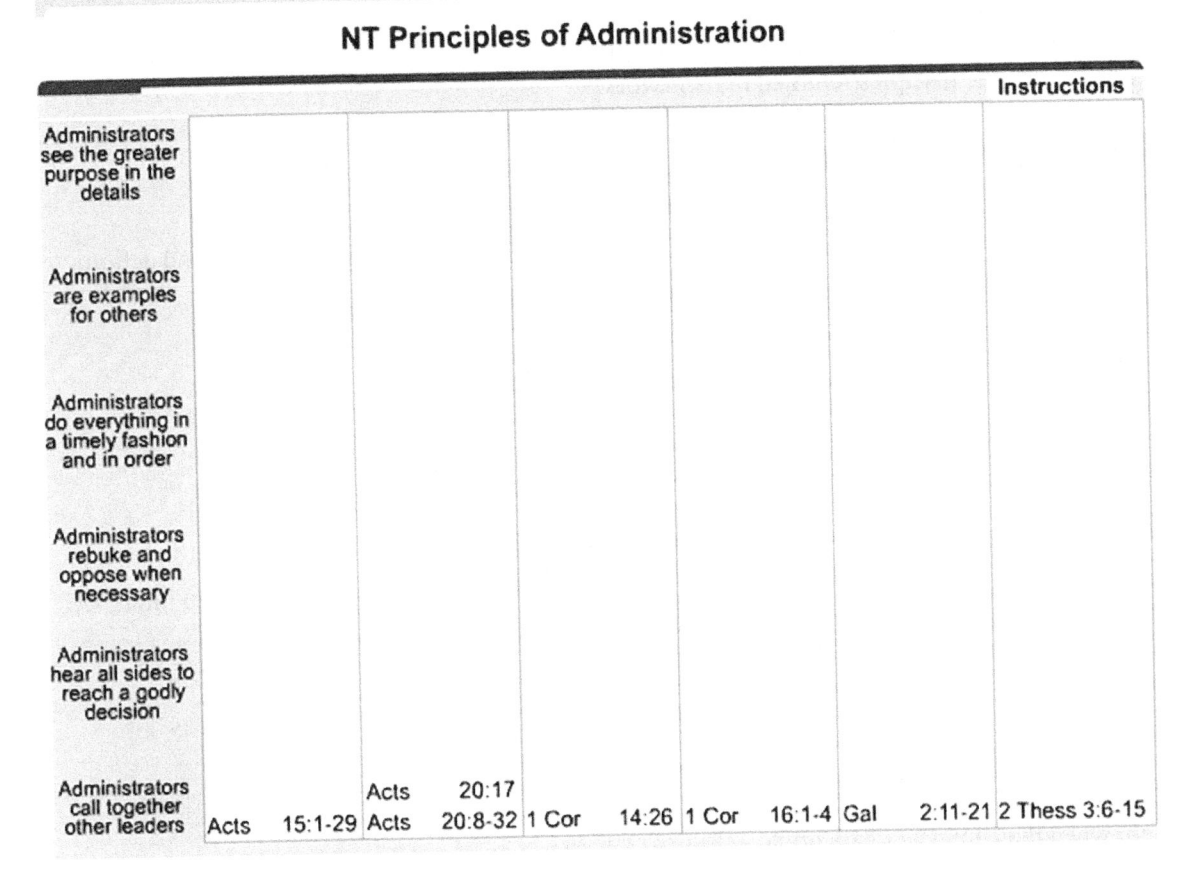

NT Principles of Administration

							Instructions
Administrators see the greater purpose in the details							
Administrators are examples for others							
Administrators do everything in a timely fashion and in order							
Administrators rebuke and oppose when necessary							
Administrators hear all sides to reach a godly decision							
Administrators call together other leaders	Acts 15:1-29	Acts 20:17 Acts 20:8-32	1 Cor 14:26	1 Cor 16:1-4	Gal 2:11-21	2 Thess 3:6-15	

Reading Assignment

Please read the textbook chapter titled "Chapter 13: Biblical Examples of Administration and Organization" in *Sharpening the Focus of the Church* in the Articles section at the end of this lesson.

Before you go on in this lesson, try to use Getz' example to add to your own study of the passages in this exercise.

QUESTION 5

Briefly state the problem, solution, and results of the dilemma for "Moses in the Wilderness" (Ex 18:13-27; Deut 1:9-18).

The next two questions are about the issue of "The Neglected Widows" (Acts 6:1-7).

QUESTION 6

A main problem concerning the neglected widows was that the apostles were distracted from their other responsibilities. *True or False?*

The results of the solution for the neglected widows are: The people's needs were met, unity was restored, and the disciples returned to their work.

Topic 1 Key Points:

- Seek wisdom and help from God in solving problems
- Develop your strategy first, and then motivate other people to involvement and action.
- Establish priorities and delegate responsibility to qualified people.
- Supervise closely and help solve problems.
- Use temporary organizational structures to meet needs

Topic 2: Principles of Administration

With these biblical examples of administration and organization from the first topic in mind, we will interact with Getz' principles of administration, and then guide you in the application of these principles to your church situation.

Reaching **rock bottom**: Often this is what it takes for a person to turn his or her life around. Most have heard stories of drug addicts, alcoholics, etc., only seeking help when they are near death or have destroyed their families. Finally, at this point, they are ready to listen to advice and motivated to deal with their problems.

However, most people are responsive to subtler signs of trouble, even if they need a Jethro to point out the problem and suggest a solution (Ex 18:13-27). To avoid problems in the future, we need to learn how to identify and apply biblical principles to administrative and organizational needs in the church today *before* encountering serious problems.

Reaching Rock Bottom

Reading Assignment

Please read the first section of "Chapter 14: Principles of Biblical Administration and Organization" in *Sharpening the Focus of the Church* in the Articles section at the end of this lesson.

In this chapter, Getz outlines seven principles of administration which emerge from four of the biblical case studies you considered earlier.

QUESTION 7

Which of the following principles would you apply if you had a theological disagreement in your church? *(Select all that apply.)*

A. Face the reality of problems
B. Develop a proper perspective of the problem before reaching a concrete solution
C. Establish priorities and delegate responsibility to qualified people
D. Maintain a proper balance between divine and human factors
E. Take an approach to problem-solving and decision-making that considers the attitudes and feelings of those directly involved
F. Solve every problem both with creativity and the guidance of the Holy Spirit, and never get locked into administrative routines simply because they have worked before

QUESTION 8

Which of the following principles would you apply if you or one of your church leaders was overloaded and overwhelmed with responsibilities? *(Select all that apply.)*

A. Face the reality of problems
B. Develop a proper perspective of the problem before reaching a concrete solution
C. Establish priorities and delegate responsibility to qualified people
D. Maintain a proper balance between divine and human factors
E. Take an approach to problem-solving and decision-making that considers the attitudes and feelings of those directly involved
F. Solve every problem both with creativity and the guidance of the Holy Spirit, and never get locked into administrative routines simply because they have worked before

Topic 2 Key Points:

In Topic 2, we learned biblical principles to successfully handle organizational and administrative issues you may encounter in your church. The principles we learned for church administration are:

- Face the reality of problems
- Develop a proper perspective of the problem before reaching a concrete solution
- Establish priorities
- Delegate responsibility to qualified people
- Maintain a proper balance between divine and human factors
- Take an approach to problem-solving and decision-making that considers the attitudes and feelings of those directly involved
- Solve every problem both with creativity and the guidance of the Holy Spirit, and never get locked into administrative routines simply because they have worked before.

QUESTION 9

You may be facing several problems or tough decisions in your ministry. Choose one problem which needs immediate attention, and then complete this exercise:

- 1. Apply the principles from the list above (Topic 2 Key Points) to the situation you have selected. Which principles are the most helpful?
- 2. Pinpoint the element in this problem that is the most difficult for you to deal with. Explain briefly why you are having difficulty, and what additional assistance you feel is needed to resolve the matter.
- 3. Write a short paragraph stating specifically what steps you will take to solve the problem you are examining.

Topic 3: Principles of Organization

Pastor Eugene has noticed in his studies that there are very few patterns of church organization provided in the Bible, but he has also noticed how principles of organization are gleaned from its many passages. "Organization" is a universal phenomenon that involves efficiencies in the way separate elements are arranged into a coherent whole or process. Leaders automatically operate with some degree of organization to help their group achieve desired objectives. The many examples of leaders in the Bible provide us with needed insights to enable us to become more efficient and productive as church leaders.

Much of today's church scene, however, has organizational structures determined by tradition or culture. There is nothing necessarily wrong in these organizational structures because, as we have learned, all three lenses are necessary for clear focus on the church of today. The three lenses (worship, edification, multiplication) provide us with the ability to create a balanced and functional church grounded in relevant biblical teachings. Biblical principles help us evaluate the contributions which tradition and culture make to our actual practices.

Staying on Course

In Topic 3, you are encouraged to think biblically about the actual dynamics of the structures you are involved with and their impact on your church.

Sailors often determine their course by sight. But what do they do when they cannot see? When a thick fog rolls in, it is often impossible to see anything. Good sailors evaluate their position with instruments so that they do not become lost. If they do not have compasses or similar instruments, they will go off course or "drift away" (Heb 2:1). The writer of Hebrews compares his readers to a ship that has drifted off course, but the pilot is unaware of any problem.

Using the biblical principle of organization in this topic will help you keep on track with running your church and prevent you from losing your way.

Reading Assignment

Please read the remaining section of "Chapter 14: Principles of Organization" from *Sharpening the Focus of the Church* in the Articles section at the end of this lesson.

The following is a broad perspective on tendencies that are true in many different countries of the world: "Principles Organized" from the Lesson 9 Articles section.

In some cultures, people tend to over-organize. In other cultures, there is a substantial lack of organization. In both cases, this has its effect on church structures. Over-organization is recognizable by bureaucratic mentalities in church, as reflected in our discussion on institutionalization. On the other hand, lack of emphasis on organization can often be recognized through the habits of leaders having too much direct personal control over things. In this case, the structure provided is not "organizational" but rather "personal." The Bible is silent on this matter, and any biblical evaluation must come from the threefold purpose of the church.

Please interact with these principles by answering the following questions (refer back to the textbook if you need assistance).

QUESTION 10

The local church's organizational structures should be established to meet the needs of the congregation and the community. *True or False?*

QUESTION 11

Why is keeping an organization flexible probably the most difficult principle to apply?

Example for Question 11:

A church establishes an evangelism committee to plan strategy and organize activities to reach a selected group in the city. After three years of operation, the original goal has been accomplished. But now the evangelism committee has become a form that has taken on the identity of a function. Attempts to dissolve the committee are met with stiff resistance. The chairman of the committee would have to give up his position of authority. Some people complain that the leaders of the church are no longer interested in evangelism. Though the purpose is met, people confuse God's purpose with their personal purpose.

QUESTION 12

Churches can fall along a spectrum from being highly organized (tending toward bureaucratic) to being much less organized (relying upon people to get things done). Open your Life Notebook and answer the following questions:

- Which end of this spectrum does your church fall within?
- What steps can you take to find a balanced approach to church organization?

Topic 3 Key Points:

In Topic 3, we learned about biblical principles of organization that will help you to keep on track spiritually:

- Organize to apply New Testament principles and to reach New Testament purposes
- Organize to meet needs
- Keep organization simple
- Keep organization flexible

In Topics 1, 2, and 3 of this lesson, you looked at biblical principles for administering and organizing your ministries. The principles are unchanging, but the way each church applies these principles is often quite different. God gives us tremendous freedom to develop creative ministry forms to fit the culture and the resources available to His servants in the community.

In this lesson, Getz raises questions to help church leaders consider changing the organizational structure of their ministries when it benefits the church as a whole. He is not suggesting making changes just to make changes. Rather, he suggests evaluating the organization to see if it meets needs.

Freedom to Create Ministry Forms

Topic 4: Developing Character— Greet, Serve, Carry One Another's Burdens

Earlier in this lesson we looked at Daniel's administrative skills. One of the reasons King Darius trusted him with such a high administrative position is that he "was distinguishing himself above the other supervisors for he had an extraordinary spirit and uncompromising character" (Dan 6:3).

Greet

Reading Assignment

Please read the article titled "Greet One Another" in the Articles section at the end of this lesson.

QUESTION 13

In the reading for "Greet One Another," the "holy kiss" is described as a biblical absolute practice. *True or False?*

Serve

Reading Assignment

Please read the article titled "Serve One Another" in the Articles section at the end of this lesson.

QUESTION 14

In the reading for "Serve One Another," Paul says we were called to freedom, so we are now free from servanthood. *True or False?*

Carry One Another's Burdens

Reading Assignment

Please read the article titled "Carry One Another's Burdens" in the Articles section at the end of this lesson.

QUESTION 15

From the reading for "Carry One Another's Burdens," match the verse in the left-hand column with the teaching from the verse in the right-hand column.

Verse	Teaching
Galatians 5:25	Restoration must be done by a spiritual Christian.
Galatians 6:1	Restoration is the task of more than one person.
Galatians 6:3	Restoration is based on our salvation by God's mercy.
Titus 3:2-5	Restoration must be done with humility.
James 5:15-16	Restoration must be done prayerfully.

QUESTION 16

Evaluate your own ministry. Organizational questions to help you are provided. Please open your Life Notebook, number the lines 1-4, and answer the following questions:

1. What is the strongest basis for the organizational structure in your church? Is it primarily biblical, historical, cultural, or a combination of these? Are you organized to fulfill priorities and meet congregational and community needs?
2. How many meetings does your congregation have weekly? How many monthly? What types of meetings are they? How many of the same people attend most meetings? How does this affect the family life of these busy people?
3. Which ministries are done well by your current organizational structure? Which are not done at all or are poorly done? What adjustments are needed?
4. Which ministry adjustments would be readily accepted by the people? Why do you think so? Which ministry adjustments are likely to receive opposition? Why? What might be done to minimize people's concerns?

In Lesson 10, you have learned to:

- Identify biblical principles to apply to the local church's administrative and organizational needs
- Estimate the degree of spiritual maturity of your local church using the three criteria of faith, hope, and love, as presented by Getz
- Discuss the relationship between the major elements covered in this course:
    The major purposes for the church in the world today
    What constitutes a balanced church ministry
    The internal leadership needed for a local congregation of believers to function
    The place of evaluation in the local church
- Develop a strategy for ministry evaluation and spiritual growth toward maturity in Christ to use within your ministry context

Pastor Eugene realizes that just wanting to be a good administrator and to be organized are *not* enough. As a church leader, he must make a concerted effort to gain the knowledge, skills, and experiences in the area of administration and organization to successfully lead his congregation toward maturity in Christ. No longer is saying "I'll get to it" acceptable! He must find a way, through efficient administration and organizational practices, to actually accomplish God's mission.

Lesson 10 Self Check

QUESTION 1
When the satraps and supervisors in King Darius' service sought to charge Daniel before the king they found they could only charge him in connection with keeping God's _____.

QUESTION 2
In Exodus 18, when Jethro advised Moses to appoint qualified men to help him, the people's needs were met and they were satisfied. *True or False?*

QUESTION 3
In Acts 6, the apostles faced the problem of the widows. According to the passage, what was the main concern for the apostles?

    A. Their leadership style was being challenged.

    B. There was theological division in the church.

    C. They were distracted from their main duties.

    D. Their prayers were hindered.

QUESTION 4
Biblically, in a multiracial church, if one group has an issue it may be wise to appoint leaders from the same race to help solve it. *True or False?*

QUESTION 5
Since the purpose of the church never changes, the church should not change when the community changes. *True or False?*

QUESTION 6
Which factor causes a disproportionately negative reaction to change?

    A. People's natural resistance to change

    B. People's practices become institutionalized.

    C. People's natural irrationality

    D. People's security is threatened by change.

QUESTION 7
Believers in New Testament times were told to greet each other with a holy _____.

    A. Kiss

    B. Handshake

    C. Hug

    D. Bow

QUESTION 8
Christ has set us free, so we should never again consider ourselves servants of anyone else. *True or False?*

QUESTION 9
Restoration should be done privately by the church leader. *True or False?*

QUESTION 10
Churches should form permanent organizational structures based on biblical examples. *True or False?*

Lesson 10 Answers to Questions

QUESTION 1: True

QUESTION 2:

C. Spirit

It was not just Daniel's skill as an administrator that impressed the king, but his character that made him stand out among the other administrators. Developing Christ's character will also make us stand out—witness—to both believers and unbelievers.

QUESTION 3:

Scripture	OT Principles on Administration
Genesis 41:33-49	Pharaoh looked for a wise and discerning man.
Exodus 18:13-27	Choose capable, God-fearing, truthful men.
Ruth 4:1, 12	Everything is done by procedure and with witnesses.
1 Kings 5:1-6	Administration is best done by someone not fighting battles.
Ezra 7:25-26	Administrators appoint proven men to help them.
Haggai 1:1-15	Administrators can reason with the people from God's Word.
Nehemiah 2:1-10	Administrators have a heart for God's work.

QUESTION 4:

Scripture	NT Principles on Administration
Acts 15:1-29	Administrators hear all sides to reach a godly decision.
Acts 20:8-32; 20:17	Administrators call together other leaders.
1 Corinthians 14:26	Administrators see the greater purpose in the details.
1 Corinthians 16:1-4	Administrators do everything in a timely fashion and in order.
Galatians 2:11-21	Administrators rebuke and oppose when necessary.
2 Thessalonians 3:6-15	Administrators are examples for others.

QUESTION 5:

Moses was overwhelmed by trying to arbitrate issues for two million people. Jethro suggested Moses delegate his responsibilities to qualified men. Moses received help, the people's needs were met, and they were satisfied.

QUESTION 6: True

Yes, the disciples were neglecting teaching the Word of God (Acts 6:2). Again, this principle is important for guiding the church.

QUESTION 7:

A. Face the reality of problems

B. Develop a proper perspective of the problem before reaching a concrete solution

C. Establish priorities and delegate responsibility to qualified people

D. Maintain a proper balance between divine and human factors

E. Take an approach to problem-solving and decision-making that considers the attitudes and feelings of those directly involved

F. Solve every problem both with creativity and the guidance of the Holy Spirit, and never get locked into administrative routines simply because they have worked before.

In the situation in Act 15, the apostles applied all the principles listed above. If you use this story as an example, be sure you can identify how each principle is used.

QUESTION 8:
A. Face the reality of problems
B. Develop a proper perspective of the problem before reaching a concrete solution
C. Establish priorities and delegate responsibility to qualified people
D. Maintain a proper balance between divine and human factors
E. Take an approach to problem-solving and decision-making that considers the attitudes and feelings of those directly involved
F. Solve every problem both with creativity and the guidance of the Holy Spirit, and never get locked into administrative routines simply because they have worked before.

In the situation in Exodus 18, all of the above principles were applied by Moses. If you use this situation as a guide, be sure you can identify their use in this example also.

QUESTION 9: *Your answer*

QUESTION 10: True
If the needs of the church or the community change, the local church's organizational structure should fluctuate to meet the current needs.

QUESTION 11:
There is a natural resistance to change. People develop a sense of security in the way things are done so that any change threatens their security. That is why sometimes even the smallest change can generate such a disproportionately large amount of resistance. Think back over the discussion of form and function in Lesson 2 and institutionalism in Lesson 3. Forms tend to become institutionalized. They are then extremely hard to change.

QUESTION 12: *Your answer*

QUESTION 13: False
The holy kiss was the culturally acceptable greeting in New Testament times, but the supra-cultural concept is for Christians to greet each other appropriately and enthusiastically for their culture.

QUESTION 14: False
Paul was totally free in Christ and yet called himself a slave of Christ. Paradoxically, enslaving ourselves to Him frees us (Mark 8:34-35). That also means that we are the servants of other Christians (Ephesians 5:21; 1 Peter 5:5).

QUESTION 15:

Verse	Teaching
Galatians 5:25	Restoration must be done by a spiritual Christian.
Galatians 6:1	Restoration is the task of more than one person.
Galatians 6:3	Restoration must be done with humility.
Titus 3:2-5	Restoration is based on our salvation by God's mercy.
James 5:15-16	Restoration must be done prayerfully.

QUESTION 16: *Your answer*

Lesson 10 Self Check Answers

QUESTION 1: Law
QUESTION 2: True
QUESTION 3:
C. They were distracted from their main duties.
QUESTION 4: True
QUESTION 5: False
QUESTION 6:
D. People's security is threatened by change.
QUESTION 7:
A. Kiss
QUESTION 8: False
QUESTION 9: False
QUESTION 10: False

Lesson 10 Articles

Chapter 13: Biblical Examples of Administration and Organization

The Bible is relatively silent regarding organizational and administrative patterns. But this is not without design, for nothing becomes obsolete as quickly as administrative and organizational forms. They are but a means to divine ends. Furthermore, life is made up of so many variables and unpredictable events that creativity in this area must be constant.

But the Bible does speak in this area, and when it does, its examples yield some dynamic and powerful principles.

Both Old and New Testament illustrations of organization and administration surface the same basic principles. This again helps to show that the patterns are not absolute, but the principles are.

The purpose of this chapter is to present four structural examples—two from the Old Testament and two from the New Testament. First we'll look at an Old Testament example and a New Testament example in close alignment, to show how clearly they compare in the nature of the problems, the solutions, and the results. The second two examples are uniquely different, but again demonstrate similar principles.

A Comparative Study

Two of the most obvious problems calling for organization and administration are found in Exodus 18 and Acts 6. The former involved a mass of people, no doubt 2 million plus, camped in the wilderness. The latter involved a rapidly multiplying group of Christians in Jerusalem, by then numbering in the thousands.[1]

The following chart will help to isolate the problems, the solutions, and results recorded in these passages.

---

[1] It is interesting to note the references to numbers in the first part of the book of Acts. The church was launched with approximately 120 (Acts 1:15); in 2:41 about 3,000 were added to the original 100; in 4:4 we are told that "the number of men came to about 5,000." Some believe that the mention of "men" refers to 5,000 households. If so, the number of disciples would have been five to ten times this number, or maybe more, at the time the events in Acts 6 took place.

Moses in the Wilderness (Exod. 18:13-27; Deut. 1:9-18)	The Neglected Widows (Acts 6:1-7)
Problem	**Problem**
• v. 13—The people stood about Moses from morning until the evening. • v.14—Moses sat alone trying to do the job all by himself. • vv.15-16—Moses was attempting to resolve the problem of the people's interpersonal relationship and taught the people the laws of God. • v.18—This laborious process caused undue stress for Moses and for the people as well.	• v.1—The disciples were increasing rapidly. With such growth: the communal system was put under stress. Certain individuals among Hellenistic Jews were being overlooked in the daily serving food. Consequently, the Hellenists began to complain. • v.2—The twelve Apostles got involved in the details of this discussion and the results of this discontentment caused them to begin to neglect their primary responsibility—To teach the Word of God
Solution	**Solution**
• v.19—Moses' father-in-law, Jethro served as his consultant. Jethro advised Moses to establish priorities—to serve as a mediator between the people. • vv.20-21—To delegate the responsibility to men for handling the interpersonal problems of everyday needs of life to a select group of qualified men—"able who fear God, men of truth, who hate dishonest gain." • v.22—These men were to handle the minor matters, and only the major problems would be filtered through to Moses. Deuteronomy 1 • vv.9-12—Moses communicated his problem to the people. • v.13—Moses instructed each tribe to "choose wise and discerning and experienced men"; Moses in turn appointed them as heads. • vv.16-18—Moses carefully instructed the leaders in everything they were to do.	• v.2—The Twelve called a meeting of the disciples. • vv. 3-4—In this meeting they informed the people regarding their God. The major task as the twelve apostles was to teach them as a group the statutes, prayer, and the ministry of the World of God. • v.3—They instructed the Christians to select seven qualified men to care for the needs of life—"men of reputation who fear God, men of truth, full of the Spirit and wisdom. • v.5—The congregation chose seven men—obviously Hellenists. • v.6—The apostles confirmed the choice of the people through prayer and the layin on of hands.
Results (Exodus 18)	**Results** (Acts 6)

• v.22—Moses was assisted in his responsibilities.
 	
• v.23—Moses was able to endure the demands of his leadership role—The people's needs were met and they were satisfied.
	• v.7—the needs of the people were met; unity was restored; the apostles were able to fulfill their primary work:
	  -the number of believers kept on increasing greatly.
	  -the Word of God kept on spreading

Though these two events took place at different times, in different settings, and under different sets of circumstances, and though there were many other differences surrounding the details of these two situations, the nature of the problems, the way in which the problems were solved, and the results are strikingly similar.

The Nature of the Problem

Both Moses and the apostles had more than they could do personally, and both were becoming involved in details that kept them from fulfilling their primary responsibilities. Moses, particularly, was unable to endure the physical and psychological stress.

Furthermore, in both situations the people themselves were under stress and became discontented because their personal needs were being neglected. The children of Israel came to Moses to be instructed, to have him work out problems among them, to state their grievances, and to make their petitions. Evidently, some people stood in line all day long and perhaps even then did not get a chance to have a hearing with their leader (Ex 18:13).

In view of the previous problems Moses had with these people—their desire to return to Egypt, their complaints against him for getting them into this wilderness experience, their carnality and sin—it does not take too much imagination to reconstruct the tense mood and emotional outbursts that must have taken place among them.

The disciples in Jerusalem must have faced similar problems.

Though hopefully more spiritually mature than their forefathers, these new Christians also became very unhappy when their physical needs were not met. Furthermore, it may be that we see, in Acts 6, favoritism being shown toward a certain class or group.

It was the Hellenistic Jews against the Hebrews. The Hebrews were Palestinian Jews, whereas the Hellenists were residents of other countries, such as Syria, Egypt, and Asia Minor. The Palestinian Jews spoke their own language, whereas the Hellenists spoke Greek. Furthermore, the Hebrews probably composed the majority of Christians, and the Grecians were in the minority. Added to this, the Palestinian Jews no doubt reflected the more rigorous aspects of pure Judaism, while the Hellenists reflected the influence of Greek customs.

Consequently, we have a combination of factors that may be strongly parallel to some of the problems of prejudice that exist in today's church. But perhaps of more importance was the fact that the growth of the church was so rapid that the natural tendency to neglect certain people may have become the primary factor in causing this problem.

The Way the Problem Was Solved

Though the specific steps taken to solve the problems that existed differed in certain particulars, there were four important similarities. First, both Moses and the apostles established priorities. In Moses' case it was his father-in-law, Jethro, who helped him see and analyze the problems. He advised Moses to give primary attention to serving as a mediator between the people and God (Ex 18:19), and to be the one who taught the people the Word of God (Ex 18:20).

When the apostles became aware of the problems in Jerusalem, they immediately communicated to the multitude of Christians that they could not be burdened with the details of waiting on tables, but must continue to give primary attention to teaching the Word of God and to prayer (Acts 6:2-4). They were not negating the importance of these details, but knew they would be unable to carry out their primary spiritual objectives and be personally involved in meeting the physical needs of the people as well.

The second similarity is the delegation of responsibility to qualified men. Moses chose able men—men who were God-fearing, honest, and also men who hated dishonest gain (Ex 18:21).[2] The apostles instructed the people to select seven men who had a good reputation, who were filled with the Holy Spirit, and who were wise (Acts 6:3). Here it is important to note the high spiritual standards set for selecting men to fulfill the responsibility of meeting the physical needs of people.

Actually, these high standards in both situations were the secret to effectively solving the problem. Moses and the apostles needed men they could trust. Men who were dishonest, unspiritual, selfish, and tactless would have only made the problem worse. Qualified men, on the other hand, would resolve the problems.

The third similarity is that they organized to meet the need that existed at that moment and in those peculiar circumstances: In the Old Testament situation, "Moses chose capable men from all Israel, and he made them heads over the people, rulers over thousands, rulers over hundreds, rulers over fifties, and rulers over tens" (Ex 18:25). This was the best strategy for the occasion. This organizational plan was a fitting structure for a nation on the move, and "this arrangement was linked to the natural division of the people and the tribes and families, etc."[3]

Robert Jamieson comments:

> *The arrangement was an admirable one, and it was founded on a division of the people which was adopted not only in civil but in military affairs; so that the same persons who were officers in war were magistrates in peace (see Num. 31:14).... Care was thus taken by the minute subdivision to which the judicial system was carried, that, in suits and proceedings at law, every man should have what was just and equal, without going far to seek it, without waiting long to obtain it, and without paying an exorbitant price for it.*[4]

The apostles, on the other hand, instructed the people to select from among themselves seven men. This was a wise move, for the people themselves knew those who would meet the qualifications that the apostles had prescribed. Moreover, if the people selected these men, there would be no accusation of a prejudicial choice on the part of the Twelve (note that all seven men chosen had Greek names).

Again the structure set up on this occasion was appropriate to the situation. The number seven is significant only in that it was recommended because the apostles estimated that this was the number it would take to do the job.[5]

A fourth similarity is that in both of these circumstances, the structure set up was temporary. When the children of Israel settled in the land, the organizational plans changed. Also in a relatively short period of time, persecution drove the Christians out of Jerusalem, and some of the men who were serving tables became evangelists (Acts 7–8). The whole situation changed, creating new needs, which called for new forms and structures, particularly as permanently located churches were established in various communities.

---

[2] In Deuteronomy 1:13, these men are described as "wise and discerning and experienced men."

[3] C. F. Keil and F. Delitzsch, *The Pentateuch*, 2:87.

[4] Robert Jamieson, *Genesis–Deuteronomy*, Eerdmans, pp. 348–49.

[5] It is true that a committee or board of approximately seven is a very workable number for efficient operation, particularly when group decision-making is involved.

The Significance of the Results

The results of the organizational steps taken to resolve the problems in Exodus 18 and Acts 6 are clearly delineated in the Word of God. Simply stated, the problems were resolved—at least for the time being (organizational problems are never permanently solved since the needs of the organization change). Moses and the apostles were able to carry out their primary tasks. The people's needs were met and they were satisfied.

Moses' physical and psychological needs were also met, and as a result of the appointment of the seven men in Acts, the "Word of God kept on spreading; and the number of the disciples continued to increase greatly in Jerusalem, and a great many of the priests were becoming obedient to the faith" (Acts 6:7, NASB).

Another Example: The Book of Nehemiah

Another example of a problem calling for organization and administration is found in the book of Nehemiah. The walls of Jerusalem were in shambles and called for strong leadership on the part of Nehemiah.

The Book of Nehemiah: Rebuilding the Wall

Verses	The Problem
Nehemiah 1:2-3	Nehemiah, cupbearer to the king of Persia, received a report that the remnant in Judah who had returned were in great distress and reproached because the walls of Jerusalem were broken down and burned with fire.
Nehemiah 1:4	Nehemiah's response was one of depression and sadness.

Verses	The Solution
Nehemiah 4:1-11	Nehemiah fasted and prayed
Nehemiah 2:1-2	He did not hesitate to reveal his sadness to the king.
Nehemiah 2:3	He told the king why he was depressed.
Nehemiah 2:4	The king asked Nehemiah: "What would you request?"
Nehemiah 2:4	Nehemiah asked God for guidance in responding to this question.
Nehemiah 2:5	He asked the king to send him to Judah to rebuild the walls.
Nehemiah 2:6	The king responded positively.
Nehemiah 2:7-8	Nehemiah asked the king for official letters so he could travel freely and also obtain timber from the king's forest.
Nehemiah 2:12-16	When Nehemiah arrived, he spent three nights secretly surveying the situation. At this time, he developed a strategy for rebuilding the walls.
Nehemiah 2:17-20	Nehemiah then revealed his plan and asked the people to help him rebuild the walls.
Nehemiah 3:1-32	
Nehemiah 4:1-13	When the enemies of Israel tried to stop their work, the people did two things: they prayed and set up a guard day and night.
Nehemiah 4:14	When the people grew fearful, Nehemiah told them (1) not to be afraid, (2) to remember the greatness of God, and (3) to fight for the sake of

	their families.
Nehemiah 4:15	When their enemies learned that the people were ready to defend themselves, their plans were frustrated so the people were able to return to the wall to continue building.
Nehemiah 4:16-23	Nehemiah devised a new plan for working and guarding so that they could continue building, but also be ready for war.
Nehemiah 6:15	They completed the walls in fifty-two days.

Verses	*The Immediate Results*
Nehemiah 12:27-29, 31-42	The people sang and praised God.
Nehemiah 12:30	The people purified themselves and the city.
Nehemiah 12:43	They offered sacrifices to God.
Nehemiah 6:16	When the enemies of Israel witnessed this impossible feat and heard the rejoicing of Israel, "they lost their confidence." They recognized that this could have been achieved only "with the help of God."

The Nature of the Problem

The problems in Jerusalem focused on the broken walls. This condition resulted in ridicule, reproach, and humiliation for the people of Judah. They were mistreated and abused. Many of the Jews were afraid to even live within the city. They remained a scattered, fearful people, even though they were living in the land of Judah. They had little security from their enemies and lived in constant fear and anxiety.

Consequently, many were living out of fellowship with God.

They did not worship God nor were they being exposed to the laws of God. Some of the Jews were even taking advantage of their own people (Neh 5). Neither did they pay tithes, nor did they keep themselves pure and separated from the paganism and idols that surrounded them.

The Way the Problem Was Solved

Nehemiah's approach to solving this problem was a tremendous example of organizational and administrative skill that included both the human and divine dimensions. They are so carefully blended throughout the narrative that it is difficult to separate the two, but they are both there.

First, Nehemiah sought wisdom and help from God (Neh 1:4-11).

Struck with the terrible plight of his people, Nehemiah's initial step was to pray and fast. He acknowledged God's greatness, confessed their sins (including his own), recalled God's promises to regather the children of Israel if they repented, and then asked the Lord to grant him mercy before the king whom he served.

Second, Nehemiah built bridges to the king (Neh 2:1-10).

He had already laid the groundwork for this bridge. He had been a good servant. His sadness was very obvious to the king against a backdrop of his constantly happy countenance. And furthermore, Nehemiah was not afraid to reveal his true feelings to the king, evidence of a certain degree of rapport—and faith. Nehemiah's prayer was answered. The king asked why he was so downcast. But even at this moment Nehemiah relied on God.

Moving from a purely human factor (revealing his sadness), he breathed a prayer to God for wisdom to answer the king's question. Here was the opportunity he had been hoping for. His response and the way he answered and what he said were critical!

God answered Nehemiah's prayer as quickly as he had prayed.

Nehemiah's answer was clear-cut but tactful. He asked that the king might send him to rebuild the walls.

When given a favorable reply, Nehemiah took another step—a bold one! He asked for official letters from the king to be able to pass through various countries unhindered. He even went so far as to ask for the privilege of cutting down trees from the king's forest.

Request granted! And with these credentials Nehemiah had not only built bridges to the king, but he had built bridges all the way to Jerusalem and to his own people. To the surprise of the enemies of Judah, he even arrived with army officers and horsemen assigned to him by the king.

Third, Nehemiah secretly surveyed the situation in Jerusalem and developed his strategy (Neh 2:11-16; 3:1-32).

On three successive nights, he quietly, but carefully, inspected and evaluated the damage to the walls. Nehemiah knew that he needed to have his facts in hand before he challenged the people to rebuild the wall. Furthermore, to even let them know the purpose of his coming before developing his strategy would be lethal. Humanly speaking, he might have lost the people before he even got the plan off the ground. And to release the information early would have unveiled the plan to the enemies of Israel, who would have scoffed even more. The people, of course, didn't need any more demoralization. They were already at low ebb.

Nehemiah's great challenge was to build their morale and convince them the job could be done. So he proceeded to develop a strategy that was unique. The priests were to work on the Sheep Gate, inferring that this was an assignment that appealed to them personally. Scholars note that this gate was near the temple and it would be through this gate that they would bring small livestock for sacrifice. In like manner, if archeological speculation is correct, the goldsmiths and perfumers were assigned a section of the wall nearest their shops.

Whatever the specifics, it is clear that Nehemiah had mapped out his plan carefully and with wisdom. Every person or group who could work, including women, was assigned to a task.

Fourth, Nehemiah expounded on the plan to the people, motivating them with both human and divine factors (Neh 2:17-20).

He appealed first to their wretched condition—the reproach they were bearing because of the broken walls, and the desolate condition of Jerusalem. Next, he told them how God had helped him to win the favor of the king and his support in this venture.

The results were positive. "Let us arise and build!" was the response, and so they did. When their enemies heard about it and saw the people taking their places around the wall, they responded with mockery and hatred! But the people were prepared. Their goals were set—their strategy outlined! They did not succumb to their enemies' demoralizing attacks.

Note how Nehemiah said "we" will arise and build (Neh 2:20). He was their leader, but he was also "one" with them. He was a part of the team, and he, too, was on the front line engaging in the same difficult work (Neh 5:16). This is dynamic leadership. This is a basic reason why these people saw this project through to completion against almost impossible odds. Nehemiah's example went far beyond what is ordinarily expected.

Fifth, Nehemiah supervised the work closely, facing and solving unforeseen problems as they arose during the process (Neh 4:1-12; 6:15).

Laying the groundwork for any venture is only part of the organizational–administrative picture. Even though the people "had a mind to work," they were to face constant ridicule and hostility. The work went on, and when it became obvious the enemies were planning to attack in order to stop the work, Nehemiah prepared for the battle by placing people all around the wall. He stationed them by families (Neh 4:13). This was shrewd—but necessary. If their families had been in another place in the city or outside the walls, the temptation would be to run to them. Now they would have to fight to protect them—on location!

This is exactly what Nehemiah knew would motivate them. So when he saw their fear, he gave them three charges: (1) "Do not be afraid of them;" (2) "Remember the Lord who is great and awesome;" and (3) "Fight for your brothers, your sons, your daughters, your wives, and your houses" (Neh 4:14, NASB).

Fortunately, the battle never materialized. The enemy, evidently overawed by this determination and the bold stand of the Jews, backed away from their threat (Neh 4:15). And everyone, once again, took up his task at the wall.

Nehemiah devised a new strategy. From then on, some worked and some guarded; some worked with one hand and carried their weapon in the other; those who had to work with both hands kept their swords at their sides. A trumpet would be used to gather the people together quickly in case of attack. No one was to go out of Jerusalem at night; rather they were to stand guard. And in the final days of building, Nehemiah and many of his workers and guards never removed their clothes nor laid down their weapons, even when they stopped for a drink of water (Neh 4:23). Against almost impossible odds, they completed the wall in fifty-two days!

The Significance of the Results

The results of Nehemiah's organizational and administrative skills are obvious all the way through the building program. This was a long-range project, and at every step along the way he achieved certain significant goals. He won the favor of the king, motivated the people to begin the work, kept the people at the task in spite of threats from their enemies, and finally they rebuilt the wall.

The final results of this project were intensely rewarding. Nehemiah must have been overwhelmed with thanksgiving and praise to God; for, all the way through this intense experience, he praised the God of heaven for every accomplishment.

Imagine the thrill when he heard the people singing and praising God at the dedication of the wall (Neh 12:27-29; 31:42). The two great choirs on top of the walls must have been an incredible sight to the enemies of Judah. The sounds of their voices and rejoicing were so loud that they could be "heard from far away" (Neh 12:43). In the words of Nehemiah himself, "They recognized this work had been accomplished with the help of our God."

There were more social reforms, as they were able to reorganize and develop order in the community (Neh 11:1-2). And most important, there were religious reforms. The people were once again able to come together to hear the Law of God (Neh 8:1-18). And the most rewarding result for Nehemiah was to see the people—as a reunited people—confessing their sins, worshiping the God of heaven, and making a covenant with Him.

Another Example: The Jerusalem Council

Not only can problems calling for organization and administration be found in the Old Testament, but in the New Testament, as well. The Church had grown tremendously since Pentecost and now a controversy had arisen about the nature of the gospel itself.

The Jerusalem Council: Acts 15:1-35	
Verses	**Problem**
Acts 15:1	Certain men were teaching false doctrines in Antioch—"you must be circumcised to be saved."
Acts 15:2	Paul and Barnabas debated the issue publicly but could not solve the problem.
Verses	**Solution**
Acts 15:2-3	The church at Antioch decided to seek guidance from the apostles and elders at Jerusalem.
Acts 15:4	The Antioch delegation reported how Gentiles were being converted through faith alone.
Acts 15:6	The apostles and elders met in a closed session to discuss the matter.
Acts 15:7-11	Peter reminded the people of what God did for Cornelius and his household.
Acts 15:12	Paul and Barnabas gave specific testimony regarding the "signs and wonders God had done through them among the Gentiles."
Acts 15:13-18	James made reference to the work of the Old Testament prophets and how they had predicted Gentile conversion.
Acts 15:19-21	James proposed a solution to the problem.
Acts 15:22	The apostles, elders, and the whole church agreed to this proposal.
Acts 15:22-30	A letter was written spelling out the solution.
Acts 15:22	Judas and Silas were chosen by the church to deliver the letter.
Acts 15:30, 32	Judas and Silas delivered the letter and also a "lengthy message."
Verses	**Results**
Acts 15:31	The congregation rejoiced when they heard the contents of the letter.
Acts 15:33	Judas and Silas were sent back to Jerusalem in peace.
Acts 15:35	The work of God continued unhindered.
Acts 16:4-5	The instructions in the letter were delivered by Paul, Silas, and Timothy to many of the new churches.

The Nature of the Problem

Here was a problem that was destined to affect all of the newly formed churches. Antioch was a prominent center of Christian activity, and it would not be long until the news of the disagreement and debate would spread to the new believers scattered throughout the New Testament world. The result would be confusion, disillusionment, and disunity.

This was no minor eruption! Here were Paul and Barnabas in open debate against men from Jerusalem, the birthplace of the whole Christian movement. The issue was just as crucial—either man was "saved by grace through faith," or it also involved works.

It could not be both. The results of this controversy would either unite the churches or split them.

The Way the Problem Was Solved

It did not take long for the leaders in the Antiochian church to recognize the explosive nature of this problem. They acted quickly and with wisdom. They faced the problem head on. They met together and decided this problem was beyond their ability to handle. They needed assistance. Acting with perception, they decided to take the problem back to its original source. They chose a delegation to accompany Paul and Barnabas—and set off for Jerusalem.

Note their approach when they arrived. No attack on personalities! No accusation against the Jerusalem church! They simply reported what God was doing in the Gentile world.

The immediate result was disagreement from certain people whom Luke identified as coming from the "religious party of the Pharisees" (Acts 15:5). But rather than allowing the issue to become a matter for public debate which would have quickly degenerated into emotional name calling, the apostles and elders went into a closed session to discuss the matter.

Exact sequences and what was involved are somewhat unclear in the biblical account. But there is sufficient information to draw some accurate conclusions. There was more discussion and debate, probably within the smaller group (Acts 15:6-7).

Eventually, Peter stood up publicly before the whole congregation (Acts 15:7-12) and substantiated the initial report by reminding the people of something they already knew (Acts 15:7): his own personal experience with Cornelius. God had saved this Gentile and his household "by faith" and gave them the Holy Spirit, just as He had done at Pentecost (Acts 15:9). There were the same "signs" as at the beginning (Acts 10:44-46).

At this juncture Paul and Barnabas added more support to Peter's case by relating what signs and wonders God had done through them among the Gentiles. The next move was crucial! James (undoubtedly the brother of Christ, and obviously the most respected leader in the church in Jerusalem) spoke on the issue. He began by adding support to Peter's testimony, and then in a marvelous demonstration of wisdom and insight, summarized the teachings of several Old Testament prophets that related directly to the problem. He then made a proposal—in actuality suggesting a compromise—one that would not violate "justification by faith," but one that would also pacify the Jewish Christians who still found it difficult to understand "freedom from the law" (Acts 15:19-21).

Step by step, under the leadership of men who were seeking God's will, the immediate problem was solved. No one could really predict what was going to happen in the actual process. An objective approach to the problem, being willing to face the issue squarely and openly, and using much wisdom and administrative skill—all made the meeting in Jerusalem successful. They accomplished there what they were unable to accomplish in Antioch, achieving results that were more far-reaching and significant than had they merely stilled the local storm.

The Significance of the Results

The results of a problem well solved were immediately obvious. People were happy and content. There was peace among the brethren, and the work of God continued without interruption and without being sidetracked onto peripheral issues. It is perhaps most significant that the apostle Paul was happy with the decision. He, personally, with his missionary team, delivered the letter from Jerusalem to all the churches which he had established.

Previous encounters with Paul had evidently convinced Peter and James that he would tolerate no inconsistency in crucial theological matters.

Summary

Here, then, are four biblical examples of organizational and administrative structure and skill. Though all vary, they all have several things in common: a problem arose, a solution was sought, and results were achieved. More than that, each problem was attacked with a variety of approaches which yielded basic principles. And it is to these principles we turn in the chapter to follow.

Carry One Another's Burdens

"Carry one another's burdens, and in this way you will fulfill the law of Christ" (Gal 6:2, emphasis added).

Dealing with sin in the lives of other believers is a difficult task. Consequently, many churches ignore the responsibility entirely. This is the main idea Paul has in mind, as shown in the previous verse: "Brothers and sisters, if a person is discovered in some sin, **you who are spiritual** restore such a person in a spirit of gentleness. Pay close attention to yourselves, so that you are not tempted too" (Gal 6:1, emphasis added). We have a responsibility when other believers sin. We should attempt to restore that person by getting him or her to acknowledge and overcome the sin.

Paul's guidelines:

Restoration is a task for spiritual Christians (Gal 5:25). Not only are there two kinds of people described in the New Testament, there are also two kinds of Christians: carnal and spiritual. Although Paul clearly described the Corinthians as saved, he also called them carnal (1 Cor 3:1-3). Carnal Christians are not to attempt to deal with sin in the lives of others (Lk 6:39-42).

Restoration is the task of more than one person as Paul used the plural pronoun in Galatians 6:1 (see also Mt 18:15-17). Generally, start with confronting the person, then take witnesses, then the entire church.

Restoration must be with genuine humility. "Gently," Paul wrote (Gal 6:1, 3). We must remember that we were saved by God's mercy (Tit 3:2-5). If we understand the grace of God's salvation, we will approach someone else with humility (2 Cor 10:1).

Restoration must be done cautiously because you, too, may be tempted (Gal 6:1). Christian leaders can fall in counseling situations and must choose wisely (1 Cor 10:13).

Restoration must be done prayerfully (Jas 5:15-16). Sometimes sickness is caused by sin, but James says healing can come by prayer.

Note: This material is adapted from Gene A. Getz, *The Measure of a Man*. (Ventura, CA: Regal Books, 1984).

Greet One Another

*"**Greet one another** with a holy kiss. All the churches of Christ greet you"* (Rom 16:16, emphasis added).

At the end of his letter to the Romans, Paul greeted twenty-six people by name, and his exhortation to "greet one another with a holy kiss" is made five times in the New Testament (1 Cor 16:20; 2 Cor 13:12; 1 Thess 5:2; 1 Pet 5:14). The holy kiss was the culturally acceptable greeting in New Testament times, but the universal–cultural concept is for Christians to greet each other appropriately for their culture. In some cultures, this type of greeting is still appropriate, as is seen when certain heads of state greet each other.

Paul's concern is that it is a genuine showing of Christian love between siblings in Christ and not just a routine gesture that reflects society's social graces. It is always appropriate and important for Christians to greet one another. It should be "holy" because it reflects deep meaning and sincere Christian love. This is in contrast to the usual greetings between people that are often hypocritical or insincere. A Christian's greetings must be from pure motives. If we cannot greet one another in this way, we are admonished to confess our sins to one another, pray for each other, and forgive one another (Col 3:13; Jas 5:16). We must live in harmony with one another.

Note: This material is adapted from Gene A. Getz, *The Measure of a Man*. (Ventura, CA: Regal Books, 1984).

Chapter 14: Principles of Biblical Administration and Organization

As Christian leaders, we face a multitude of problems. The rapidly changing world has not helped to reduce the number of problems nor their complexity. But God's people have always faced problems, and in many instances those that face us today are—in their roots—the same old problems. But all problems—old or new—call for certain administrative actions and organizational structures to solve them. This was true both in the Old and New Testaments and still applies in contemporary times.

There are relatively few examples of administrative action and organizational structure in the Bible and those that do appear vary greatly. Because of the lack of conformity, these patterns and structures cannot be classified as normative. But the Bible does contain several examples, which provide us with profound and normative principles of organization and administration. It is these biblical principles which can provide us with guidelines in developing patterns and structures, and, in turn, can help us carry out biblical directives.

Principles of Administration

Face Reality

First, face the reality of problems. Do not ignore them. If we do, they will not go away! They get worse! We may "sweep them under the rug," but eventually they reappear in double measure.

We can "hide our heads in the sand," but when we develop enough courage to "look up," they will be bigger and more foreboding than ever. It does not take much creative imagination to project what could have happened in Israel if Moses had ignored Jethro's advice. What if the

Antiochian Christians had looked the other way and not faced the heresy that was being taught by the Judaizers? It could have had negative repercussions all over the New Testament world.

Nehemiah's problems were different! He could have conveniently ignored the plight of his people. But he could never have gotten away from his conscience and the pain he felt in his heart. Though the task was tough and filled with unpredictable events, he fulfilled the will of God. And the people benefited from his selfless efforts.

There are occasions—but very few—when we, as Christian leaders, can ignore problems in the church, sometimes without too many outward repercussions. But, in our hearts we must live with the decision to withdraw from desperate situations in order to have an easier path to walk. When people's needs go unmet because of our selfishness and our unwillingness to face problems, we must live with our decisions. And as often happens, God bypasses us to achieve His purposes through another vessel that is far more sensitive to human needs as well as to His Spirit.

Today, as in the New Testament, churches are facing problems. Some are purely organizational; some are theological; some are cultural. Many, of course, involve all three. Though some of these problems are as old as man himself, and though some are new and contemporary, they are problems and they must be solved for God's richest blessing to rest on the local church.

Never ignore problems. For, if you do, they may overwhelm you, defeat you and cause you to leave the work of God, feeling hostile and bitter or depressed and discouraged. Worst of all, you may rationalize your failure, putting the blame on others for your own unwillingness to face problems as they arise.

Develop a Proper Perspective

Second, develop a proper perspective on the problem before reaching a concrete solution. Sometimes this can be done quickly, and at other times it takes a period of careful evaluation.

In Acts 6 it did not take the apostles long to pinpoint the nature of the problem and to arrive at a solution. The cause was obvious, as well as what was and what was not the best approach to solving it. It did not take a long period of prayer, evaluation, and seeking God's will to arrive at a solution.

For Nehemiah it was a different story. He was far removed from the actual environment in which the problem existed. His only source of information was an oral report (Neh 1:1-2), and what he actually learned from this report was very limited (Neh 1:3). Consequently, he spent a lengthy period of time seeking God's guidance, and his first step when arriving in Jerusalem was to spend three nights carefully inspecting and evaluating the walls of Jerusalem. Because of the complexity of the problem and the explosive nature of the situation, he, in wisdom, decided to get a personal perspective before publicly announcing his strategy.

For the leaders in the Antiochian and Jerusalem churches, the problem in Acts 15 was yet different. It was a theological problem—one that had grown out of Judaism and the Law of Moses. It emerged in the transition from Old Testament days to the New, as the apostles themselves attempted to clarify even in their own minds "how a man is saved."

In Jerusalem, it took time to solve the problems of Judaism *vis-à-vis* Christianity. It involved a process of reports, debate, and discussion, both in private and in public. It involved historical and biblical research as well as an analysis of what God was doing on the contemporary scene. And it was the result of this process that led to perspective and an organizational and administrative answer—a letter and its deliverance to the churches.

Moses, as he led the people through the wilderness, appears to have been totally unaware that he even had a problem, or that it could be solved with a good organizational and administrative plan. It took his father-in-law, Jethro, to identify and solve the problem.

One of the problems of being a leader is that sometimes we get so close to a situation that "we can't see the forest for the trees." This was Moses' difficulty. He knew he had a lot of work to do and that he was working with a group of unspiritual and unpredictable people, but he did not have the "big picture" that would have helped him execute his responsibilities. Here is where others can help us solve problems. It took Jethro to help Moses even see his problem. *It took the Jerusalem church to help the Antiochian church solve the problem they were already aware of.* Pinpointing it more specifically, it took the assistance of Peter and James to help Paul and Barnabas to bring the problem of law versus grace into clear focus.

A great danger that faces every Christian leader is to become threatened by advice. Somehow we feel it is a reflection on our competence, so we try to solve the problem alone. Unfortunately, if the problem is beyond us, we will probably end up a failure, far more humiliated than if we had admitted needing help. To seek advice is a sign of strength and not weakness. This does not mean that we execute every bit of advice we get from others. Rather it means listening, sorting ideas carefully, and selecting a course of action in dependence upon the Spirit of God.

Establish Priorities

Third, establish priorities. This may actually be one of the main reasons we cannot solve our organizational and administrative problems. We try to solve all the problems by ourselves.

This was Moses' problem until he took his father-in-law's advice. He was in the process of physical and psychological deterioration caused by undue stress. He could not do everything. Fortunately, he recognized this fact with Jethro's help and did something about it.

The apostles, in Acts 6, were also aware of this principle. They quickly established their priorities and made them known to the people. This did not mean that serving tables was unimportant—far from it—but it did mean that they had certain essential spiritual responsibilities that they had to fulfill. They could not do both.

Today, pastors and other spiritual leaders are bombarded with many demands on their time. Contemporary culture and its pressures have complicated the lives of people, creating greater needs. A "big society" and "big business" have created a "big mentality." We automatically demand more of our leaders and ourselves. Therefore, it is absolutely essential, especially for spiritual leaders in the church, to establish priorities. If we don't, we will neglect our primary callings to shepherd and to teach.

Delegate Responsibility

Fourth, delegate responsibility to qualified people. This principle follows naturally the establishment of priorities. We have seen it demonstrated by Moses, by the apostles, and by Nehemiah.

This principle, we can conclude, has been the secret to every leader's success. Peter Drucker, who has made a careful study of executives, concludes that a significant mark of every successful leader—whether he be the President of the United States or the president of Nanjing

Automotive—is that he knows how to "use all the available strengths—the strength of associates, the strength of supervisors, and one's own strength."[6]

But notice that the Bible clearly emphasizes that delegation of responsibility must be to spiritually qualified people. This is what Moses and the apostles did in Exodus 18 and Acts 6. They looked for people who were honest and full of faith, people who were wise and discerning and experienced. They knew that to appoint a person of weakness rather than of strength would be devastating to the whole operation. They also knew that people of quality could handle organizational problems.

Nehemiah, of course, had a similar problem. However, he needed every available person to rebuild the walls and he used them. But when it came to administering the affairs of Jerusalem after the walls were rebuilt, he appointed Hananiah, who had been commander of the forces, to be in charge of Jerusalem. Nehemiah chose this man because "he was a faithful man and feared God more than many" (Neh 7:2). He had already proved himself as a qualified leader.

The selection of spiritually and psychologically qualified people for leadership positions in the church is one of the most important administrative principles in the New Testament. This is why most all of the qualifications of elders and deacons in 1 Timothy 3 and Titus 1 relate to the person's reputation, ethics, morality, temperament, habits, and spiritual and psychological maturity.

Many churches today are guilty of filling positions with people—but not qualified people. We often make judgments based on "skills," but if these skills are practiced in a context of carnality, it can be devastating. It is much better to have a person with as yet undeveloped skill but who is strong spiritually.

Maintain a Proper Balance

Fifth, maintain a proper balance between divine and human factors.

The temptation for all leaders is to go to extremes. On the one hand, we may rationalize indecision and inaction on the basis of God's sovereign will and grace. This can easily become a cop out for irresponsibility and—God forbid—even laziness. On the other hand, we may take matters into our own hands and ignore the will of God, His power, wisdom, and guidance.

Both extremes are inappropriate. Nehemiah, of all the biblical examples, demonstrates the balance most forcefully. He prayed and then acted. And sometimes he acted and then prayed. And at times he prayed while he acted. As he consistently sought guidance from God he, at the same time, proceeded to use the mind and energy that God had given him to do what needed to be done.

Today's Christian leaders must maintain the same balance. How easy it is to go to extremes, to attempt to solve problems in our own strengths and with our own abilities and to neglect prayer, God's help, direction, and blessing. On the other hand, how easy it is to withdraw, spend time in prayer or in Bible reading, and neglect human responsibility. May God help us to put a proper emphasis on both the divine and human—and in that order.

---

[6] Peter F. Drucker, The Effective Executive, *Harper & Row*, p. 71.

Consider Attitudes and Feelings

Sixth, take an approach to problem solving and decision making that takes into consideration the attitudes and feelings of those who are directly involved.

Basic to effectively applying this principle is communication. Before taking specific steps to solve his problem, Moses explained to the people he was not able to bear up alone under the heavy responsibility (Deut 1:9). At the appropriate time, Nehemiah called the people together and explained his strategy to rebuild the walls (Neh 2:17). The apostles in Jerusalem summoned the congregation and explained the situation (Acts 6:2), and in Acts 15 the whole church was ultimately involved in solving the problem of law and grace. Organizational and administrative problems cannot be satisfactorily solved without proper communication.

Another factor which appears in all four biblical case studies is group involvement in the decision–making process. We see variance in the particulars, but there was always group participation and ultimate agreement. Moses instructed each tribe to select leaders to represent and rule them (Deut 1:13). The apostles charged the congregation to choose seven men to serve tables (Acts 6:1-3).

Nehemiah's problem was a different one, indeed. The primary responsibility of rebuilding the walls lay on his shoulders. He was the leader. *It was his idea and strategy.* But Nehemiah knew he could never achieve his goal without the cooperation of the people. Consequently, he carefully communicated his ideas and then issued a call to come as a team to rebuild the walls of Jerusalem. The results of his success as a leader are reflected in their response: "Arise! Let's rebuild!" (Neh 2:18).

Many problems are created in the church by ignoring this important biblical principle. We are only asking for trouble if we attempt to railroad things through and operate as a dictator. Naturally, there are many problems which need not be brought to the whole congregation for debate and discussion, but again our biblical examples give us significant guidelines in applying the principle of congregational involvement.

In Exodus 18 and Acts 6 minor details were solved by people selected by the group. This was the crucial point at which there was group involvement. Note, however, that in Acts 6 it is conceivable that only the Grecian Christians were involved in solving the problem.[7] There was no need to call the whole Jerusalem church together to solve a problem that affected only a certain segment of the church. In Acts 15, the whole church seemed to be made aware of the problem, but the basic proposal was formulated as a result of debate and discussion by the apostles and elders. However, it was the whole church that affirmed the proposal and was involved in the selection of men to implement the plan.

Here in Scripture we see four significant guidelines in determining when the whole group should be involved:

1. In general, it is best to involve only people who are directly related to and affected by a particular problem.
2. Clearly communicate the nature of the problem.
3. Involve this group in selecting qualified people to represent them in helping to

---

[7] The argument for this is based on the fact that only men who had Greek names were selected. It is further supported by the fact that it was the Grecian Jews who were being neglected. It seems the apostles called these people together and helped them solve their particular problem.

solve the problem.

4. Secure the group's approval of the final solution.

Be Creative

Seventh, solve every problem creatively under the leadership of the Holy Spirit. Never allow yourself to get locked into administrative routines that may have worked before.

We must remember that in the Bible there was no one way of either attacking or solving a problem. Every situation was different. Circumstances varied, the nature of the problem varied, and, therefore, solutions varied.

Christian leaders today frequently allow themselves to get locked into administrative patterns. They attempt to borrow patterns and approaches from other churches, or they continue to use patterns that have worked before. When we do, we are closing our minds and hearts to God, who has always used creative means throughout history to administer His work. In order to find the will of God in every matter, we must be guided by biblical principles, current circumstances, and the Holy Spirit.

Administration Summary

1. Face the reality of problems.
2. Develop a proper perspective on the problems before seeking concrete solutions.
3. Establish priorities.
4. Delegate responsibility to qualified people.
5. Maintain a proper balance between divine and human factors.
6. Take an approach to problem solving and decision making that takes into consideration the attitudes and feelings of those who are involved.
7. Solve every problem creatively under the leadership of the Holy Spirit.

Principles of Organization

Set Principles as Goals

First, organize to apply New Testament principles and to reach New Testament purposes.

Throughout these chapters, principles are stated which are believed to be biblical principles. If the principles are applied, they will provide the twenty-first-century church with New Testament guidelines.

Organizational structures in the Bible are always presented as a means to an end. They were never ends in themselves. Therefore, the first and most important biblical principle of organization is always to develop structures for the church which will help us to reach New Testament objectives.

This, in fact, becomes one of the criteria whereby we are able to evaluate our organizational structures. Are we truly functioning according to New Testament principles? Are we reaching New Testament purposes?

Meet Needs

Second, organize to meet needs. This was a distinctive mark of the New Testament church. The church did not just organize to organize. Rather it organized when the need arose, whether it was to feed the people in need or to solve a theological problem.

The first, most inclusive and continuous need faced by the New Testament church was to carry out the Great Commission. They were under obligation to make disciples and to teach those disciples. They organized to do so. But, as pointed out already, very few illustrations are given as to how this was done.

True, there is limited reference to organizational structure in the Scriptures, but again, this is not without design. There are sufficient illustrations to show it is necessary, and there is sufficient variance to show that particular structures are not absolute. The illustrations we do have yield dynamic principles that are applicable to any culture, and at any time in history. All of this points to freedom to design and create organizational structures that will be the most effective to reach New Testament objectives in today's world.

It has already been demonstrated that Paul was more concerned about qualified people than specific patterns of organization. Nevertheless, he was also interested in organization, for he charged the Corinthians to "do everything in a decent and orderly manner" (1 Cor. 14:40). He also instructed Titus to remain in Crete so he could "set in order the remaining matters" (Tit 1:5).

Paul also knew that every culture (even the various subcultures in the New Testament world) called for different approaches to specific organizational problems. He therefore bore down on the absolutes—qualifications for leadership positions—knowing that people of God who are wise and prudent could develop the structures necessary to meet the specialized demands of any culture at any time in history. As Dr. Francis Schaeffer has said, "Anything the New Testament does not command, and regard as church forms, is a freedom to be exercised under the leadership of the Holy Spirit for that particular time and place."[8]

Keep It Simple

Third, keep organization simple. This principle is closely aligned with the former; that is, organizing to meet needs. If organization is to be functional, it must be as simple as possible.

This does not mean that organizational patterns are never complex. For example, the pattern in Exodus 18 was very intricate, but it was also designed for over 2 million people who were traveling through the wilderness. Though complex, it was functional and was carefully designed to meet the needs of the Children of God at that particular time in their lives.

A good test of whether or not simplicity is being lost, even in a complex pattern, is whether or not the structure is serving biblical objectives. If it is not, it needs to be carefully evaluated in the light of scriptural criteria.

Keep It Flexible

Fourth, keep organization flexible. The structures set up in the wilderness for a people "on the move," were changed when they "settled in the land." When the walls were complete, a new approach was devised to govern Jerusalem. When persecution hit Jerusalem, the structure of Acts 6 was terminated, and when the specific "law and grace" problems recorded in Acts 15 were

---

[8] Schaeffer, Francis. *The Church at the End of the Century*, 67.

solved, they went on to new ways of solving *new* problems. *Biblical leaders were never locked into organizational structures.*

Organizational patterns that develop rigidity and "hardening of the categories" are in danger of being treated as authoritative and absolute. This is wrong. We are not free to make unchangeable what God intended to be changeable.

There are many areas today where the evangelical church needs to rethink its organizational structures—areas that we have allowed to become absolute and inflexible. The following questions are designed to probe our thinking and to "break us loose" from rigidity and inflexibility.

How Many Meetings and When?

Who is to say *how many* meetings should be conducted in a given week in the church? The Bible certainly does not dictate any patterns in this area.

Furthermore, who is to say when these meetings are to be held?

Other than a few references to meetings on the "first day of the week" (Acts 20:7; 1 Cor. 16:2), there is little said in Scripture about when the New Testament church met. Some would even question that meeting on Sunday is an absolute guideline for the church, but rather an example of when the church met. Remember that the Jerusalem church met daily in its initial days.

The Corinthians, no doubt, met on Sunday evening to partake of the Lord's Supper and to exercise their spiritual gifts (1 Cor. 11), but is this an absolute pattern? I think not! If so, the majority of churches have been out of step with Scripture for many years. But even in view of this scriptural evidence (or lack of it) regarding when believers are to meet, there are many Christians who feel you are tampering with scriptural authority if it is suggested, for example, that the Sunday night service be cancelled in favor of a more qualitative meeting at some other time.

Midweek prayer meeting has probably become one of the most rigid patterns of all, for to suggest a change (in the minds of some) is synonymous with being opposed to prayer. The fact is, there is no biblical injunction for the church to meet for a midweek prayer meeting. It may be an excellent idea, but there is nothing sacred about a midweek prayer meeting per se. What makes it sacred is what happens there, for there is no question but that believers are to pray. But when they meet to pray is not specified in the Bible.

It is interesting, too, that many Christian leaders evaluate the spiritual climate of the church by how many attend midweek prayer meeting. There may be some truth to this, but a more basic question is whether or not the body of believers represents a *praying* church. *When* they meet or *how many* meet at one time is not nearly so significant. A quantitative answer to how many attend midweek prayer meeting may be an indicator of spiritual maturity—or the *lack of it*. But it may also be true that a midweek prayer meeting, as it has come to be traditionally practiced, may no longer be the best means or pattern for our culture and times. Because of work schedules, school activities, and other cultural changes, perhaps the hour and evening chosen in a previous era is no longer the best time. This is probably a major reason why believers are not actively attending the service as they once did.

What Kinds of Meetings

In recent years, the various *kinds* of meetings conducted by the American Evangelical church have multiplied. We have meetings for children, meetings for youth, and meetings for adults. We have Bible classes, fellowship meetings, training sessions, worship periods, preaching services, and prayer meetings. We have Sunday school sessions, vacation Bible schools, training hour, children's church, youth church, adult church, women's missionary meetings, home Bible studies, child evangelism classes and youth rallies. We have board meetings, committee meetings, teachers' meetings and choir practice. Other types of meetings, of course, could be added to this list depending on the church and situation.

Actually, it is impossible to find any pattern in the New Testament that illustrates the present approach to meetings and agencies in our average church today. We know the first-century Christians had meetings, but what kind and what the specific characteristics of these meetings were is very difficult to determine.

This, of course, does not mean it is wrong to have the different kinds of meetings and agencies we have today. The very freedom allowed in the New Testament is the basic reason there is so much variety. The important New Testament principle is why these meetings are held; in other words, do they exist to achieve New Testament objectives.

The point I am making here is that the very freedom that has allowed us to develop the forms and structures we have today has been stifled by allowing what we are doing at the present time to become *the only way for "doing" church*. It is time for the church to evaluate the kinds of meetings it has, and to justify their existence on the basis of New Testament principles and purposes.

What About the Patterns and Format?

In some churches, if you dare change the order of the morning worship service, you get the distinct feeling you are tampering with the Scriptures themselves. Who is to say how a service is to be ordered? There is very little in Scripture to suggest specific answers to this question.

We do have mention of what *experiences* Christians should have when the body of Christ meets, but *how* all of this is put together is not illustrated in detail. We do have some reference to what the Corinthians did in their Sunday evening meetings, but the specific format is difficult to reconstruct.

It is my opinion that what we see in Corinthians is illustrative of the way they met and, with the exception of certain aspects of what they did, provides no absolute guidelines for the church. This is logical when we realize that the whole tone of Scripture emphasizes freedom in organizational structure.

The body of Christ, therefore, needs to determine its meeting patterns and format, first of all by setting forth clear-cut biblical objectives for these meetings. The patterns which are chosen should then be the best possible means to achieve these biblical objectives within the context of the contemporary culture, taking into consideration the many variables which affect a group of people who live in a particular time in history, and in a particular part of the world, and in particular communities. This is also true in determining the number of meetings, *when* the meetings are held, and the various *kinds* of meetings. To allow our present patterns to lock us into a particular approach is to make non-absolutes absolute, and this is a definite step in the direction of institutionalism.

What About the Place for Meetings?

An interesting trend in churches today is to conduct meetings off the church property. But more interesting than this phenomenon is the attitude of certain Christians toward this trend. Some people are highly threatened, for they feel the church hierarchy may lose control of what is happening. To some, anything that decentralizes the body of Christ rather than centralizing it (that is, bringing everyone together in one place) is a danger signal.

It is enlightening to get feedback from some Christians that the church building is *the* scriptural place to meet. This is of special interest since the New Testament Christians had no church buildings to meet in. At first, they met in the temple in Jerusalem and in homes. When the Jewish leaders eventually rejected Christianity, some Christians had to meet in their homes. This is one reason why we have many references to "house churches" in the New Testament.

Does this mean that a house church is the New Testament way—an absolute pattern which we must go back to if God's richest blessing is to rest upon the church? Again, I think not!

To say that the church building is *the* biblical place to meet is to be totally unscriptural. To say that any particular place is the biblical place is to make a non-absolute an absolute. Because of the various cultural changes and the needs of people today, the body of Christ needs to be flexible as to where it meets. A Sunday school class for college youth meeting on the university campus may be far more effective than meeting in the church building. Using a number of homes for midweek Bible study and prayer sessions, led by a number of mature lay Christians, may be far more significant than trying to get everyone to meet at the church building under the leadership of the pastor.

The important point is that the body of Christ must be flexible in determining where its meetings are to take place. There are no biblical absolutes dictating the answers to these questions.

Summary

What forms and patterns are developed to carry out these administrative and organizational principles is a matter of creative leadership under the direction of the Holy Spirit. It is impossible to derive specific patterns and structures from the New Testament (which is also abundantly demonstrated by the many different types of church governments in existence today among evangelical believers).

It seems, however, that the Holy Spirit definitely planned this ambiguity. Because of the variety of environments, cultures, and mentalities in the world today, God knew that to issue absolutes in the area of structure and form in organization and administration would be to provide specific guidelines that would be difficult to implement in various areas of the world. In fact, if God had dictated form, He would have locked the church into the Middle-Eastern culture in a first-century world. It would have greatly restricted the spread of Christianity to other cultures.

But God has not locked us into culture. The principles He has given us are absolutes that can and should be applied to today's church, wherever it may be. The principles of organization are:

1. Organize to apply New Testament principles and to reach New Testament purposes.
2. Organize to meet needs.
3. Keep organization simple.
4. Keep organization flexible.

Serve One Another

*"For you were called to freedom, brothers and sisters; only do not use your freedom as an opportunity to indulge your flesh, but through love **serve one another**"* (Gal 5:13, emphasis added).

Freedom is a major theme in Paul's letter to the Galatians. They must not allow themselves to "be subject again to the yoke of slavery" (Gal 5:1). They, like the entire unsaved world, were prisoners of sin (Gal 3:22). Christ fulfilled the requirement of the law— death— and it was "for freedom Christ has set us free" (Gal 5:1a).

Our freedom in Christ is not freedom to sin (Gal 5:13). Like Christians today, the Galatians had reverted to two extremes: either they tried to become righteous by keeping the law or they felt free to do whatever they wanted, even indulging their sin nature (Gal 5:13; Rom 6:1-2). Instead, "it trains us to reject godless ways and worldly desires and to live self-controlled, upright, and godly lives in the present age" (Tit 2:12-14). It is not freedom from our sin nature and its attraction to sin (Gal 5:16-21).

It is also not freedom from servanthood. Paul was totally free in Christ and yet called himself a slave of Christ. Paradoxically, enslaving ourselves to Him frees us (Mk 8:34-35). That also means that we are the servants of other Christians (Eph 5:21; 1 Pet 5:5). The way of love—living by the Spirit—is what sets us free (Gal 5:22-25).

Note: This material is adapted from Gene A. Getz, *The Measure of a Man*. (Ventura, CA: Regal Books, 1984).

Lesson 11: Testing the Dynamics

Lesson Introduction

Unbelievers are won to Christ through the Word and life presentation of the Gospel message—as if a love-letter from God—by concerned believers (2 Cor 2:14–3:6). Then they are taught how to grow and develop in their Christian faith (2 Cor 5:15). Growth toward maturity in Christ is the goal for all believers, both individually and collectively, in their local congregations (Heb 5:11–6:1).

This lesson looks at how God evaluated maturity in first-century churches. It considers what criteria seemed most important to Him in order to help you test the present degree of maturity in your church. It also takes an in-depth look at the insidious threat to the physical and spiritual growth of your church: legalism.

Lesson Outline

Lesson 11: Testing the Dynamics
- Topic 1: The Measure of Success—Spiritual Growth
- Topic 2: The Origin of Legalism
  - The Concept of Law
  - The Concept of Grace
  - Law and Grace Contrasted
- Topic 3: Recognizing the Threat of Legalism
  - The Meaning of Legalism
  - Going Back under the Law
- Topic 4: Grace against Legalism
  - Freedom from Law
  - Life under Grace
- Topic 5: Developing Character—Bearing With, Submitting To, Encouraging One Another
  - Bearing with One Another
  - Submitting to One Another
  - Encouraging One Another

Lesson Objectives

Pastor Eugene must assess the degree of success or failure of his church, but he doesn't know what measurements to use. He sees that some churches assess their success by numbers, but some of those churches remain immature even while having new members and many activities. Other churches are improving the walk of their believers, but are not reaching out to the lost. Therefore, he feels that neither measure is adequate. He wants to determine God's criteria for measuring success by studying the first-century church. Additionally, he is concerned about the threat of legalism. He wants to learn as much as he can about it to prevent it from inhibiting the spiritual growth of his flock.

When you have completed this lesson, you should be able to:
- Biblically measure spiritual growth and maturity in your own church
- Explain the concepts of law, grace, and legalism
- Recognize the threat of legalism in yourself and in your church
- Use grace as a teaching tool to stop your church from going back under the law
- Continue the growth of your Christian character by bearing with, submitting to, and encouraging other Christians

Topic 1: The Measure of Success—Spiritual Growth

Most church leaders want productive churches or ministries that are growing spiritually and numerically. Look at the contrast in Scripture between the following two churches: one vibrant, growing, and healthy and the other sluggish and stagnant.

> They were devoting themselves to the apostles' teaching and to fellowship, to the breaking of bread and to prayer. Reverential awe came on everyone, and many wonders and miraculous signs came about by the apostles. All who believed were together and held everything in common, and they began selling their property and possessions and distributing the proceeds to everyone, as anyone had need. Every day they continued to gather together by common consent in the temple courts, breaking bread from house to house, sharing their food with glad and humble hearts, praising God and having the good will of all the people. And the Lord was adding to their number every day those who were being saved (Acts 2:42-47)

> On this topic we have much to say and it is difficult to explain, since you have become sluggish in hearing. For though you should in fact be teachers by this time, you need someone to teach you the beginning elements of God's utterances. You have gone back to needing milk, not solid food. For everyone who lives on milk is inexperienced in the message of righteousness, because he is an infant. But solid food is for the mature, whose perceptions are trained by practice to discern both good and evil. Therefore we must progress beyond the elementary instructions about Christ and move on to maturity, not laying this foundation again: repentance from dead works and faith in God (Heb 5:11–6:1)

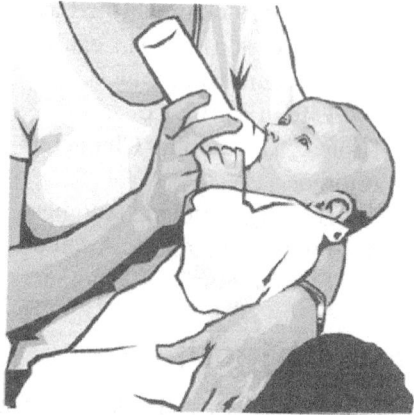

Infant's Perceptions are Untrained

Please take a few minutes now to reflect upon these passages and briefly complete the sentences in Questions 1 and 2 below. Try to identify several indicators of spiritual health, or the lack of it, in your church before proceeding. Remember to record your answers in your Life Notebook.

QUESTION 1

"I consider my church to be growing spiritually because..."

QUESTION 2

"My church is **not** growing as much as it could spiritually because..."

Pastor Eugene will now look to Paul's epistles and to the book of Acts for a way to measure spiritual growth in his church.

Reading Assignment

Read the textbook chapter titled "Chapter 6: Building the Church" from *Sharpening the Focus of the Church* in the Articles section at the end of this lesson.

QUESTION 3

Based on 1 Corinthians 13: 13, which virtue would be the best measurement of spiritual maturity of a church?

    A. Prophesying

    B. Faith

    C. Love

    D. Hope

QUESTION 4

Why does the church exist as a gathered community?

    A. To live our lives in greater comfort with believers around us

    B. To make it easier to fight the enemies of the Christian faith

    C. To have greater resources for distribution of food to the needy

    D. To become mature though the process of edification

QUESTION 5

The spiritual maturity of a church can be measured by the virtues of faith, hope, and love. Key verses for each are listed below. Read them, then open your Life Notebook and identify at least three ways each of these virtues could be demonstrated in the life of your church. Note: *Some of the verses tell us what faith, hope, and love are NOT like. Understanding what they are NOT will help clarify how the opposite should manifest itself in the life of the church*:

Faith

Mark 2:3-12

1 Thessalonians 1:3, 8-10

Hebrews 11

Describe how FAITH could be demonstrated in the life of your church.

Hope

1 Thessalonians 4:13

Hebrews 6:17-20

1 Peter 1:3-6

Describe how HOPE could be demonstrated in the life of your church.

Love

Romans 14:13-15

1 Corinthians 13:4-8

1 John 3:10-18

Describe how LOVE could be demonstrated in the life of your church.

Topic 1 Key Points:

- The church is a "gathered community" in order to become mature through the process of edification.
- Maturity is measured by the virtues of Faith, Hope, and Love.
- Love is the most important measure of spiritual growth.

Topic 2: The Origin of Legalism

God wants His church to mature, each local church genuinely demonstrating faith, hope, and love. Reaching the goal of maturity is not without its difficulties, and few hindrances are as powerful as *legalism*. Legalism is an insidious enemy of the church; it is even more dangerous because it often masquerades as spirituality.

Legalism Masquerading as Spirituality

When legalism infects a local church, it short-circuits the work of God in that church. Rather than faith, hope, and love, legalism produces pride, hypocrisy, self-righteousness, a judgmental spirit toward other believers, and a lack of love. It destroys the ability of the church to reach out to unbelievers, crushes the fellowship of believers within the church, and poisons the heart of the church's worship.

Pastor Eugene has heard of legalism but really does not understand what it is. Therefore, he will start with an examination of the concepts of "law" and "grace" in both the Old and New Testament to help him understand how it came about.

The Concept of Law

Reading Assignment
Please read the article titled "The Concept of Law" in the Articles section at the end of this lesson.

QUESTION 6
Use a pen or pencil to write the text in the left column in the appropriate Scripture column.

Shortcoming of the Law

	Rom. 3:20	Gal. 3:3	Acts 15:10	Gal 3:2-5	Jas 2:10	Instructions
The law cannot give us the Spirit						
Seeking law-righteousness obligates us to the whole law						
The law cannot sanctify						
The law cannot save						
The law became an unbearable burden						

QUESTION 7
Which of the following indicate usefulness of the Law of Moses. *(Select all that apply.)*

A. It reveals our sinfulness

B. It leads us to Christ, in whom we find justification by faith.

C. By obeying the law, we can be declared righteous in God's eyes.

D. It can provide a motive for righteous behavior.

QUESTION 8
No matter what historical age a person lives in, there are always principles for conduct. *True or False?*

Lesson 11: Testing the Dynamics

The Concept of Grace

Reading Assignment

Please read the article titled "The Meaning of Grace" in the Articles section at the end of this lesson.

QUESTION 9

Which of the following best describes the word "grace" in the Old Testament?

    A. The bestowing is independent of merit

    B. Forgiveness through Christ's sacrifice

    C. Obligation on the part of the giver

    D. The recipient's claim to the gracious act

QUESTION 10

What is the ultimate expression of grace in the New Testament?

    A. The birth of Jesus in a humble stable

    B. The healing of the sick by Jesus and His disciples

    C. Jesus' death, resulting in our salvation

    D. Making a sacrifice to pay for our sins

Law and Grace Contrasted

Reading Assignments

- Please read Galatians chapters 3–6.
- Please read "Law and Grace Contrasted" in the Lesson 11 Articles section.

Answer Question 11 based on Galatians 3-6 and Question 12 based on the article.

QUESTION 11

Which statements below truly represent the message that Paul is trying to convey to the Galatians in Chapters 3-6? *(Select all that apply.)*

    A. Those who try to be justified by the law are alienated from Christ.

    B. The law was put in charge to lead us to Christ that we might be justified by faith.

    C. If you are led by the Spirit, you are under the law.

    D. The entire law is summed up in one command: "Love your neighbor as yourself."

    E. True freedom comes from following the law.

    F. All who rely on the law are under a curse.

QUESTION 12

According to the author of the article, the problem lies in trying to turn the shortcomings of the Law into good uses. How do people often do this?

- A. By making it a means to salvation, rather than letting it show the need for salvation as God intended.
- B. By allowing it to reveal the holiness of God and the requirements for entering into His presence
- C. By loving their neighbors as themselves
- D. By seeking sanctification through the law

QUESTION 13

Write some specific examples of how people attempt to earn salvation by their works.

Topic 2 Key Points:

- Legalism derives its existence from the law.
- The law of the Bible can reveal our sinfulness, but it cannot save.
- Grace, the opposite of law, exists throughout the Bible as unmerited favor from God.
- God's grace reaches its peak through Jesus Christ.
- The problem lies with trying to make the law, rather than grace, a means to salvation.

Topic 3: Recognizing the Threat of Legalism

Having learned the meanings of law, grace, and their biblical relationship, Pastor Eugene realizes now that there is a problem related to law and grace. That problem is called legalism.

The Real Problem of the Law

The real problem has never been the idea or the presence of law. It has always been the human perversion of the law of God; whether it was the Mosaic Law or the law of Christ. Men have taken something good and made it the great enemy of the grace of God. It was true particularly of the Pharisees in biblical times, and it is true of many churches and Christian groups today.

The legalistic teachers of Jesus' day were not only good at their legalism, but they were so good at teaching it to others that Jesus said, "You cross land and sea to make one convert, and when you get one, you make him twice as much a child of hell as yourselves!" (Mt 23:15b).

Pastor Eugene now wants to learn how to recognize the symptoms of legalism in his church, as well as in himself.

The Meaning of Legalism

In the entire chapter of Matthew 23, Jesus teaches clearly on His feelings about legalism. The following is one example: "Woe to you, experts in the law and you Pharisees, hypocrites! You give a tenth of mint, dill, and cumin, yet you neglect what is more important in the law—justice, mercy, and faithfulness! You needed to do these things without neglecting the others. Blind guides! You strain out a gnat yet swallow a camel!" (Mt 23:23-24).

Straining Out a Gnat!

Reading Assignments

- Please read Matthew 23.
- Please read the article titled "The Meaning of Legalism" in the Articles section at the end of this lesson.

QUESTION 14

Match the verse in the left-hand column to the corresponding woe to the Jewish leaders in the right-hand column.

Verse	Woe
Matthew 23:13-14	Tithing but ignoring justice, mercy, and faithfulness
Matthew 23:15	Cleaning the outside but not the inside
Matthew 23:16-22	Locking people out of the kingdom
Matthew 23:23-24	Making converts into children of hell
Matthew 23:25-26	Swearing to the truth
Matthew 23:27-28	Whitewashed tombs full of hypocrisy

QUESTION 15

By reading Matthew 23:25, what can you conclude about Legalism? *(Select all that apply.)*

A. It is ceremonially unclean.

B. It is self-centered.

C. It requires a pure heart.

D. It emphasizes appearance.

QUESTION 16

Review the characteristics of a legalist in the article. Do any of these characteristics apply to you? Ask your spouse or a friend if you show any of these characteristics in your life. If so, what can you do to change?

QUESTION 17

Think about your church situation. Then open your Life Notebook and list all the rules and regulations, if any, which might be called legalistic. Then give at least one reason why you think it might (or might not) be considered legalistic.

Going Back Under the Law

Reading Assignment

Please read the article titled "Going Back Under the Law" in the Articles section at the end of this lesson.

QUESTION 18

Based on Galatians 3:23-29 and Heb 5:12-6:1, the law treated us as immature children under its watchful care. *True or False?*

QUESTION 19

Are you acquainted with believers who have put themselves back under a law system? In your Life Notebook, list the reasons why you think they gave up the wonderful freedom in Christ in order to live under the law again.

Topic 3 Key Points:

- Legalism is self-centered.
- Despite their knowledge that salvation comes through grace alone, people are still motivated to return to a system of law.

Topic 4: Grace Against Legalism

The Jewish leaders had immediate conflicts with Jesus; His view of the law and of grace was a particular snare for them:

> Now Jesus went again into the synagogue, and a man was there who had a withered hand. They watched him carefully to see if he would heal on the Sabbath, so that they could accuse him. And he said to the man who had the withered hand, "Stand up among everyone." Then he said to them, "Is it lawful to do good on the Sabbath, or evil, to save a life or destroy it?" But they were silent. After looking around at them in anger, grieved by the hardness of their hearts, he said to the man, "Reach out your hand." He stretched it out and it was restored. So the Pharisees went out immediately and began plotting with the Herodians, as to how they could assassinate him (Mk 3:1-6)

Pastor Eugene has identified several areas in which legalism has already started to infect his church. He wants to understand the role of grace in the Christian life in order to properly teach his flock and remove all reasons for going back under law.

Grace vs Legalism

Freedom from Law

Reading Assignment

Please read the article titled "Freedom From the Law" in the Articles section at the end of this lesson.

QUESTION 20

The common motivations for churches or individuals to go back under the law are listed on the left. Match each one with the characteristic of grace that removes the reason.

Motivation	Characteristic of Grace
The fear of an unholy life	We already have salvation; we need not earn it.
Our basic rebelliousness toward God	Know that we cannot achieve salvation on our own.
A fear of rejection	We are freed from the obligation to obey that we might gratefully obey.
Our desire for security	Nothing we could ever do, or not do, would make Him love us any more or less, because He already loves us perfectly and promises He always will.

Life Under Grace

Reading Assignment

Please read the article titled "Life Under Grace" in the Articles section at the end of this lesson.

QUESTION 21

There are several specific biblical principles that help us decide whether to do something or not. Match the verse in the left-hand column with the principle taught in the right-hand column.

Verse	Principle
1 Corinthians 10:31	Will it enslave you?
1 Corinthians 10:23	Is it a weight?
Hebrews 12:1	Is your conscience clear?
1 Corinthians 9:19-23	Will it glorify God?
Romans 14:23	Will it hinder God's purpose?
1 Corinthians 6:12	Is it profitable for one's spiritual life?

QUESTION 22

On a spectrum of 1-10, does your church lean toward being more law oriented (1) or grace oriented (10)? What observations can you make that support your rating? What do you think can be done to help your congregation be more grace oriented? Record your response in your Life Notebook.

Topic 4 Key Points:

- Grace removes the motivation to go back under the law.
- We are free to do anything that God does not forbid, but not all freedoms are to be exercised.

- We can live with the freedom given by grace if we put the love of God above everything else.

Topic 5: Developing Character—Bearing With, Submitting To, Encouraging One Another

Because God extended His grace to each of us, we must extend it to one another.

The essence of the mature Christian life is not in seeking glory for ourselves (Mk 8:34-38). We must follow the example of Jesus who "did not come to be served but to serve, and to give His life as a ransom for many" (Mk 10:45). "Who though he existed in the form of God did not regard equality with God as something to be grasped, but emptied himself by taking on the form of a slave, by looking like other men, and by sharing in human nature. He humbled himself, by becoming obedient to the point of death—even death on a cross!" (Phil 2:6-8).

Christ's Example: Washing Each Other's Feet

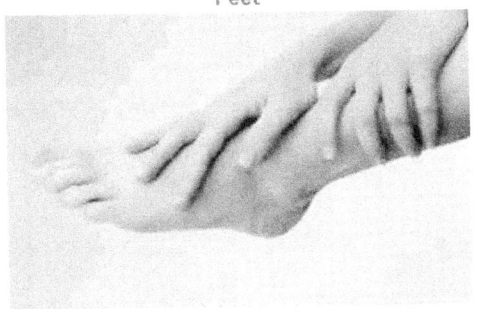

We will continue developing Christ's character by focusing on bearing with one another, submitting to one another, and encouraging one another.

Bearing With One Another

Reading Assignment

Please read the article titled "Bearing with One Another" in the Articles section at the end of this lesson.

QUESTION 23

The word that consistently appears before the phrase "bearing with one another" in Scripture is

_____

QUESTION 24

Take a good look at yourself. In all honesty, make a list of your weaknesses and idiosyncrasies. To help you, open your Life Notebook and answer these questions:

1. What do I do (or not do) that irritates my friends, family, co-workers, or schoolmates?
2. Do you expect more from other Christians than you do from yourself? Do you criticize others in areas where you are weak?
3. Think of a fellow Christian who often irritates you. Make a list of all things that this person does that bother you. Compare this list to a list of your own sins that God has forgiven you through the death of His Son on the cross. Which list is greater? And which sacrifice is greater—for you to bear with the weaknesses of this Christian or for Christ to die on the cross?

Submitting to One Another

Reading Assignment

Please read the article titled "Submitting to One Another" in the Articles section at the end of this lesson.

QUESTION 25

The essence of Christian service (submission) is shown in Mark 10:45. *True or False?*

Encouraging One Another

Reading Assignment

Please read the article titled "Encouraging One Another" in the Articles section at the end of this lesson.

QUESTION 26

A Christian's primary means of encouragement is _____
- A. The Word
- B. Our Lives
- C. Heaven
- D. Miracles

QUESTION 27

Now that you have examined the biblical teaching and summarized some ways to demonstrate faith, hope, and love, consider the following questions. Write your answers in your Life Notebook.

- If Paul were to write a letter to your church, how would he begin the letter? What would he thank God for?
- List the ways your church already reflects faith, hope, and love.
- Complete the following statement: "I thank God for my church because…"
- Complete the following statement: "I believe my church could become more mature if…"
- When you evaluate your church in relation to legalism and grace, what is the outcome? If it is a church that models grace, then you should thank God heartily. If it is legalistic, how can you encourage change toward grace?

Lesson 11 Self Check

QUESTION 1

Which virtue is the most important measure of Christian maturity?

QUESTION 2

The main purpose of the church as a "gathered community" is to comfort us in our lives as aliens in this world. *True or False?*

QUESTION 3

Which of the following is NOT a proper use of the Law of Moses?

    A. It reveals our sinfulness.

    B. It leads us to Christ, in whom we find justification by faith.

    C. It can declare us righteous in God's eyes.

    D. It can provide a motive for righteous behavior.

QUESTION 4

The Spirit-led believer must still keep the Law of Moses. *True or False?*

QUESTION 5

All Christians are saved by faith, but remain under the Law of Moses for sanctification. *True or False?*

QUESTION 6

By reading Matthew 23:25, what can you conclude about legalism?

    A. It is ceremonially unclean.

    B. It is self-centered.

    C. It requires a pure heart.

    D. It emphasizes inner change.

QUESTION 7

A clear conscience is important under grace. *True or False?*

QUESTION 8

One biblical principle that helps us decide whether we should or should not do something is whether it will enslave us. *True or False?*

QUESTION 9

The essence of Christian service is shown in _____.

QUESTION 10

One principle under grace is that we are free to do anything that God does not forbid, as long as our actions do not enslave us or others. *True or False?*

Lesson 11 Answers to Questions

QUESTION 1: *Your answer*
QUESTION 2: *Your answer*
QUESTION 3:
C. Love
QUESTION 4:
D. To become mature though the process of edification
The answer to this question is clear-cut in the New Testament: The church is to become a mature organism through the process of edification to honor and glorify God, and in the process become a dynamic witness in the world.
QUESTION 5: *Your answer*
QUESTION 6:

Scripture	Shortcomings of the Law
Romans 3:20	The law cannot save.
Galatians 3:3	The law cannot sanctify.
Acts 15:10	The law became an unbearable burden.
Galatians 3:2-5	The law cannot give us the Spirit.
James 2:10	Seeking law-righteousness obligates us to the whole law.

QUESTION 7:
A. It reveals our sinfulness.
B. It leads us to Christ, in whom we find justification by faith.
D. It can provide a motive for righteous behavior.
QUESTION 8: True
In our times, the laws and principles for conduct are found in the New Testament.
QUESTION 9:
A. The bestowing is independent of merit
Graciousness is clearly independent of merit and finds its motivation in God, not in the person: "I will be gracious to whom I will be gracious, and will show compassion on whom I will show compassion" (Ex. 33:19).
QUESTION 10:
C. Jesus' death, resulting in our salvation
In the New Testament, grace expresses the same idea of undeserved blessing or unmerited favor. But here this concept of grace reaches its heights, being exhibited supremely in the gift of Jesus Christ and His offer of complete, eternal salvation by faith alone, made possible through His death on the cross.
QUESTION 11:
A. Those who try to be justified by the law are alienated from Christ.
B. The law was put in charge to lead us to Christ that we might be justified by faith.
D. The entire law is summed up in one command: "Love your neighbor as yourself."
F. All who rely on the law are under a curse.
QUESTION 12:
A. By making it a means to salvation, rather than letting it show the need for salvation as God intended
QUESTION 13: *Your answer*

QUESTION 14:

Verse	Woe
Matthew 23:13-14	Locking people out of the kingdom
Matthew 23:15	Making converts into children of hell
Matthew 23:16-22	Swearing to the truth
Matthew 23:23-24	Tithing but ignoring justice, mercy and faithfulness
Matthew 23:25-26	Cleaning the outside but not the inside
Matthew 23:27-28	Whitewashed tombs full of hypocrisy

QUESTION 15:
B. It is self-centered.
D. It emphasizes appearance.

QUESTION 16: *Your answer*

QUESTION 17: *Your answer*

QUESTION 18: True

The law's children practiced dead works along with their faith in God. Maturing Christians must practice righteousness by applying God's Word to situations in their daily life. This trains their conscience and perceptions to make better decisions in the future.

QUESTION 19: *Your answer*

QUESTION 20:

Motivation	Characteristic of Grace
The fear of an unholy life	We are freed from the obligation to obey that we might gratefully obey.
Our basic rebelliousness toward God	Know that we cannot achieve salvation on our own.
A fear of rejection	Nothing we could ever do, or not do, would make Him love us any more or less, because He already loves us perfectly and promises He always will.
Our desire for security	We already have salvation; we need not earn it.

QUESTION 21:

Verse	Principle
1 Corinthians 10:31	Will it glorify God?
1 Corinthians 10:23	Is it profitable for one's spiritual life?
Hebrews 12:1	Is it a weight?
1 Corinthians 9:19-23	Will it hinder God's purpose?
Romans 14:23	Is your conscience clear?
1 Corinthians 6:12	Will it enslave you?

QUESTION 22: *Your answer*

QUESTION 23: Patience

We know each other's idiosyncrasies, but Paul tells us to bear with one another in love. The example for Paul was always the Lord's great patience with him (1 Tim 1:15-17). We must not carry grudges against others considering the Lord's total forgiveness of us (Mt 18:21-35). How many times should we forgive our brother? Seventy times seven!

QUESTION 24: *Your answer*

QUESTION 25: True

The essence of all Christian service is submission, just as Jesus submitted Hill will to the Father's (Mark 10:45; Hebrews 10:7). He, though Lord of the universe, "did not regard equality with God as something to be grasped, but emptied himself by taking on the form of a slave" (Philippians 2:6b-7a).

QUESTION 26:
A. The Word
God's truth is our primary means of encouragement (Eph. 4:15)
QUESTION 27: *Your answer*

Lesson 11 Self Check Answers

QUESTION 1: Love
QUESTION 2: False
QUESTION 3:
C. It can declare us righteous in God's eyes.
QUESTION 4: False
QUESTION 5: False
QUESTION 6:
B. It is self-centered.
QUESTION 7: True
QUESTION 8: True
QUESTION 9: Correct answers include:
Submission
Obedience
QUESTION 10: True

Lesson 11 Articles

Bearing with One Another

*"With all humility and gentleness, with patience, **bearing with one another** in love"* (Eph 4:2, emphasis added).

The word "bear" here means to tolerate other Christians, to bear with their idiosyncrasies and be patient, kind, and forgiving. It is easier to do this when you have a good picture of your own weaknesses. But there will be many Christians you meet who seem unlovable, and it is difficult to bear with them. Colossians 3:12-13 instructs us here:

> *"Therefore, as the elect of God, holy and dearly loved, clothe yourselves with a heart of mercy, kindness, humility, gentleness, and patience, **bearing with one another** and forgiving one another, if someone happens to have a complaint against anyone else. Just as the Lord has forgiven you, so you too forgive others"* (emphasis added)

Patience is always the word right before this phrase and forgiveness is the key (Eph 4:2; Col 3:12-13). All of us fail, particularly in human relationships. We do not want to expect more from others than from ourselves. As Christians, we are family so we see each other at our best and worst. We know each other's idiosyncrasies, but Paul tells us to bear with one another in love. The example for Paul was always the Lord's great patience with him (1 Tim 1:15-17). We must not carry grudges against others, considering the Lord's total forgiveness of us (Mt 18:21-35). How many times should we forgive our brother? Seventy times seven!

Patience, forbearance, and forgiveness are not automatic actions for Christians, but deliberate acts of the will. Everyone with an unforgiving spirit chooses to be that way. If we ignore, avoid, or talk sharply to someone, we do all those by choice. Instead, Christians who care about each other and truly desire God's best must strive "to keep the unity of the Spirit in the bond of peace" (Eph 4:3).

Note: This material is adapted from Gene A. Getz, *The Measure of a Man*. (Ventura, CA: Regal Books, 1984).

Chapter 6: Building the Church

Disciples were to be taught! This is the second great task spelled out in Christ's commission. Believers were to meet as a "gathered community" in order to become a mature organism.

Just as there are a variety of words used to describe the activities of the disciples as they went about evangelizing, there are also a number of different words used to recount their ministry of edification. They, of course, baptized and taught the new believers as Jesus had commanded in the Great Commission. But this process of growth and development also involved fellowshipping with one another, breaking bread, uniting their hearts in prayer, and praising God. They were encouraged, strengthened, implored, exhorted, admonished, and established in the faith.

As you move from the study of the functions and results among believers in the book of Acts to an analysis of the Epistles, once again, functions often become directives, and results often become objectives. "Encourage one another," "build up one another," "admonish the unruly," "encourage the fainthearted," "help the weak," "seek after that which is good for one another" are all examples of Pauline directives to the local church (1 Thess 5:11-15). All believers were to be involved in the edification process, ministering to each other. They were to always abound "in the work of the Lord" (1 Cor 15:58) and to "teach and admonish one another with psalms and hymns and spiritual songs" (Eph 5:19).

Frequently directives regarding edification in the Epistles were followed immediately with a statement of expected results or objectives, just as in the area of evangelism. Paul wrote to the Corinthians that he, along with Timothy and Silas, had exhorted and encouraged and implored them so that they might "walk in a manner worthy of the God" (Col 1:10) who had called them. Later he said (1 Thess 3:10) that they constantly prayed that they might see the Thessalonians again so as to "complete" what was lacking in their faith. Paul urged the Roman Christians to present themselves to God to be able to "prove what the will of God is" (Rom 12:1, 2). Paul prayed for the Ephesians that they might be "filled up to all the fullness of God" (Eph 3:19). And in Colossians 1:10, he instructed the Colossians to "bear fruit in every good work." "Let us press on to maturity," said the writer to the Hebrews (Heb 6:1).

Why then does the church exist as a gathered community? The answer to this question is clear-cut in the New Testament. The church is to become a mature organism through the process of edification to honor and glorify God, and in the process become a dynamic witness in the world.

Luke recorded that "the church throughout all Judea and Galilee and Samaria enjoyed peace, and thus was strengthened [that is edified]" (Acts 9:31). Paul informed us that gifted leaders were given to the church to equip all Christians for service so that the body of Christ would be built up [edified] (Eph 4:11-12, 16).

Some form of the word "edification" appears more times in Paul's letter to the Corinthians (particularly in his first epistle) than in any other New Testament book(1 Cor 8:1; 10:23; 2 Cor 14:4-5, 12, 17, 26; 2 Cor 12:19). This, of course, is not surprising, for of all the churches in the New Testament world, this church was the most carnal and immature and in need of spiritual growth and development (1 Cor 3:1-3).

Edification should lead to maturity or completeness in Christ. "We proclaim Him," wrote Paul to the Colossians, "by instructing and teaching all men with all wisdom, so that we may present every man mature in Christ" (Col 1:28). The apostle's primary concern for the body of Christ was that we "all attain to the unity of the faith, and the knowledge of the Son of God—a mature person, attaining to the measure of Christ's full stature" (Eph 4:13).

A Mature Church—What Is It?

How can we recognize a mature church? By what criteria can we measure ourselves as a local body to see if we have arrived at a degree of completeness? Again, the New Testament is explicit.

"But now abide faith, hope, love, these three; but the greatest of these is love" (1 Cor 13:13). Maturity in the body of Christ can be identified by the enduring virtues. The degree of completeness can be measured by the degree to which the church manifests faith, hope, and love. This is quite clear from Paul's writings, since he frequently used these three virtues to measure the maturity level of the New Testament churches.[1] Notice these introductory paragraphs in his letters to various churches.

---

[1] For an in–depth study of the concepts of faith, hope, and love, see Gene A. Getz, *The Measure of a Church* (Regal, 1975).

Lesson 11 Self Check Answers

The First Thessalonian Letter

"We give thanks to God always for all of you, making mention of you in our prayers, constantly bearing in mind your work of FAITH and labor of LOVE and steadfastness of HOPE in our Lord Jesus Christ in the presence of our God and Father" (1 Thess 1:2-3, NASB, emphasis added).

The Second Thessalonian Letter

"We ought always to give thanks to God for you, brethren, as is only fitting because your FAITH is greatly enlarged, and the LOVE of each of you all toward one another grows even greater; therefore, we ourselves speak proudly of you among the churches of God for your perseverance and FAITH in the midst of all your persecutions and afflictions which you endure" (2 Thess 1:3-4, NASB, emphasis added).

The Colossian Letter

"We give thanks to God, the Father of our Lord Jesus Christ, praying always for you, since we heard of your FAITH in Christ Jesus and the LOVE which you have for all the saints; because of the HOPE laid up for you in heaven, of which you previously heard in the word of truth, the Gospel" (Col 1:3-5, NASB, emphasis added).

The Ephesian Letter

"For this reason I too, having heard of the FAITH in the Lord Jesus which exists among you, and your LOVE for all the saints; do not cease giving thanks for you, while making mention of you in my prayers; that the God of our Lord Jesus Christ, the Father of glory, may give to you a spirit of wisdom and of revelation in the knowledge of Him. I pray that the eyes of your heart may be enlightened, so that you may know what is the HOPE of His calling, what are the riches of the glory of His inheritance in the saints" (Eph 1:15, NASB, emphasis added).

The Letter to the Hebrews

"Let us draw near with a sincere heart in full assurance of FAITH.... Let us hold fast the confessions of our HOPE.... Let us consider how to stimulate one another to LOVE and good deeds" (Heb 10:22–24, NASB, emphasis added).

It is clear what the New Testament criteria is for determining the maturity level of a local body of believers. First of all, is there love manifested toward other members of the body of Christ? Second, is there a strong and vital faith? Third, is there a demonstration of hope? But these words can be merely theological concepts. What do they mean? It is only as we reinforce these words with meaning and content that we get the complete picture. Once again the New Testament speaks articulately.

Love

"The greatest of these is love," concludes Paul (1 Cor 13:13). The apostle consistently drives home this truth in his correspondence with the churches, which agrees with Christ's exhortation recorded in John 13:34, to "love one another."

The Colossian Letter

"And so, as those who have been chosen of God, holy and beloved, put on a heart of compassion, kindness, humility, gentleness, and patience; bearing with one another, and forgiving each other,

whoever has a complaint against any one; just as the Lord forgave you, so also should you. And beyond all these things put on LOVE, which is the perfect bond of unity" (Col 3:12-14, NASB, emphasis added).

The Ephesian Letter

"As a result, we are no longer to be children, tossed here and there by waves, and carried about by every wind of doctrine, by the trickery of men, by craftiness in deceitful scheming; but speaking the truth in LOVE, we are to grow up in all aspects into Him, who is the head, even Christ, from whom the whole body, being fitted and held together by that which every joint supplies, according to the proper working of each individual part, causes the growth of the body for the building up of itself in LOVE" (Eph. 4:14-16, NASB, emphasis added).

The apostle Peter also elevates love to the greatest level when he says, "Above all, keep fervent in your LOVE for one another, because love covers a multitude of sins" (1 Peter 4:8, NASB, emphasis added). And there is no question as to John's concern, for in his first epistle alone, he states four times that believers are to "love one another" (1 Jn 3:11, 23; 4:7, 11).

But what is love? How is it manifested? How can it be recognized in the body of Christ? The most prominent passage portraying the particular aspects of love is, of course, 1 Corinthians 13. Here Paul spells out for the immature Corinthian church exactly what love is and how it is to be manifested by the body of Christ. Unfortunately, this great love chapter is often lifted out of context and used in isolation. To get the full meaning and impact of Paul's words, you must see his description of love in the light of the whole Corinthian epistle, and you must interpret his definitions in the light of the Corinthian carnality. Then, too, we must observe Paul's words in 1 Corinthians 13 in relationship to the body of Christ, not just to individual Christians.

First, note that the Corinthians were not lacking in any gift (1 Cor 1:7). Yet, they were an immature church. Paul classified them as "infants in Christ" (1 Cor 3:1), carnal and fleshly (1 Cor 3:3). Obviously, the manifestation of spiritual gifts in a local church is not synonymous with spirituality and maturity. It certainly was not true with the Corinthians.

Paul described how to recognize love in the body of Christ:

- *Love is patient* (1 Cor 13:4). In other words, it is the opposite of what the Corinthians were demonstrating. They were impatient with one another, and there were disagreements and divisions among them (1 Cor 1:10).

- *Love is kind and is not jealous* (1 Cor 13:4). Earlier in his letter Paul had written about the "jealousy and strife" among the Corinthians (1 Cor 3:3).

- *Love does not brag and is not arrogant* (1 Cor 13:4). Paul had to warn the Corinthians against false boasting (1 Cor 1:29). "If any man among you thinks that he is wise in this age, let him become foolish that he may become wise....Let no one boast in men.... What do you have that you did not receive? But if you did receive it, why do you boast as if you had not received it?" (1 Cor 3:18, 21; 4:7, NASB).

- *Love ... does not act unbecomingly* (1 Cor 13:5). There was immorality in the church at Corinth and, said Paul, "immorality that is not permitted even among the Gentiles" (1 Cor 5:1; 6:15-20). Furthermore, they were acting in a most unbecoming way at the Lord's table—some even overeating and overdrinking—even to the point of drunkenness (1 Cor 11:20-21).

- *Love . . . does not seek its own, is not provoked, does not take into account a wrong suffered* (1 Cor 13:5). Here were believers who were taking each other to court (1 Cor 6:1-7). They were wronging and defrauding each other (6:8). They were also insensitive to the weaker members of the body of Christ and some allowed their liberty in Christ to become a "hindrance to the weak" (1 Cor 8:9). Some, in fact, were actually participating in idolatry (1 Cor 10:14).

- *Love ... does not rejoice in unrighteousness but rejoices with the truth* (1 Cor 13:6). It is hard to conceive of such gifted Christians bragging about the immorality in the church, but Paul states emphatically, "You have become arrogant [about this immorality, and have not mourned instead" (1 Cor 5:2, NASB).

After defining love and contrasting its ingredients with what the Corinthians so glaringly lacked, Paul gave some positive statements about love (1 Cor 13:7). It "bears all things" (that is, it suffers and bears up under pressure). It "believes all things" (that is, it is "always eager to believe the best," Moffatt). It "hopes all things" (that is, it demonstrates a forward look, not hopeless pessimism). It "endures all things" (that is, it is steadfast and enables a Christian to continue on in the thick of battle).

Now as we approach verses 8-12 in 1 Corinthians 13, some aspects of Paul's statements are somewhat difficult to understand. But in context, certain truths become very obvious. Paul naturally and logically concludes that "love never fails" (1 Cor 13:8). Gifts are temporal, but love goes on forever (1 Cor 13:8).

Notice the contrasting words and phrases he used in these verses just quoted and the ones to follow (that is, in verses 9-12):

Part or Partial	*Perfect or Complete*
Child	Grow up
Childish	Put away childish things
We see in a mirror dimly	Clarity
I know in part	I will know completely

Looking at the whole of 1 Corinthians and comparing it with the epistles Paul wrote to other churches, several conclusions stand out. These believers had not reached the degree of maturity and completeness or perfection that other New Testament churches had reached. They were still babes or infants. They were childish in their behavior. They had made very little progress in becoming conformed to the image of Jesus Christ.[2] They had not yet reached the place in their spiritual development where Paul could write to them as he did to the Thessalonians, the Colossians, the Ephesians, and the Philippians and thank God for their faith, hope, and love. Rather, it seems they were almost void of these virtues as a local body of believers. In order to correct the situation, Paul admonished them to refocus their priorities. First, he told them to strive for the "more excellent way"; they were to "pursue love" (1 Cor 12:31; 14:1, NASB).[3]

---

[2] Note that Paul utilizes the same literary technique throughout this chapter. He uses personal pronouns and applies these statements to himself: "If I speak ... I have become ... I'll have the gift ... I am nothing... And if I give ... it profits me nothing.... When I was a child, I used to speak as a child.... When I became a man, I did away with childish things.... Now I know in part, but then I shall know fully." In the light of the context it is obvious he is speaking of the deep spiritual needs of the Corinthians, but he illustrates these truths by referring to his own life. The Corinthians had no problem in getting the point.

[3] The concept of the "greater gifts" is developed at length in chapter 7.

Faith and Hope

Faith and hope, the other two virtues set forth as standards by which we can measure the maturity level of the local church, are also uniquely described in the New Testament. Though there is no central passage describing these virtues such as 1 Corinthians does for love, there are a number of descriptive words and phrases used by the New Testament writers to add significant meaning and content to these words. Following are some of these phrases:

Faith

- Work of faith (1 Thess 1:3)
- Breastplate of faith (1 Thess 5:8)
- Faith in Jesus Christ (Col 1:4)
- Faith in the Lord Jesus (Eph 1:15)
- Faith in God (1 Pet 1:21)
- Faith greatly enlarged (2 Thess 1:3)
- Faith without hypocrisy (1 Tim 1:5)
- Faith toward the Lord Jesus and toward all the saints (Phm 5)
- Full assurance of faith (Heb 10:22)

Hope

- Steadfastness of hope (1 Thess 1:3)
- Hope of salvation (1 Thess 5:8)
- Hope laid up for you (Col 1:5)
- That you may know what is the hope of His calling (Eph 1:18)
- Hope in God (1 Pet 1:21)
- Hold fast the confession of our hope without wavering (Heb 10:23)
- Christ Jesus who is our hope (1 Tim 1:1)
- We fixed our hope on the living God (1 Tim 4:10)
- Not to fix our hope on the uncertainty of riches but on God (1 Tim 6:17)
- Hope of eternal life (Tit 1:2)

Even a casual reading of this list reveals that faith and hope are closely aligned in meaning and significance. The writer of Hebrews clarifies this relationship when he says, "Faith is the assurance of things hoped for, the conviction of things not seen" (Heb 11:1, NASB). Faith has to do with Christians themselves—their personalities—that is, their minds, their attitudes, their wills. It involves inner convictions and assurance. The primary object of our faith is God the Father and His Son Jesus Christ, but it also includes faith in our fellow Christians (1 Cor 13:7; Phm 5).

Hope on the other hand, though linked to faith, has to do with the object and content of faith. It is most frequently used to refer to salvation and ultimate deliverance from this world into the presence of Jesus Christ when He comes again.

The word hope is also used to describe the state of Christians. It is used in conjunction with such words and phrases as "steadfastness" (1 Thess 1:3), "without wavering" (Heb 10:23), and "fixed" (1 Tim 4:10; 6:17; 1 Peter 1:13). It is used to describe certainty and stability.

Lesson 11 Self Check Answers

In conclusion it is obvious why Paul refers to faith, hope and love as the primary virtues by which we may measure the maturity level of a local church. Love has to do with Christlike relationships among members of the body and toward all men—an attitude that creates unity and one-mindedness.

Faith has to do with the confidence that the body of Christ has in its Head—the Lord Jesus Christ. There is that unified conviction and assurance that God is, that He answers prayer, and that He is our divine source of life and existence.

The presence of hope is manifested in stability, steadfastness, and certainty, and particularly looks beyond the present to that day when Jesus Christ shall come again for the church, and in turn, to set up His eternal kingdom.

Summary

Why then does the church exist as a gathered community? The church is to become a mature organism through the process of edification, and this maturity is reflected, first of all by the degree of love that exists in the body of Christ, and second, by the degree of corporate faith and hope that is manifested.

"Be careful how you build!" warned Paul. A church can be weak and immature—constructed of wood, hay, and stubble. Or it can be strong and mature composed of gold, silver, and precious stones (1 Cor. 3:10-15). If it is immature, it reflects impatience, jealousy, strife, divisions, pride, arrogance, and unbecoming behavior. If it is mature, it reflects a growing love, a unity of faith, and a steadfast hope.

Encouraging One Another

*"Therefore **encourage one another** and build up each other, just as you are in fact doing"* (1 Thess 5:11, emphasis added).

The concern always on Paul's mind was to build up the body of Christ. He encouraged every Christian to develop this concern for Christians by building up and edifying one another (Eph 4:15, 16; Col 2:2; 4:8). The Thessalonian church learned the importance of mutual encouragement, exhortation, and comfort.

God's truth is the primary means of encouragement (Eph 4:15). A qualification for eldership is to "hold firmly to the faithful message as it has been taught, so that he will be able to give exhortation in such healthy teaching and correct those who speak against it" (Tit 1:9, see also 1 Thess 2:11-13; 2 Tim 2:4).

The Christians in Thessalonica illustrated mutual encouragement by God's Word more than any other New Testament church:

1. **By the truths regarding the dead in Christ.** The Thessalonians were discouraged because they thought those who had died would somehow miss out on Christ's Second Advent (1 Thess 4:13-14). After Paul explained they would not, he said to encourage one another with these words (1 Thess 4:18).

2. **By the truth regarding the rapture of the church.** The Thessalonians knew about the day of the Lord, but apparently did not know they would be raptured before it (1 Thess 5:9-10). Again, this was to encourage them (1 Thess 5:11).

3. **The truth regarding the day of the Lord.** In the second epistle, a false teacher

troubled them by teaching that the day of the Lord had already come (2 Thess 2:2). Through belief in the truth, Paul taught that they would share in His glory (Second Coming, see 2 Thess 2:13-14).

God's Word is an eternal encouragement that will encourage and strengthen (2 Thess 2:15-17).

Note: This material is adapted from Gene A. Getz, *The Measure of a Man*. (Ventura, CA: Regal Books, 1984).

Freedom From the Law

Let us consider the same fears of legalism from the perspective of grace:

The fear of an unholy life. In one sense this is a valid fear. We saw above that grace is so free that we are free to obey and free to sin; we are free to choose righteousness or unrighteousness. As one person put it, "If grace is not amenable to abuse, it is not truly grace."

That Paul clearly taught this freedom is seen in the question of the objector in Romans 6, who apparently had this fear: "Are we to continue in sin that grace may increase?" (Rom 6:1 NASB). The question seems to be, "If grace abounds wherever sin appears, why not sin more in order to experience more grace?" To this idea Paul gives a resounding "No!" Such an idea severely misunderstands grace.

Paul warns that grace was never intended to lead to ungodliness (Rom 6:1; Tit 2:11-14). Peter also warns believers not to let their liberty be used as a pretext for sin (1 Pet 2:16). But neither Paul nor Peter would take away the believer's freedom under grace! As we must use the law responsibly, so we must use grace responsibly.

Do not forget that grace does not advocate the absence of standards. The New Testament is full of commands and instructions that the Lord and the apostles meant for obedience. So the issue is not *if* we should obey or *what* we should obey (though we do have many different rules) but *why*. Do we obey out of obligation or gratitude?

God wants our obedience out of love, not obligation. And the freedom that allows obedience from love also allows the possibility of disobedience for whatever reason. But when people put themselves once again under the control of law, they may achieve outward conformity to the law, but the love is gone. Then what do they have? They have a Pharisaism that does not please God.

Thus, the answer to this fear is that a system of law keeping no more preserves a person from sin than does grace. Indeed, there is much in Scripture that suggests that law promotes sin (Rom 3; 7). It can be stated unequivocally that grace will no more lead to sin than will law and that it is more likely than law to lead to obedience. We might say that we are freed from the obligation to obey that we might gratefully obey.

Our basic rebelliousness toward God. We must remember that we can never merit God's approval, neither before salvation nor after. His standards are too high—infinitely high—so there is no use trying. What we can do is please Him by our obedience and accomplish His will by Jesus' power and enjoy His blessings (1 Cor 15:9-11).

In fact, trying to merit His approval or acceptance, before or after salvation, is an affront to Him and the expression of His grace in the death of Christ. God gave the priceless gift of His Son to provide salvation *cost free*, as a gift and only as a gift. For us to try to earn it in any way is simply saying to Him that His gift was not sufficient, not good enough. It maligns what God accomplished through Christ on the cross (Heb 10:26-31).

Lesson 11 Self Check Answers

In terms of going back under law to achieve this, at a minimum, no list is good enough. And at a maximum it would lead to pride, which is contrary to all that God is. Thus, once again, going back under law is not superior to living by grace. Indeed, it is much worse.

A fear of rejection. The main result of seeking to appease this fear through keeping the law is loveless conformity to the law. There is no expression of gratitude in this effort.

Keeping the law, in and of itself, is not pleasing to God. A brief look at the Old Testament will show several places in which God says that He hates their law keeping (1 Sam 15:22; Isa 1:10-17; Mic 6:6-8; Mt 15:7-9; 23:23). But did God not command them to bring sacrifices? Yes. But His intent was that they bring them out of gratitude, not in hypocrisy or rote ritualism.

So with us obedience itself is not the only issue. An important issue is motive. Forcing a person to conform to a set of rules is not biblical sanctification or spirituality. God hates such "obedience" as much as He hated false sacrifices in the Old Testament. Obedience by faith out of gratitude is most acceptable to Him.

More important, God has already fully accepted us in Christ. He knows everything about us, inside and out, and yet has brought us into His family forever. Nothing we could ever do, or not do, would make Him love us any more or less, because He already loves us perfectly and promises He always will. Our obedience should come from seeking to please, enjoying fellowship with Him, and not trying to win His acceptance.

Our desire for security. This fear fails to claim God's total acceptance of the person. Our real security comes from the knowledge of God's complete love, forgiveness, and acceptance of us in Christ. We need seek security nowhere else. We already have it; we need not earn it.

This fear also relates to maturity. In human life, external rules and controls are removed as we get older and internalize them. We stop doing things because we are told to and start doing them because we are trained in righteousness. We have learned the wisdom and value of mature and wise decisions.

For example, a child must be told to keep his room clean. As he grows up and sees the value of having everything orderly, he chooses this without supervision. The former stage is supervision; the latter stage is maturity.

The same is true in the Christian life. As spiritual children we need more external rules and controls. But as we grow, these should become internalized and done because we love God, not because someone tells us we must. The former is law living; the latter is grace living.

Going Back Under the Law

Most believers seem to have no problem understanding and accepting that we have been saved by grace and not by law ("if righteousness comes through the Law, then Christ died needlessly" Gal 2:21 NASB). One would think that, in light of this and all we have read above about legalism, it would be avoided at all costs, seeing its potential damage to the church and its people. But ironically the tendency is to return to the law for living the Christian life and obtaining sanctification.

This was Paul's concern with the Galatians. Certain teachers among them tried to convince them that they must keep the law to grow in the Spirit. But Paul responded, "Having begun by the Spirit, are you now being perfected by the flesh?" (Gal 3:3, NASB). Paul is not saying that they should not obey the commands of Christ. He is concerned about their going back under a system of obligation, not gratitude, to achieve a holy life.

Under grace, a person empowered by the Holy Spirit obeys out of a desire to please God and demonstrates gratitude for his salvation. Under law, people obey out of fear and obligation. This is what Paul meant when he said we are "not under law but under grace" (Rom 6:14). There is a new system in operation. We have been made to "die to the law" (Rom 7:4) so that we might be "released from the law" (Rom 7:6) to live by grace. We are free from legal obligation.

In spite of the clarity of those distinctions and in spite of the joy of the knowledge that salvation comes from grace alone, and not works, people still have a desire to return to a law system. How can this be? There are at least five motivations for placing ourselves back under a law system. We will examine these motivations first from a law perspective, then from a grace perspective:

- **The fear of an unholy life**. It seems that the greatest fear of grace is that if Christians really follow the principles of grace, they will live any way they want; therefore, that grace will lead to careless, ungodly Christian lives, not true sanctification. They fear that if there is no external pressure from a list of laws, rules, and regulations to encourage obedience, they will probably fall into sin. It is particularly tempting for church leaders, who have a genuine concern that believers under their care live godly lives, to fear that giving up the tremendous pressure of the law will result in a lack of holiness/discipline in believers' lives.

- **Our basic rebelliousness toward God**. We do not like hearing that we cannot merit His approval. We want some credit for ourselves. We want to believe that we are acceptable to God, if not for salvation, at least in our Christian lives.

- **A fear of rejection**. This causes us to conform or obey to gain or maintain the favor of the authorities in our lives. Often this produces a very performance-oriented personality in which the sense of well-being is based upon achievement. People are often afraid that God will reject them if He sees their true inner motives. Therefore, they try to hide their inner failures by emphasizing outward actions hoping that God will give them credit for their hard work. Other people rebel by simply attempting to prove that they do not have this fear of authority.

- **Our desire for security**. While we want independence and freedom of choice, there is a lot of security in well-defined guidelines and familiar structure. We grow used to external pressure, such as threats or actual experiences of punishment, to produce right conduct.

- **Control over others**. We can also control others and define who is spiritual and who is not (Gal 2:4). This is maybe the most insidious: the question is often subtly suggested that if someone does not follow the established rules that "maybe they are not really saved."

When these external pressures are suddenly removed, we have a hard time adjusting. We expect God to take up where our parents left off. To a certain extent He does this (He disciplines us like a father, though a perfect one, Heb 12:5-10), but He treats us as responsible people, responsible for our own choices, given the guidelines in the Bible.

For the insecure person, the biblical guidelines are not enough. They are not complete enough; they still require us to think for ourselves, with the guidance of the Holy Spirit. Such a person wants every little detail clearly spelled out in a "rule" so that there are no "tough questions" which call for the individual's commitment in the midst of some ambiguity.

Thus, for some a law system is an easy way out. By emphasizing a few externals, a person can avoid the heavier problems of justice, love, and concern for others (see Gal 5:6, in which faith and love are pitted against circumcision). So a person does not need to "grow up" and gain experience and maturity by choosing wisely (Heb 5:11–6:1). A person can remain like a child and have the rules tell him what to do (Gal 3:23-26).

Law and Grace Contrasted

If both law and grace are valid concepts in the Bible, both given by God, where is the problem? Why are grace and law treated as opposites in the New Testament? The answer lies in recognizing their differences and respective purposes, and primarily seeing that men tried to use them in a way God did not intend.

As we saw in the previous section, "Going Back Under the Law," law has good uses but also shortcomings. The problem lies in trying to turn the shortcomings into good uses. God meant for the law to show us our **need** of salvation; man sought to make it the **means** of salvation (and sanctification). It is the grace of God in Jesus Christ—not the law—that provides salvation as a free gift.

The law can never save us. According to **Romans 3–5**, the law gives the knowledge of sin, shows the magnitude of our separation from a holy God, and makes us accountable to Him (Rom 3:19). Thus, there is nothing we can ever do through the law to earn or merit our salvation (Rom 3:24, 28; 5:15). The only thing we deserve is condemnation.

But because of the grace of Christ we can be freed from that condemnation, not by working for it, but by accepting it by faith as grace—a gift from the Lord. That is the wonder and joy of the grace of God—totally unmerited, undeserved blessing. Only grace saves and gives life, both before **and after** salvation (Gal 3:1-5).

Life Under Grace

As mentioned previously, living under grace is **not** living with an absence of law. We looked briefly at the various kinds of laws and instruction present during this age of grace (Jas 1:22-25; 2:12). But life under grace is freedom from law as obligation, as the means of acceptance before God (Rom 6:6; 8:2). We are free from the condemnation of the law (Rom 8:1-4) and from man's use of it to enslave us (1 Cor 9:19). At the same time Scripture speaks of our being enslaved by choice to righteousness (Rom 6:18), to Christ (1 Cor 7:22), and to all men (1Cor 9:19).

Therefore, liberty does **not** mean that we are autonomous individuals with no responsibilities outside of our desires. Liberty means that we are freed from things that enslaved us destructively, so we can choose commitment and enslavement to that which is true and just (see Mt 22:37-40; 1 Cor 13; Jas 2:8).

There is liberty in freedom within the bounds of responsibility to God, His Word, and others. Think, for example, of a mother who tells her child not to play in the street. Her desire is not to enslave her child to a law. She is not denying her child anything good. She wants to protect her child from harm.

As long as the child obeys that "law," he can play safely anywhere else with great security and joy. Within the boundaries of that law there is peace and security. But the minute the child breaks that law, he is in danger.

That is an illustration of life under grace. There are laws, instructions, and guidelines, not to enslave us but to free us. They tell us where sin's danger lies and free us from those dangers by letting us know where we can live in safety. If we stay within those boundaries, there is peace and security. When we venture beyond them, we enter a danger zone.

None of these, therefore, has to do with winning God's approval and acceptance or proving to Him how spiritual we are. They have to do with enjoying God and His blessings as we obey His guidelines.

To develop the thought mentioned above, living under grace is like living as an adult rather than as a child. When one is a child, he needs limited freedom and lots of specific rules to control his actions and guide his path. This is why Paul says that the law was our tutor for the earlier years, before the son was officially recognized as the adult son by faith in Christ (Gal 3:23-25). As an adult, there is still responsibility to do what is right, and there are some laws to identify the difference between right and wrong, but there are also larger areas of freedom which require mature judgment to live wisely.

Returning to our illustration of the child playing in the street, as a child he obeys his mother's instructions because his mother says so. But as he grows older, he sees the wisdom of the rule and decides for himself to not go into the street. He does not need mother's rule any more. Or, more accurately, his mother's rule is now internalized. She does not need to tell him to do it; he does it freely because it is right and wise to do. The rule remains; the reason for obeying has changed. It is no longer obligation; it is now desire.

Handling the Freedom of Grace

Through handling these areas of freedom, legalism finds an opportunity to infect the church and destroy its ministry. As adult believers in Christ, we must learn how to handle our freedom under the guidance of the Holy Spirit and the principles of Scripture, and not through a great list of do's and don'ts, rules of external conformity. The great temptation we face is making absolute those things that God has left as areas of freedom.

There are some things that are right, and these things are specifically commanded and encouraged in the Scripture. There are other things which are clearly wrong, and these things are clearly identified as sins and forbidden in the Scripture. In between these two ends of the spectrum there is a large area of freedom. In this area fall all of those actions and activities which are not prohibited in Scripture but are not commanded either.

For example, sobriety is clearly commanded (1 Tim 3:2, 11; Tit 2:2), and drunkenness is clearly forbidden (Gal 5:21). But in between these two extremes is a large area of freedom, namely, drinking wine in moderation, where God has left the decision to us. This example is, of course, dealing with a strongly cultural issue. Nevertheless, it illustrates the spectrum clearly.

For us, the issue is how we make wise decisions in the areas in which God has given us freedom. To help in this process, there are three general principles and at least seven specific principles to provide guidance for our decision making in this area.

We are free to do anything which the Word of God does not forbid.

Paul indicates that we are free to make our own decisions in those areas where the Scripture does not restrict us. For example, he observes that "all things are lawful" (1Cor 10:23, NASB) and "nothing is unclean in itself" (Rom 14:14, NASB). In these passages, he deals with situations in which some believers attempted to take away the freedom of other believers. Paul asserts that there are large areas of life in which God has given us freedom to choose. He is not indicating that we have freedom to sin.

Not all freedoms must be exercised.

The exercise of personal freedom is not the highest value in the Christian life. Though we are free to do many things, our Christian life will not be impoverished if we voluntarily choose not to do them because there are things we value in life more than choosing every freedom.

We are not free to impose our decisions on others in areas of freedom.

These areas of freedom are not intended to become means of judging other believers (Rom 14:10; 1Cor 10:29). Believers may come to different conclusions about certain activities, but they are not free to impose their conclusion upon the lives of others and thus take away their liberty before God (Gal 2:4).

These general principles are supported by several specific principles. These principles can be expressed as questions which may be used to evaluate a given activity.

Will it glorify God? (1Cor 10:31). This is the most crucial question to ask, for glorifying God with our lives should be our primary goal in life. It is God's goal for human history (Eph 1:12, 14). One should ask whether the activity in question honors God. Does it reveal His character? If we are truly His ambassadors (2Cor 5:20), does our participation in this represent Him well and accurately to the world? Upon this principle all of the following principles depend.

Is it profitable for one's spiritual life? (1 Cor 10:23). While Paul recognized that all things were lawful for him, he also knew that all things he had a right to do were not profitable for him. Will the activity in question build up or strengthen believers? Will it encourage us toward what is right and true and honorable? Am I, or others, helped in their walk with Christ? We are commanded not to seek our own good but that of others (1Cor 10:24).

Is it a weight? (Heb 12:1). Scripture compares the Christian life to a race. It is not a sprint but a distance race, which requires great endurance. Our goal is to run the race successfully without dropping out along the way. To do this, we must leave behind anything which would weigh us down.

The writer of Hebrews reminds us to lay aside every encumbrance and sin which weighs us down and entangles us so that we might run with endurance. It is obvious that sin should be left behind. An encumbrance, on the other hand, could refer to those things which might not be sinful in themselves but which might slow us down in the Christian life. A runner in the race may have the right to carry a large rock with him, but it would certainly not be wise if he wanted to race well.

Interestingly, it is only by running that one can determine whether something is a weight.[4] Those who are not running the race will not experience an activity as weighing them down. Believers not walking with the Lord may be unaware of the detrimental effects of some of their activities.

Our conduct as believers is guided by whether it would cause a younger or less mature believer to stumble in his Christian life. By stumbling, Paul means that the weaker believer is not just offended by your conduct, but he is caused to fall into sin. Stumbling describes a weaker brother (or sister) being led by your example to violate his conscience by doing something he thinks is wrong, thus entering into sin.

Often people interpret stumbling as simply being offended (that is, disagreeing strongly with your action). But if this is the case, then a manipulative Christian may control the activities of everyone in the church simply by being "offended."

In dealing with this question, your values are determinative. What is most important to you? Paul says that the kingdom of God is not in eating and drinking, activities which you are free to engage in but which some may not feel free to do (Rom 14:17). In other words, there are things more

---

[4] Ryrie, p. 66.

important than the exercise of your freedom. Your Christian life will not be hurt by choosing not to do the activity (in Paul's day eating meat which had been offered to idols) by which another is led to act contrary to his conscience.

Will it hinder the fulfillment of God's purpose? (1 Cor 9:19-23). God's purpose is the spreading of the Gospel and the bringing of salvation to people everywhere. Paul was willing to subject all of his activities to the fulfillment of this great purpose. We are told to conduct ourselves wisely toward unbelievers (Col 4:5) and to cause our lives to present the truth of God in the clearest, most attractive way (Tit 2:10). Any activity we are free to do but which will, in a given situation, prevent a person from understanding the truth about God or coming to trust Christ as his Savior ought to be rejected.

Is there any doubt in your own heart about the activity? (Rom 14:23). If you think an activity is wrong, but you do it anyway, you have sinned—**even if the activity is not wrong in itself!** By doing what you thought was wrong, you have transgressed your conscience and rebelled against your concept of God's will. Therefore, Paul warns us not to do something which we are not fully convinced is alright to do.

Will it enslave you? (1Cor 6:12). While Paul vigorously asserts his freedom, he equally vigorously refuses to be mastered by anything, **even his freedom!** He will not allow anything but God to dominate his life. There are things which we are perfectly free to do but which, if we are not careful, can master us. We must not be enslaved by any activity, even permissible ones.

If we were to summarize all that we have just said, the words of an old saint might be the best. He said, "Love God with all your heart . . . then do as you please." Pastor Charles Swindoll comments: "The healthy restraint is in the first phrase, the freedom is in the second. That's how to live a grace-oriented, liberated life."[5]

Grace Against Legalism

In light of the previous discussion, we emphasize that the purpose of grace is far more important than justifying participating in "stronger brother" activities without feel guilty.

At its heart the meaning of grace is that God accepted into His family people who on their own merits were totally unacceptable. Paul's great statements in Ephesians 2:1-11 show that God's grace reached down to us when we were lost in our trespasses and sins (2:1-2), when we were living in the lusts of our flesh (2:3), and brought us into intimate, personal relationship with Him (2:5-6). God's process takes guilty sinners where they are, receives them to Himself by His grace, and then enables them by this same grace to become His children in reality.

Unfortunately, man's process in far too many churches demands that new believers become our concept of holiness before we accept them. When Christians truly understand grace, it allows them to accept people whom they could not accept before. *Grace allows churches to accept new believers into their fellowship as they are, with all of the blemishes of their immaturity, and then lovingly disciple them to become what God wants them to be.*

A legalistic church places heavy demands upon new believers to conform to its rules before they can be accepted into the fellowship of the church. In so doing, they refuse to extend to the new believer the grace God extended to them when they were enemies of God (Rom 5:8-10). Such a church grieves the heart of the Savior.

---

[5] Charles R. Swindoll, *The Grace Awakening* (Dallas, TX: Word Publishing, 1990), p. 50. The entire book is an outstanding popular treatment of the subject of law, grace, and legalism.

Submit to One Another

*"**Submitting to one another** out of reverence for Christ"* (Eph 5:21, emphasis added).

In essence, submission is a synonym for obedience and yielding to someone else. Submission is used to describe Christians' relationships to one another; young men's relationships with older men; all believers relationships to their leaders; wives to their husbands; slaves to their masters; children to their parents; and Christians to secular authority (Rom 13:1; Eph 5:21-22, 6:1, 5; 1 Pet 5:5; Heb 13:17).

But the essence of all Christian service is submission, just as Jesus submitted His will to the Father's (Mk 10:45; Heb 10:7). As Jesus pointed out, this is diametrically opposed to the way the world works: "'You know that those who are recognized as rulers of the Gentiles lord it over them, and those in high positions use their authority over them'" (Mk 10:42b).

Mutual submission is a distinct concept brought into the world and made possible by Jesus Christ. He, though Lord of the universe, "did not regard equality with God as something to be grasped, but emptied himself by taking on the form of a slave" (Phil 2:6b-7a).

Note: This material is adapted from Gene A. Getz, *The Measure of a Man.* (Ventura, CA: Regal Books, 1984).

The Concept of Law

Legalism derives its existence from law. To understand legalism, therefore, we need to understand the concept of law in the Bible. Much, of course, could be said about law, but we will limit our discussion to our purposes for this course.

"Law" has been defined as "a system of rules or principles for conduct."[6] As such, law refers to a common standard by which those under its authority live. Laws can be good or bad, but they are the standards set up to govern life.

No matter what historical age a person lives in, there are still principles or rules of conduct. In the Bible, the most famous law is the Law of Moses (Ex 20–40), given by God at Mount Sinai. It contains 613 commandments[7] and is both good and useful. Paul said that the law is holy, righteous, and good (Rom 7:12) and that the law is spiritual (Rom 7:14).

In the New Testament, the law of Moses has been exchanged for the law of Christ, "though not being without the law of God but under the law of Christ" (1 Cor 9:21 NASB). "The law of Christ is the 'system of rules or principles for conduct' of the Christian today."[8] There are hundreds of commands contained in the New Testament governing every area of our lives. These commands are meant to be obeyed just as much as the law of Moses was. In fact, the penalty for disobedience to the law of Christ is more severe than disobedience to the law of Moses!

---

[6] Charles C. Ryrie, *The Grace of God* (Chicago, IL: Moody Press, 1963; reprint ed., 1975), p. 52.

[7] For a complete listing of all 613 commands, see John H. Sailhamer, *The Pentateuch as Narrative* (Grand Rapids, MI: Zondervan, 1992), pp. 481–516.

[8] Ryrie, p. 63.

> For if we deliberately keep on sinning after receiving the knowledge of the truth, no further sacrifice for sins is left for us, but only a certain fearful expectation of judgment and a fury of fire that will consume God's enemies. Someone who rejected the law of Moses was put to death without mercy on the testimony of two or three witnesses. How much greater punishment do you think that person deserves who has contempt for the Son of God, and profanes the blood of the covenant that made him holy, and insults the Spirit of grace? For we know the one who said, **"Vengeance is mine, I will repay,"** and again, **"The Lord will judge his people."** It is a terrifying thing to fall into the hands of the living God. (Heb 10:26-31)

All but one of the Ten Commandments are restated in the New Testament.[9] However, **a spiritual Christian will never have his/her actions directed by the Ten Commandments**.

> But the fruit of the Spirit is love, joy, peace, patience, kindness, goodness, faithfulness, gentleness, and self-control. **Against such things there is no law** (Gal 5:22-23, emphasis added).

> For the whole law can be summed up in a single commandment, namely, **"You must love your neighbor as yourself."** (Gal 5:14)

The law of Christ contains:

1. Positive commands (1 Thess 5:16-18)

2. Negative commands (prohibitions) (Rom 12:2)

3. Principles: Many of the particular questions which come up in the Christian life are not covered by any of the positive or negative commands. Therefore, they must be settled by applying general biblical principles. In Christ we are now adults; while under the law we were children and prisoners with our behavior determined by a (legal) guardian:

   > Thus the law had become our guardian until Christ, so that we could be declared righteous by faith. But now that faith has come, we are no longer under a guardian (Gal 3:24-25)

4. Rules: Those in positions of authority in the church are given the power to rule on matters of procedure (Eph 4:11-12; 1 Tim 3:5; Heb 13:7; 17), though these rules are not infallible.

So the concept of law is present throughout the Bible. There is never a time when rules of conduct are not valid. The question then becomes the purpose and use of law. Law in the Bible has several good uses:

1. It reveals our sin and thus our utter helplessness and hopelessness before a holy God (Rom 7:7-11)

2. It reveals the holiness of God and the requirements for entering into His presence (Rom 3:21-28)

3. It leads us to Christ, where we find justification by faith in Christ, not by the law (Gal. 3:24)

---

[9] Lewis Sperry Chafer, *Grace* (Grand Rapids, MI: Zondervan, 1922, 1950; 13th ed., 1970), pp. 153–54.

But the law also has several shortcomings:

1. The law cannot save (Rom 3:20; Acts 13:39; Gal 2:21).
2. The law cannot sanctify (Gal 3:3).
3. The law cannot provide a sufficient motive for righteous conduct.
4. The law became an unbearable burden (Acts 15:10) which produced a curse (Gal 3:13) and became a yoke of slavery (Gal 5:1).
5. The law cannot give us the Spirit or work miracles among us (Gal 3:2-5).
6. The law cannot provide righteousness and those who seek righteousness by it are alienated (cut off) from Christ and obligated to keep the whole law (Gal 5:3-4; Jas 2:10).

Though the law in itself is good and holy, it actually stirs up sin rather than righteousness (Rom 7:8-9). The law interacts with our rebellious, sinful nature and actually excites our fallen nature toward evil. This is why even the best law system (God's law) will ultimately fail.

The Meaning of Grace

The opposite of law in the New Testament is grace. This concept must be understood along with law to understand the problem of legalism. The concept of grace begins in the Old Testament, where it is expressed primarily in two word groups: the verb *chanan* and its related forms, and the noun *chesed*. **Chanan** expresses the idea of favor or graciousness, "a heartfelt response by someone who has something to give to one who has a need."[10] The term often has the idea of showing kindness to the needy or unfortunate. It describes the action of a superior to an inferior who has no real claim to favorable treatment.

The majority of the uses of **chanan** have the Lord as the subject, the One being gracious. For example, God graciously gave Jacob children and prospered him (Gen 33:5, 11). The Lord also dealt with David in the same way (Ps 25:16; 31:9; 51:1). And Isaiah appeals to the Lord on behalf of Israel asking for God's graciousness (Isa 33:2).

The related noun *chen* denotes an unexpected and undeserved favor or grace. It is found most often in the phrase "to find favor in the eyes of." The focus of the word is not on the giver but on the recipient: "The LORD gives grace and glory; no good thing does He withhold from those who walk uprightly" (Ps 84:11 NASB).[11]

The adjective *channun*, "gracious," is often used in conjunction with "merciful" or "compassionate," and all uses of this term refer to God as gracious. The free, undeserved favor of a superior is always the idea in this term (Ex 22:27; see also Ex 34:6; 2 Chr 30:9; Ps 86:15; 103:8; 116:5; 145:8; Joel 2:13).[12]

All of these related terms carry the idea of unmerited favor or supreme graciousness and condescension on the part of the giver. There is absolutely no obligation on the part of the one

---

[10] Edwin Yamauchi, "*chanan*," in *Theological Wordbook of the Old Testament*, ed. R. Laird Harris, Gleason L. Archer, Jr., and Bruce K. Waltke, 2 vols. (Chicago, IL: Moody Press, 1980), 1:302.

[11] Ibid., p. 303.

[12] Ibid., pp. 303-4.

being gracious, nor has the recipient claim to the gracious act. Graciousness is clearly independent of merit and finds its motivation in God, not in the person: "I will be gracious to whom I will be gracious, and will show compassion on whom I will show compassion" (Ex 33:19, NASB).

The focus of the second word, **chesed**, is kindness or loyal love, especially shown to a person related to God by covenant. God is not required to express this love; He is free to give it however He desires (Ex 20:6). There are several things to note about this term:

1. It involves intensity of feeling.
2. It involves a relationship between those involved in the act of lovingkindness performed (David and Jonathan, 1 Sam 20:8, 14-15; 2 Sam 1:26; 9:1, 3, 7).
3. There is, therefore, a strong idea of "faithfulness" in this term.

Only because of God's loyal love can we have a covenant relationship with Him (2 Sam 7:15; 1 Chr 7:13), enjoy daily fellowship with Him (Ps 5:7; also Ps 48:9), and experience such important outworkings of God's **chesed** as deliverance (Ps 31:7) and enlightenment in the form of daily guidance (Ps 143:8).

In the New Testament, the Greek word *charis*, which translates **chanan** and **chesed** in the Greek translation of the Old Testament, expresses the same idea of undeserved blessing or unmerited favor. But here this concept of grace reaches its heights, being exhibited supremely in the gift of Jesus Christ and His offer of complete, eternal salvation by faith alone, made possible through His death on the cross:

> You know the grace of our Lord Jesus Christ, that though He was rich, yet for your sake He became poor, so that you through His poverty might become rich (2 Cor 8:9 NASB)

In Him are all of the same elements of grace in the Old Testament: the superior One, the Son of God Himself, expressing His lovingkindness by becoming poor so that we, the inferior ones (all of us, impoverished, lost in our sin, deserving judgment, having no claim whatsoever on God's riches) might become rich, a benefit we could never earn or deserve.

It is not that there was no grace before the incarnation of Christ but that in Christ grace reaches its peak, for "the law came through Moses," but grace and truth were fully realized only in Jesus Christ (Jn 1:14-17). To the Jews of John's day, hardly anything was more important than the law, and they revered Moses as the giver of the law. But the law was never meant to be a permanent fixture governing the relationship between man and God. It was a temporary expedient until the appearance of Jesus Christ (Gal 3:23-25). The law brought obligation, guilt, debt, and bondage; Jesus Christ brought freedom and forgiveness.

One writer[13] has defined grace in these terms:

> Grace is God's inclination to give good things to people who do not deserve them, who cannot earn them, and who can never do enough to pay for them.

---

[13] Richard L. Strauss, "Getting What You Don't Deserve" *Kindred Spirit.*

The Meaning of Legalism

The previous article entitled "The Concept of Law" said that law is "a system of rules or principles for conduct." Building on his definition of law, Ryrie gives this succinct definition of legalism:

> A fleshly attitude which conforms to a code [a set of laws or rules] for the purpose of exalting self [14]

The self-centeredness of legalism is one of its distinguishing elements. Rather than allowing the law to expose our sin and need for God's grace, the legalist uses his rules to construct a system through which he can, by his own efforts, assure himself that he is acceptable to God. Essentially, legalism allows man to be "righteous" by his own efforts without needing God. Bruce Narramore and Bill Counts describe this process in these words:

> Legalism is a human life-style contrived to resist God's attempts to show us we're failures. Legalism tries to demonstrate our goodness. We substitute our keep-able rules for God's impossible standards. We substitute observable externals for the hidden purity of heart he demands, and we cling to a human righteousness in place of unattainable divine holiness [15]

In legalism, a person, or a group, develops his own list of rules (laws) that he can keep by his own efforts. These rules may be good or bad, wise or unwise. The problem is that keeping these rules, generally focusing on elements of external behavior or dress, is made the measure of spirituality. This allows the person or group to believe that they are spiritually virtuous, when in fact their heart may be far from God. It is precisely for this external appearance of righteousness, disguising an internal rottenness and hypocrisy, that Jesus severely criticized the Pharisees (Mt 23:25-28).

Legalistic rule-keeping also promotes a feeling of pride in oneself and a judgmental spirit toward other believers. Narramore and Counts express it this way:

> We want to **perform** to get acceptance. If we keep the rules we feel more "righteous" or "spiritual." Those who fail to keep them are "sinful"

In this way, rules tend to create a rash of contradictions and hypocrisy. They cater to our craving for acceptance by our own efforts. They focus our attention on a few externals instead of the great biblical issues like love, justice, and humility. And they may lead to a form of pride and a tendency to judge others.[16]

Legalism has a disastrous effect in the lives of believers. Characteristics of a legalist include the following:

> He is motivated by guilt rather than by a love response to God.

> Rules for rules' sake are highly important. He keeps the letter, not the spirit of the law.

> He can't tell the difference between freedom and license.

---

[14] Ryrie, p. 76.

[15] Bruce Narramore and Bill Counts, *Guilt and Freedom* (Santa Ana, CA: Vision House, 1974), p. 117.

[16] Ibid., p. 101.

He wishes to impose his rules on others.

He supports his system of law by proof texts.

He belongs to an in-group of similar minds who exclude others.

His compulsive rule keeping usually gets in the way of meaningful witness; He tends to repel people rather than draw them to Christ.[17]

When legalism infects a church, the results are equally disastrous. Here are some characteristics of a legalistic church:

1. The church has a list of "rules" that it believes to be essential behaviors for spirituality. The list has little to do with righteousness or justice or love for the Lord and other people. It has a lot to do with specific, observable, external actions. Things like personal habits (drinking, smoking, chewing gum), manner of dress and appearance (wearing of cosmetics or jewelry, dress length, length of hair), recreational activities (movies, television, theater, dancing, going to restaurants, type of music, playing sports on Sundays, working on Sundays), and other more intangible things that people in the church call "worldly" make up most of the list. Most of the rules are negatives, prohibitions, because it is always easier to be "against" something than to be "for" something.

2. More attention is given to the list and to people's conformity to it than to determining what their needs are and ministering to them.

3. Ministry becomes a rigid, uncreative process of encouraging conformity to the rules. Ministry often degenerates into nothing more than attempting to impose one's own standard of righteousness upon others. The preaching of the church then becomes pressure to conform to the rules, not an appealing invitation to grow deeper in relationship to God.

4. A feeling of pride grows insidiously within the people of the church who see themselves as spiritual and pure; everyone else is worldly.

5. There is a judgmental spirit toward others—those within the church who are not as rigid in keeping the rules and those in other churches who do not have the same rules.

6. Unbelievers are viewed as a part of the "world," and believers, therefore, should have only limited contact with them so that the believers will not be infected with worldliness. Few believers in the church have any non-Christian friends.

7. There is little evangelistic outreach by the church, lest the people be stained by contact with unbelievers. Unbelievers would not feel comfortable in the services of the church, so they do not come. Unbelievers are expected to "clean up their lives" to be acceptable to God, and any new believer who wants to become part of the church must be willing to undergo a microscopic examination of his life before being accepted as a church member. Most new believers feel so unwelcome they do not come back.

8. The worship of the church is often fairly rigid, dull, and predictable.

9. There is little joy in the church.

---

[17] Lloyd Ahlem, "Rules," *Moody Monthly*, January 1976.

10. The church has almost no ministry to the community in which it lives.

11. The church is one step away from being an irrelevant fossil in its culture.

Lesson 12: Your Biblical Philosophy of Ministry

Lesson Introduction

The purpose of this final lesson is to help you develop a strategy for spiritual growth for your church or area of responsibility in the church. All you have studied so far will help.

Early in the course, we gained scriptural direction from defining what the church is and should be. This provides the reason for the existence of the church and its many activities. Throughout the course, we have developed a biblical study of all church relationships, both with God and fellow Christians. We have looked at this scripturally, traditionally, and culturally.

The first topic in this lesson reviews your study so far. We provide an overview before applying the whole perspective to your service within your church.

Some of you serve as overseers. Others are responsible for prayer meetings, Sunday school, or a particular evangelistic outreach. Whatever your role, these lessons should give you a full three-lens perspective on why you do what you do and why you will do what you plan. Whatever area you choose, the course should help you develop your ideas to help the church conform to its threefold purpose.

Gazing in the Mirror...Then Living It Out

It would be easy at this point in the course to become discouraged. Translating principles into life situations is a difficult, yet vital, aspect of ministry. Be encouraged by James 1:22-25:

> But be sure you live out the message and do not merely listen to it and so deceive yourselves. For if someone merely listens to the message and does not live it out, he is like someone who gazes at his natural face in a mirror. For he gazes at himself and then goes out and immediately forgets what sort of person he was. But the one who peers into the perfect law of liberty and sticks with it, and does not become a forgetful listener but one who lives it out—he will be blessed in what he does

Lesson Outline

Lesson 12: Your Biblical Philosophy of Ministry
- Topic 1: A Review of Biblical Principles
- Topic 2: Developing a Relevant Strategy
  - Determining Current Needs
  - Formulating Goals
- Topic 3: Changing Familiar Church Practices
- Topic 4: Discovering and Using Resources
- Topic 5: Formulating Your Strategy
- Topic 6: Conclusion

Lesson Objectives

When you have completed this lesson, you should be able to:

- Summarize all the principles learned in this course
- List your ministry's current needs based upon your review of the principles learned in this course
- Select at least one ministry form in your church which you think needs to be changed and, state briefly how you would introduce this change
- Maximize the use of available resources within your church
- Propose a strategy for the ongoing spiritual growth of your ministry by writing your own philosophy of ministry

Topic 1: A Review of Biblical Principles

Pastor Eugene has learned a lot about God's vision and purpose for the church, and he wants to apply his newfound knowledge to his own congregation. He wants to develop a ministry strategy as a guiding document for his church's spiritual growth, but he doesn't know what to include in the strategy or how it should be written. He wants to write a personal and practical statement of how these biblical teachings help him minister effectively. His initial direction came from defining what the church should be and studying the church's relationships with God and men. To write the strategy he must use the lenses of history, culture, and Scripture, as well as, all of the biblical teachings that he's studied in this course.

Many principles were discussed in this course, but how do they relate to one another? Here is a brief explanation of the relationship between the various principles we discussed.

Worship, edification, and evangelism are the threefold purpose of the church. Adequate leadership enables us to accomplish our purpose. Leaders growing toward maturity in Christ are needed to plan, organize, and administer the programs and to inspire and train others to share in all aspects of church life. The end result is a body of believers growing more Christlike each day by serving one another and fulfilling their roles in their church and community.

To learn more about a subject, we break it down and analyze its individual parts. Once we know about each of its parts, we may be able to find ways to improve those individual parts. Then through synthesis we may be able to find ways to improve the original subject's performance.

The parts make up the whole. If we develop organization but lose sight of its bigger purpose, we fall short of what God wants our churches to accomplish. All aspects work together to build the church. So let us briefly review the areas discussed in this course.

Reading Assignment

Please read the textbook chapter titled "Chapter 20: Developing Proper Perspective, Step by Step" from *Sharpening the Focus of the Church* in the Articles section at the end of this lesson.

We have studied the church, breaking it down into smaller pieces. We have studied it from many different perspectives. Now it is time to put it back together and improve its performance. To help you with putting together your biblical ministry strategy, please continue with this topic and lesson.

QUESTION 1

Based on what you learned in this course, record in your Life Notebook a one or two sentence purpose statement for each of the three purposes of the church (worship, edification, and multiplication).

QUESTION 2

Open your Life Notebook and review all your notes and answers to questions in previous lessons. Write three practical lessons you've learned that will help you to minister more effectively.

Topic 1 Key Points:

- We have learned about God's purpose for the church by breaking it down into its essential parts.
- In order to develop an effective ministry strategy, we need to review all major aspects of our local church, make adjustments and then put it back together again to improve the church's performance, as measured against God's purpose.

Topic 2: Developing a Relevant Strategy

You have just reviewed biblical principles relevant to your situation. Yet as you learned, the way those principles are applied will vary in different situations and churches. Although principles are universal, the specific ministry forms are not. Forms can be changed to implement principles more effectively, reaching current needs much better.

Most church leaders recognize that planning is important, though difficult for many. The demands of ministry often crowd out time for good planning. Furthermore, few leaders are trained to plan their ministries, and fewer know where to begin. Getz suggests five steps for planning:

1. Determine current needs
2. Develop both long-range and short-range goals
3. Change ministry forms where necessary
4. Discover and use all relevant and legitimate resources
5. Evaluate the ministry continuously to focus biblically, historically, and culturally

Determining Current Needs

Most of you have met three-year-old children. If you've ever lived in the same household with them, you have likely been worn out by their constant question of *why?* They learn by asking questions about everything.

In this topic, you will do a similar activity to analyze current needs in your church. For help in determining those current needs, please continue with this topic.

QUESTION 3

In Chapter 20 of Getz' book, there is a section on "Determining Current Needs." That section provides a set of questions to ask yourself about whether your church is meeting biblical purposes and following biblical principles. Read the list of questions and make a list of the principles that are not being met or followed in your church. This will be your list of current needs.

Formulating Goals

Reading Assignment

Please read the article titled "Formulating Goals" in the Articles section at the end of this lesson.

QUESTION 4

What are two primary characteristics of goals? *(Select all that apply.)*
- A. They are a synthesis.
- B. They are measurable.
- C. They have a time limit.
- D. They are adaptable.

QUESTION 5

According to the principles you learned in the previous article, which of the following statements is an appropriate goal? *(Select all that apply.)*
- A. We will provide basic biblical training for all new believers within two months of their acceptance of Christ as their savior.
- B. We will only choose elders who meet biblical criteria for church leadership.
- C. We will have better youth programs so that the kids learn to enjoy church.
- D. We will create an Internet site to share our sermons via Podcast by the end of the year.
- E. From this day forward, our worship services will focus on God's character and glory.

QUESTION 6

Review the list of current needs that you wrote in Question 3. Select up to six needs and write goal statements in your Life Notebook to alleviate those needs. Remember to make your goals measurable and time limited.

Topic 3: Changing Familiar Church Practices

One of the most difficult parts of any ministry is making changes in the usual way things are done. As discussed previously, changes make people insecure. Changes are often met with resistance and sometimes even hostility. If you are to implement ministry changes successfully, you must carefully plan how to introduce these changes. You will need to prepare people.

God prepared His people by providing a forerunner for His Son, Jesus Christ. Before Jesus came preaching the Gospel of the kingdom, John the Baptist came with the same message:

Making Changes

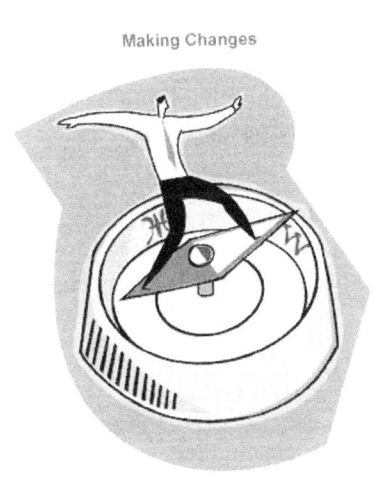

As it is written in Isaiah the prophet, "**I am sending my messenger ahead of you, who will prepare your way, the voice of one calling out in the wilderness, 'Prepare the way for the Lord, make his paths straight.'** In the wilderness John the baptizer began preaching a baptism of repentance for the forgiveness of sins. People from all over Judea and Jerusalem were going out to him and were being baptized by him in the Jordan River as they confessed their sins" (Mark 1:2-5).

The coming of the Messiah would bring major changes and God was preparing His people (Mk 1:7-8; 2:18-22; 3:20-3:35). There are multitudes of ways God used to get people ready for a new way of living, but some of them are through the promise of a deliverer (Gen 3:15), through the many prophecies of His ministry, and through His forerunner.

QUESTION 7

Open your Life Notebook, select one ministry activity practiced as part of your church program that you think needs changing, but would be difficult to change. How would you prepare your congregation to participate in this change? What biblical, historical, and cultural evidence would you use to convince them of the need?

Reading Assignment

Please read the article titled "Changing Familiar Church Practices" in the Articles section at the end of this lesson.

QUESTION 8

When introducing change, it is important to have good arguments against existing goals and programs. *True or False?*

QUESTION 9

Match the order of those who most easily adapt to change as ranked in the left-hand column with descriptions of people in a church in the right-hand column.

Category of Person	Description
Innovators	The majority who respond to proposals of others
Early Adopters	New ideas seldom, if ever, adopted by this group
Middle Adopters	The last in a church to endorse an idea
Late Adopters	The dreamers
Laggards	Those who know a good idea when they see it

QUESTION 10

Review the goals that you wrote in Question 6. If you were to meet these goals, what changes would need to be made? How will these changes affect the members of your congregation? Based on the principles in the article you just read, write a plan in your Life Notebook for the steps you will take to make the transition smoothly.

Topic 4: Discovering and Using Resources

Resources are necessary for effectively building the church. God gives each church a limited supply of precious resources—people, money, spiritual gifts, buildings, and time. To build successfully, we must identify and effectively use His resources.

It is inspiring to read how Solomon built the Lord's temple (1 Kgs 5–6). He used all the best materials and skilled men. And the outcome was exactly according to God's plan. The New Testament temple God builds is not physical, but it is built with God's resources and He uses His saints to help build it.

Reading Assignment

Please read 1 Kings 5–6 about Solomon building the temple.

QUESTION 11

Use a pen or pencil to write the text in the left column in the appropriate Scripture column on the right.

Solomon's Temple

Instructions

- God's Promise to Solomon
- 1st Description of the Temple
- Description of the Finished Temple
- Solomon's Request of Hiram
- The Work Crews
- Hiram's Response

1 Kings 5:1-6	1 Kings 5:7-12	1 Kings 5:13-18	1 Kings 6:1-10	1 Kings 6:11-13	1 Kings 6:14-38

QUESTION 12

Open your Life Notebook and number the lines 1-5. For each of the following areas within your particular ministry, think of one additional resource you have which is not being used to full advantage at the present time.

1. Worship
2. Evangelism
3. Edification
4. Leadership

5. Organization and administration

Topic 5: Formulating Your Strategy

Evaluation is the final step. Evaluation can be threatening, but we must know whether or not we are aiming at biblical objectives for ministering to people, both in the world and in the church. Then we need to know whether or not we are actually accomplishing these objectives. Since circumstances are always changing, we must check periodically to see if our current strategies and structures are the best in view of the changing needs around us.

God evaluated every king that ruled over Judah and Israel. If he did good, his deeds were described and praised. If he did evil, his deeds were described and condemned. The good kings were compared to the standard of King David (2 Kgs 21:1-17; 2 Chr 24:2; 33:1-20). The evil kings were compared to the standard of evil done by King Ahab (e. g., 2 Chr 21:6-7; 22:3; 28:2).

In like manner, we will evaluate our current strategies and structures. To continue these processes please proceed with this topic.

QUESTION 13

Match the verse in the left-hand column with the king described in those verses in the right-hand column.

Verse	King
2 Kings 21:1-17	Manasseh
2 Chronicles 24:2	Ahaz
2 Chronicles 34:1-2	Ahaziah
2 Chronicles 21:5-7	Josiah
2 Chronicles 22:2-3	Jehoram
2 Chronicles 28:1-2	Joash

QUESTION 14

How do you go about evaluating your ministry now? Who besides yourself is involved in the evaluation? How could others be involved in ministry evaluation as you strive together to grow toward maturity in Christ? Record your thoughts in your Life Notebook.

Topic 6: Conclusion

In this lesson, you reviewed all of the major topics covered in the course and started to think through the various aspects of your ministry to consider evaluation. It is exciting to be part of God's eternal purpose of making disciples, and we are grateful that God left us with directions for how to proceed!

Throughout this course, you have had opportunity to think through your existing church ministry and to dream of implementing a ministry plan. These two efforts are not the same, but they are related. With your experience in ministry to date, as well as the work you have put into this course, you can develop a realistic approach to ministry, either for your present church as a whole, for any particular one of its activities, or even for a totally new ministry you propose to start.

We hope that through your work in this course you have discovered many helpful principles which will become part of your ministry and help you more effectively participate in building the church. May the Lord bless and keep you as you build your ministry on the sure foundation of His Word and give you wisdom and opportunity as you implement your ministry plan!

You are at the same point in this course as Pastor Eugene. You have completed all the work and planning, and now it is time to write your biblical ministry strategy. For help with completing your project, please continue with this topic.

QUESTION 15

With the input gained from each unit of study, you should be able to write out your biblical ministry strategy. To do this, you may want to write it all out in paragraph form so that all of the major ideas are included and organized.

Your strategy should describe what your church believes about:

- The nature and purpose of the church
- The role of function and form, and how the church will relate to the Bible, history, and culture
- The meaning, purpose, and process of worship
- Edification
- Multiplication
- Church leadership and organization
- The measure of the maturity of your church

If you are in a seminar group, be ready to share your biblical ministry strategy and your plan for implementation. Listen for thoughts and ideas from your colleagues; they may have insights you have not yet thought of to benefit your ministry.

Remember, this is not the last statement you will ever write! But having gone through the discipline of putting your convictions and ministry strategies down on paper once, the resulting document will serve you well in the future. In this way, you can clearly assess areas of strength and weakness in your ministry six months, one year, or two years from now and make changes accordingly.

As you may recall, Pastor Eugene had been assigned to become the pastor of a church in a small town about forty kilometers from the capital. He found himself being tossed about, not by winds of doctrine, but by the "winds of the times." Everything was changing. A new generation of Christians had arisen, and many of them were not comfortable with the old ways of "doing church" that he had learned as a youth and which had been reinforced in Bible school. This was causing a considerable amount of internal conflict for Pastor Eugene, as well as causing tension within the church between the older Christians and the newer or younger Christians.

By taking this course, Pastor Eugene has learned the biblical definition of the word "church" and plans to educate his congregation about this definition as well as the difference between function and form. In his next sermon series, Pastor Eugene plans to get back to the basics and teach the congregation about biblical worship, edification, and multiplication. After the sermon series, he plans to prayerfully focus the church elders on what changes need to be made in order to meet biblical mandates for the church.

Pastor Eugene is filled with a new sense of awe of God's wisdom and passion for executing His vision for the church in his own congregation.

May God bless Pastor Eugene, and you, in your endeavors to lead your congregation toward the vision that the Bible reveals to us. May you sense the Spirit's leading and rely on God's strength and wisdom as you and your congregation grow closer to Christ.

Lesson 12 Self Check

QUESTION 1

The threefold purpose of the church is worship, edification, and _____.

QUESTION 2

Spiritual leaders should maintain their priorities and delegate cultural responsibilities to other qualified men and women. *True or False?*

QUESTION 3

The church gathered should be the primary place to preach the Gospel. *True or False?*

QUESTION 4

The two primary characteristics of goals are measurability and _____.

    A. Synthesis

    B. Time limit

    C. Adaptability

    D. Visionary

QUESTION 5

Respect is earned through concern for people, competence at your ministry, and _____ to the church and Scriptures.

QUESTION 6

Of the five categories of people in the church who respond to change, which category "knows a good idea when they see it"?

    A. Innovators

    B. Late Adopters

    C. Early Adopters

    D. Laggards

QUESTION 7

God chose Solomon to build His temple instead of David because Solomon was a man of peace. *True or False?*

QUESTION 8

In successfully implementing change, what helps you maintain God's viewpoint on the process and a proper attitude toward those who oppose the change?

    A. Prayer

    B. Education

    C. Feedback

    D. Comparison

QUESTION 9

God evaluated every king of Israel and Judah, and the king that set the standard for evil kings was named _____.

QUESTION 10

God evaluated every king of Israel and Judah, and the king that set the standard for good kings was named _____.

Unit Four Exam: Church Dynamics

QUESTION 1

The concepts that are important to include in defining the word "church" are community of believers, worship, edification, and _____.

QUESTION 2

A group of people who meet on Sunday for good purposes can be defined as a "church." *True or False?*

QUESTION 3

A biblical purpose for ministry is called a _____.
- A. Function
- B. Mandate
- C. Method
- D. Form

QUESTION 4

When you create a ministry strategy, it is helpful to view your church through the lenses of Scripture, history, and _____.
- A. Nature
- B. Dynamics
- C. Culture
- D. Others

QUESTION 5

Every growing movement eventually faces the challenge of institutionalism. *True or False?*

QUESTION 6

Which of the following is a remedy to institutionalism?
- A. Emphasizing how someone lives over what someone believes
- B. Moving non-absolutes toward becoming absolutes
- C. Emphasizing the gifted Bible teaching of one main leader
- D. Emphasizing the church's role as a soul-winning station

QUESTION 7

Worship times and formats should change if one or more members disagree with the proposed changes. *True or False?*

QUESTION 8

Worship must have priority in our personal lives, and it should take precedence in our ministries. *True or False?*

QUESTION 9

Proper worship is focused on _____.

    A. The blessings we have received

    B. The character of God

    C. Christ's sacrifice for us

    D. Our sinful behaviors

QUESTION 10

Which of the following is an essential element for the edification of believers?

    A. Sunday school

    B. Weekly sermons

    C. Small groups

    D. Teaching the Bible

QUESTION 11

Which of the following elements is NOT an important factor for spiritual growth and maturity?

    A. Learning experiences with the Word

    B. Inspirational, Spirit-led prayer meetings

    C. Relational experiences with God and one another

    D. Individual and corporate witnessing experiences

QUESTION 12

Who is responsible for equipping the believers of the church?

    A. Believers

    B. Pastors

    C. Elders

    D. God

QUESTION 13

The best way to discover your spiritual gift is through _____.

    A. Prayer

    B. Pastoral discernment

    C. Serving

    D. Asking your friends

QUESTION 14

For effective evangelism, what do the New Testament epistles emphasize?

    A. The oral message

    B. Having the gift of evangelism

    C. Showing unity and love

    D. Having altar calls

QUESTION 15

Which of the following traits is essential for a church leader?

- A. Lack of sin
- B. Educational achievement
- C. Spiritual maturity
- D. Regular church attendance

QUESTION 16

The Bible supports the concept of having multiple elders. *True or False?*

QUESTION 17

When there are multiple elders, then all the elders should have equal authority. *True or False?*

QUESTION 18

What is the proper goal of admonishing a fellow Christian?

- A. To cleanse the church of sin
- B. To help him or her become mature in Christ
- C. To set the proper example for others
- D. To make sure Christians are united

QUESTION 19

Training a new convert to be a church leader should take several years. *True or False?*

QUESTION 20

Which factor causes a disproportionately negative reaction to change?

- A. People's natural resistance to change
- B. People's practices become institutionalized
- C. People's natural irrationality
- D. People's security is threatened by change

QUESTION 21

Churches should form permanent organizational structures based on biblical examples. *True or False?*

QUESTION 22

Based on 1 Corinthians 13:13, which virtue would be the best measurement of spiritual maturity of a church?

- A. Prophesying
- B. Faith
- C. Love
- D. Hope

QUESTION 23

Grace is_____.

    A. Unmerited favor from God

    B. Earned through our good works

    C. People being nice to us unnecessarily

    D. A good deed that goes unnoticed

QUESTION 24

The two primary characteristics of goals are measurability and _____.

    A. Synthesis

    B. A time limit

    C. Adaptability

    D. Visionary

QUESTION 25

In successfully implementing change, what helps you maintain God's viewpoint on the process and a proper attitude toward those who oppose the change?

    A. Prayer

    B. Education

    C. Feedback

    D. Comparison

Lesson 12 Answers to Questions

QUESTION 1: *Your answer*
QUESTION 2: *Your answer*
QUESTION 3: *Your answer*
QUESTION 4:
B. They are measurable.
C. They have a time limit.
Briefly stated, a goal is a statement of what you want to see happen and when.
QUESTION 5:
B We will only choose elders who meet biblical criteria for church leadership.
C. We will have better youth programs so that the kids learn to enjoy church.
E. From this day forward, our worship services will focus on God's character and glory.
QUESTION 6: *Your answer*
QUESTION 7: *Your answer*
QUESTION 8: False
To avoid unnecessary controversy that distracts you and the congregation from the important issues you need to deal with, do not argue against existing goals and programs. Simply teach biblical goals and principles and let them (the leaders and congregation) discover what needs changing, once they are convinced of the purpose and principles.

QUESTION 9:

Category of Person	Description
Innovators	The dreamers
Early Adopters	Those who know a good idea when they see it
Middle Adopters	The majority who respond to proposals of others
Late Adopters	The last in a church to endorse an idea
Laggards	New ideas seldom, if ever, adopted by this group

QUESTION 10: *Your answer*

QUESTION 11:

Scripture	Title of Verses
1 Kings 5:1-6	Solomon's Request of Hiram
1 Kings 5:7-12	Hiram's Response
1 Kings 5:13-18	The Work Crews
1 Kings 6:1-10	1st Description of the Temple
1 Kings 6:11-13	God's Promise to Solomon
1 Kings 6:14-38	Description of the Finished Temple

QUESTION 12: *Your answer*

QUESTION 13:

Verse	King
2 Kings 21:1-17	Manasseh
2 Chronicles 24:2	Joash
2 Chronicles 34:1-2	Josiah
2 Chronicles 21:5-7	Jehoram
2 Chronicles 22:2-3	Ahaziah
2 Chronicles 28:1-2	Ahaz

QUESTION 14: *Your answer*
QUESTION 15: *Your answer*

Lesson 12 Self Check Answers

QUESTION 1: Correct answers include:
Evangelism
Multiplication
QUESTION 2: True
QUESTION 3: False
QUESTION 4:
B. Time limit
QUESTION 5: Correct answers include:
Commitment
Dedication
QUESTION 6:
C. Early Adopters
QUESTION 7: True
QUESTION 8:
A. Prayer
QUESTION 9: Ahab
QUESTION 10: David

Unit 4 Exam Answers

QUESTION 1: Multiplication
QUESTION 2: False
QUESTION 3:
A. Function
QUESTION 4:
C. Culture
QUESTION 5: True
QUESTION 6:
A. Emphasizing how someone lives over what someone believes
QUESTION 7: False
QUESTION 8: True
QUESTION 9:
B. The character of God
QUESTION 10:
D. Teaching the Bible
QUESTION 11:
B. Inspirational, Spirit-led prayer meetings
QUESTION 12:
B. Pastors
QUESTION 13:
C. Serving
QUESTION 14:
C. Showing unity and love
QUESTION 15:
C. Spiritual maturity
QUESTION 16: True
QUESTION 17: False
QUESTION 18:
B. To help him or her become mature in Christ
QUESTION 19: True
QUESTION 20:
D. People's security is threatened by change.
QUESTION 21: False
QUESTION 22:
C. Love
QUESTION 23:
A. Unmerited favor from God
QUESTION 24:
B. A time limit
QUESTION 25:
A. Prayer

Lesson 12 Articles

Changing Familiar Church Practices

Now that you have given some thought to at least one activity in your church which you think needs changing and how you might introduce change, we would like to suggest a procedure for introducing change in a local church. For the sake of simplicity of presentation, we will refer to you in the role of a pastor. The principles, of course, apply to elders and those in leadership in any ministry group.

Earn the respect of all. The first thing you must have to successfully lead the church through the difficult process of change is the respect of those you lead. There are three primary things you must do to earn this respect.

First, demonstrate *concern* for people. In your ministry you must show concern for people's needs. Your ministry should clearly demonstrate that people are more important than programs.

Second, you must *demonstrate competence*. You should exhibit skill in "doing the work of the ministry." Your performance in ministry should develop the congregation's confidence in you and make them more willing to follow your leadership through a change. This is critical to the process of change because the congregation finds it easier to follow church leaders they are confident in.

Third, you must *demonstrate commitment to the Scriptures* and the church. You must teach the authority of the Scriptures and live a life personally submitted to them. The church must not be seen as a stepping-stone to greater and more glamorous ministries. You must demonstrate your intention to live with the results of a change.

Develop support among the leaders. Obviously, without the support of your leaders it will be difficult, if not impossible, to introduce change in a church. We have three suggestions for accomplishing this important objective.

    1. *Develop personal relationships.* Spend as much formal and informal time as possible with the leaders of the congregation. By gaining their personal support, you lay the foundation for gaining their support for the needed changes. An open, honest, and free relationship should be sought in which you communicate interest in their ideas. Seek their evaluation of the present situation, and as appropriate, stimulate their thinking concerning improvement through needed change. Keep in mind that you cannot gain their support without communicating respect for them. Express appreciation for their contribution, and seek their counsel as appropriate.

    2. *Develop a shared philosophy of ministry.* There are at least three aspects to this:

        First, teach the biblical purposes of the church to leaders and the congregation. This will determine the ultimate objectives for the local church and thereby eliminate many secondary matters.

        Second, teach biblical principles of ministry to leaders and congregation. These basic principles will strongly influence methods of ministry. The principles will provide orientation for less experienced believers and will help avoid possible danger areas in ministry.

Third, transfer loyalty from traditional programs and methods to biblical purposes and principles. This important step can be done slowly and unobtrusively. To avoid unnecessary controversy that distracts you and the congregation from the important issues you need to deal with, do not argue against existing goals and programs. Simply teach biblical goals and principles, and let them (the leaders and congregation) discover what needs changing once they are convinced of the purposes and principles. The goal is developing the congregation's commitment to biblical functions and principles and the willingness to evaluate cultural forms in light of biblical functions.

3. *Develop a shared involvement in the ministry.* Teach the biblical concept of the functions of the body, and encourage church leaders to be active in personal ministry. Then teach them ministry skills, if necessary. Take them with you on visitation. Give them responsibilities in conducting the service. The pastor should not assume all the ministry responsibility; he should, instead, share the responsibility with others. People involved in personal ministry are more likely to appreciate the need for changes than those focusing on the church's ministry to them.

Introduce change at a rate suited to the church. When someone has a new idea, he is usually excited about implementing it. In some cases, it is acceptable to move quickly; in others, caution is preferable. Normally, however, introducing change in a church setting requires a cautious approach. Note the following thoughts about introducing change in your ministry.

BE PATIENT! Do not attempt to change too quickly. Change is a long-term process, and **any** change produces some anxiety. Some people, for example, feel insecure because they are invested in the way things are, in exciting forms of ministry, and change will upset stability. They may also fear the new or uncertain outcome of decisions and new procedures.

Others are secure in relationships which they fear will change. Some enjoy power or authority which they fear losing. While everyone may be convinced that they will gain from the change, most also fear that they will lose something. To help avoid these insecurities, go slowly.

Carefully evaluate changes before making them. Be sure you are clear on the goals of the church before you suggest changes. It is helpful to develop a priority list for changes so the temptation to change everything at once is avoided.

It may be necessary to make changes in small steps rather than in one giant leap. This makes the overall change less apparent and seems less threatening. People will adjust more easily to incremental change.

Justifying changes with sound reasons does two valuable things: First, it helps avoid unnecessary changes. But more important, explaining the changes to concerned people removes the fear of the unknown, and studying needs for change involves more people in the process.

Always anticipate what needs will not be met if the change takes place. Then seek to meet them in other acceptable ways.

Work through the leaders. An effective means of bringing about change is planting the seeds for change with responsible people and letting them suggest a different way of doing things as their own idea. People are always more enthusiastic about their own ideas.

In addition, it is essential to never bypass an elder or department head. Doing so weakens their leadership position and creates resentment, which hinders change. Responsible leaders should be involved in any discussion or planning which touches their area of responsibility.

Focus on those who will change. Dr. Win Arn has identified five categories of people in a church by the way that they respond to change.

1. Innovators: The dreamers
    a. They are often responsible for new ideas but seldom receive the credit.
    b. They are generally not acknowledged as leaders or policy makers.
    c. Many have the spiritual gift of faith (1 Cor. 12:9).
2. Early Adopters: Those who know a good idea when they see it
    a. Their opinions are generally respected in the church.
    b. They often receive credit for new ideas that may not have been theirs.
    c. Many have the gift of wisdom (1 Cor. 12:8).
3. Middle Adopters: The majority who respond to proposals of others
    a. They are generally reasonable in their analysis of a new idea but inclined to maintain the status quo.
    b. They are more easily influenced by those opposing change than those supporting it.
4. Late Adopters: The last in a church to endorse an idea
    a. They often speak against and vote against proposed changes, ideas, and innovations.
    b. They may never verbally acknowledge acceptance, but they generally adopt if the majority has demonstrated support.
5. Laggards: New ideas seldom, if ever, adopted by this group
    a. Their commitment is to the status quo and to the past.
    b. They often sow discord after change.
    c. They are often the leaders of division within the church.[1]

In view of these different responses, Arn has made important suggestions, which we have outlined for you:

1. Put Early Adopters in positions of leadership (boards, committee chairpersons, etc.).
2. Solicit support of Early Adopters before the change is publicly introduced.
3. Seek out suggestions for refinement before the change is publicly announced.
4. Emphasize the change as an addition, not an alteration or subtraction.[2]

Prepare the people. As indicated above, uncertainty breeds insecurity, and insecurity breeds resistance to change. Therefore, lower the resistance and avoid misunderstanding, thus creating an atmosphere of security, by explaining proposed changes thoroughly. Focus particularly on the

---

[1] Win Arn, *The Pastor's Manual for Effective Ministry*, (Monrovia, CA: Church Growth Incorporated, 1988), p. 50. The content of the five categories of people is essentially a direct quote, but some adaptations have been made to create the outline format in this workbook.

[2] Ibid., p. 51. The content of the four responses is an exact quote, but the original format has been altered somewhat to fit the outline format in this workbook.

motivations and reasons for changes. Whenever helpful, refer to changes as "experiments." Do not promote changes as "the final answer," but present them as a better attempt to meet the purposes of the church in harmony with the principles of ministry adopted.

Get continuous feedback before and after implementing change. This brings into play almost everything said above. By seeking out opinions among the people, you demonstrate respect for them, you involve them in the process, you lead them to make the ideas their own, and in other ways you draw them into a mode of acceptance. In this process, be alert for areas of tension and misunderstanding. It is much better and easier to handle emerging problems than ones that have had time to fester.

Approach changes prayerfully. Though listed last, it is certainly not the least important part of the process. Prayer is the channel, the means through which God works and enacts His will. You must keep this channel open.

In addition, prayer helps you keep your perspective. God may have given you the idea, but you also must proceed according to His plan. Prayer will often help you maintain His viewpoint on the process.

It also helps you maintain a proper attitude toward those who opposed the change. Whether your proposed change is accepted or not, the process should not lead to division and strife. Prayer will help you keep a proper attitude toward your brothers and sisters in Christ.

Chapter 20: Developing Proper Perspective, Step by Step

How can we renew our church? Or how can we launch a new church that is characterized by New Testament life and vitality?

These are questions that are being asked today by numerous concerned Christians: by pastors, ministerial students, and laymen representing all segments of church life.

The two chapters in this final section are designed to help answer these questions. They present a step-by-step plan for renewal—strategy for developing proper perspective and a practical approach for implementing change.

At this juncture it is *important* to remember that church renewal within the evangelical church means dealing with the "body of Christ." Each member is part of "us"—and a part of Him. To hurt the body is to hurt ourselves and Jesus Christ, the head. Furthermore, to approach the church with brutal force and insensitivity is to violate the very principles we believe in.

There will be those, of course, who are carnal and insensitive and inflexible. We cannot move forward for Jesus Christ without hurting someone. But this may be a necessary hurt, and one that in the end will help transform that person into the image of Jesus Christ.

But the important concern before us is how can we approach the need for renewal in a way that is biblical and Christlike, and help the majority see what must be done—and then, as a body, move forward in oneness and unity.

The Lens of Scripture

To start a new work or to renew an established church, it is important to begin with the perspective of the Word of God. Bible-believing Christians, particularly since they believe the

Bible is the Word of God, are responsive to the Scriptures. It is to this Book we must turn as our authoritative base. The problem in many churches is that Christians (including both pastors and people) don't really know what the Bible teaches about New Testament church life. The principles that grow out of such a study are not clearly focused in their thinking.

You must begin, then, where we began in this study: with the *lens of Scripture*. You must start with the Great Commission and help people see *why* the church exists, both as a church "in the world" and as a "gathered community." Christians must see clearly the five important areas in the New Testament that relate to the church: worship, edification, evangelism, church leadership, organization and administration. As they study the church's functions and the results of those activities in the book of Acts, and as they carefully consider the directives and objectives given to the church in the Epistles, the New Testament principles we have discovered will also emerge in *their* thinking.

It should be noted, that, to this point, we have identified these concepts as *principles*. However, as will be shown later, they must be translated into New Testament purposes; that is, biblical objectives which need to be clearly focused and set up as targets for the twenty-first-century church.

These New Testament principles and purposes are summarized as follows:

Principles and Purposes of Worship

1. Worship leads to edification, which leads to multiplication. These church functions are tightly interrelated.
2. Giving glory to God through worship is the foundation for the endeavors of the church.
3. Worship must have priority in our personal lives, and it should take precedence in our ministries.
4. Proper worship is focused on the character of God. Hypocritical worship is focused on our own selfish motives.
5. Worship forms can become empty and/or used for the wrong purpose.
6. Worship is part of our broader service to God and therefore is continuously expressed in both public and private settings.

Principles and Purposes of Edification

1. The local church must be kept in focus as the primary means by which edification is to take place.
2. Believers must be provided with a basic knowledge of the Word of God.
3. Believers must be provided with an in-depth knowledge of the Word of God.
4. Believers must be provided with opportunities to develop capacities that go beyond knowledge.
5. Believers must be provided with the sum total of experiences, which will help them get beyond the knowledge level—vital learning experiences with the Word, vital relational experiences with one another and with God, and vital witnessing experiences both individually and corporately.
6. All believers must be equipped for Christian service.

7. Believers must be encouraged and assisted in developing a high quality family life.
8. Today's church must develop its own contemporary forms and structures for applying the biblical principles and purposes just outlined.

Principles and Purposes of Evangelism

1. Every body of believers must be responsible for its own community first.
2. Corporate evangelism is basic to personal evangelism.
3. When possible, presenting the gospel to the unsaved is to take place against the backdrop of a loving and unified body of Christians.
4. The primary target for evangelism should be adults and consequently whole households.
5. The church is responsible to identify those who have a desire to carry the Good News in a special way out into the community and beyond the immediate community, even to "the remotest parts of the earth."
6. New believers, as soon as possible, should be integrated into the life of the church.
7. The church must develop its own contemporary forms and approaches to evangelism utilizing the principles and purposes just stated as biblical guidelines.

Principles and Purposes of Leadership

1. The first step in assisting local churches in their spiritual growth is to appoint spiritually qualified people to lead these churches. These leaders must be first of all selected on the basis of spiritual qualifications–not gifts, talents, and abilities.
2. Spiritual leaders must function as managers and pastors and not merely as administrators and decision makers.
3. Spiritual leaders should maintain their priorities and delegate cultural responsibilities to other qualified men and women.
4. Churches should appoint certain spiritual leaders to serve in staff positions and adequately remunerate them for their efforts.
5. When feasible, churches should be led by more than one spiritual leader, but it is important to designate one spiritual leader as the primary leader.
6. Churches should be free to develop creative forms and structures to apply the functions and principles just outlined.

Principles and Purposes of Administration and Organization

Administration

1. Face the reality of problems.
2. Develop a proper perspective on the problem before reaching a concrete solution.
3. Establish priorities.

4. Delegate responsibility to qualified people.
5. Maintain a proper balance between divine and human factors.
6. Take an approach to problem solving and decision making that considers the attitudes and feelings of those who are directly involved.
7. Solve every problem creatively, under the leadership of the Holy Spirit.

Organization
1. Organize to apply New Testament principles and to reach New Testament purposes.
2. Organize to meet needs.
3. Keep organization simple.
4. Keep organization flexible.

The Lens of History

Christians today need to look through the lens of history. Obviously in this study it has been impossible to treat every lesson that today's church can learn from history. We have attempted to open up the area by selecting one major section which relates particularly to church forms and structures — that of institutionalism. There are many other areas in history that will also challenge our thinking. But from the study of institutionalism in history, we can isolate at least five important lessons:

1. Our greatest strength — our emphasis on teaching and learning the content of the Bible— has also helped create some of our greatest problems. In our attempt to teach the Bible we have neglected two other vital experiences: relational experiences with God and with one another and the vital experience of corporate witness.
2. We have made the church a soul-winning station rather than a life-building station, thus weakening both the functioning body of Christ and our witness in the world.
3. We support the institution, rather than its reason for existence.
4. We have emphasized correct doctrine and neglected the quality of one's life. Furthermore, the criteria for evaluating spirituality has often been based on externalities rather than on inner spiritual qualities.
6. We have fallen into the subtle trap of allowing non–absolutes to become absolute; of making forms and structures, methods and approaches ends in themselves, rather than means to biblical ends.

The Lens of Culture

If we are to renew the church, we must also help believers understand contemporary culture— how it affects our thinking, and how easy it is to confuse purely cultural values and biblical values. Of all the influences that shape our thinking, culture can blur it more than any other.

Culture, too, is a large subject. Consequently we have limited our study to the American culture, which in many respects is reflective of an emerging world culture.

From this analysis we arrived at least ten implications for the twenty-first-century church. They are as follows:

1. The church must develop a correct perspective regarding the multiple factors at work in our society.
2. The church must develop a correct view of history. We are moving on target toward the climax of history and the return of Jesus Christ.
3. The church must understand clearly why Jesus Christ has left us on earth and strive with His help to fulfill that purpose. Culture can blur this purpose and sidetrack us onto peripheral issues.
4. The church must show a vital concern for government leaders, giving primary attention to prayer for them, as well as living an exemplary life.
5. The church must provide an atmosphere where Christians can relate to one another in a noninstitutionalized environment.
6. The church must provide security and stability for people, something which culture is increasingly failing to do.
7. The church must help Christians to live in the world, without being a part of the world. Christians must not, consciously or unconsciously, adopt the aspects of the cultural value system that are contradictory to a Christian value system.
8. The church must recognize, understand, and adapt to the cultural effects of the communications revolution.
9. The church must understand the cultural effects on lifestyle particularly of our youth—and learn to differentiate between what is a violation of biblical principles, and what is a violation of the cultural norms we have come to accept as absolute.
10. The church must do all it can to strengthen the home and counteract the devastating cultural attacks on this basic of all institutions.

Once we have clearly communicated biblical principles, significant lessons from history, and the most important cultural implications that relate to our own community, our next move in church renewal is to help Christians develop greater perspective by looking at five important steps which must be taken to develop a contemporary strategy: (1) to determine current needs in their own churches; (2) to formulate and set up both immediate and long-range objectives and goals; (3) to change, reshape, and develop functional forms and structures; (4) to discover and utilize all relevant and legitimate resources; and (5) to constantly evaluate to see if total perspective is in focus biblically, historically, culturally, and functionally.

Determining Current Needs

In order to determine current needs in our local church, we need to reshape each biblical principle into significant and penetrating questions, incorporating our insights from history and culture.

These questions will form the criteria by which we can evaluate our present situation. This process will help us to spot strengths as well as weaknesses in our church.

The following section illustrates the kinds of questions which can be formulated:

Worship

1. Is worshipping God and glorifying Him the first priority in our church?
2. Does our worship focus on the character of God, and not our own selfish motives?

3. Is worship to God continuously expressed by the church in both public and private settings?

Edification

1. Are we providing a conducive place for edification to take place? Does it provide a warm inviting atmosphere? Do we exclude people or make them feel uncomfortable because of our own cultural hang-ups and prejudices?
2. Are we providing new believers with a basic knowledge of the Word of God? Are they taught basic Bible doctrine that will stabilize them in the Christian faith?
3. Are we providing believers with an in-depth knowledge of the Word of God? Are we helping them to understand and appropriate the deep truths of the Scriptures?
4. Are we helping Christians to get beyond the Bible-knowledge level to develop capacities that include wisdom, enlightenment, appreciation, and awareness and sensitivity to the Holy Spirit; as well as a sensitivity to members of the body of Christ, and a sensitivity to the needs of all people? Are Christians developing the sensitivity to be able to differentiate between values that are cultural and those that are Christian?
5. Are we providing believers with the sum total of experiences that will help them get beyond the knowledge level—vital learning experiences with the Word of God, vital relational experiences with one another and with God, and vital witnessing experiences, both corporately and individually?
6. Are all believers being equipped for Christian service—both in the world and within the church?
7. Are we helping husbands and wives, fathers and mothers, and children develop qualitative Christian family life? Are we doing all we can to unite families, to encourage families, and to provide them with the spiritual equipment to combat the negative influences of the secular and materialistic culture?
8. Are we developing contemporary church forms and structures that will enable us to apply New Testament principles in the today's culture? Do we have forms and structures that provide a sense of Christian community—an atmosphere that is in contrast to the institutionalized environment in the American culture?

Evangelism

1. Is our church concerned about its immediate community? Or, are we substituting a program of foreign missions and neglecting those who live within the context of our local witness?
2. Are we active "as a body" in local evangelism? Are we providing a backdrop against which individual evangelism can take place? Or do we expect individual Christians to witness in a vacuum?

3. Are we substituting the "church gathered" as the *primary* place to preach the gospel, rather than a place to develop Christians and serve as a dynamic example of Christian love and unity to the world?
4. Are we reaching whole households with the gospel, concentrating first on reaching parents? Or are we substituting a program of child and youth evangelism for adult evangelism?
5. Are we discovering and recognizing those in the church who feel especially called to evangelism, and are we encouraging them in their community and worldwide witness through moral and financial support?
6. Are new believers integrated into the life of the local church as soon as possible?
7. Are we utilizing contemporary strategies and approaches to carry out community and worldwide evangelism, that are distinctive and unique to our particular twenty-first-century problems in reaching people for Christ?

Leadership
1. Are we selecting local church leadership based first and foremost on spiritual qualification rather than gifts, talents, and abilities?
2. Are the spiritual leaders in our church functioning as managers and pastors in the true sense of the word and not merely as administrators and decision makers?
3. Are our spiritual leaders maintaining their priority functions and delegating day-to-day responsibilities to other qualified men and women?
4. Are we appointing an adequate number of spiritual leaders to staff positions in the church and remunerating them adequately?
5. Are we practicing the principles of multiple leadership but yet designating one person as the primary leader?
6. Are we developing adequate forms and structures to enable our church leadership to adequately carry out their biblical and cultural functions?

Administration
1. Do we face problems realistically, doing something about them as soon as possible?
2. Do we develop a proper perspective upon problems before trying to arrive at concrete solutions?
3. Do we establish priorities, especially as spiritual leaders in the church, determining where primary attention must be given?
4. Do the spiritual leaders in the church delegate responsibility to qualified people?
5. Do leaders in the church maintain a proper balance between divine and human factors in performing their administrative roles?
6. Do we use an approach to problem solving and decision making in our church that takes into consideration the attitudes and feelings of everyone directly involved?

7. Do we solve problems creatively under the leadership of the Holy Spirit? Or are we hampered by approaches that have worked in the past or that have worked for someone else?

Organization

1. Is organization used primarily as a means to apply New Testament principles and reach New Testament purposes? Or has organization become an end in itself?
2. Do we organize to meet needs? Or do we organize just to organize?
3. Do we keep our organizational structures simple and functional?
4. Do we keep our organizational structures flexible? Or do we get locked up by structures that are outdated, outmoded, and nonfunctional?

Formulating Objectives and Goals

Once we have evaluated the overall function of our local church, and isolated both strengths and weaknesses, we then need to formulate both immediate and long-range objectives and goals. This is the most important step in the whole process of renewal, and a step that will call for some very careful thinking, as well as time and effort. When approached correctly, it can help to create unified thinking in the local body of Christ—an element which is basic to effective change and renewal.

On the other hand, if this step is not taken prayerfully, carefully, and thoroughly, all of the efforts put forth in focusing biblical principles, historical lessons, cultural implications, and current needs may achieve very little.

Changing Functional Forms and Structures

If formulating objectives and goals is a crucial step in the process of renewal, then changing, reshaping, and developing functional forms and structures is the most *difficult*. *It is at this point that we begin to tamper with tradition and emotion*. Forms and structures represent our way of doing things. And they have provided us with a great deal of security. We know what is going to happen next; that is, how things are going to be done because of our forms and structures.

But if certain forms and structures are no longer or even halfway achieving New Testament purposes because they are no longer functional, they *must* be changed. *If they are not changed, we are failing to be New Testament*. We have allowed ourselves to become chained to non-absolutes. We are resisting the Holy Spirit.

If you have proceeded carefully to this point—and particularly if you have helped people clearly focus on New Testament principles—most will begin to see the difference between absolutes and non-absolutes. The Holy Spirit Himself will use the Word of God to clear away fuzzy thinking and to renew vision.

This does not mean there will not be those who will *resist* change. This is natural among all people, whether Christian or non-Christian. Management studies show that about 10 percent of a group of people in an organization are innovators—people willing to try most any new form or structure or idea. About 80 percent are conservative—people who are hesitant to change, until they have all the facts and have their feet firmly planted on projections that seem to be completely feasible. Only about 10 percent are inhibitors—people who are against any kind of change, whether they have the facts or not.

If we approach a body of believers with biblical, historical, and cultural facts, theoretically 90 percent will be ready to change when they see God's plan clearly. And hopefully, since we have the authoritative Word of God and the Holy Spirit on our side, we can reduce the number to less than 10 percent who resist just to resist. *In other words, people who are Christians should shatter the world's statistical norms.*

Discovering and Utilizing Resources

We live in a technological age that has provided the church with unusual resources. They should never, of course, be thought of as being more important than the spiritual resources available to the church; that is, the Word of God, prayer, and the Holy Spirit, and the dynamic of the body of Christ itself. But to ignore the human and technological resources available to us is to be less than spiritually alert.

Jesus Christ used the resources available in His day. Whether it was a well, the wind, a sower, a child, or a temple, all were used to communicate His eternal message. Paul used Greek logic, various literary styles, parchments, ships, and a messenger service. Limited, yes, but he used them all to carry out the Great Commission.

Today the church needs to use every relevant and legitimate means to reach the same New Testament objectives that captured the minds and hearts of our biblical forefathers. Literature, CDs, DVDs, films, radio, TV, the Internet—whatever! We need to consider new methods, new approaches, new ideas to communicate the eternal and never-changing message. The communications revolution in our culture has set the stage for a communications revolution in the church.

This is not to say that preaching is no longer relevant or necessary. But what we need to do is preach in new and more creative ways. The Bible does not tell us how to preach; it just tells us to preach and gives us a variety of illustrations as to the way it was done. So it is with teaching. If we are to keep up with a media-oriented society, we cannot sit idly by and continue to perform in the same old way. Many will not listen to us. Their boredom will win out. What's more, some will become drop outs, especially if the problem is not counteracted within the home. At the same time we may become guilty of sitting back and complaining about the unresponsive and spiritually-hardened generation.

We live in a different world. People's cognitive and perceptive abilities have changed. We think faster, know more, and ask more questions; and in many instances, ironically, we are more confused. But our hearts are the same! We still cry out for understanding, sympathy, support, and security. And what every person needs is what the church of Jesus Christ can give. Our challenge is to use every resource available to meet these human needs.

Evaluating

The word evaluation is a threatening word, but it is a biblical concept. In the King James Version, Paul exhorted the Corinthians to "prove" themselves (2 Cor 13:5): to put themselves to the test, examine themselves, scrutinize themselves. To the Galatians, he wrote, "Let every man examine his own work" (Gal 6:4); and he admonished the Thessalonians to "examine everything carefully" (1 Thess 5:21).

Paul also practiced this concept in his own ministry. He sent Timothy back to Thessalonica to evaluate the state of the church to see how they were (1 Thess 3:5). He was constantly anxious to get reports from various sources as to what was happening in all the churches, regarding their problems, their needs, their concerns, and their progress.

Several things should be noted regarding the process of evaluation.

First, it should be constant. The process of evaluation applies to every aspect of the process of developing a biblical philosophy of the ministry. We must constantly search the Word of God to see if we have clearly focused biblical principles. We must constantly reconsider history in the light of contemporary culture. We must constantly determine current needs against the backdrop of biblical principles, historical lessons, and cultural implications.

We must constantly refocus our objectives and goals, particularly in the light of biblical purposes. We must constantly evaluate our forms and structures to see if they are appropriately applying biblical principles and reaching New Testament goals and objectives. We must constantly look for resources to help us apply New Testament principles in the twenty-first-century. And finally, we must evaluate, evaluate, evaluate!

Second, evaluation should be carried out by the whole body of Christ. It is only as all are involved in this process that all will want to change. This is why it is important to help each member of the body to know what is and what is not a New Testament principle; what is and is not a biblical norm or absolute; what is and what is not cultural. When every member of the body of Christ is involved in the process, it also provides assurance that we are arriving at a correct perspective on our problems. It is dangerous for one individual to evaluate alone. All of us are, to a certain extent, in bondage to subjective feelings. We need the body of Christ and its many members to help correct any incorrect perceptions.

Third, though evaluation is threatening, it is ultimately rewarding. We are afraid of evaluation, because we are afraid we will discover that we have done something wrong.

But let's face reality! Not one of us is perfect. We all make mistakes. This is why we need the "body." When all are involved, all are to blame when we make mistakes. Together we must evaluate and together we must plan and together we will become what God want us to become.

Summary

To renew and help your church step by step:
1. Focus biblical principles and purposes by looking through the lens of Scripture.
2. Focus lessons of history by looking through the lens of history.
3. Focus implications from culture by looking through the lens of culture.
4. Determine its current needs in the light of biblical, historical, and cultural perspective.
5. Formulate immediate and long-range objectives and goals.
6. Develop contemporary forms and structures.
7. Discover and utilize relevant resources.
8. Use this step-by-step process to constantly evaluate and to prove themselves.

Formulating Goals

Briefly stated, a goal is a statement of what you want to see happen and when. A goal has two primary characteristics: it is measurable and has a time limit. If a goal is measurable, you will know when you have accomplished it.

For example, if your goal is "to train more people for evangelism," you must ask yourself how you will know when you have accomplished this goal. As the goal is now stated, it is difficult to know when it has been accomplished! It is not measurable. How many people must you train before you reach your goal? When do you want to have these people trained? Next week? Next month? Even better, restate the goal as "to teach five additional people how to share the Gospel by July 31." This goal is both measurable and time limited. On July 31, you will know whether you have taught five additional people how to share the Gospel.

But is it spiritual to set goals and make plans? Should not the Spirit tell us what to do? It is true that we can make plans which are neither for the glory of God nor sensitive to God's leading. But planning is not unspiritual in itself and the more biblical your orientation, the more your plans will prosper (Ps 1:3).

God urges us to depend on Him as we plan. He does not commend us for not planning: "Commit your works to the LORD, and your plans will be established" (Prov 16:3). For a Christian, to surrender to God does not mean "chaotic planning" but rather the conviction that "the mind of man plans his way, but the LORD directs his steps" (Prov 16:9 NASB).

In fact, it can be a step of faith. By faith we can allow the Holy Spirit to use us as His instruments as we aim to be good leaders. This means using the resources available to us, including biblical principles of administration and organization.

Planning a strategy for our churches is an opportunity to dream big dreams for God, to think about great things to accomplish for His kingdom and glory. As we plan, we step out in faith, giving God the opportunity to work through us. Of course, He may choose to change our plans! But it is better to plan and have God change our plans than to make no plans and be disorganized.

We are stewards of God's resources. The wise steward plans how to best use the resources God entrusts to him. When we do it from love for God (and not our plans), planning becomes a wonderful means of serving God (Mt 22:37).

Made in the USA
Columbia, SC
05 July 2024